PERSUASIVE COMMUNICATION

Persuasive Communication

Second Edition

JAMES B. STIFF
PAUL A. MONGEAU

THE GUILFORD PRESS
New York   London

© 2003 The Guilford Press
A Division of Guilford Publications, Inc.
72 Spring Street, New York, NY 10012
www.guilford.com

All rights reserved

No part of this book may be reproduced, translated, stored in a
retrieval system, or transmitted, in any form or by any means,
electronic, mechanical, photocopying, microfilming, recording,
or otherwise, without written permission from the Publisher.

Printed in the United States of America

Library of Congress Cataloging-in-Publication Data

Stiff, James B. (James Brian)
    Persuasive communication / by James B. Stiff and Paul A. Mongeau.—
2nd ed.
        p. cm.
Includes bibliographical references and index.
    ISBN 1-57230-702-1
    1. Persuasion (Rhetoric)   2. Persuasion (Psychology)   3. Attitude
(Psychology)   I. Mongeau, Paul A.   II. Title.
    P301.5.P47 S75 2003
808—dc21   2002007093

Library
University of Texas
at San Antonio

To Gerald R. Miller (1931–1993),
a good friend and mentor

WITHDRAWN
UTSA Libraries

Acknowledgments

To begin, Jim would like to acknowledge the addition of Paul Mongeau as an important contributor to this edition of the book. After Jim left academia to pursue a career as a litigation consultant, it became apparent to him that this second edition would require the insights and perspective of a scholar who was actively teaching persuasion to undergraduate and graduate students. Those of you who know us understand our long friendship and similar academic pedigrees. We were colleagues in the graduate programs at Arizona State University and Michigan State University and we have coauthored several publications and convention papers. Consequently, we came to this project with similar perspectives and agreement about changes that were necessary to improve the book.

It bears mentioning that while Jim is listed as the first author on this edition, Paul completed the lion's share of the work in revising the book. Without Paul's considerable contributions, the second edition of *Persuasive Communication* would never have become a reality.

We would like to thank several friends who made important contributions to this project. First, we would like to acknowledge the contributions of Jim Dillard and an anonymous reviewer. Jim, in particular, provided us with thoughtful and pointed feedback, helpful recommendations, and yet-to-be published chapters and sources to help us amplify and clarify our discussion. We would also like to thank Kristal Hawkins and Laura Patchkofsky of The Guilford Press for their help and patience. Most important, Jim would like to thank Kathy Miller for her support throughout the original project and during this most recent revision. Kathy offered valuable feedback about conceptual issues and suggestions about how to convey them in a coherent manner. Jim would also like to thank Kalena Miller for her love and irreverence. Paul would like to thank the graduate students in Communication 633: Persuasion Theory and Research at Miami University during the fall semester of 2001 for their detailed comments on the first edition of this book. Last, but certainly not least, Paul would like to thank Arta Damnjanovic and Mike Mongeau for their love and for putting up with him (in general as well as during the time he worked on this book).

Preface

Our goal in creating a second edition of this book was to keep the strongest elements of the first edition while updating and clarifying the presentation. Jim's primary motivation for writing the first edition of this book was to have a textbook for his students that reflected the way he organized the persuasion literature in his persuasion courses. Instead of organizing the literature around classic theories, Jim initially preferred an organization that emphasized important issues. Thus, unlike many persuasion textbooks, there were (and are) no chapters in the book devoted to the Theory of Reasoned Action, Cognitive Dissonance Theory, Social Judgment Theory, and the like. Instead, readers found a review of essential characteristics of persuasion and a discussion of how these characteristics are effectively used in persuasive transactions.

We have attempted to maintain the focus of the first edition while expanding and clarifying the presentation. For example, Chapter 6 in the first edition focused on message factors in persuasion. In this edition, the discussion of message factors has been expanded into two separate chapters: Chapter 6 examines the effects of rational appeals, while Chapter 7 focuses on the effects of emotional appeals. In addition, we expanded our discussion of Models of Interpersonal Compliance (Chapter 10 in the first edition) into two separate chapters. In this edition, Chapter 11 retains the name "Models of Interpersonal Influence," but now focuses exclusively on the effectiveness of various compliance-gaining strategies, while Chapter 12 focuses on the theory and research on generating and resisting influence messages. In addition, we have made a number of substantive changes in the amount of attention we devote to various avenues of research and we have made every effort to update our discussions by combining the seminal works included in the first edition with recent developments in persuasion theory and research.

Two additional features of the book bear mentioning. First, the book is not intended to be an encyclopedic review of prior persuasion research. Such reviews are already available. Instead, we review enough research to clearly explain the issues under consideration, but not so much that the ideas under discussion become lost in a surfeit of studies. For most topics, we describe a typical study in the research area and then summarize the important findings of remaining studies in that area. Finally, where it was possible to summarize the findings of an area without becoming embroiled in a methodological debate, we avoid the debate and focus on drawing substantive conclusions about the research findings. Sometimes, however, substantive conclusions are affected by researchers' methodological choices. In these cases, we examine the methods and describe their influence on a study's findings.

There are three major sections in the book. The four chapters in Part I discuss fundamental issues in persuasion research and lay the foundation for the topics discussed later. Chapter 1 defines several essential concepts of persuasion and draws distinctions among several types of persuasive activity. The broad definition of persuasion presented in Chapter 1 reflects the diversity of the types of communicative activities that are examined in subsequent chapters. Chapter 2 reviews the research methods that are most common to persuasion investigations. The book is written for students who have a basic knowledge about social scientific research methods and Chapter 2 is meant as a review of, rather than an introduction to, these methods. In our persuasion classes, we generally review fundamental issues in quantitative research methods to ensure that students are informed consumers of the investigations we discuss. For students with an advanced understanding of research methods, Chapter 2 may be the least valuable part of the book. For students with more limited experience, Chapter 2 may be essential to understanding the literature reviews that follow.

The next two chapters examine the relationship between attitudes and behavior, which is a central focus of the attitude construct. Consequently, researchers have devoted considerable effort to investigating the relationship between them. In Chapter 3, we consider the conditions under which attitudes predict behavior. In Chapter 4, we turn the table and describe the conditions under which behaviors affect attitudes.

Having described the basic elements of persuasion research, we focus attention on the essential features of persuasive transactions in the five chapters of Part II. Chapter 5 examines features of persuasive sources. Chapters 6 and 7 describe persuasive message characteristics.

Chapter 8 discusses important characteristics of message receivers. Chapter 9 reviews persuasive settings.

Part III of the book examines several contemporary approaches to persuasion theory. In these chapters we examine how the concepts and research findings described in Parts I and II have been integrated into theoretical perspectives for studying persuasive communication. Chapter 10 describes cognitive models of persuasion. Chapters 11 and 12 discuss models of interpersonal influence. Chapter 13 examines models that have been effectively applied in media influence campaigns. Each of these chapters reflects contemporary programs of persuasion research that have evolved from knowledge of the basic elements of persuasion that were examined in Part II of the book.

We hope that you enjoy reading the book and find that our review of persuasion research is relevant, clear, and thorough.

Contents

Part I

Fundamental Issues in Persuasion Research

This part introduces the essential concepts of persuasive communication. Chapter 1 introduces and defines persuasive activity. Chapter 2 reviews the research methods that are common to persuasion research; included in this review are criteria for evaluating the quality of research investigations. Chapter 3 investigates the relationship between attitudes and behavior and answers the question, "Under what conditions do attitudes predict behavior?" Chapter 4 concludes this part of the book by describing the conditions under which changes in behavior will produce attitude change.

Concepts, Definitions, and Basic Distinctions

L OOKING AHEAD ...

This chapter introduces the concept of persuasion and provides a definition of the persuasion process. Next, two related definitions of the attitude construct are discussed. The chapter concludes with a discussion of functional approaches to studying attitudes and the role of attitudes in the development of theories of persuasion.

As connoisseurs of late-night "junk TV" we routinely subject ourselves to the worst that television advertising has to offer. The number and variety of advertisements that can be aired in a single commercial break often amaze us. Not too long ago, Jim watched seven different messages during one break. One ad encouraged Jim to purchase a particular brand of batteries and another described the many household uses for baking soda. Of course, there were the obligatory late-night beer and pizza commercials. However, there was also an ad that promoted the virtues of labor unions, and, because it was an election year, there were two political advertisements. One campaign ad encouraged Jim to vote for Al Gore for president, and another supported a proposition to eliminate the gun show loophole for conducting background checks on people purchasing firearms.

There were marked differences in the style, substance, and objectives of these advertisements, but they shared one important characteristic: they were all intended to persuade late-night television viewers like ourselves. The goals of these different television advertisements underscore the variety of functions that persuasive messages can serve.

For example, the baking soda commercial was designed to teach viewers about "new uses" for an old product. The beer and battery advertisements were intended to reinforce buying decisions and promote "brand loyalty." The political and pizza advertisements promoted a specific behavior, that is, voting for the candidate or proposition, or calling to order a late-night pizza. Finally, the union advertisement was designed to project a favorable image of organized labor.

The variety of goals and message characteristics apparent in these television commercials is evidence of the large number of communicative options available to people in everyday persuasive transactions. The diverse nature of this type of communication is also reflected in the variety of academic fields, ranging from communication and social psychology to political science and advertising, that study persuasive messages and their effects. Given the professional and intellectual diversity of people interested in this process, the term *persuasion* has taken on a number of different meanings. Thus, a clear definition of the concept of persuasion seems a logical way to begin a review of this literature. After describing the persuasion concept, we examine the concept of attitude, which has been the conceptual cornerstone of many theories of persuasion. Finally, we integrate these concepts by examining the functions that attitudes serve in the persuasion process.

Before we begin this discussion, however, it is important to note that no single, universally accepted definition of persuasion exists. What we present is a definition that we find useful in introducing the breadth and complexity of persuasive communication. As a consequence, what we suggest is not the objectively "best" definition of persuasive communication (however that could be determined), but rather one that works for us.

DEFINING PERSUASION

G. R. Miller (1980) recognized the breadth of communicative activities that are potentially persuasive. To reflect this range of persuasive activities, he advocated a definition of persuasion that is broader than the definitions reflected in prior reviews of the literature (Insko, 1967; Kiesler, Collins, & Miller, 1969/1983; C. W. Sherif, Sherif, & Nebergall, 1965; Triandis, 1971). Specifically, G. R. Miller (1980) defined persuasive communication as *any message that is intended to shape, reinforce, or change the responses of another, or others*. This definition limits persuasive activity to intentional behavior. Although one can argue that all communication is by its very nature persuasive and that many activities might inadvertently affect the responses of others, this discussion of persuasive activity will only consider communicative behaviors that are *intended* to affect the responses of others. Given this limitation, G. R. Miller identified three dimensions of persuasive activity: the processes of response shaping, response reinforcing, and response changing. A description of each process will provide a more complete understanding of this definition.

Response-Shaping Processes

In the autumn of 1975, Jimmy Carter was virtually unknown to U.S. voters. Because he was a newcomer to the national political scene, few people could correctly identify him as a former governor of Georgia. In January 1976, a Gallup poll indicated that fewer than 5% of Democratic voters supported Jimmy Carter for their party's presidential nomination (Gallup, 1977). Ten months later he was elected president of the United States.

In the short time between the January Gallup poll and the November election, Americans witnessed one of the most remarkable persuasive campaigns in the history of U.S. politics. As a relative unknown and an outsider to Washington politics, Jimmy Carter enjoyed the advantages of anonymity while his advisors methodically introduced him to the U.S. public. Together, they successfully created an image of Jimmy Carter as an intelligent, honest, and competent alternative to the Watergate-ravaged Republican Party. Like many mass media campaigns, the Carter campaign was designed to foster positive responses to a new stimulus object. In this instance, the stimulus object was Jimmy Carter and the *response-shaping process* was represented by the creation of a favorable image.

G. R. Miller (1980) argued that this emphasis on response-shaping processes is important because we are routinely exposed to new objects, people, and issues that require our evaluation. For example, the structure of the DNA molecule was not discovered until 1953 (Watson, 1968) and at that time very few people considered the possibilities of cloning. Over time, people developed favorable and unfavorable opinions about the use of cloning technology. Today, scientists are cloning mammals such as sheep, cows, and mice and controversy abounds as to the medical, moral, and ethical issues surrounding cloning humans.

The Gulf War provided another example of the importance of response-shaping processes. In January 1990, few Americans had ever heard of Saddam Hussein. A year later, most Americans had been convinced to support a war against him and to destroy much of his country. This transformation was largely caused by the images created by the first President Bush and relayed through mass media. Hussein was characterized as an evil dictator and the second coming of Adolph Hitler. These images were so powerful that they motivated Americans to support a war in a region of the world that 12 months earlier was largely unknown to them.

Response-shaping processes are also critical for people entering new professions. Large corporations develop extensive socialization and training programs that shape the desired values, goals, and objectives of new employees. Though less formally established, socialization processes are also prevalent in smaller businesses as well as in religious and social organizations.

Like socialization, many response-shaping processes take place through social learning (cf. Bandura, 1977, 1986; J. K. Burgoon, Burgoon, Miller, & Sunnafrank, 1981). Social learning theories describe how people form responses to stimuli by modeling the behaviors of others and observing the positive and negative outcomes associated with a model's behavior (see Chapter 13, this volume).

Though notable situations provide the clearest examples, response-shaping processes are typical of everyday persuasion. We routinely develop impressions about people we meet and form opinions about new consumer products. Many of these impressions are formed on the basis of intentional behaviors (e.g., behaviors designed to impress a job interviewer). Although they are not considered in traditional, change-based definitions of persuasion, response-shaping processes are a prominent feature of human social influence.

Response-Reinforcing Processes

More than 500,000 self-help groups in the United States offer support to people who are coping with crises, role transitions, or problems (Naisbitt, 1982). Many of the 15 million Americans attending these self-help groups are recovering alcoholics and drug addicts who meet across the country in the basements of churches and community centers. For many people these weekly meetings provide the only meaningful encouragement they receive as they struggle to maintain their sobriety (Cline, 1990, p. 74).

Like many self-help groups, Alcoholics Anonymous reinforces the sobriety of alcoholics and assists them on the road to recovery. For most alcoholics, the decision to stop drinking is just the first step in the recovery process. Self-help groups provide social support and reinforce an individual's decision to remain sober. These support activities reflect the *response-reinforcing* dimension of G. R. Miller's (1980) definition of persuasive communication.

Response-reinforcing processes are also the mainstay of the advertising industry. Although some advertising campaigns introduce new products and services, most advertising dollars are spent maintaining "brand loyalty." Jackall and Hirota (2000) claim that developing brand loyalty is the "bread and butter" of traditional advertising. Along a similar line, Tellis (1987) concluded "that advertising is more effective in increasing the volume purchased by loyal buyers than in winning new buyers" (p. 22). Recognizing that repeat customers are critical to their success, advertisers fill the mass media with jingles and slogans that increase the salience of products ranging from toothpaste to Cadillacs. Airline commercials promote frequent flyer programs that offer substantial rewards for returning customers. These commercials are an excellent example of the response-reinforcement dimension of persuasion.

Likewise, politicians recognize the importance of reinforcing the opinions and values of their constituents. As political campaigns near Election Day, politicians spend a disproportionate amount of their time in precincts and districts where they already enjoy widespread support. Returning home to friendly districts, political candidates reinforce existing political opinions and motivate people to go to the polls on Election Day.

Response-reinforcing processes extend well beyond self-help groups and persuasive campaigns: they play a central role in the development of our social, political, and religious institutions. Most religious services, for example, are designed to reinforce belief in a prescribed doctrine and to maintain lifestyles consistent with that doctrine. Elementary and high school curricula in the United States reinforce the positive attributes of capitalism while describing socialist and communist economic and political systems much less favorably.

Like the response-shaping function, the response-reinforcing dimension of persuasion has not been emphasized in traditional definitions of persuasion. However, G. R. Miller (1980) emphasized the importance of response-reinforcing processes in his broad-based definition of persuasive communication.

Response-Changing Processes

After breaking up with her boyfriend, Debbie left home on the East Coast to start summer school at a college in California. She was optimistic, if also a bit apprehensive, about her upcoming adventure. Her parents expected her to do well in the school environment, as she had dealt quite successfully with high school and the first year in a local college. Before summer school began, though, she was befriended by a group of youths who suggested that she get to know members of their informal organization dedicated to promoting "social ecology and world peace." Within a month she was spending all her spare time with the group. Only at this point did they tell her that the group was associated with a small religious cult with an elaborate and arcane theology. She was asked by the group's leader to adopt its idiosyncratic beliefs and leave school. Interestingly, she agreed to all of this without hesitation, and began to devote herself full time to raising funds for the cult. For the next three months her parents could not locate her. In the midst of their anxiety, they could offer no explanation as to why she "threw away" the family's values and her own stake in her future. Five years later Debbie described the period as a difficult but meaningful time, and the friends she made there as the best she ever had. (Galanter, 1999, p. 2)

Debbie's story is just one illustration of the dramatic changes in personal and religious values that often coincide with cult indoctrination. Each year, thousands of adolescents and young adults abandon their traditional values, along with their family and friends, to become members of religious and political cults. In fact, estimates indicate that, in the United States, there may be as many as 5,000 cults and cult-like organizations involving more than 3,000,000 people (Allen & Metoyer, 1987).

The belief, value, and lifestyle changes that cult members experience clearly reflect the *response-changing* dimension of persuasion. Though these changes are often extreme, marking a critical event in a person's life history, indoctrination into cults and cult-like organizations employs the same basic processes of attitude change underpinning many of our daily interactions.

Reliance on a charismatic leader, manipulation, and coercion are some of the persuasive characteristics that distinguish cults from other highly cohesive groups and organizations (MacHovec, 1989). Though perhaps more extreme, the persuasive strategies employed by cults are often reflected in mainstream political and religious communication as well. For example, both politicians and cult leaders are often described as "charismatic." Like cult leaders, politicians and mainstream clergy have been known to use coercive strategies to achieve their goals. Although significant differences distinguish politicians and clergy from cult leaders, it is worth considering the similarities of many of their underlying influence strategies.

Although some response-alteration experiences are sudden and extreme, most response-changing processes evolve slowly over time. Consider, for example, two significant statements made by Robert Kennedy about the United States's military involvement in Viet Nam: in 1964, he stated that, "this kind of warfare can be long-drawn-out and costly, but if Communism is to be stopped, it is necessary. And we mean to see this job through to the finish" (Shannon, 1967, p. 101), but in 1966 Kennedy said, "A negotiated settlement means that each side must concede matters that are important in order to preserve positions that are essential" (Shannon, 1967, p. 101).

Because he helped shape the United States's Viet Nam policy as a member of the Kennedy administration, his public opposition to the war in February 1966 reflected a dramatic change in Robert Kennedy's position and signaled a clean break from the policies of the Johnson administration. Johnson's open-ended commitment to keeping ground troops in Viet Nam coincided with a growing number of casualties and a worsening of the conflict. Kennedy concluded that a U.S. victory was not imminent and that our national interests would be best served by a negotiated settlement to end the war (Shannon, 1967, pp. 101–109).

Like many response-changing processes, Kennedy's shift on the United States's involvement in Viet Nam was motivated by new information in the form of multiple messages from a variety of sources that caused him to reevaluate his previously held beliefs (Beran, 1998). Many persuasive theories, including Information Integration Theory (Anderson, 1971) and Social Judgment Theory (M. Sherif & Hovland, 1961) have helped to explain these response-changing processes that have been the central focus of traditional research in persuasion.

There are similarities between response shaping and response changing. Specifically, they both involve a change in one's responses from one position to another. The difference between these outcomes, of course, is that in response shaping the change is from *no* response to *some* response. In response changing, the change is from *one*, already established, position to *another*, different, position. This is an important distinction because research on some theories allegedly focusing on attitude change (e.g., the Elaboration Likelihood Model; see Chapter 10) intentionally focuses on issues about which message recipients have little knowledge. Thus, these theories focus on response-forming rather than response-changing processes.

Related Issues

Two additional features of this definition bear mentioning. First, the term *response* underscores G. R. Miller's (1980) concern about approaches to studying persuasion that define persuasive outcomes solely in terms of attitudes and attitude change. Indeed, titles of traditional reviews of the persuasion literature such as *Theories of Attitude Change* (Insko, 1967), *Attitudes and Attitude Change* (Triandis, 1971), *Attitude Change* (Kiesler et al., 1969/1983), and *The Psychology of Attitudes* (Eagly & Chaiken, 1993) reflect this emphasis. As we explain in Chapter 3, one overriding limitation of prior persuasion research stems from an emphasis on attitudes. However, G. R. Miller's

(1980) use of the term *response* reflects an emphasis on other types of persuasive outcomes such as perceptions, emotions, beliefs, behavioral intentions, and behaviors.

The response-shaping, -reinforcing, and -changing processes described above reflect the variety of outcomes that are consistent with G. R. Miller's definition of persuasion. For example, Al Gore's presidential campaign reflected a concern with belief, attitude, and behavior formation. Voting behavior was the eventual desired outcome of the campaign, but attitude and belief formation were critical initial steps in that persuasion process. Organizational socialization, another response-forming process, emphasizes the development of employee values. Response-reinforcing processes apparent in self-help groups such as Alcoholics Anonymous often emphasize the maintenance of desirable behaviors. Advertising campaigns that promote brand loyalty are also geared toward the reinforcement of targeted behaviors. Finally, the example of Debbie's experience with a religious cult reflects a response-changing process that targets a person's values and beliefs. In short, a broader definition of persuasion, such as that offered by G. R. Miller (1980), is consistent with the wide range of cognitive, emotional, and behavioral outcomes that are routinely associated with persuasive communication.

Finally, although some scholars prefer to distinguish persuasion from the concepts of manipulation and coercion, this definition makes no attempt to draw conceptual distinctions among these related concepts. Attempts to differentiate persuasion from coercion typically center on the receiver's free will. The distinction typically goes like this: In persuasion, the receiver has the ability to accept or reject the persuasive attempt; however, in coercion, the receiver does not. This distinction between persuasion and coercion, however, is rarely satisfactory. One reason that it is difficult to separate these constructs is that "much persuasive discourse is *indirectly* coercive" (G. R. Miller, 1980, p. 12, emphasis in original). For example, a parent might threaten to cut off his or her child's allowance if the son or daughter does not improve his or her grades. This persuasive attempt is indirectly coercive because a punishment is promised if the child does not conform.

Though you might not consider the request of an armed robber to "hand over your wallet" as an instance of "persuasive communication," studies of interpersonal compliance examine similarly coercive messages that are generally placed under the umbrella of persuasive communication. As such, we examine message strategies such as manipulation and coercion as possible strategies for achieving persuasive outcomes in Chapter 11. In summary, persuasive communication represents *any message that is intended to shape, reinforce, or change the responses of another, or others.*

DEFINING THE ATTITUDE CONSTRUCT

A variety of responses are consistent with G. R. Miller's (1980) definition of persuasion (e.g., attitudes, behaviors, behavioral intentions, values, beliefs, moods, and emotions). Though affective and emotional responses are consistent with the definition of persuasion described above, attitudes, and, to a lesser extent, behaviors have been the focus of most prior studies of persuasion. Over the past 60+ years, attitudes have become a central component in many theories of persuasive communication.

There are important differences between attitudes and behaviors. *Behavioral responses* (e.g., donating to a charity or buying a particular product) are relatively concrete, and as such are often accessible to direct observation by researchers. Cognitive responses such as *attitudes*, however, are more abstract and relatively difficult to observe directly. Given the important roles that attitudes play in persuasion theories and their hidden nature, it is important that we spend some time discussing attitudes in some detail. As a consequence, in this section of the chapter, we present two definitions of the attitude concept, discuss the functions of attitudes in human interaction, and indicate how attitudes are measured within each perspective.

The definition and study of attitudes has a long history (Eagly & Chaiken, 1993). The attitude construct initially gained prominence through the writings of Gordon Allport (1935), who used it to help understand and explain human behavior. In the nearly 70 years since Allport's ideas were published, attitudes have become a central component in many theories of persuasive communication. An attitude is a theoretical construction created by social scientists to explain the different reactions that people have toward similar objects or situations. Unlike behaviors, which are directly observable, attitudes are not directly observable, and hence are more difficult to measure. Nevertheless, the explanatory power of the attitude construct has helped lay the foundation for contemporary persuasion research.

In its infancy, the attitude construct was defined as "a mental and neural state of readiness, organized through experience, exerting a directive or dynamic influence upon the individual's response to all objects and situations with which it is related" (Allport, 1935, p. 810). Thus, the utility of attitudes depends on their ability to predict overt behaviors. About this time, Thurstone (1928, 1931) identified methods for "measuring" people's attitudes. Since these early efforts, the attitude construct's evolution is evidenced by the number of definitions that have been proposed as ways of thinking about attitudes (Zanna & Rempler, 1988). As was true with the definition of persuasion, none of these definitions of attitude have received universal acceptance.

Rokeach's Definition

One of the most parsimonious definitions of an *attitude* was provided by Rokeach, who defined it as "a relatively enduring organization of beliefs around an object or situation predisposing one to respond in some preferential manner" (1968, p. 112). There are several important implications of Rokeach's (1968) definition. First, *attitudes are relatively enduring*. Most scholars agree that attitudes represent more than a fleeting thought about or a momentary evaluation of an object. Attitudes are developed over a long period of time and are frequently reinforced. As such, they are relatively stable and are difficult to change. This does not imply that attitudes are not susceptible to sudden and dramatic shifts, only that such changes are exceptional.

The second implication of Rokeach's definition is that *an attitude is an organization of beliefs*. Rather than conceptualizing an attitude as a single element within a person's cognitive or mental framework, Rokeach conceptualizes an attitude as a cluster or combination of several related cognitive elements. These cognitive elements are defined as beliefs that cluster around a central attitude object, and the entire cluster of beliefs is the attitude about the object.

A *belief* is a single proposition (or statement) about an object or a situation. The content of a belief usually describes the object as something that is correct or incorrect, good or bad, moral or immoral, and so forth. Rokeach identified three types of beliefs: descriptive, prescriptive, and evaluative.

Descriptive beliefs are verifiable statements about people, objects, and situations. Like factual statements, descriptive beliefs are objective statements that, in principle, can be shown to be correct or incorrect. For example, the statement, "*The Jerry Springer Show* is produced in Chicago" is a descriptive belief because its validity can be established.

Prescriptive beliefs are statements about the appropriateness of a position or an activity in a given situation. These subjective statements reflect the values, morals, or ethics of the person or persons advocating them. For example, the statement "*The Jerry Springer Show* sets a bad example for children by glorifying immoral lifestyles" may reflect the degree to which a person values traditional versus alternative ways of living. It may also reflect a belief about the role of the media in reinforcing moral and ethical standards in our culture. Regardless, beliefs like these cannot be demonstrated to be incorrect, as they reflect subjective feelings about the attitude object.

Evaluative beliefs, according to Rokeach, are statements that reflect a general evaluation of an attitude object—for example, "*The Jerry Springer Show* is good." Evaluative beliefs are very similar to the general conceptualization of attitudes. Like prescriptive beliefs, evaluative beliefs cannot be shown to be objectively correct or incorrect.

The third implication of Rokeach's definition reflects the behavioral component of these individual beliefs. The attitude reflected in the combination of beliefs around an object or situation represents a *predisposition to respond.* Once established, this predisposition guides our behavior as we encounter similar attitude objects. For example, if you have a negative attitude toward drug use, you are likely to refuse a friend's offer of the drug ecstasy at a party. If this attitude is extremely negative, you might also be motivated to join a community organization and promote drug resistance among adolescents and young adults.

Rokeach's definition, like many others, presumes that attitudes have affective, behavioral, and cognitive components. Because this view defines attitudes as having three components, it is referred to as the "tripartite" model of attitudes (Zanna & Rempler, 1988). The cognitive component of attitudes represents the beliefs (particularly descriptive beliefs) that a person has about an attitude object. The affective component of attitudes represent the positive, negative, or neutral evaluations people have about attitude objects. Rokeach's evaluative beliefs are a good example of the affective components of attitudes. Finally, attitudes have a behavioral component because they are considered as closely linked to behaviors. This is best represented by Rokeach's claim that attitudes are "predispositions to respond."

While Zanna and Rempler (1988) argued that the tripartite model of attitude was popular, it is not without its problems. In their view, the most important problem is that the tripartite model presumes that attitudes, by definition, are related to behaviors. For a long period of time, however, research on the relationship between attitudes and behaviors was less than convincing (as we will discuss in Chapter 3). As a consequence, Zanna and Rempler prefer a definition that does not presume an attitude–behavior relationship. As a consequence, they defined attitudes "as the categorization of a stimulus object along an evaluative dimension based upon, or generated from, three general classes of information: (1) cognitive information, (2) affective/emotional information, and/or (3) information concerning past behaviors or behavioral intentions" (p. 319). This revised view differs from Rokeach's definition in two important ways. First, while Zanna and Rempler argue that attitudes can be based upon past behaviors, there is no assumption that attitudes, by definition, predict behaviors. Second, in their view, attitudes are composed of a single dimension (an evaluative judgment—e.g., good–bad) rather than three. Put another way, Zanna and Rempler's definition is unidimensional (i.e., composed of a single unit or dimension). Zanna and Rempler's definition maintains Rokeach's three components, but consider them the information upon which attitudes are based.

How Are Attitudes Measured?

Students often ask how internal characteristics like attitudes can be measured. Whether attitudes are defined using the tripartite model (e.g., Rokeach, 1968) or unidimensionally (e.g., Zanna & Rempler, 1988), most measures of attitudes focus on the global evaluation of a person, object, or idea rather than trying to measure specific beliefs. Two of the most popular measures of attitudes are Likert scales and semantic differentials.

Attitude measurements using *Likert scales* contain a number of positive and negative opinion statements. Each statement is accompanied by a set of response scales ranging from "strongly disagree" to "strongly agree." Assume that we are trying to measure attitudes toward *The Jerry Springer Show* using two Likert-type scales. In a questionnaire, we might use two items provided in the upper portion of Figure 1.1.

Respondents are asked to indicate which response most clearly matches their opinion on each statement. The numbers to the right of each response option represents the score that an individual would receive for each response (and would not be presented in an actual ques-

The Jerry Springer Show is entertaining.
_____ Strongly agree [5]
_____ Agree [4]
_____ Neither agree nor disagree [3]
_____ Disagree [2]
_____ Strongly disagree [1]

The Jerry Springer Show is the worst that television has to offer.
_____ Strongly agree [5]
_____ Agree [4]
_____ Neither agree nor disagree [3]
_____ Disagree [2]
_____ Strongly disagree [1]

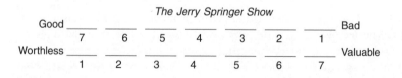

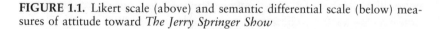

FIGURE 1.1. Likert scale (above) and semantic differential scale (below) measures of attitude toward *The Jerry Springer Show*

tionnaire). In this example, high scores reflect positive attitudes toward the show and low scores represent negative attitudes.[1] The scoring is reversed in the second Likert item because the wording of the statement is opposite to that of the first item. A person with a very positive attitude would likely "strongly agree" with the first statement and "strongly disagree" with the second.

Semantic differential scales come in the form of the attitude object accompanied by a number of bipolar adjective pairs (i.e., opposites). These opposites are separated typically by seven response options. To indicate an attitude, the respondent would mark the response option that most clearly indicated his or her opinion. Two semantic differential attitude scales toward *The Jerry Springer Show* are provided at the bottom of Figure 1.1.

Using these semantic differential scales, a person with a very positive attitude would likely check a response close to the "good" and "valuable" ends on the two scales. The numbers associated with each option represent the score that particular response would generate (and would not be provided in the questionnaire). Again, high scores represent positive attitudes.

Fishbein and Ajzen's Definition

Adopting the perspective that an attitude is a combination of beliefs representing a predisposition to respond, Fishbein and Ajzen (1975) provided a more precise description of the influence of individual beliefs on people's attitudes and behavioral intentions. Fishbein and Ajzen argued that an attitude toward a particular behavior was a function of the perceived consequences of performing the behavior and an evaluation of those consequences. This relationship is represented in the equation

$$A_B = \Sigma \ (b_i \times e_i) \tag{1.1}$$

where A_B is the attitude toward performing behavior B; b_i is the belief that performing behavior B leads to the outcome specified in belief statement i (where i represents each belief statement; i.e., the first, second, third, all the way to the last one); and e_i is the person's evaluation of the outcome specified in belief statement i. To estimate a person's attitude toward performing a particular behavior, numbers ranging from 0 to +3 are assigned to the belief value (b) component. A zero would indicate that it is considered highly unlikely that the behavior would lead to the particular outcome, while a +3 would indicates that the outcome is a highly likely result of the behavior. The evaluation (e) components for each belief statement (i) is measured using a –3 (extremely negative evaluation of the outcome) to a +3 (extremely positive evaluation of the outcome) scale. The product of the belief and evaluation values ($b_i \times e_i$) for each belief statement (i) are summed (Σ) to produce a single value representing the attitude toward performing behavior B (Fishbein & Ajzen, 1975, p. 301).

To understand the contribution of beliefs and their evaluation to a person's attitude, let's consider an example. In this example, the behavior in question is participating in a demonstration to prevent additional offshore oil exploration along the Florida coastline (Table 1.1).[2] Consider the beliefs and evaluations of two people, an environmentalist and an industrialist.

Our hypothetical industrialist and environmentalist share some beliefs, but differ on others, about the merits of demonstrating against offshore drilling. They also differ in their evaluation of these belief statements. For example, the two differ in their belief that coastal wildlife needs protection from oil companies. The industrialist believes this to be somewhat true (+1), but the environmentalist strongly believes this statement (+3). However, both strongly agree that the prevention of offshore drilling will decrease oil company profits. Notice, however, that although they share the same belief about oil company profits (+3), they differ in their evaluation of this belief. The industrialist has a negative evaluation of this statement (−3), whereas the environmentalist views the loss of company profits favorably (+2).

TABLE 1.1 Hypothetical Beliefs about Participating in a Demonstration to Prevent Off-Shore Oil Exploration

Belief statement	Industrialist views		Environmentalist views	
	b	e	b	e
Coastal wildlife needs protection from oil companies.	+1	−1	+3	+3
Public demonstrations will cause politicians to vote against off-shore drilling.	0	−2	+3	+3
Prevention of off-shore drilling will increase development of alternative energy resources.	+1	−1	+2	+2
Prevention of off-shore drilling will decrease profits of oil companies.	+3	−3	+3	+2
	$\Sigma (b \times e) = $ −11		$\Sigma (b \times e) = $ +28	

Note. b represents belief in the statement (ranging from 0 to +3) and e represents evaluation of the belief statement (ranging from −3 to +3).

Consequently, their attitudes about participating in the demonstration are likely to differ.

The attitude of the industrialist can be estimated with Fishbein and Ajzen's (1975) formula. To do this, first multiply the belief and evaluation score for each belief statement, then add these scores together. In this example, the products $(b \times e)$ of the industrialist's views on the four belief statements are −1, 0, −1, and −9, respectively. The sum of these products is −11, and this number represents the industrialist's moderately negative attitude about participating in the demonstration against offshore drilling along the Florida coast. Conversely, the products of the environmentalist's views on each of the four belief statements are +9, +9, +4, +6, respectively. Adding these four products produces an estimate of +28, which represents the environmentalist's positive attitude about participating in the demonstration.

This definition permits a precise, quantitative estimate of a person's attitude about a particular behavior. However, such estimates only become meaningful when they are compared with other attitude estimates. In the example, the industrialist's rating (−11) is difficult to interpret by itself. However, compared with the value for the environmentalist (+28), the industrialist's attitude is 39 units more negative than the attitude of the environmentalist. Indeed, this model provides an estimate of both the valence (positive or negative) and strength of a person's attitude. Specifically, the sign (+ or −) associated with the final score indicates the valence of an attitude. The strength of an attitude is indicated by the absolute value of the final score. Strong attitudes differ substantially from zero, while weak attitudes cluster close to zero.

When plotted over time, one can track changes in a person's attitude toward a particular behavior through these attitude estimates. For example, if the public demonstration had little or no influence on the voting behavior of politicians, the environmentalist's belief regarding the effects of public demonstrations on political decisions might change, for example, from +3 to +1. This belief change would result in a less favorable attitude about participating in public demonstrations, that is, from +28 to +22.

In the example about offshore drilling, the different attitudes held by the industrialist and the environmentalist are due in large part to differences in their belief systems and how they value those beliefs. It is easy to understand the different attitudes of these hypothetical people given their beliefs about offshore drilling and the utility of public demonstrations. However, it is possible for people to hold the *same* beliefs about a particular object or situation and yet maintain different attitudes toward it.

Americans often decide who they will vote for based on a single issue. For example, a pro-life activist may decide not to vote for a particular candidate who publicly supports abortion rights for women. This same position may cause a pro-choice activist to support the candidate. It is possible that the different attitudes pro-choice and pro-life activists have toward a candidate may be based on similar beliefs about the candidate (Table 1.2). In this example, the hypothetical pro-choice and pro-life activists hold identical beliefs about the likely effects of voting for the candidate; however, their evaluations of those beliefs differ. In the case of the pro-life activist, the negative evaluation assigned to these beliefs results in a negative attitude (−24) about voting for the candidate. Conversely, the positive evaluations of these belief statements by the pro-choice activist lead to a positive attitude about voting for the candidate (+24).

Though it is unlikely that *all* of the salient beliefs of pro-choice and pro-life activists are identical, this example clarifies an important distinction between a person's belief in a particular statement and the evaluation of that statement. In so doing, it also highlights the important contributions of beliefs and evaluations to the formation of attitudes.

Comparing Rokeach's and Fishbein and Ajzen's Definitions

The definitions of attitude provided by Rokeach (1968) and Fishbein and Ajzen (1975) share a number of conceptual similarities. First, both definitions conceptualize an attitude as a combination of beliefs about a

TABLE 1.2. Hypothetical Beliefs about Voting for a Political Candidate

Belief statement	Pro-life activist's views		Pro-choice activist's views	
	b	e	b	e
Candidate will support laws guaranteeing abortion rights.	+3	−3	+3	+3
Candidate will support federally funded abortions.	+2	−3	+2	+3
Abortion will increase if candidate is elected.	+2	−3	+2	+3
Teenage women will have more abortion rights if candidate is elected.	+1	−3	+1	+3
	$\Sigma\ (b \times e) = -24$		$\Sigma\ (b \times e) = +24$	

Note. b represents belief in the statement (ranging from 0 to +3) and *e* represents evaluation of the belief statement (ranging from −3 to +3).

particular object, situation, or behavior. Fishbein and Ajzen's definition is much more precise because it specifies how these beliefs and evaluations combine to form an attitude.

Like Rokeach, Fishbein and Ajzen allow for some beliefs to be more influential than others in determining the overall attitude. Rokeach describes the most influential beliefs as being more centrally clustered around the attitude object, whereas Fishbein and Ajzen argue that highly influential beliefs receive more extreme evaluations than less influential ones. According to Fishbein and Ajzen, the multiplicative relationship between individual beliefs and their evaluation reflects the relative contribution of each belief to the overall attitude.

Finally, both definitions are consistent with Hovland, Janis, and Kelley's (1953) assertion that attitude change is dependent upon the addition to or alteration of a person's belief system. For Rokeach, adding to or restructuring a person's system of beliefs clustered around the attitude object is the best way to accomplish attitude change. Fishbein and Ajzen argue that attitude change is accomplished through the addition of new belief statements, or by altering a person's evaluation or belief in an existing belief statements. The more strongly an attitude is bolstered (i.e., the more beliefs compose the attitude), the more difficult it will likely be to change that attitude.

In summary, Fishbein and Ajzen provide a more precise definition of attitude that represents an extension of Rokeach's earlier thinking about the issue. Moreover, both definitions are consistent with the widely accepted position that an attitude reflects more than a single belief statement; it is a combination of all the salient beliefs a person may have about an attitude object. We will return to Ajzen and Fishbein's view of attitudes when we discuss the relationship between attitudes and behaviors in Chapter 3.

THE ROLE OF ATTITUDE
IN PERSUASION RESEARCH

Attitudes have become a central focus of many persuasion theories because social scientists believe that attitudes guide and direct human behavior. The attitude construct was originally introduced to explain why people respond differently to similar stimuli. One approach that emphasizes the predictive and explanatory power of an attitude is labeled the *functional approach*.

Functional Approaches to Studying Attitudes

Why do people hold particular attitudes? What functions do attitudes serve? Questions like these led to the development of the functional approach to studying attitudes. "Functional approaches attempt to identify the various psychological benefits that people can and do derive from forming, expressing, and changing their attitudes" (Lavine & Snyder, 2000, p. 98). The functional approach was developed in the 1950s, primarily through the work of Katz (1960) and Smith, Bruner, and White (1956). These researchers studied attitudes by examining the psychological functions they serve.

Katz (1960) identified four psychological functions that attitudes serve: (1) an *instrumental, adjustive, or utilitarian* function; (2) an *ego-defensive* function; (3) a *knowledge* function; and (4) a *value-expressive* function. Each of these functions is associated with a set of implicit goals that people would like to reach by holding attitudes.

For example, people want to experience a pleasant state of existence and are motivated to pursue those pleasant states by maximizing rewarding experiences and minimizing negative ones. Consequently, Katz suggests that the *instrumental* (sometimes called *adjustive* or *utilitarian*) function is reflected in the positive attitudes people develop toward objects or situations that are rewarding and the negative attitudes that are associated with situations that produce unfavorable outcomes. For example, college students usually develop an affinity for specialty courses in their chosen major, and they are less enthusiastic about general studies courses they perceive to be unrelated to their major field of study.

Second, developed from psychoanalytic theory, the *ego-defensive* function serves to protect people from basic truths about themselves and their environment that they don't want to face or deal with (Katz, 1960; Sarnoff, 1960). The attitudes people develop toward objects or situations sometimes allow them to insulate themselves from their insecurities or emotional conflicts. Prejudicial attitudes often serve this function. Negative evaluations of people from different ethnic and racial groups allow prejudiced people to maintain the belief that they are superior to "outgroup" members who threaten their egos.

Third, attitudes also serve a *knowledge* function. They allow us to organize information and structure evaluations of novel stimuli. In situations where uncertainty is high, attitudes can bridge an information gap and permit the interpretation and categorization of new information into preestablished general categories. This process, referred to as *stimulus generalization*, involves the stereotyping of people or stimulus objects into categories based on the perceived similarities among them. For example, the knowledge function of attitudes is reflected in the generalizations people make about strangers during initial interactions. Automobile salespeople, for example, attempt to "size up" potential customers soon after meeting them in the showroom in an effort to determine how serious they are about purchasing a car. A salesperson may have a positive attitude toward a well-dressed couple carrying an automobile pricing guidebook because he or she judges them to be prospective customers. The salesperson might have a negative attitude toward an individual dressed in blue jeans and a sweatshirt because he or she might be thought of as a mere windowshopper. In an effort to categorize people who enter their showroom, auto salespeople rely on well-established, but sometimes erroneous, attitudes about the appearance and behavior of potential customers. Salespeople who pay little attention to the person dressed in blue jeans and a sweatshirt may miss an opportunity to sell a car to a qualified but casually dressed potential customer.

Finally, the *value-expressive* function was conceptualized as a means for establishing and maintaining norms of social appropriateness. Katz argued that social forces applied through interaction mold self-concepts. Attitudes serve as reminders of the values and orientations of groups and organizations. When people identify with a reference group, they adopt the values and orientations of that group. For example, a devout member of the Catholic Church may hold attitudes about family planning that reflect the church's values about procreation and family development.

Also adopting a functional perspective, Smith and colleagues (1956) provided a list of attitude functions that parallel the list generated by Katz. Though important conceptual differences exist between the two lists, articulation of an exhaustive list of such functions is not the primary objective of functional theorists. Indeed, social scientists may never be able to present a truly exhaustive list of functions served by different attitudes.

The initial work produced by Smith and colleagues (1956) and Katz (1960) provided scholars with a finite number of functions that attitudes might serve. However, they provided insufficient guidance on how the functions might be measured. As a consequence, research from the functional perspective languished (Eagly & Chaiken, 1993; Maio & Olson, 2000a). Due to advances in both conceptual and measurement issues, however, the last decade has seen a strong resurgence in functional approaches to attitudes (see Maio & Olson, 2000b; Shavitt & Nelson, 2002, for recent overviews).

Recent work on functional theory has increased both the number of functions identified and the number of terms used to describe similar functions (Maio & Olson, 2000b). This recent functional research seeks to understand the psychological foundations underlying attitudes and to identify specific persuasive strategies that may be effective for changing those attitudes.

Understanding the functions that attitudes serve is important for persuasion practitioners. For example, a politician may favor racial segregation because it expresses a value (value-expressive function) or because most of the politician's constituents live in racially segregated neighborhoods (utilitarian function). These two functions have very different implications for attitude change. If the politician's attitude expresses a value, then persuasive messages designed to change the politician's attitude must address his or her prescriptive beliefs about segregation. If, on the other hand, the politician's attitude reflects a utilitarian function, then persuasive messages must convince the politician that although his or her constituents live in segregated neighborhoods, they would support programs that encourage racial integration. Put another way, it is important to match the persuasive appeal to the particular function(s) that receivers have for attitudes (Lavine & Snyder, 2000). Of the many functional studies of attitudes, one particularly interesting application is the nature of attitudes toward gay men and lesbians.

Functions of Attitudes toward Gay Men and Lesbians

Many people maintain latent prejudicial attitudes toward people from different ethnic, religious, or racial backgrounds; people of the opposite sex; and people with different sexual orientations. Although some prejudicial attitudes remain subconscious and undetected, others surface in the form of discrimination and physical abuse. In a survey of 2,000 lesbians and gay men, more than 90% of the males and 75% of the females reported that they had been verbally abused because of their sexuality (National Gay Task Force, 1984). This violence has shown no signs of abatement; indeed, "gay-bashing" is on the rise throughout the United States (J. D. Wilson, 1992).

The growing number of violent acts against lesbians and gay men has produced an increasing interest in *homophobia*, a colloquial term for negative attitudes toward gay men and lesbians. Adopting a functional framework, Herek (1984a, 1984b, 1987, 1988) has described the psychological functions served by experiential, ego-defensive, and symbolic attitudes. As part of this research, Herek (1988) developed a Likert measure of attitudes toward lesbians and gay men (Table 1.3).

Herek's (1988, 2000) concept of an *experiential attitude* is consistent with the knowledge function identified by Katz (1960). According to Herek (1984b, 1987), experiential attitudes are formed whenever affects and cognitions associated with specific interpersonal interactions are generalized to all lesbians and gay men. People with mostly positive experiences will form positive attitudes, whereas those with mostly negative experiences will form negative attitudes. Because face-to-face interactions are more informative than stereotypical information, such interactions will serve to refute stereotypes and reduce ignorance (Herek, 1984b, p. 8). Consistent with this argument is the finding that hetero-

TABLE 1.3. Herek's (1988) Measure of Attitudes toward Lesbians and Gay Men (ATLG Scale)

Attitudes Toward Lesbians (ATL) subscale

1. Lesbians just can't fit into our society. (Short-form item)
2. A women's homosexuality should *not* be a cause for job discrimination in any situation. (R)
3. Female homosexuality is detrimental to society because it breaks down the natural divisions between the sexes.
4. State laws regarding private, consenting lesbian behavior should be loosened. (R) (Short-form item)
5. Female homosexuality is a sin. (Short-form item)
6. The growing number of lesbians indicates a decline in American morals.
7. Female homosexuality in itself is no problem, but what society makes of it can be a problem. (R) (Short-form item)
8. Female homosexuality is a threat to many of our basic social institutions.
9. Female homosexuality is an inferior form of sexuality.
10. Lesbians are sick. (Short-form item)

Attitudes Toward Gay Men (ATG) subscale

11. Male homosexual couples should be allowed to adopt children the same as heterosexual couples. (R)
12. I think male homosexuals are disgusting. (Short-form item)
13. Male homosexuals should *not* be allowed to teach school.
14. Male homosexuality is a perversion. (Short-form item)
15. Just as in other species, male homosexuality is a natural expression of sexuality in human men. (R) (Short-form item)
16. If a man has homosexual feelings, he should do everything he can to overcome them.
17. I would *not* be too upset if I learned my son was a homosexual. (R)
18. Homosexual behavior between two men is just plain wrong. (Short-form item)
19. The idea of male homosexual marriages seems ridiculous to me.
20. Male homosexuality is merely a different kind of lifestyle that should *not* be condemned. (R) (Short-form item)

Note Scoring for items followed by an (R) should be reversed. People's attitudes about lesbians often differ from their attitudes about gay men. Herek recommends using separate subscales for measuring attitudes about lesbians and gay men. Items used in the short version of each subscale are indicated. From "Heterosexuals' attitudes toward lesbians and gay men: Correlates and gender differences" by G. Herek, 1988, *Journal of Sex Research*, a publication of The Society for the Scientific Study of Sex, 25, 451–477. Copyright 1988 by The Society for the Scientific Study of Sex, P.O. Box 208, Mount Vernon, IA 52314. Reprinted by permission.

sexuals with gay male and lesbian friends can more readily recognize inaccurate stereotypes and express more tolerant attitudes (Herek, 1984a). A poll indicated that only 43% of U.S. adults know someone who is openly gay, and only 20% work with someone they know is gay (Wilson, 1992). Unfortunately, people with no gay male or lesbian friends may never experience the favorable interactions that are needed to eliminate their negative stereotypes.

Herek's concept of *defensive attitudes* is consistent with Katz's ego-defensive function. Defensive attitudes result from insecurity about one's sexual identity and sexual orientation. Herek (1984b, 1987) argues that protection of insecure sexual identities and the perceived threat of homosexuality is the primary function of defensive attitudes toward lesbians and gay men. Herek (1984b) argues that insecure heterosexuals should feel more threatened by similar homosexual men and hence be more negative toward them. Consistent with this argument, San Miguel and Millham (1976) reported that men with anti-gay attitudes were more punitive toward gay men who were described as being similar to themselves than they were to gay men who were described as being different from themselves.

Researchers often separate measures of attitudes about gay men from measures of attitudes about lesbians. The reason for this is that heterosexual women tend to hold more negative attitudes toward lesbians than toward gay males, whereas heterosexual men tend to hold more negative attitudes toward gay males than toward lesbians (Herek, 1988). This distinction is further evidence of the defensive function that attitudes toward gay men and lesbians serve.

Herek's *symbolic attitudes* are similar to Katz's (1960) value-expressive function because they represent values and beliefs that are reinforced by important reference groups. Herek (1984b, 1987) argues that sexual attitudes often symbolize a person's larger ideologies, a claim that is consistent with research findings that correlate negative attitudes toward gay men with positive attitudes toward authoritarianism and religiosity and negative attitudes about pornography and erotic material (Herek, 1988). Not surprisingly, people with negative attitudes toward gay men and lesbians also tend to be less tolerant of other minority groups.

To reflect these experiential, defensive, and symbolic functions of attitudes toward gay men and lesbians, Herek (1987) developed and validated the Attitude Functions Inventory (AFI) to measure the psychological foundations of attitudes (Table 1.4). Three dimensions of the AFI, experiential-schematic, defensive, and value-expressive (symbolic), reflect Herek's three original functions of attitudes toward lesbians and gay men. An additional function, social-expressive, emphasizes the role of attitudes in the maintenance of social norms. Herek emphasizes that the AFI is a general measure of attitude functions and can be modified when used in different attitude domains.

A study examined the prominent influence of attitudes on learning about AIDS and HIV transmission. Using Herek's (1988) measure of attitudes toward lesbians and gay men, Stiff, McCormack, Zook, Stein, and Henry (1990) measured college student attitudes. Shortly after this

TABLE 1.4. Herek's (1987) Attitude Functions Inventory (AFI)

Experiential-schematic function

1. My opinions about gay men and lesbians mainly are based on whether or not someone I care about is gay.
2. My opinions about gay men and lesbians mainly are based on my personal experiences with specific gay persons.
3. My opinions about gay men and lesbians mainly are based on my judgments of how likely it is that I will interact with gay people in a significant way.
4. My opinions about gay men and lesbians mainly are based on my personal experiences with people whose family members or friends are gay.

Defensive function

5. My opinions about gay men and lesbians mainly are based on the fact that I would rather not think about homosexuality or gay people.
6. My opinions about gay men and lesbians mainly are based on my personal feeling of discomfort or revulsion at homosexuality.

Value-expressive (symbolic) function

7. My opinions about gay men and lesbians mainly are based on my concern that we safeguard the civil liberties of all people in our society.
8. My opinions about gay men and lesbians mainly are based on my beliefs about how things should be.

Social-expressive function

9. My opinions about gay men and lesbians are based on my perceptions of how the people I care about have responded to gay people as a group.
10. My opinions about gay men and lesbians mainly are based on learning how gay people are viewed by the people whose opinions I most respect.

Note. The AFI is not a measure of attitude toward gay men and lesbians. Rather, it is a measure of the psychological functions served by such attitudes. The value-expressive dimension of the AFI is most similar to the symbolic function described by Herek. From "Can functions be measured?: A new perspective on the functional approach to attitudes" by G. Herek, 1987, *Social Psychology Quarterly, 50,* 285–303. Copyright 1987 by the American Sociological Association. Reprinted by permission.

pretest, these students received an extensive lecture on psychosocial issues related to the AIDS epidemic and methods of HIV transmission.

Because the AIDS epidemic was originally associated with gay men (mass media once referred to it as "The Gay Plague" and "Gay Cancer"), we hypothesized that attitudes toward gay men and lesbians might influence learning about AIDS and HIV transmission. We found that students with extreme positive attitudes about lesbians and gay men learned more about the psychosocial issues surrounding the AIDS epidemic than students with extreme negative attitudes. However, attitudes toward gay men and lesbians were unrelated to learning about HIV transmission. Presumably all students, including those with extreme negative attitudes, were motivated to learn about "protecting themselves from the virus," whereas only those with extreme positive attitudes were motivated to learn about the psychosocial aspects of the disease itself. These findings suggest that the effects of prejudicial attitudes may extend beyond overt discrimination and violent behavior; they may also influence people's motivation to process information that has been associated with the attitude object.

SUMMARY

This chapter began with a definition of persuasion. Persuasion was defined as involving response-shaping, response-reinforcing, and response-changing processes. Examples of each process were provided along with a discussion of their implications. Following this, attitudes were defined using definitions developed by Rokeach (1969) and Fishbein and Ajzen (1975). Rokeach defined an attitude as a combination of beliefs centered around an attitude object. Fishbein and Ajzen's definition was presented as an extension of Rokeach's definition. They provided a formula for defining an attitude, arguing that a person's attitude about performing a particular behavior is a function of his or her salient beliefs and evaluation of those beliefs. Finally, Katz's functional approach to studying attitudes was discussed. Herek's description of the psychological foundations of prejudicial attitudes toward lesbians and gay men exemplified the merits of this approach.

NOTES

1. These Likert items could also be scored with values ranging from –2 to +2. While this scoring more clearly reflects the positive and negative aspect of the attitude underlying the response, it is equivalent to the 1 to 5 scoring we discussed.
2. Fishbein and Ajzen (1975) provide more extensive discussion and examples of this expectancy-value model of attitude formation. For the sake of simplicity, we include only four beliefs in this example. Fishbein and Ajzen, however, emphasize that attitudes are determined by all the salient beliefs a person may hold about a particular attitude object. In many instances, there are likely to be a large number of relevant beliefs that contribute to an attitude.

2

Investigating Persuasive Communication

Looking ahead ...

This chapter examines the scientific approach to studying persuasive communication. The chapter begins by distinguishing between commonsense observation and social science. The chapter continues with a discussion of scientific methods employed in individual investigations of persuasive communication. This discussion emphasizes design and observational procedures that are frequently employed in persuasion research. The chapter ends with a discussion of narrative and meta-analytic procedures for cumulating the findings of individual investigations.

The previous chapter reflected our beliefs that the scientific method can be used fruitfully to increase knowledge of persuasive communication. In this chapter, we intend to explain why this is the case. Before we go too far into the chapter, we need to ask the question "What is science?" Rather than viewing science as the accumulated body of knowledge, our view is that science is a way of knowing or a way of finding things out about the world. Everyone needs knowledge to survive. Almost every waking moment we are faced with having to describe, explain, and predict what is going on around us. Scientific inquiry is one way of knowing or finding out about persuasive communication.

Students frequently challenge the role of academic research in understanding persuasion. They question the utility of investigations that draw what are thought to be commonsense conclusions: "Why conduct an experiment that produces findings that everyone already knows to be true?" Responding to challenges like this is an excellent way to introduce the concept of scientific inquiry. This chapter discusses the superiority of scientific inquiry over commonsense methods for generating knowledge about persuasion. Characteristics of scientific investigations of persuasion are introduced and criteria for evaluating and cumulating findings across research investigations are discussed.

COMMON SENSE VERSUS SOCIAL SCIENCE

Persuasion is the primary function of many communicative transactions. The social systems we live in are predicated on the development and maintenance of normative behavior. As participants in these social systems, we are routinely involved in the process of shaping, maintaining, and changing the thoughts and behaviors of those around us. Implicitly or explicitly, we communicate with one another in order to create, reinforce, or change behavior.

Commonsense Theories

Through frequent involvement in persuasive transactions, we develop commonsense or "implicit theories" about strategies and tactics that are useful to achieve desired outcomes. For example, children quickly learn that the timing of their requests is essential to gaining parental compliance: sensing that a parent's foul mood is likely to produce a negative response, a child may wait for a better opportunity to ask if a friend can spend the night. As children develop cognitively, they become more sophisticated managers of social interaction (Delia & Clark, 1977; Delia, Kline, & Burleson, 1979; Marshall & Levy, 1998). Meanwhile, parents learn through trial and error which rewards and punishments are likely to influence a child's behavior; moreover, parents with multiple children learn that what is rewarding for one child may not be rewarding for another.

Over time, we come to view ourselves as experts in social influence. Armed with years of personal experience and countless opportunities for testing and validating these implicit theories, we gain confidence in our understanding of the process of persuasion. We develop and maintain these implicit theories because they help us to explain the world around us. They allow us to describe, explain, and predict what will happen to us in many persuasive exchanges. Indeed, we become so strongly attached to these implicit theories that we develop routine patterns of social influence. Salespeople, for example, can precisely describe the sequence and timing of specific compliance strategies that they believe are most likely to result in a sale. Expert teachers know when to apply sanctions for noncompliance and when to provide rewards that reinforce behavior. Politicians have discovered that "10-second sound bites" are more persuasive than 30-minute speeches. However, although they are also often insightful and frequently correct, these implicit theories are also often inadequate representations of human behavior.

Social Scientific Theories

Social scientists are also interested in theories. However, social scientists adopt a more public, systematic, and disciplined approach to developing and testing theories of human behavior. Social science theories attempt to describe, explain, and predict human behavior (for a detailed discussion of theory construction, see K. I. Miller, 2002).

For example, Inoculation Theory (McGuire, 1961a, 1961b, 1964) was developed to explain the effectiveness of techniques that are designed to increase a person's resistance to persuasion. Using a biological metaphor, McGuire described how weak attack messages can act like an inoculation (or vaccine) to help message receivers build resistance to a stronger persuasive attempt.

For over 40 years, scholars of persuasion have studied Inoculation Theory, tested its propositions, and offered modifications that expanded the theory's application and refined its predictions (McGuire, 1999; Pfau, 1992, 1995). In Chapter 13 we will discuss the evolution and application of Inoculation Theory. For now, we simply choose to use the theory as but one example of social scientific theory construction.

Comparing Social Science and "Implicit" Theories

Compared to the explanations derived from social scientific inquiry, implicit theories of persuasion have several important deficiencies. First, social science theories are explicit and publicly stated. For example, William McGuire did not develop Inoculation Theory and keep it to himself. Instead, he published several articles and research studies testing the theory and its propositions (McGuire, 1961a, 1961b, 1964). This public-nature aspect of social science research enables other scholars to scrutinize the theory and assess its validity. Implicit theories rarely receive such scrutiny.

Second, implicit theories of human interaction are not objective. Because they are derived from personal experience, commonsense observations are inextricably woven with the biases of the observer. For example, a woman who has been sexually harassed by a previous employer might respond suspiciously to her current employer's request to work late in order to complete an important project. However, the same request might not arouse the suspicions of a woman who had not been sexually harassed. These different interpretations are likely to result in the development of different theories to explain the supervisor's request. In this example, one implicit theory may be that the supervisor is interested in exploring the possibility of an amorous relationship. However, a competing implicit theory might be that the supervisor's request to work late reflects confidence in the subordinate's ability to work effectively under the pressure of a deadline. Clearly, the different experiences of these two hypothetical employees can produce dramatically different explanations for the same behavior. In this regard, an implicit theory is likely to reflect the biases of the person who develops it.

In contrast to implicit theories, social science strives to make objective observations about phenomena that are not encumbered by the biases and experiences of the people making them. For example, since McGuire first described Inoculation Theory in the early 1960s, the theory and its scope of application have been subjected to repeated tests by many different scholars studying a variety of persuasive contexts (see Chapter 13, this volume; K. I. Miller, 2002). Third, implicit theories are not derived from systematic observation. Instead, they rely on commonsense observation that is less likely to recognize or explore counterintuitive explanations of human interaction. Though many useful theories are intuitively obvious, some are not. For example, Dissonance Theory (Festinger, 1957) offered a counterintuitive prediction about the amount of attitude change people experience after advocating a position they do not believe (see Chapter 4, this volume). Over the years, Dissonance Theory has been one of the most influential and provocative theories of attitude change. However, without systematic observation it is unlikely that Dissonance Theory would have ever been developed.

Finally, though commonsense and social science explanations are both fallible, only science has a built-in self-correcting function (M. R. Cohen, 1949, p. 51; Kerlinger & Lee, 2000, p. 7). Scientists are human. They are prone to the same biases as everyone else (Gould, 1983). Through replication by different investigators, however, social science explanations are frequently reexamined. Over time, errors caused by biases and other factors are detected. When necessary, theories are modified, even discarded.

In contrast, as commonsense explanations become reified through experience, errors in reasoning become more difficult to change as time passes. Although many commonsense observations may be accurate, people often cling tenaciously to beliefs derived from commonsense observations that are incorrect. For example, for many years, people maintained a widely held belief that women are more easily persuaded than men (and many people probably still cling to this belief). Indeed, many scholars of persuasion subscribed to this belief until the careful investigations by Alice Eagly and her colleagues (Eagly, 1978; Eagly & Carli, 1981) debunked that belief (see Chapter 8, this volume).

Formal distinctions between science and commonsense observation are often based on Peirce's discussion of the scientific method. Peirce claimed that it is important to separate observations from biases and personal experiences because objectivity is an important underlying goal of science. Specifically, Peirce claimed, "The method must be such that the ultimate conclusion of every man shall be the same. Such is the method of science" (quoted in Kerlinger & Lee, 2000, p. 7).

Peirce's definition allows for only one approach to scientific inquiry. However, there are a variety of methods consistent with this approach that scientists employ to avoid the deficiencies of commonsense observation (Kerlinger & Lee, 2000, pp. 7–8). At the level of the individual investigation, the scientific approach provides specific standards for making systematic and objective observations that are capable of producing counterintuitive findings. However, scientific discovery involves more than careful attention to the design and conduct of specific investigations. It also suggests that scientists work within a community of scholars, replicating and cumulating findings over time. This self-correcting function requires different methods than those used to generate primary research findings.

The next section describes several scientific methods that are frequently used in persuasion research. For individual studies, methods of observing persuasive phenomena are presented along with criteria for evaluating the quality of those observations. Following this, two procedures for reviewing and cumulating the findings of individual studies are discussed.

SCIENTIFIC METHODS OF PERSUASIVE COMMUNICATION INQUIRY

Designing Scientific Investigations

Over the past 50 years, a variety of experimental, quasi-experimental, and nonexperimental research designs have been employed to test theoretical hypotheses about persuasive communication (Campbell & Stanley, 1966; Cook & Campbell, 1979). Regardless of their nature, research designs serve three scientific functions: (1) structuring the investigator's observations, (2) providing a logical rationale for making comparisons among observations, and (3) establishing a procedural record for other scholars who wish to examine or replicate a study's findings.

Variables

Before the specific research design categories are discussed, it is important to consider the term *variable*. Variables are an important component in social scientific theory and research. Put simply, a variable is anything that can take on more than one level (i.e., anything that is not a
constant). Sex, race, source credibility, and argument quality (among
many others) are all variables because they can take on at least two levels. Sex, for example, is a variable because people are either male or female.

In persuasion research, there are four common types of variables:
independent, dependent, intervening, and moderator variables. First, the
independent variable is a variable that is hypothesized by the researcher
to cause changes in some other variable. As we will discuss shortly, Janis
and Feshbach (1953) were interested in the persuasive impact of fear-
arousing message content on behavior change. They manipulated fear by
creating three messages that varied in the amount of fear-arousing content they contained. The amount of fear in the message, then, was the independent variable.

The second type of variable in an experiment is the *dependent variable*. Most often, the independent variable is the hypothesized cause
while the dependent variable is the hypothesized effect. Janis and
Feshbach (1953) were interested in the persuasive impact of fear-arousing message content (the independent variable) on behavior change.
Since behavior change is what the messages were supposed to influence,
they represented the dependent variable (or effect) in that study.

All studies that test causal relationships will have at least one independent variable and at least one dependent variable. In addition, some
studies have two other types of variables, intervening variables and moderator variables. An *intervening variable* (sometimes called a *mediating
variable*) is a variable that comes between the hypothesized cause and effect in a causal relationship. Consider the example in which the amount
of fear-arousing persuasive content in a message is the independent variable and behavior change is the dependent variable. It is possible, however, that there is not a direct relationship between these two variables.
Instead, it might be that the amount of fear-arousing content affects the
level of physiological arousal that message receivers experience. In turn,
it is the level of physiological arousal that motivates behavior change. In
this example, physiological arousal serves as an intervening variable because it mediates the relationship between message content (independent
variable) and behavior change (dependent variable) (see Figure 2.1).

The fourth variable type is a *moderator variable*. A moderator variable is any variable that influences the direction and/or strength of rela-

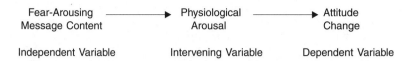

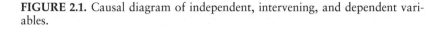

FIGURE 2.1. Causal diagram of independent, intervening, and dependent variables.

tionship between two other variables. Moderator variables, then, influence the correlation between independent and dependent variables. Hale, Lemieux, and Mongeau (1995) found that trait anxiety influenced the relationship between the amount of fear-arousing content in a message (the independent variable) and attitude change (the dependent variable). Specifically, these researchers found that for message recipients who were typically anxious people (i.e., high in trait anxiety), fear appeals had a weaker effect on attitudes than they did for people who were low in trait anxiety.

Research Design Categories

Now that we have defined the four types of variables found in studies of persuasive communication, it is time to turn our attention to the ways in which studies of persuasion are performed. There are three basic research design categories: experimental, quasi-experimental, and non-experimental (Campbell & Stanley, 1966). Two design characteristics distinguish these categories. Experimental and quasi-experimental investigations control (or manipulate[1]) at least one independent variable (hypothesized to be the cause) and measure its influence on one or more dependent variables (hypothesized to be influenced by the independent variables). Nonexperimental designs involve no such control. Instead, investigators measure one or more independent variables and assess their influence on one or more dependent variables. In short, if a study involves the *experimental control* of a variable, then it is classified as an experimental or quasi-experimental investigation.

The difference between an experiment and a quasi-experiment rests on the use of *random assignment* of research participants to experimental conditions. Random assignment means that every research participant has an equal chance of being placed in each of the experimental conditions. In some investigations, it is possible to randomly assign participants to experimental treatments. This procedure allows investigators to assume that participants assigned to different experimental conditions are similar when the study begins.[2] This assumption is useful in assessing the effects of experimental treatments (manipulations) on research participants. If there are no systematic differences among participants assigned to different experimental conditions before the experiment, then any differences arising after the experiment can be attributed to the experimental treatment (manipulation) because everything else besides the independent variable is assumed to be constant across conditions.[3]

In many investigations, however, random assignment is not possible. Participants are often assigned to treatment conditions on the basis of their membership in some predetermined group. For example, a field experiment on the effectiveness of two different television advertising campaigns may be conducted in two separate, but similar, cities. Although the communities may be randomly assigned to the treatment conditions, there are likely to be important differences in the characteristics of people in these two conditions. Thus, the effectiveness of the two campaigns can only be compared after differences between the two treatment groups are measured and *statistically controlled*. For example, if socioeconomic status (SES) is considered to be an important factor in the campaign's effectiveness, then comparisons must statistically control for differences in SES across the two communities. In this case, statistical control replaces random assignment as a means of equating the two treatment groups.

Thus, experimental control and random assignment of research participants are two factors that determine the nature of a research design. These factors are summarized in the decision tree in Figure 2.2.

In addition to the differences among experimental, quasi-experimental, and nonexperimental designs, there are also important variations in design characteristics within each of these general categories. The studies described below underscore these differences and reflect the variety of procedures employed to investigate persuasive communication. Three experimental studies help distinguish between single-factor, factorial, and repeated-measures designs. Following this discussion, two investigations are presented as examples of quasi-experimental and nonexperimental research designs.

Single-Factor Experimental Designs. The most basic experimental design involves the control (manipulation) of a single independent variable (factor) and the assessment of its influence on a dependent variable. One of the first fear-appeal experiments employed this design. As we noted above, Janis and Feshbach (1953) were interested in the effects of a single independent variable, *fear-arousing message content*, on a dependent variable, *adherence to message recommendations*.

To study this relationship, Janis and Feshbach varied the amount of

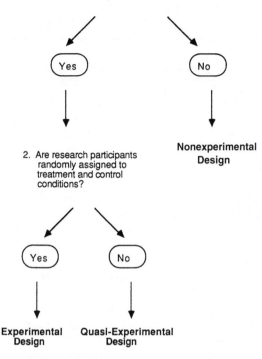

1. Does the study involve the control (manipulation) of one or more independent variables?

Yes

No

2. Are research participants randomly assigned to treatment and control conditions?

Nonexperimental Design

Yes

No

Experimental Design

Quasi-Experimental Design

FIGURE 2.2. Decision tree for categorizing study designs.

fear-arousing content in three persuasive messages. High school students were randomly assigned to one of three message (experimental) conditions or a control group. In the strong fear condition, students heard a lecture that emphasized "the painful consequences of tooth decay, diseased gums, and other dangers that can result from improper dental hygiene" (Janis & Feshbach, 1953, p. 79). The moderate fear-arousing message contained a milder and more factual presentation of these issues, and the minimal fear message contained a minimal fear appeal that "rarely alluded to the consequences of tooth neglect" (Janis & Feshbach, 1953, p. 79). Each of these messages was accompanied by a number of slides designed to match the verbal message's fear-arousing content. Participants in the no-treatment control group heard a factual lecture about the functions of the eye that was similar in intensity to the low fear message.

One week prior to the experiment, every student completed a survey of personal dental hygiene practices, such as the type of brushing strokes they used and the amount of time they spent brushing their teeth. A week following the experiment, students once again reported on these practices. Comparison of the premessage and postmessage surveys revealed that some students changed their dental hygiene practices. The difference between the percentage of students who adopted better dental hygiene and those who became worse represented the "net effect" of the message on behavior.

Results indicated that the minimal fear-arousing message was most effective in changing the actual behavior of participants. The net change in conformity was +36% in the minimal fear condition (i.e., 36% more students improved compared to those who became worse), +22% in the moderate fear condition, and +8% in the strong fear condition. There was no net change in the control condition. To explain these unanticipated findings, Janis and Feshbach (1953) speculated that "when fear is strongly aroused but is not fully relieved by the reassurances contained in the mass communication, the audience will become motivated to ignore or minimize the importance of the threat" (p. 90).

The independent variable manipulated by these investigators was the amount of fear-arousing information presented in the three persuasive messages. By using random assignment of participants to experimental treatments and holding constant all other features of the message, Janis and Feshbach were able to argue that differences in the hygiene practices of participants across the three experimental conditions following the experiment were attributable to differences in the fear-arousing content of the persuasive messages. While there may be alternative causal explanations for their results, the experimental design renders these explanations unlikely. This allowed Janis and Feshbach to conclude that the most likely explanation was that the independent variable caused the dependent variable.

The Janis and Feshbach experiment also included a no-treatment control condition. Participants assigned to this condition completed the pretest and posttest surveys of dental hygiene practices. Thus, in addition to estimating the relative effectiveness of the three experimental messages, Janis and Feshbach were also able to compare the survey results in each experimental condition with those in the control condition and estimate the absolute effectiveness of the three experimental messages. It should be noted that although many single-factor experiments contain a no-treatment control condition, this feature is not a requirement of the design. Investigators who are only concerned with the relative effects of various experimental treatments need only to include the various treatment groups in the design.

Janis and Feshbach employed a single-factor experimental design because they were only concerned with assessing the persuasive effect of a single independent variable. However, researchers soon became interested in estimating the separate and combined effects of two or more independent variables on a dependent variable, and factorial designs were developed to accomplish this objective. For example, if one wanted to determine if fear appeals are more persuasive when they come from highly credible sources, a factorial design that manipulates both the amount of fear-arousing information and the credibility of the source would be useful. Agricultural researchers of the 1930s and 1940s first employed factorial designs; by the 1960s they had become a prominent tool of persuasion scholars as well.

Factorial Experimental Designs. Often researchers are interested in investigating the separate and joint effects of two or more independent variables in a single study. Factorial designs satisfy the demands of such an investigation.

The basic requirement of a factorial design is that two or more of the independent variables must be crossed with one another. An experimental design is said to be "completely crossed" when a separate condition is created for every possible combination of all the levels of all the independent variables. For example, if one independent variable (A) has three levels (A_1, A_2, and A_3) and another (B) has two levels (B_1 and B_2), then a completely crossed design will have six experimental conditions or cells (A_1B_1, A_2B_1, A_3B_1, A_1B_2, A_2B_2, and A_3B_2; see Figure 2.3). This particular design is called a 3×2 (read as "three-by-two") factorial design because the first independent variable has three levels and the second independent variable has two levels.

Factorial designs allow researchers to identify both separate and combined impacts of the independent variables on dependent variables.

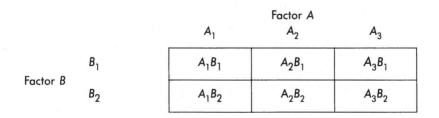

FIGURE 2.3. Diagram for a 3×2 factorial design.

The separate effects of the independent variables are called *main effects* and the combined impact of two or more independent variables are called *interaction effects*. An interaction effect occurs when a moderator variable influences the relationship between the independent and dependent variables.

Petty, Cacioppo, and Goldman (1981) employed a factorial experimental design to test the combined effects of source credibility, argument quality, and involvement on attitude change. They argued that when messages are highly involving (i.e., personally relevant), message receivers are motivated to scrutinize the quality of message arguments. They also argued that when message topics have little personal relevance, message receivers are unwilling to think carefully about the issue and instead base their attitudes on more superficial cues such as a source's expertise. Thus, Petty and colleagues hypothesized that when persuasive messages are personally relevant for receivers (i.e., high involvement), argument quality should have an important influence on attitudes. Conversely, when persuasive messages lack personal relevance for receivers (i.e., low involvement), the source's expertise should be more important in changing attitudes. Stated differently, they hypothesized two interaction effects: one specified that the level of personal relevance would "interact" with argument quality to influence attitudes and the other specified that personal relevance would "interact" with source credibility to influence attitudes.

These hypotheses specified that certain combinations of involvement and argument quality or involvement and source credibility would produce attitude change and that other combinations would produce little or no attitude change. Hence, a three-way factorial design (i.e., an experimental design with three fully crossed independent variables), which completely crossed high and low levels of involvement, argument quality, and source credibility, was employed to test these hypotheses.

Two levels of involvement (high, low), two levels of argument quality (strong, weak), and two levels of source expertise (expert, inexpert) were completely crossed to create an eight-condition experimental design (Table 2.1). Petty and colleagues (1981) then created eight experimental messages on the topic of comprehensive exams, one for each condition. For example, students in one condition heard a high-involvement message containing strong arguments that was attributed to an expert source. Students in another condition heard a high-involvement message containing strong arguments that was attributed to an inexpert source, and so on.

Participants were randomly assigned to one of the eight experimental conditions and then listened to a recorded message. Participants com-

TABLE 2.1. Three-Way Factorial Design from Petty, Cacioppo, and Goldman (1981)

	High involvement		Low involvement	
	Expert source	Nonexpert source	Expert source	Nonexpert source
Strong arguments				
Weak arguments				

pleted an attitude questionnaire (among other measures). The use of random assignment permitted the assumption that the attitudes of participants across the eight experimental conditions were similar prior to hearing the message. Hence, any differences across conditions after the message presentation could be attributed to the message presentation itself.

Petty and colleagues (1981) observed their hypothesized effects. As Table 2.2 reveals, participants hearing the high-involvement message were influenced primarily by the quality of the message arguments and not by the source's expertise. Specifically, on the left side of Table 2.2 (i.e., high involvement), average scores are higher in the upper two cells (corresponding to the strong arguments) when compared with the lower two cells (i.e., weak arguments). Participants hearing the low-involvement message were influenced primarily by the source's expertise and were relatively unaffected by the quality of message arguments. In the right-hand portion of Table 2.2 (i.e., low involvement), left-hand-most cells (i.e., expert source) have higher means than the right-hand-most cells (i.e., nonexpert source).

TABLE 2.2. Findings from the Petty, Cacioppo, and Goldman (1981) Study

	High involvement		Low involvement	
	Expert source	Nonexpert source	Expert source	Nonexpert source
Strong arguments	.64	.61	.40	−.12
Weak arguments	−.38	−.58	.25	−.64

Note. Numbers are standardized attitude scores for participants in the experimental conditions. The score for participants in a no-message control condition was −.18. From "Personal involvement as a determinant of argument-based persuasion" by R. E. Petty, J. T. Cacioppo, & R. Goldman, 1981, *Journal of Personality and Social Psychology, 41,* 847–855. Copyright 1981 by the American Psychological Association. Reprinted by permission.

The factorial design was critical for the Petty and colleagues (1981) experiment. The design systematically controlled the levels of involvement, argument quality, and source expertise, and it assessed the separate and combined influence of these independent variables on the attitudes of message receivers. Without a factorial design, it would have been very difficult to assess the combined (interaction) effects of these variables. Because researchers are frequently interested in both the separate (i.e., main) and combined (i.e., interaction) effects of two or more independent variables, factorial designs have become a critical tool of experimental persuasion research.

Though research designs have become more sophisticated over the past 40 years, one important feature of many early persuasion experiments has been lost in contemporary persuasion research. Early researchers were frequently interested in both the immediate and the delayed effects of persuasive communication. Present-day theorists demonstrate relatively little concern for the persistence of persuasive effects, even though persistence remains an important theoretical concern. As a result, designs that assess persuasive effects over time are rarely employed in contemporary persuasion research. Nevertheless, repeated-measures designs remain an important, though underutilized, tool of persuasion research.

Repeated-Measures Experimental Designs. The critical feature of repeated-measures designs is the use of multiple assessments (or measurements) of the dependent variable. Repeated measures can be used in conjunction with both single-factor and factorial designs. Whereas the terms *single factor* and *factorial* describe the structure of the experimental treatments (i.e., manipulations), the term *repeated measures* refers to the assessment (or measurement) of a dependent variable at multiple points in time. Thus, both single-factor experiments and factorial designs can incorporate repeated measures of the dependent variable. For example, if Petty and colleagues (1981) had been interested in the persisting effects of argument quality and source credibility, they would have measured the attitudes again a few weeks later to determine the extent to which attitudes remained the same or decayed over time.

Investigations of the "sleeper effect" have traditionally relied on repeated-measures designs. Hovland, Lumsdaine, and Sheffield (1949) first observed the sleeper effect when they found that messages presented by low-credible sources were not immediately accepted, but became more influential over time. Hovland and his colleagues speculated that the negative effects of the source's credibility may initially offset the positive effects of a persuasive message, but that over time the source becomes disassociated from the message—that is, people remember the message content, but not its source. Because the message content is persuasive, attitude change at a later point in time is more positive than immediately following the message presentation.

As part of a larger study, Kelman and Hovland (1953) tested this hypothesis. They exposed students to a persuasive message from a positive or a negative communicator. The message advocated lenient treatment of juvenile delinquents. The positive communicator was described as a judge who had authored several books on juvenile delinquency and was well known for his views on the integration of the delinquent into society. The negative communicator was described as a "man on the street" who gave the impression of being obnoxious and self-centered and indicated he got into several "scrapes" as a youngster.

Before the experiment, participants in both groups had similar opinions about the treatment of juvenile delinquents. Immediately following the message presentation, participants listening to the positive communicator demonstrated significantly more agreement with the communicator ($M = 46.70$) than participants exposed to the same message attributed to a negative communicator ($M = 42.75$). After 3 weeks, participants were once again asked to indicate their opinions about the treatment of juvenile delinquents. Posttest opinions had decreased significantly ($M = -3.22$) among participants exposed to the positive communicator, while the posttest opinions of participants exposed to the negative communicator became slightly more positive ($M = +0.65$). Together, these changes represented a convergence of opinions when attitudes are measured a second time. This finding is consistent with the general pattern predicted by the sleeper effect. Over time, attitude change produced by the positive communicator decreased considerably while attitude change produced by the negative communicator increased slightly.

Relatively few studies have focused on the immediate and delayed effects of persuasive messages on attitudes and behaviors. Nevertheless, investigators who are interested in the persistence of change in attitudes and behaviors over time typically employ a repeated-measures design.

Quasi-Experimental Designs. For many investigations, it is possible to experimentally control one or more of the independent variables under consideration but impossible to randomly assign participants to experimental conditions. Field studies, for example, often involve the use of intact groups. Reliance on intact groups negates the advantages of random assignment and results in reliance on quasi-experimental designs. Because quasi-experiments do not involve random assignment of participants to treatment conditions, they preclude the assumption that participants in different treatment groups are relatively similar to one another. To alleviate this problem, statistical techniques (i.e., analysis of covariance) are used by researchers to control statistically for preexisting differences between treatment groups.

With the exception of assigning participants to treatment conditions, quasi-experimental and experimental designs are identical. Hence, one could conduct a quasi-experiment using a single-factor or a factorial design with single or repeated measures of the dependent variables. Though random assignment of participants to treatment conditions is desirable, field investigations do not always afford researchers this luxury. For example, a study of the effectiveness of a drug resistance program for high school students would be difficult to conduct with an experimental design. Most likely, a quasi-experimental design would be used and intact classes (or schools) would be assigned to the treatment and control conditions. In this instance, it would be impractical, and perhaps undesirable, to randomly assign students within the same classes (or school) to different conditions. Nevertheless, because field settings often prove to be more realistic arenas for persuasion research, quasi-experimental designs are an attractive alternative for scholars.

Hecht, Corman, and Miller-Rassulo (1993) utilized a quasi-experimental design to test the effectiveness of their Drug Resistance Strategies Project skills training program (see Chapter 12 for a more detailed discussion of this project). This program is designed to give high school students the persuasive skills they need to resist others' attempts to get them to use illegal drugs. They tested the effectiveness of their program in a high school in the southwestern United States. An approximately 30-minute skills training presentation entitled "Killing Time" was either presented live or on film. After the presentation, a follow-up discussion was performed for some groups but not for others. Still another group was not exposed to the training program at all. As a consequence, Hecht and colleagues created five experimental conditions: live presentation with discussion, live presentation without discussion, film presentation with discussion, film presentation without discussion, and a control (i.e., exposed to neither presentation nor discussion). A variety of variables, including drug use, attitudes toward drug use, and confidence in refusing drug offers were measured 1 month before, immediately after, and 1 month following the presentations. Because of restrictions created by the school setting, they could assign classrooms, but not participants, to five conditions. This is the factor that makes this a quasi-experimental, rather than an experimental, design.

Results of the Hecht and colleagues (1993) investigation indicated that 1 month following the program, students in all of the conditions except live performance without discussion exhibited less drug use when compared with control students. Moreover, when compared with control conditions, both discussion conditions created more negative attitudes toward drug use, perceptions that fewer of their peers were using drugs, and increased confidence in refusing future drug offers.

While their findings were not particularly strong, the Hecht and colleagues (1993) investigation indicates that a single presentation of an anti-drug program can produce changes in various attitude, belief, and behavioral outcomes. Moreover, given the restrictions of the research setting (i.e., a high school) an experimental design was not possible. In such cases, researchers have no choice but to use a quasi-experimental design.

Though experimental and quasi-experimental designs have several desirable features, in many situations it is impossible or impractical for investigators to control or manipulate the theoretical variables of interest. In these situations, researchers rely on nonexperimental procedures for estimating relationships among variables and testing hypotheses. Though a variety of procedures exist, the study described below illustrates the utility of nonexperimental procedures for persuasion research.

Nonexperimental Designs. For over 50 years, persuasion scholars have devoted considerable effort to understanding the relationship between attitudes and behaviors (see Chapters 3 and 4). One popular strategy has been to identify factors that influence the strength of the attitude–behavior relationship. For example, Sivacek and Crano (1982) hypothesized that *vested interest*, the extent to which the message topic influences a person's life, would moderate the strength of this relationship. They argued that when people had a vested interest in a topic, their attitude about the issue would correspond with their behavior about the issue (i.e., the attitude–behavior correlation would be strong). Conversely, Sivacek and Crano predicted a weak attitude–behavior relationship when people had no vested interest in a topic.

To test this hypothesis, Sivacek and Crano (1982, Study 1) asked college students to complete an attitude survey that included questions about a state ballot initiative to raise the legal drinking age from 18 to 21 years. After 7 to 10 days, students were contacted by a different person and asked if they were willing to work to defeat the proposal to raise the drinking age. The amount of time students volunteered to work was the measure of their behavior (actually of their behavioral *intention*, as students did not actually participate in the campaign against the proposal).

Most of the students (80%) reported a negative attitude toward the proposal. Demographic information allowed students to be classified into three groups. Students who would be unaffected by the proposal (i.e., those who would be 21 when the law was enacted) were placed in the low-vested-interest group. Students who would be legally prevented from drinking for at least 2 years (i.e., 18- and 19-year-olds) were placed in a high-vested-interest group. Finally, a few students were placed in a moderate-vested-interest group because the new law would affect them for less than 2 years. Notice that this categorization scheme produced three groups of participants who were analytically equivalent to participants in three experimental conditions without randomly assigning participants to groups.

Sivacek and Crano (1982) reported that the attitude–behavioral intention relationship was strongest for students in the high-vested-interest group ($r = .61$), followed by those in the moderate-vested-interest group ($r = .40$), and by those in the low-vested-interest group ($r = .16$).[4] Thus, without the use of an experimental treatment, Sivacek and Crano were able to statistically create three groups that represented varying levels of vested interest and estimate the effect of vested interest on the relationship between attitude and behavior. Although these procedures may appear similar to those used in experimental investigations, the Sivacek and Crano study did not involve the experimental control or manipulation of independent variables. Nevertheless, the statistical controls employed by Sivacek and Crano permitted a scientific examination of the relationship between attitudes and behaviors.

Critics of nonexperimental investigations sometimes engage in fallacious reasoning. These critics have argued that one cannot draw causal inferences with correlational data. Causal inferences, they argue, can only be derived from experimental investigations. Such claims reflect a basic misunderstanding of causal inference and experimental design.

John Stuart Mill identified three requirements for inferring causation: time ordering, covariation, and elimination of alternative interpretations for the relationship. That is, before variable A can be inferred to cause variable B, A must precede B in time, A and B must be conceptually and empirically related, and all alternative explanations for the relationship between A and B must be examined (Cook & Campbell, 1979, pp. 18–19). For example, if attitudes are hypothesized to cause behaviors, then attitudes must be formed before the behavior occurs, attitudes must be conceptually and empirically related to behaviors, and all rival explanations for the attitude–behavior relationship must be examined.

Notice, however, that Mill's criteria suggest nothing about the method of observation to be used in gathering the necessary information for causal inference. Individual experiments or quasi-experiments are helpful in meeting the first two criteria, time ordering and covariation, but by themselves they cannot rule out all rival explanations for the hypothesized causal relationship. Nonexperimental observations can also be used to establish temporal ordering and covariation. Statistical procedures such as causal modeling and time-series analyses are effective substitutes for experimental control. Once again, however, the application of these techniques in a single investigation is inadequate for eliminating rival explanations. Thus, regardless of its design, no single investigation is capable of meeting Mill's criteria for inferring a causal relationship. Instead, the process of causal inference occurs over time and with converging evidence generated from many different observations made by a variety of researchers. Clearly, the observation of a correlation between two variables is inadequate for drawing a causal inference. Instead, careful procedures must be employed to meet all three of Mill's criteria.

Many additional designs have been employed in prior persuasion research and could have been included in this review. However, the purpose of this section was to describe the basic designs that have contributed to our understanding of persuasive communication. The designs discussed in this chapter reflect a variety of analytical problems investigators face when structuring observations of persuasive phenomena. Although they provide the structure necessary to make systematic and objective observations, these designs provide only a partial picture of the observation process. The next section reviews methods of observation frequently employed in persuasion research and identifies criteria for evaluating these methods.

Evaluating Observational Procedures

Just as there are a variety of ways of creating an experimental design, there are many ways of observing (or measuring) dependent variables. Each of these observational methods can be placed on a continuum ranging from direct to indirect. Direct observational procedures typically involve the coding of actual behavior by trained observers. For example, an investigation of the nonverbal correlates of high- and low-credible speakers might involve the videotaped recording of message presentations by speakers who are judged to have high or low credibility. Trained raters could then code these videotaped messages and identify the frequency and/or duration of various nonverbal behaviors. Such coding procedures are relatively direct because there are few opportunities for slippage between the actual and the measured behavior.

Less direct procedures involve self-reports of prior behavior. For example, memory-recall procedures may ask participants to remember a time when they persuaded a friend to do a favor for them and describe the strategies they used. Though they focus on actual behavior, these procedures depend on accurate memories and can be biased by memory lapses and willful distortion. Hence, the opportunity for measurement error is greater with self-report and recall procedures than with observation of actual behavior.

Because attitudes are constructs that cannot be directly observed, assessment of their existence is often based on the indirect self-reports of research participants. The Gallup Poll, for example, routinely assesses the opinions and attitudes of Americans about a variety of topics. Because self-reports of attitudes or opinions cannot be verified, this measurement technique is placed at the indirect end of the continuum.

Regardless of its placement along the direct–indirect continuum, the utility or quality of any observational procedure is determined by its *reliability* and its *validity*. The application of these criteria is discussed below.

Reliability

In a measurement or observation context, reliability means consistency. An observational procedure is said to be reliable if it produces consistent and stable estimates of the phenomenon under investigation. For direct observation procedures, having at least two people observe the behavior of interest and then compare their ratings typically assesses reliability. If there is considerable agreement among the coders' ratings (generally 85% or more is acceptable), the coding is considered reliable. However, the amount of agreement among coders depends in part on the number of categories in the coding scheme. If a coding scheme includes only three categories, then 33% agreement among coders should be expected by chance alone. If a coding scheme has only two categories, chance agreement is 50%. The extent of agreement among coders will be inflated by these chance agreements. Cohen's kappa, a more sophisticated reliability statistic, was developed to account for chance probabilities in agreement percentages (J. Cohen, 1960). Kappa values never exceed 1.00. Typically, coding procedures that produce kappa values above .75 are considered to be sufficiently reliable, though higher values are always desirable.

When self-report procedures are used, researchers often assess reliability by comparing the responses among two or more items (e.g., questions or opinion statements) that were designed to measure the same construct, that is, an attitude or behavioral intention. If a measurement scale is reliable, then a person's responses to one item measuring the construct will be similar to his or her responses to all other items in the scale. For example, a correlation of .80 between two items reflects a high degree of association between peoples' responses to the two items. Coefficient alpha is a statistic that represents the proportion of measurement error (or inconsistency) in a scale and is a function of the degree of association among all the items in a scale or measure. Alpha values range from .00 to 1.00. Typically, self-report measures that produce alpha levels exceeding .70 are considered to be sufficiently reliable, though once again higher alpha values are desirable.

Validity

An observational procedure is said to have validity if it precisely measures the phenomenon of interest. Though there are few statistical procedures for assessing the validity of a measure, four criteria—face validity, content validity, pragmatic validity, and construct validity—are frequently employed to evaluate the validity of an observational procedure (Kerlinger & Lee, 2000).

Face validity is a "commonsense" criterion. Most often, checks for face validity consist of reviewing the questions contained in a measure to determine if they seem to be measuring the construct they are intended to measure. Although it is the least important of the four criteria, a check for face validity is an important step in the validation process. If a measure lacks face validity, it will probably also fail to meet the other checks for validity. Even if a researcher can provide evidence of the other forms of validity, scholars will likely remain skeptical due to the lack of face validity.

Content validity reflects the extent to which the measure or observational procedure fully represents the phenomenon under consideration. In other words, does the measure of observation procedure tap the entire variable as it was conceptually defined? For example, the content validity of a midterm exam depends on the extent to which questions on the exam reflect the scope and depth of issues covered in the course. When students complain that an exam "did not cover the material discussed in class," they are essentially criticizing the content validity of the exam.

Pragmatic validity refers to the utility of a measure or observational procedure. Measures that discriminate between groups of people at the present time are said to have concurrent pragmatic validity. For example, a final exam in a persuasion course has concurrent pragmatic validity if it discriminates between students who understand the course material and those who do not. A measure is said to have predictive pragmatic validity if it helps to predict or forecast differences among people at some point in the future. Standardized exams such as the Scholastic Aptitude Test are part of the entrance requirements to many universities and colleges because they help predict how students will perform in university settings.

Construct validity is the most important form of validity and refers to the relationship between the measure under consideration and measures of other variables. A measure has construct validity if it is positively correlated with measures of variables that are conceptually similar, negatively correlated with measures of conceptually opposite variables, and unrelated to measures of variables that are conceptually independent. For example, responses to a valid measure of attitudes toward Cuban president Fidel Castro should be negatively related to a measure of attitudes toward capitalism, positively related to a measure of attitudes toward Marxism, and unrelated to a measure of intelligence.

Unfortunately, most persuasion studies fail to document the validity of the measures used. Though it is common practice to discuss the reliability of measures, for a number of reasons most studies provide little or no evidence to establish the validity of measurement instruments. Nevertheless, validity and reliability are essential features of effective observation, and consequently the quality of the investigation.

Evaluating Experimental and Quasi-Experimental Treatments

Validity and reliability concerns are not limited to the observation of independent and dependent variables. Experimental controls (manipulations) also vary in the degree to which they produce their intended effects. Reports of experimental and quasi-experimental studies typically include information regarding the effectiveness of the manipulations.

Manipulation checks are often used to evaluate the quality and strength of a treatment. Frequently, manipulation checks involve asking research participants to evaluate the effects of the treatment. For example, a study of fear appeals may manipulate the amount of fear-arousing content in persuasive messages. To check the quality of the manipulation, a researcher might ask participants to indicate how fearful the message made them feel. If participants exposed to the high fear message treatment perceived substantially more fear than those exposed to the low fear message treatment, evidence exists for the quality of the treatment.

A prevalent limitation of persuasion research stems from the weak correlation between the intended and the actual effects of experimental treatments. The pervasiveness of this problem is apparent in several quantitative literature reviews. For example, a review of the fear-appeal literature found only a moderate average correlation ($r = .36$) between manipulated and perceived fear (Boster & Mongeau, 1984). Though manipulation checks in most fear-appeal experiments were statistically significant, a correlation of $r = .36$ means that the average manipulation accounted for less than 13% of the variance in participant reports of aroused fear.

Findings such as these raise two essential concerns about experimental treatments. First, when ineffective treatments are employed, it is very difficult to examine the hypothesis in question. For example, if fear-appeal experiments fail to create messages that differ considerably in the amount of fear they arouse, then it is difficult to determine whether differences in fear-arousing content account for observed changes in attitudes and behaviors. Second, the use of ineffective treatments raises questions about the conceptual development of the variable or construct under consideration. Perhaps researchers have difficulty creating effective fear-appeal treatments because they do not clearly understand what makes a message arouse fear in message receivers.

Together, these issues underscore a point raised earlier in this chapter: though experimental treatments are often referred to as "manipulations," we don't really "manipulate" people in our research. Instead, we manipulate levels of the independent variable and assess the effects of these treatments on relevant attitudes and behaviors. The fact that our treatments are always less than perfect in creating their intended effect (e.g., the arousal of fear) underscores the importance of viewing a treatment as the manipulation of a variable rather than as the manipulation of research participants.

Even when they achieve their intended effects, experimental treatments may fail because they also produce unanticipated effects. This problem arises most frequently in experiments that cross two or more treatments in a factorial design. Treatments in factorial designs are usually intended to be independent of one another. However, when used in combination, they may produce perceptions that are highly related. For example, in one of the seminal investigations of the Elaboration Likelihood Model (ELM) of persuasion (Petty et al., 1981), the argument quality treatment had a stronger effect on perceived source expertise than the source expertise treatment! Clearly, the perceptions created by the source expertise and argument quality treatments were confounded, so that the strength of the arguments had more influence on perceived source expertise than the source's credentials did. These problems are not limited to investigations of the ELM, but are prevalent throughout the persuasion literature.

In the fear-appeal arena, Dillard, Plotnick, Godbold, Freimuth, and Edgar (1996) investigated the affective (i.e., emotional) reactions created by fear appeals in the form of AIDS public service announcements (i.e., PSAs). They found that AIDS PSAs influenced a host of affective reactions in receivers including, of course, fear, but also surprise, puzzlement, anger, happiness, and sadness. As a consequence, experimental manipulations of fear may create a number of unexpected affective and emotional processes. This is important because the varying reactions may amplify, interfere with, or eliminate the impact of fear on attitude and behavior change. As a consequence, it may be difficult to determine the impact of fear (alone) on persuasive outcomes.

Up to this point, the issues discussed in this chapter have focused on the generation and interpretation of scientific data in single study investigations. However, the generation of effects is only part of the scientific process. Once numerous studies have investigated a particular phenomenon, scholars face the task of combining findings from individual studies and integrating them with a larger body of persuasion literature. The next section discusses two methods for combining or cumulating findings of individual investigations.

Cumulating Findings of Individual Investigations

The most difficult requirement for drawing causal inferences is the elimination of rival explanations for the findings of an individual investigation. Many rival explanations can be routinely discounted through careful design and analysis of observations. However, rival explanations that are derived from alternative theoretical perspectives often require researchers to develop and conduct several investigations before they can confidently choose among competing explanations. Examination of self-perception and dissonance explanations for attitude change following counterattitudinal advocacy provides a clear account of this process. As discussed in Chapter 4, Bem's (1967, 1972) Self-Perception Theory provided a plausible rival account for the findings from many tests of Dissonance Theory conducted during the 1960s. After a decade of investigations pitting the two competing explanations against one another, researchers concluded that both explanations may be correct, but that each is applicable in certain circumstances (Fazio, Zanna, & Cooper, 1977).

The process of testing rival explanations exemplifies the continuous nature of scientific inquiry. Through replication and extension of prior investigations, scientists accumulate knowledge about phenomena of interest. The knowledge generated by individual investigations is then codified in reviews of the literature. Two types of reviews—narrative summaries and meta-analysis—appear frequently in the persuasion literature; both are described below.

Narrative Summaries

Traditional reviews of the persuasion literature consist of narrative descriptions of studies investigating the same phenomenon. These summaries critically evaluate the quality of individual investigations, highlight conceptual differences among them, and organize their findings along unifying dimensions.

Ajzen and Fishbein's (1977) review of the attitude–behavior literature exemplifies the narrative review. They attempted to reconcile the contradictory conclusions of studies investigating the relationship between people's attitudes and their behaviors. As discussed in Chapter 3, Ajzen and Fishbein developed several conceptual and empirical explanations for the apparent discrepancies among the findings of studies in their review.

Eagly's (1978) review of studies investigating the effects of gender on persuasability (see Chapter 8, this volume) is another example of a narrative review. In addition to evaluating the conceptual and methodological characteristics of studies in her review, Eagly counted the number of investigations that found women to be more easily persuaded, less easily persuaded, and no more or less persuasible than men. This counting procedure allowed her to draw inferences about the relationship between gender and influenceability based on a large number of investigations.

Although such counting procedures can be insightful, they represent only rough approximations of the actual relationship among variables of interest. As such, narrative reviews can result in more erroneous conclusions than reviews employing meta-analytic procedures.

Meta-Analytic Summaries

During the 1980s, meta-analytic procedures were developed to provide more quantitative literature reviews (Glass, McGaw, & Smith, 1981; Hunter & Schmidt, 1990; Hunter, Schmidt, & Jackson, 1982). Meta-analytic reviews begin with a critical assessment of the quality of individual investigations and the conceptual differences among them. This leads to a more complete understanding of the relationship between the independent and the dependent variables. Once the important study features have been identified, the empirical review takes place in two stages. The first stage of this review involves the estimation of the strength of relationship among variables of interest for each study. This estimation is called a *study effect size* (e.g., a correlation coefficient). After the effect sizes have been computed for each study in the review, they are averaged into a set of statistics that summarizes the entire body of literature.

Meta-analysis has a number of empirical advantages over traditional counting procedures. Counting procedures rarely consider the strength of the relationship among variables of interest. Hence, a small, but significant, effect is counted the same as a very strong effect. Meta-analysis, on the other hand, is predicated on estimating the strength of relationships among variables. In addition, "Hunterian" meta-analysis (Hunter et al., 1982; Hunter & Schmidt, 1990) provides formulas for correcting these estimates for measurement error (e.g., unreliability) and other factors. Measures used in persuasion research are never perfect and the presence of measurement error always reduces the size of the observed relationship among variables. Correcting individual study estimates for measurement error produces a more accurate (and larger) estimate of the relationship between variables. Finally, although counting procedures weigh all studies equally, the procedures developed by Hunter and colleagues correct for sampling error. By weighing each estimate by the study sample size, meta-analysis places more emphasis on the findings of studies with large samples than on those with smaller samples.

In addition to its statistical prowess, meta-analysis has the added advantage of giving consideration to every study included in the review. Narrative reviews are sometimes biased by the findings of one or two studies published in prominent journals. To correct this problem, meta-analysis requires the analysis of every investigation that meets the conceptual criteria for inclusion in the review. With meta-analysis, an investigation conducted by the most prominent persuasion scholar and published in a high-quality journal receives the same attention as one conducted by a little-known scholar that appears in an obscure journal.

Meta-analyses allow researchers to draw much more specific conclusions about the nature of a body of studies than would be possible with narrative reviews. For example, following up on Eagly's (1978) narrative review, Eagly and Carli (1981) performed a meta-analysis on the same set of studies. After meta-analyzing the studies, they were able to make much more precise statements about the issue of sex differences in persuasibility.

Kim and Hunter (1993a, 1993b) meta-analyzed the literature related to the relationship between attitudes and behaviors (see Chapter 3, this volume). Not only were the estimates of the correlation between attitudes and behaviors more precise in their meta-analysis, the results (particularly after effect sizes were corrected) indicated that the correlation between attitudes and behaviors was much stronger than most scholars would have expected.

Because they do not always concur with prevailing wisdom, or the conclusions of prior narrative reviews, meta-analytic reviews are sometimes controversial. Two meta-analytic reviews (Johnson & Eagly, 1989; Stiff, 1986) produced findings that questioned the validity of the Elaboration Likelihood Model of persuasion (see Chapter 10, this volume), and these reviews were met with intense criticism from the authors of the model (Petty & Cacioppo, 1990; Petty, Kasmer, Haugtvedt, & Cacioppo, 1987). Critiques such as the latter often focus on the appropriateness and utility of various meta-analytic techniques. As these exchanges indicate, meta-analytic reviews are subject to the same reinterpretation and scrutiny as original investigations of persuasive communication. Moreover, as with any narrative review, the validity of a meta-analytic review is dependent on the quality of the individual investigations included in the review. Though procedures for correcting measurement and sampling error exist, other limitations of primary research are often reflected in the quality of the conclusions emerging from these reviews.

SUMMARY

This chapter began with a discussion of the differences between scientific and commonsense observation. It was argued that scientific observations are a superior method for generating knowledge because they are systematic and strive for objectivity, are capable of producing counterintuitive findings, and have a self-correcting function. Consistent with the scientific method, several experimental, quasi-experimental, and nonexperimental research designs were described. These designs reflect strategies for structuring observations about persuasive phenomena. Following this was a discussion of several procedures for observing persuasive phenomena along with criteria and procedures for assessing the reliability and validity of these observations. The chapter concluded with a discussion of narrative and meta-analytic methods for cumulating the findings of individual investigations in a review of the literature.

NOTES

1. The term *manipulation* here is used in an emotionally neutral fashion. To manipulate means that the experimenter creates at least two levels of the independent variable. People are exposed to the various levels of the independent variable. As a consequence, variables are being manipulated, and not people.
2. It should be emphasized that random assignment does not guarantee equivalence among participants in different experimental conditions. Random assignment reduces systematic differences among the participants in experimental conditions but it cannot eliminate them. In addition, the procedures used for random assignment in many experiments are not truly "random." As a result, random and nonrandom differences may exist in many investigations that are labeled experiments.
3. Such conclusions should not be taken lightly, however. To assume that there

are no threats to the validity of a design or research procedure is akin to assuming a perfect world. In almost any experiment there are several issues that can be raised to challenge the internal or external validity of the findings. Given this reality, researchers strive to minimize such threats and replicate their findings by conducting multiple investigations with different samples and procedures. Only after repeated replication with various methods should researchers become confident of the findings they observe. Campbell and Stanley (1966) and D. T. Cook and Campbell (1979) provide excellent discussions of these issues.

4. The letter r stands for a statistic called the Pearson product–moment correlation coefficient (or, more simply, the correlation). The correlation coefficient measures the linear association between two variables. Correlations range from −1.00 (a perfect linear association between variables where as one variable increases, the other variable decreases) to +1.00 (a perfect linear association between variables where as one variable increases, the other variable increases). A correlation of 0.00 indicates that there is no linear association between variables. The larger the correlation (either positive or negative), the more accurately you can predict one variable by knowing the level of the other.

3

Examining the Attitude–Behavior Relationship

LOOKING AHEAD ...

This chapter examines the attitude–behavior literature with an eye toward establishing the boundary conditions under which attitudes predict behavior. The chapter begins with a description of the first classic investigation of the relationship between attitudes and behaviors. Next comes a discussion of Ajzen and Fishbein's (1977) review of this literature, which serves as a framework for assessing this relationship. Fishbein and Ajzen's (1980) Theory of Reasoned Action is then presented to describe factors that attenuate the attitude–behavior relationship. Finally, the chapter closes with a discussion of several factors that moderate the strength of the attitude–behavior relationship.

Persuasion scholars have traditionally focused their attention on predicting attitudes and attitude change and have exhibited relatively little concern for assessing persuasive effects via behavioral measures. According to G. R. Miller and Burgoon, "So pervasive has been the tendency of persuasion researchers to employ attitude change as their principle measure of persuasive effect that the terms 'persuasion' and 'attitude change' are virtually synonymous" (1978, p. 34). As we discussed in Chapter 1, the attitude construct was created by social scientists who sought an intervening process to explain behavioral reactions to stimuli. Both the Rokeach (1968) and the Fishbein and Ajzen (1975) views of attitudes discussed in Chapter 1 highlighted the close conceptual link between attitudes and behaviors. As a consequence, the utility of the attitude construct rests largely on its ability to predict and explain behavior. Consequently, the utility of any persuasive theory emphasizing attitudes is dependent on the predictive strength of the corresponding attitude–behavior relationship. If attitudes do not predict behaviors, there may not be sufficient reason to keep the attitude concept.

If the relationship between attitudes and behaviors is consistently strong, then reliance on attitudes as a sole measure of persuasive effect permits the prediction of consequent behaviors. Unfortunately, the relationship between attitudes and behaviors has been difficult to establish. Since the early 1930s, investigations of this relationship have produced mixed findings and stimulated considerable debate about the utility of the attitude construct.

THE LAPIERE STUDY

LaPiere (1934) performed one of the first investigations of the relationship between people's attitudes and their corresponding behavior. LaPiere was intrigued by earlier research suggesting that people's attitudes on racial issues were not closely related to their behaviors. In addition, he was concerned about the utility of questionnaires as a valid method of measuring attitudes. To investigate these issues, LaPiere traveled the West Coast for parts of 2 years with a Chinese couple. During their travels, they stayed in hotels and roadside campgrounds that varied in quality. They also ate at cafés and restaurants, some of which were much nicer than others. On some occasions, LaPiere entered the service establishments with the Chinese couple and asked for service. On other occasions, he asked the Chinese couple to enter the establishments on their own and to ask for service. Sometimes the trio was well dressed, other times they dressed casually, and sometimes they were dusty from the road.

LaPiere kept a diary of the group's interactions with people they encountered. He noted that of the 251 hotels, campgrounds, restaurants, and cafés they entered, they were only refused service once. Moreover, LaPiere found that the overall quality of service they received was quite good and that there was no pattern of discriminatory service in the establishments they visited.

Several months after they completed their travels, LaPiere sent questionnaires to the establishments they had visited and several that they had not visited. The questionnaires asked whether the establishment would provide service to a Chinese couple. Responses from 92% of the restaurants and cafés and 91% of hotels and campgrounds that they had visited indicated that the establishment would *not* provide service to Chinese.

Clearly, the attitudes reflected in the questionnaire responses were incompatible with the pattern of behavior LaPiere observed when traveling with the Chinese couple. Though this investigation is not without its methodological limitations, the findings are generally considered to be incontrovertible: the attitudes reflected in the questionnaire responses were inconsistent with, indeed the opposite of, the behaviors LaPiere observed.[1]

The LaPiere investigation raised questions about the validity of self-report attitude measures and about the relationship between attitudes and behavior. Investigations that followed contributed to the controversy over the utility of the attitude construct. Results of subsequent studies on the relationship between attitudes and behaviors were hopelessly inconsistent. Some studies found strong relationships while others found no relationship at all. Early optimistic assessments of the importance of attitudes (e.g., Allport, 1935) faded into critical evaluations of the attitude construct. By the 1960s, contradictory findings from many investigations caused some scholars to seriously question the viability of the attitude construct for predicting behavior (Festinger, 1964; Wicker, 1969). Wicker (1969) went so far as to suggest that if strong relationships between attitudes and behaviors were not found more consistently, then one possibility was "to abandon the attitude concept in favor of directly studying overt behavior" (p. 75).

By 1970, things were looking grim for the attitude construct. Persuasion scholars, however, were unwilling to let go of attitudes as an explanatory construct. In response to Wicker's (1969) call to abandon attitudes, scholars developed two separate streams of research (Greenwald, 1989). First, one set of researchers (Ajzen & Fishbein, 1977; Fishbein & Ajzen, 1975) emphasized methodological explanations for the contradictory findings of prior investigations. In the other stream of research, scholars began to investigate moderator variables that affect the strength of the attitude–behavior relationship (Fazio & Zanna, 1981; D. J. O'Keefe & Delia, 1981; Sivacek & Crano, 1982). These efforts are examined in the following sections.

CHARACTERISTICS OF ATTITUDES AND BEHAVIORS

Ajzen and Fishbein's (1977) review of the attitude–behavior literature emphasized the conceptual and operational characteristics of attitudes and behaviors. Essentially, Ajzen and Fishbein argued that the weak attitude–behavior relationship found in prior research was due to a lack of specificity in both the conceptual definitions and measures of attitudes and behaviors.

Ajzen and Fishbein described attitudes and behaviors in terms of their action and target entities. Ajzen and Fishbein (1977) began by arguing that "a given action is always performed with respect to a given target" (p. 889). All behaviors, then, have both an action and a target component. The action component represents the behavior being performed, while the target component represents the object toward which the action is directed. For example, a behavior of "going to church" has both target (i.e., the church) and action (i.e., attendance) components. To maximally predict a particular behavior, Ajzen and Fishbein argued that measures of attitudes must contain the same action and target components as are represented in the behavior.[2] While this seems quite simple, many early studies investigating the attitude–behavior relationship had frequently used general personality measures (e.g., religiosity) to predict specific behaviors like going to church. Such general attitude measures contained neither the target (church) nor the action (attendance) component of the behavior.

Ajzen and Fishbein (1977) argued that a strong attitude–behavior relationship should be expected only when there is a high degree of correspondence between the attitude measure and the behavior. An attitude measure is said to correspond to the behavior if two conditions are met. First, the attitude and behavior correspond to the extent that the action component contained in the attitude measure matches the action component of the behavior. Second, the attitude and behavior correspond to the extent that the target component of the attitude measure is similar to the target of the behavior. Thus, there is a low degree of attitude–behavior correspondence in the above example of attending church. The target of both the attitude and the behavior must be *church* while the action component of both must be *attending church*.

Relying on this conceptual framework, Ajzen and Fishbein (1977) reviewed prior studies investigating the relationship between attitudes and behaviors. They categorized each study as having low, partial, or high correspondence between the attitude measure and the behavior under consideration. Low-correspondence studies were defined as those that lacked correspondence on both the action and the target components of the attitude and the behavior. An example might be using a general measure of attitudes toward religion to predict church attendance. Partial-correspondence studies exhibited correspondence on either the action or the target components, but not both. For example, asking students their attitudes about church would capture the target but not the action component of a behavior. Finally, studies in the high-correspondence group had correspondence on both the action and the target components of the attitude and behavior (e.g., asking about attitudes concerning attending church to predict actual church attendance).

If Fishbein and Ajzen's explanation is correct, then studies with low correspondence should exhibit a weak attitude–behavior relationship, studies with partial correspondence should exhibit a moderate attitude–behavior relationship, and studies with high correspondence should exhibit a strong attitude–behavior relationship. Ajzen and Fishbein's (1977) findings were consistent with this analysis (Table 3.1). Of the 27 studies classified as having low correspondence, 26 produced an attitude–behavior correlation that was not significantly different from zero and only one study produced a small-to-moderate attitude–behavior correlation. Among the 71 studies in the partial-correspondence category, 20 found nonsignificant attitude–behavior correlations, 47 found small-to-moderate attitude–behavior correlations, and four studies exhibited a strong attitude–behavior relationship. Finally, among the 44 studies with high correspondence, nine found a small-to-moderate attitude–behavior correlation, and 35 found strong attitude–behavior correlations.[3] The pattern that emerged from this analysis was clear and supported the importance of correspondence in assessing the relationship between attitudes and behaviors.

In addition to these findings, a meta-analytic review of the attitude–behavior literature found a pattern of effects consistent with the Ajzen and Fishbein analysis (Kim & Hunter, 1993a). In a review of over 100 studies, the strength of the attitude–behavior relationship was a function of the relevance of the attitude measure to the corresponding behaviors. Studies that had a high degree of relevance (correspondence) exhibited

TABLE 3.1. Studies Exhibiting the Relationship between Attitude–Behavior Correspondence and the Strength of the Attitude–Behavior Relationship

Degree of correspondnce	Size of the attitude–behavior relationship		
	Strong	Small to moderate	Nonsignificant
High	35	9	0
Partial	4	47	20
Low	0	1	26

Note. Numbers reflect the number of studies that fell within each of these categories. From "Attitude–behavior relations: A theoretical analysis and review of empirical research" by I. Ajzen & M. Fishbein, 1977, Psychological Bulletin, 84, 888–918. Copyright 1977 by the American Psychological Association. Adapted by permission.

an average attitude–behavioral intention correlation that was larger (r = .69) than studies in which the relevance (correspondence) was moderate (r = .62) or low (r = .46). In addition, this review underscored the effects of measurement problems (described in Chapter 2, this volume) on the estimation of the attitude–behavior relationship. Once statistical corrections were applied, the corrected correlations for the high-, moderate-, and low-relevance studies increased dramatically (r = .90, r = .82, and r = .70, respectively)[4] (Kim & Hunter, 1993a).

In summary, the findings of these reviews (Ajzen & Fishbein, 1977; Kim & Hunter, 1993a) are consistent with earlier speculation that the weak attitude–behavior relationship found in many studies is due in part to conceptual ambiguity in the attitude and behavior measures (G. R. Miller, 1967; Wicker, 1969). Many prior studies lacked correspondence because they measured general attitudes and used them to predict behaviors toward specific people or situations—for example, by using a measure of attitudes toward labor unions to predict a union member's attendance at regularly scheduled union meetings. Essentially, these reviews found that conceptual and measurement problems attenuated the strength of the attitude–behavior relationship in prior research.

Moreover, Kim and Hunter's (1993a) meta-analysis indicated that attitudes and behaviors are strongly related (average r = .79, once corrected for measurement artifacts). One might be tempted, then, to claim that attitudes are the only important predictor of behaviors. A more prudent conclusion, however, is that there is still likely to be variation in the link between attitudes and behaviors. Thus, the viability of the attitude–behavior relationship (and, as a consequence, the attitude construct itself) was reasserted in the Ajzen and Fishbein review and reinforced in the Kim and Hunter meta-analysis. However, two issues remain. First, the specific nature of this relationship remains unexamined. The next section reviews a mathematical model of the attitude–behavior relationship. Second, there are also factors that influence the strength of the attitude–behavior relationship. The final section in the chapter discusses several moderator variables that affect the size of this relationship.

AJZEN AND FISHBEIN'S THEORY OF REASONED ACTION

By the late 1960s, researchers had focused considerable attention on understanding the specific nature of the relationship between attitudes and behaviors. Perhaps the most widely investigated model to emerge from these efforts became known as the Theory of Reasoned Action (Ajzen & Fishbein, 1980; Fishbein, 1967; see Hale, Householder, & Greene, 2002, for a recent review). Examination of this model and the research that tested it provides a clearer understanding of the relationship of attitudes to behaviors.

Examining the Ajzen and Fishbein Model

Extending Dulany's (1961, 1968) Theory of Propositional Control to examine social behavior, Fishbein (1967) argued that the best predictor of behavior (B) was an individual's intention (I) to perform a particular behavior. Hence, the Theory of Reasoned Action (Ajzen & Fishbein, 1980) was designed to predict behavioral intentions toward specific objects or situations. To understand this theory, we begin by examining the specific components that affect behavioral intentions, then apply them to the example from Chapter 1 of this volume regarding voting for a pro-choice politician.

The Theory of Reasoned Action specifies a model where two theoretical components, the individual's attitude toward performing the particular behavior (AB) and the existing subjective norms (SN), combine additively to determine a person's behavioral intention (BI). Specifically, the model holds that a behavioral intention (I) is a function (f) of the importance (W_1) of an individual's attitude (AB) plus the importance (W_2) of the subjective norms (SN). The model is represented in the following mathematical equation:

$$BI = f(W_1AB + W_2SN) \tag{3.1}$$

As we discussed in Chapter 1, a person's attitude toward performing a particular behavior (AB) is determined by the sum of his or her particular beliefs about performing the behavior and the evaluations those beliefs receive.[5] Recall the examples used to describe attitudes about demonstrating to prevent offshore oil exploration (see Table 1.1) and voting for a political candidate (see Table 1.2). Both examples described how beliefs about the consequences of performing particular behaviors and evaluations assigned to those beliefs combine to determine an individual's attitude toward performing a behavior. This relationship is represented in the following equation[6]:

$$A = \Sigma (b_i\, e_i) \tag{3.2}$$

The concept of a subjective norm (SN) has not been previously introduced. It can be defined as the influences of the social environment (i.e., other people and social norms) on a person's behavioral intentions. Although it is likely that attitudes guide behavioral intentions, Ajzen and Fishbein (1980) argued that the opinions and attitudes of a person's reference group (e.g., friends, family, coworkers, religious and political leaders) could influence behavioral intentions as well. Hence, the subjective norm represents an individual's perceptions of the social appropriateness of performing a particular behavior. Mathematically, the subjective norm is defined by the following equation:

$$SN = \Sigma \ (b_i \ m_i) \tag{3.3}$$

In this equation, SN represents the subjective norm, b_i represents normative beliefs, and m_i represents one's motivation to comply with those beliefs. Normative beliefs (b_i) are simply the attitudes that reference group members have about your performing the behavior, whereas the motivation to comply (m) represents the extent to which a person wants to act as the reference group member in question desires. Evaluations of normative beliefs and motivation to comply are multiplied for each reference group member. Then the products are added together to form the subjective norm.

Consider the example from Chapter 1 that described a person's attitude about voting for a political candidate who supported abortion rights for women. Voting intentions are likely to be influenced by the person's individual attitude and by the beliefs of his or her reference group. Who is likely to have an influence on voting decisions? Assume that the relevant reference group in our hypothetical example contains four people: a minister, a parent, a coworker, and a relational partner. Table 3.2 reflects the hypothetical beliefs (b) each of these reference group members may have about the consequences of voting for the pro-choice candidate. Because these beliefs are from members of one's reference group, they set a standard or norm for beliefs about the candidate. The beliefs of some reference group members are more influential than those of others. Thus, the importance of each reference group member's belief is reflected in the motivation to comply (m).

Referring to the hypothetical reference group in Table 3.2, the normative belief of the minister (-3) is more negative than the relational partner's belief $(+2)$. However, the person in our example feels less motivation to comply with the minister's position $(+1)$ than with the relational partner's position $(+3)$. The normative influence of each reference group member is determined by multiplying the value for the normative belief (b) by the value for the motivation to comply (m). The resulting value (bm) reveals that the influence of the minister's belief is somewhat negative (-3), but that the influence of the relational partner's belief is strongly positive $(+6)$. These products (bm) can then be added across reference group members to obtain the subjective norm (SN) for the entire reference group $(+2)$.

Included in the equation of the entire model (Equation 3.1) are two

TABLE 3.2. Subjective Norm (SN) of a Hypothetical Reference Group

Reference group member	Belief about voting for pro-choice candidate (b)	Motivation to comply (m)	Normative influence (bm)
Minister	−3	1	−3
Parent	−1	2	−2
Coworker	+1	1	+1
Relational partner	+2	3	+6

$$SN = \Sigma \ (bm) = +2$$

Note. Belief about voting for the candidate (b) scores range from −3 to +3 and motivation to comply (m) scores ranging from 0 to +3.

weights (W_1 and W_2) that reflect the relative importance of the attitude (AB) and the subjective norm (SN) in determining the behavioral intention (I). In situations where a person's own attitude is the primary determinant of the behavior intention, the weight assigned to the attitude component is larger than the weight assigned to the subjective norm component. In these instances, a person is more concerned with acting in accordance with personal beliefs than with conforming to the beliefs of others. When the subjective norm is more influential than the attitude, the weight assigned to the subjective norm is larger than the weight assigned to the attitude. In such instances, behavioral intentions are affected more by the influence of others than by one's personal beliefs. When the two components contribute equally to the behavioral intention, their weights are equal.

Evaluating the Theory of Reasoned Action

Ajzen and Fishbein (1980) described several investigations that successfully employed their model to predict behavior. Since then, the model has been tested extensively across a variety of behavioral situations. A meta-analytic review of these investigations found that the attitude and subjective norm components explained much of the variance in behavioral intentions ($R = .66$)[7] and that behavioral intentions explained much of the variance in actual behavior ($r = .53$) (Sheppard, Hartwick, & Warshaw, 1988). These findings suggest that the model is an excellent device for predicting and understanding behavior. However, in many of these investigations, the attitude component was a much stronger predictor of behavioral intentions than the subjective norm component. Combined with the fact that these two components tend to be positively correlated with one another, this finding has caused some researchers (Mindred & Cohen, 1979, 1981) to question the predictive utility of the subjective norm component of the model.

Unfortunately, tests of the Theory of Reasoned Action have traditionally focused on predicting individual behaviors in relatively private settings. Some studies have focused on attitudes about abortion (Smetana & Adler, 1980), minor consumer decisions (Ryan, 1982; Warshaw, 1980), and voting decisions (Bowman & Fishbein, 1978; Fishbein & Coombs, 1974; Jaccard, Knox, & Brinberg, 1979). Given that many of the behaviors used in these studies are individual rather than social, it is not surprising that personal attitudes have been found to be stronger predictors of behavioral intentions than subjective norms. David Trafimow and his associates have recently performed a number of studies to determine if subjective norms are more important in some circumstances than others (see Trafimow, 2000, for a recent review). Specifically, Trafimow and Fishbein (1994) claimed that some behavior is "normatively controlled" (i.e., influenced more by subjective norms than by attitudes toward the behavior). For example, Trafimow and Fishbein (Study 1) found that intentions toward "going to a Korean restaurant *alone*" were influenced more by attitudes toward the behavior while intentions concerning "going to a Korean restaurant *with a date*" were influenced more by the opinions of the other person (e.g., the date partner) than by one's own attitude about going to a Korean restaurant. In addition, Trafimow and Finlay (1996) investigated the relationships between subjective norms, attitudes toward the behavior, and behavioral intentions across 30 behaviors. In a vast majority of the cases, attitudes were a better predictor of behavioral intentions than were subjective norms; however, the importance of subjective norms varied dramatically across behaviors. For the most part, subjective norms exerted a stronger impact in the prediction of social (as opposed to individual) behaviors. Social behaviors are behaviors where others' opinions were valued (e.g., "marry someone my parents would approve of") or where others are directly involved (e.g., "use condoms if I have sex") (Trafimow & Finlay, 1996).

Consistent with this line of thinking, a recent meta-analytic review of studies investigating condom use during sexual intercourse (Albarracin, Johnson, Fishbein, & Muellerleile, 2001) found that the average correlation between subjective norms and behavioral intentions was substantial (average $r = .39$). While intentions to use a condom were more strongly related to attitudes toward the behavior ($r = .58$), the results of this review support the contention that subjective norms are a more important determinant of social behaviors than of individual behaviors.

In addition to Trafimow and Finlay's (1996) claim that some behaviors are influenced more by subjective norms than other behaviors, these scholars also claimed that subjective norms influence the behavior of some people more than they influence the behavior of others. Ybarra and Trafimow (1998) found that 20% of the people in their study based their behavioral intentions more on the subjective norms of others than on their own attitudes toward the behavior. Ybarra and Trafimow asserted that individuals whose behavioral intentions are primarily determined by subjective norms tend to think about themselves in terms of how they relate to other people.

Subjective Norms and Social Influence

The recent work by Trafimow and his associates (Trafimow, 2000) on subjective norms is consistent with several normative theories of social influence (Aronson, 1999; Deutsch & Gerard, 1955; Festinger, 1954; Kelley, 1952) that describe the effects of social norms on conformity to group (i.e., social) behavior. People often find themselves performing certain behaviors in order to get along with group members and avoid group conflict. In addition, people rely on social norms to interpret ambiguous situations. Such influences stimulated research on *bystander intervention* (Latane & Darley, 1968, 1970; Latane & Rodin, 1969). In several investigations, Latane and his colleagues observed people's reactions to a variety of emergency situations. They consistently found that when more than one person was around to observe the situation, no one was likely to offer assistance. However, if only a single person observed the situation, he or she was more likely to offer assistance. One explanation for this curious finding is the hypothesis that when others do not respond immediately to an apparent emergency, a nonintervention norm is established. Again, in ambiguous situations people look to the behaviors of others to determine whether providing assistance is necessary and appropriate. Bringing this example back to the Theory of Reasoned Action, in situations like these, the influence of subjective norms on behavioral intentions may be considerably stronger than the influence of individual attitudes.

Furthermore, it is possible that normative influences dictated personal behavior in LaPiere's (1934) investigation of attitudes and behavior toward a Chinese couple. Recall that respondents to the questionnaire reported strong prejudicial attitudes, but LaPiere found no evidence of prejudicial behavior. Providing or denying service to customers is a social, rather than an individual, behavior. As a consequence, perceptions of social norms (i.e., community values against racial discrimination) may have prevented people from behaving in accordance with their personal attitudes.

In summary, existing evidence supports the Theory of Reasoned Action as a valid representation of the role of attitudes and normative influences in the formation of behavioral intentions. In addition, the model points to opportunities for behavior change. By specifying the effects of attitude and normative influences, the model provides a framework for persuasion practitioners. For example, in Chapter 13 of this volume we review persuasive campaigns, derived from Social Cognitive Theory (Bandura, 1977, 1986), that use individual attitudes and social norms to mold the behaviors of adolescents. Due to its theoretical precision and easy application across a variety of persuasive situations, the Theory of Reasoned Action remains a popular description of the relationship between attitudes and behavior.

Behavioral Intentions and Behaviors

That attitudes influence behavioral intentions that, in turn, influence behaviors is an important component of the Theory of Reasoned Action. The second of Kim and Hunter's meta-analyses (1993b) on the attitude–behavior relationship focused on the issue of whether behavioral intentions actually acted as an intervening variable between attitudes and behaviors. This is an important issue because results of Kim and Hunter's (1993a) first meta-analysis could be interpreted as indicating that attitudes and behaviors are so strongly correlated as to make any intervening variables unnecessary. Kim and Hunter (1993b) analyzed the results of studies investigating the relationships between attitudes and behavioral intentions and between behavioral intentions and behaviors. The results of the meta-analysis were consistent with the intervening role of behavior intentions (Kim & Hunter, 1993b, p. 355). Attitudes predict behavioral intentions, which in turn predict behaviors. This is, of course, consistent with the Theory of Reasoned Action.

In an effort to improve the predictability of behavioral intentions and behaviors, Ajzen (1985) extended the Theory of Reasoned Action by arguing that *perceived behavioral control*, or the belief that one can perform the behavior in question, is sometimes an important predictor of behavioral intentions and subsequent behavior. Consistent with earlier research on *self-efficacy* (Bandura, 1982; Bandura, Adams, Hardy, & Howells, 1980), Ajzen argued that people's intentions to perform a behavior are often thwarted by a lack of confidence in their ability to perform that behavior. For example, people may perceive more behavioral control over taking daily vitamins than they do over getting a good night's sleep (see Madden, Ellen, & Ajzen, 1992). Thus, the Theory of Planned Behavior (Ajzen, 1985) posits that perceived behavioral control combines with the attitude and subjective norm components to predict behavioral intention. In addition, this theory hypothesizes a direct effect of perceived behavioral control on behavior.

For example, a smoker might understand the dangers of smoking (i.e., have a negative attitude toward smoking), have strong social support for his or her efforts to quit smoking (i.e., a positive subjective norm), and *intend* to quit smoking, but he or she may also believe that smoking is an addiction so he or she cannot actually perform the behavior (i.e., low perceived behavioral control). As a consequence, the person may continue to smoke because of low perceived behavioral control even though he or she has a negative attitude toward smoking and subjective norms supporting quitting. The conceptual differences between these two models are reflected in Figure 3.1.

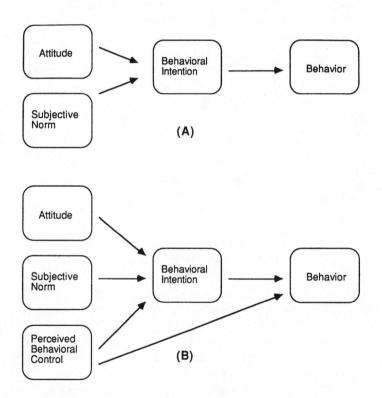

FIGURE 3.1. Comparison of the Theory of Reasoned Action (A) and the Theory of Planned Behavior (B). From "A comparison of the theory of planned behavior and the theory of reasoned action" by T. J. Madden, P. S. Ellen, & I. Ajzen, 1992, *Personality and Social Psychology Bulletin, 18*, 3–9. Copyright 1992 by Sage Publications. Reprinted by permission.

A comparison of these two theories (Madden et al., 1992) found strong support for the perceived behavioral control component. The Theory of Planned Behavior explained significantly more of the variation in behavioral intentions and behavior than did the Theory of Reasoned Action. In addition, the predictive value of perceived behavioral control was greater for behaviors that lacked predictive control than it was for behaviors where predictive control was high. In other words, when most people are certain that they can perform the behavior in question (e.g., take a daily vitamin), perceived behavioral control is not related to behavior. However, when people vary more in their ability to perform the behavior in question (e.g., get a good night's sleep), perceived behavioral control is an important predictor of their behavior.

Together, the Theory of Reasoned Action and the Theory of Planned Behavior provide strong support for the position that attitudes, subjective norms, and perceived behavioral control are important predictors of a person's behavior. Although the subjective norm and perceived behavioral control components are not always essential, these theories helped to reestablish an important role for attitudes in the prediction of behavior. Indeed, by the mid-1980s, these theories replaced speculation about the existence of an attitude–behavior relationship.

Bolstered by the success of the Theory of Reasoned Action in establishing the important role of attitudes in predicting behaviors, other researchers focused their efforts on identifying factors that affect the strength of the attitude–behavior relationship. Several of these factors are described in the next section.

FACTORS MODERATING THE
ATTITUDE–BEHAVIOR RELATIONSHIP

A second group of researchers studying the attitude–behavior relationship focused on the inconsistencies in prior estimates of the relationship between attitudes and behaviors. These scholars assumed that one of the reasons for the inconsistency in past studies was that the correlation between attitudes and behaviors varied across situations and across people. In short, these scholars presumed that there were a number of moderator variables that influenced the size of the attitude–behavior relationship. While a large number of moderators have been identified, we will discuss two factors related to the process of attitude formation, *direct experience* and *vested interest*, and two factors related to cognitive processing, *cognitive differentiation* and *attitude accessibility*, as moderators of the attitude–behavior relationship.

Factors Related to Attitude Formation

In a review of the attitude literature, Fazio and Zanna (1981) suggested that *direct experience* with the object of the attitude might influence the strength of the attitude–behavior relationship. According to this hypothesis, attitudes formed through personal experience with an object or situation will be more strongly related to subsequent behaviors than attitudes formed through the indirect experiences of others. For example, children who play a musical instrument form attitudes about music education and performance based on their direct experience with the activity, whereas children who do not play an instrument form their attitudes indirectly, through discussions with others, or perhaps by watching MTV. Consequently, Fazio and Zanna hypothesized that children with favorable or unfavorable attitudes formed through direct experience are more likely to act in accordance with those attitudes than children whose attitudes are formed through indirect experience.

Support for this proposition came from a study of college student attitudes about a campus housing shortage (Regan & Fazio, 1977). Participants in this study were Cornell University students who were experiencing an acute housing shortage. As a result, many freshmen spent the first few weeks of the Fall semester sleeping on cots in the lounge and common areas of campus dormitories. Questionnaires were sent to students who received permanent housing accommodations (i.e., a dorm room) and to those who were assigned temporary accommodations (i.e., in lounges and common areas). Almost every student was aware of the housing shortage, and most had formed negative attitudes about the university's response to the crisis. However, the manner in which these attitudes were formed differed between students assigned immediately to permanent housing and those assigned to temporary housing accommodations. Students assigned to the temporary housing accommodations formed their attitudes through direct personal experience, whereas those assigned to permanent housing accommodations formed their attitudes after talking with friends and reading articles in the student newspaper.

In addition to measuring attitudes, Regan and Fazio invited students to take a series of actions in response to the crisis. Students were given a list of six behavioral options:

1. Sign a petition urging the university to solve the problem.
2. Encourage other students to sign the petition.
3. Agree to attend a future meeting to discuss potential solutions.
4. Indicate interest in joining a committee to investigate the problem.

5. Develop a written list of recommendations for solving the problem.
6. Write a letter expressing opinions about the shortage that would be forwarded to the campus housing office.

Regan and Fazio calculated the relationship between student attitudes and behavioral intentions toward the housing crisis. As anticipated, they found that students whose attitudes were formed through direct experience exhibited significantly stronger attitude–behavior correlations than those whose attitudes were formed through indirect experience. In other words, students who formed negative attitudes because they were living in the lounge area were more willing to act on their attitudes than students who formed negative attitudes based on a friend's experience or by reading articles in the newspaper.

Though the Regan and Fazio (1977) findings are consistent with the argument that direct experience moderates the size of the attitude–behavior correlation, the method employed by Regan and Fazio to assign students to the direct and indirect experience conditions confounded the concept of direct experience with a number of other, related, variables. For example, students in these two groups may have also differed in the amount of their vested interest and ego-involvement with the situation. Most likely, students assigned to the temporary housing conditions also had more of a vested interest, or personal stake, in potential solutions to the housing shortage than students assigned to the permanent housing conditions. Thus, it is difficult to determine whether direct experience, vested interest, or both factors accounted for differences in the strength of the attitude–behavior relationship.

To test the hypothesis that vested interest moderates the attitude–behavior relationship, Sivacek and Crano (1982) assessed attitudes of college students about proposed changes in the legal drinking age (also see Chapter 2, this volume). During the course of the investigation, residents of the state of Michigan were considering a ballot proposition to increase the age for legal consumption of alcohol from 18 years to 21 years. As part of an attitude survey on a variety of topics, students at Michigan State University were asked to provide their opinions about the proposition. Students were contacted by phone 7 to 10 days after completing the opinion survey, when they were asked if they would like to volunteer time to campaign against passage of the proposition. Willingness to participate and the number of phone calls they were willing to make served as measures of students' behavioral intentions.

Sivacek and Crano reasoned that all students formed attitudes about drinking through direct experiences that were similar. After all, most students were at least 18 and had some direct experience with alcohol consumption. Thus, the topic selected for investigation provided a natural control for direct experience. Vested interest, however, varied strongly across students. Vested interest was higher among students who would not be able to legally drink for 2 years or more and lowest among those students who would soon be 21 years old. A third group, those who would not be able to drink legally for less than 2 years, fell between the low- and high-vested-interest groups. As a result, the proposition to increase the legal drinking age provided three natural levels of vested interest while controlling for the effects of direct experience.

As we noted in Chapter 2, findings were consistent with the vested-interest hypothesis. Students in the high-vested-interest group volunteered more time and exhibited a stronger attitude–behavior correlation ($r = .61$) than students in the moderate- ($r = .40$) and low- ($r = .16$) vested-interest groups.

Sivacek and Crano conducted a second study in which they assessed attitudes and behaviors toward a proposal to institute comprehensive exams as a graduation requirement for undergraduate students. Students who expected to graduate before the proposal was enacted were placed in the low-vested-interest group, whereas those who would be required to complete the exams were placed in the high-vested-interest group. Once again, the attitude–behavior correlation was significantly higher among students with a high vested interest ($r = .82$) than among students with limited vested interest ($r = .52$).

Together, the housing shortage, drinking age, and comprehensive examination studies reveal that the method of attitude formation influences the relationship between attitudes and behaviors. These studies are not without their limitations. In the housing study, the concept of direct experience was confounded with the concept of vested interest. Moreover, the effect of direct experience was held constant in the drinking age and comprehensive examination studies. Thus, although Sivacek and Crano (1982) documented the importance of vested interest, they were unable to estimate effects due to direct experience. Notwithstanding their limitations, these investigations suggest that vested interest and perhaps direct experience influence the extent to which people act in accordance with their attitudes.

Factors Related to Cognitive Processes

A number of cognitive style constructs have been developed over the years to describe differences in the ways people process information. One measure of cognitive style, *construct differentiation*, has been investigated as a moderator of the attitude–behavior relationship.

Delia and his colleagues (Delia & Crockett, 1973; B. J. O'Keefe &

Delia, 1978; D. J. O'Keefe & Delia, 1981) have argued that construct differentiation is an important characteristic of a person's cognitive style. *Construct differentiation* refers to the number of different dimensions along which people judge objects and situations. People with highly sophisticated construct systems employ a greater variety of attributes when describing a person, object, event, or situation, while those with less developed construct systems use fewer traits and characteristics.

Construct differentiation is typically measured by asking respondents to write a short paragraph describing a positive and a negative person, event, object, or situation. For example, respondents may be asked to describe someone they like and then to describe someone they dislike. These descriptions are then analyzed for the number of different dimensions the person used to describe the liked and disliked persons. Though other coding procedures are available, evaluation of these responses usually consists of counting the number of unique descriptions (i.e., constructs) included in the paragraphs. Constructs are typically reflected in the use of adjectives and adverbs. The greater the number of unique constructs, the more differentiated the construct system.[8] For example, a person with a less differentiated construct system might describe a well-liked friend as someone who was "fun" and "easy to talk with" (two constructs). Conversely, a person with a highly developed construct category system might describe the same well-liked person as a "thoughtful, compassionate, and empathic" person who is "quite entertaining" and "fun to be with" (five constructs).

D. J. O'Keefe and Delia (1981) argued that people with more developed construct systems should demonstrate lower attitude–behavior intention correlations than those with less developed systems. They reasoned that people with less developed systems are more likely to be guided by a concern for cognitive consistency. Hence, they are more likely to demonstrate a strong relationship between attitudes and behavioral intentions. People with well-developed construct systems, on the other hand, are more likely to tolerate apparent discrepancies between attitudes and behavioral intentions, because they are able to more precisely differentiate the characteristics of an attitude object from the characteristics of related behavior. By drawing precise conceptual distinctions, people with highly differentiated construct systems are able to logically behave in a manner that is apparently inconsistent with the related attitude.

To test their hypotheses, D. J. O'Keefe and Delia (1981) asked students to write a short paragraph describing a person they liked and another paragraph describing someone they disliked. These descriptions were coded for the measure of construct differentiation. After 3 months, they asked these participants to write a description of a classmate with whom they had become acquainted. There were about 15 people in the class and students got to know several other classmates.

Students then completed an attitude measure about this classmate and responded to a series of hypothetical social and work situations in which they might find themselves interacting with another person. They were asked to indicate, for each context, the extent to which they would choose the classmate they earlier described for their "social partner in that situation." Responses to this measure constituted the measure of behavioral intentions.

Results of this investigation were consistent with D. J. O'Keefe and Delia's (1981) predictions regarding the moderating role of construct differentiation on attitude and behavior consistency. First, low-differentiation participants showed more consistency in the description of their classmate (either mostly positive or mostly negative), whereas high-differentiation participants tended to provide a mixture of positive and negative characteristics in their descriptions. Compared to the high-differentiation participants, low-differentiation participants also exhibited more consistency between the attitude rankings on the survey and the attitudes reflected in their written descriptions.

Low-differentiation participants also demonstrated more consistency between the attitude and behavioral intention rankings than high-differentiation participants. On eight of the nine hypothetical situations, and for the composite measure of behavioral intentions, correlations between attitudes and behavioral intentions were higher for low-differentiation subjects ($r =. 88$) than for high-differentiation subjects ($r = .65$).[9]

These findings are consistent with D. J. O'Keefe and Delia's reasoning and suggest that cognitive style may influence individual concerns about attitude–behavior consistency. Though it may be reasonable to conclude that people desire consistency in their attitudes and actions, these findings suggest that people with highly developed cognitive systems are better equipped to tolerate apparent cognitive inconsistencies than people whose cognitive systems are less complex.

Attitude accessibility is another cognitive variable that has been hypothesized to moderate the relationship between attitudes and behaviors. "Attitude accessibility" refers to the extent to which an attitude is activated automatically from memory. Fazio and his colleagues (Fazio, Chen, McDonel, & Sherman, 1982; Powell & Fazio, 1984) have demonstrated that when a person repeatedly expresses an attitude toward an object or situation, it becomes chronically accessible. Once an attitude has become chronically accessible, it can be activated automatically from memory in response to future encounters with the object or situation (Fazio, Sanbonmatsu, Powell, & Kardes, 1986). Thus, the more frequently an attitude is expressed, the more readily it is recalled from memory. For example, a person who actively works to promote legislation about abortion rights is likely to express pro-choice or pro-life opinions more frequently than someone who holds an identical attitude but who is less actively involved on the topic. Though both people may possess similar attitudes about abortion rights, the person who frequently expresses his or her opinion will have a more accessible attitude and will respond more rapidly to abortion-relevant stimuli. It's like exercising a muscle: the more frequently you exercise a muscle, the stronger it becomes. The more you access (exercise) an attitude, the stronger it becomes as well (see Roskos-Ewaldson, Apran-Ralstin, & St. Pierre, 2002, for a recent review of the accessibility construct).

To test the influence of attitude accessibility on the attitude–behavior relationship, Fazio and Williams (1986) examined attitudes toward Ronald Reagan and Walter Mondale during the 1984 presidential campaign. Attitude accessibility was assessed by measuring the response latency (the amount of time that elapsed between the end of a question and the beginning of a response) associated with attitudes toward Reagan and Mondale. Later, Fazio and Williams measured perceptions of candidate performance in the presidential debates and conducted a post-election interview to assess voting behavior.

Consistent with their hypothesis, Fazio and Williams found that people with highly accessible attitudes toward either Reagan or Mondale exhibited more bias in their perceptions of the presidential debates than people with less accessible attitudes. Independent of attitude intensity, they also found that people in the high-attitude-accessibility group were more likely to vote in accordance with their attitudes than those with less accessible attitudes.

A recent study of attitudes toward a variety of consumer products produced similar results. Kokkinaki and Lunt (1997) found that attitude accessibility was a strong predictor of the strength of the attitude–behavior relationship; participants with highly accessible beliefs showed the strongest attitude–behavior relationship, whereas those with relatively inaccessible beliefs exhibited the weakest attitude–behavior relationship.

These findings suggest that attitude accessibility affects the extent to which attitudes predict behavior. For instance, two people may hold similar attitudes on a political issue such as gun control, but differ in their expression of this attitude: for example, one person might frequently discuss the need for gun control legislation, whereas another person with the same attitude may rarely discuss the issue. Research on attitude accessibility suggests that, although these two hypothetical people share the same attitude, the person who routinely discusses the merits of gun control is likely to have the more accessible attitude, and thus be more likely to act (e.g., vote or circulate a petition to promote gun control legislation).

It bears mentioning that attitude accessibility is conceptually distinct from both attitude extremity and involvement. Though accessibility and extremity have been statistically related in prior research (Powell & Fazio, 1984), they remain separate constructs. That is, attitudes can vary along an extremity dimension and along an accessibility dimension. In addition, Kokkinaki and Lunt (1997) found that accessibility is related to involvement, but that these two factors exert separate moderating impacts of the attitude–behavior relationship. The findings of Fazio and his colleagues suggest that highly accessible attitudes affect the perception of attitude-relevant information and moderate the strength of the attitude–behavior relationship.

Together, construct differentiation and attitude accessibility appear to be two important cognitive factors that influence the relationship between attitudes and behaviors. Given the cognitive nature of the attitude definition presented in Chapter 1 of this volume, it is not surprising that cognitive processes can influence the predictive utility of the attitude construct.

SUMMARY

Several conclusions emerge from prior investigations of the attitude–behavior relationship. First, the attitude–behavior controversy, which emerged in the early 1960s, appears to have been created by sloppy conceptual definitions and poor investigative procedures. Though their work was regarded as a theoretical review of the literature, Ajzen and Fishbein (1977) focused primarily on conceptual and operational limitations of prior investigations. By the late 1970s, this controversy had been laid to rest. Assuming that precise conceptual and operational definitions are employed, most scholars agree that attitudes are predictive of related behavior. The results of two meta-analyses (Kim & Hunter, 1993a, 1993b) reinforce the strong relationships among attitudes, behavioral intentions, and behaviors.

Researchers also turned their attention to examining moderator variables that influence the strength of the relationship between attitudes and behaviors. Research on attitude formation suggests that two factors, direct experience and vested interest, affect the strength of this relationship. Given the sheer number of attitudes people hold about a variety of issues, it is unrealistic to expect that people will always behave in accordance with their attitudes. Instead, people are most likely to act in accordance with their attitudes when the issue is central to their lives.

Investigations of cognitive processing revealed two additional factors that influence the predictive utility of attitudes. Delia and O'Keefe's investigation of construct differentiation found that people possessing complex cognitive systems tolerate apparent inconsistencies by drawing precise distinctions between attitudes and related behavior. In addition, research by Fazio and his colleagues demonstrated the importance of attitude accessibility in determining the extent to which attitudes guide behavior.

Thus, although we can safely conclude that attitudes predict behaviors, Allport's (1935) assertion that attitudes exert a directive influence on all objects with which they come in contact (p. 810) is perhaps overstated. Over the past 60+ years we have learned that, when properly defined and measured, personal attitudes guide individual behavior, but that the strength of this directive influence varies across people and situations.

NOTES

1. Many scholars have criticized LaPiere's study on a variety of grounds (e.g., see Petty & Cacioppo, 1981). For example, the measure of attitudes used in this study (i.e., Would the place of business serve a Chinese couple?) seems more like a measure of behavioral intention than of attitude. Given this and other criticisms, the LaPiere study may not be relevant to our discussion of the relationship between attitudes and behaviors. We include this seminal study because of its historical importance in the attitude–behavior "problem."

2. Ajzen and Fishbein (1975) went further to say that a specific behavior occurs in a given context and at a particular time. In our church example, the context component would focus on a particular church while the time component would focus on a particular day.

3. Actually, studies with high correspondence were divided into two groups: those that used reliable measures and those that didn't use reliable measures. Of the 18 studies with suspect attitude and behavior measures, nine reported small-to-moderate correlations and nine reported strong attitude–behavior correlations. Of the 26 studies that used reliable measures, all 26 found a strong attitude–behavior correlation. This finding emphasizes the importance of measurement qualities discussed in Chapter 2 of this volume.

4. As we pointed out in Note 4 in the previous chapter, r is a statistic called the *correlation coefficient*. The correlation coefficient measures the strength of the linear association between two variables. The closer a correlation is to 1.00 (or –1.00), the more accurately one variable can be predicted given knowledge of the other variable. A correlation of 0.0 would indicate that knowledge of one variable would be of no help in predicting the other variable. In the present context, as correlation coefficients between attitudes and

behaviors approach 1.00, behaviors can be predicted very accurately given knowledge of an individual's attitudes.

5. By specifying attitude *toward a particular behavior*, Ajzen and Fishbein ensure that they include both the action and the target component in their measurement of attitude and, by definition, closely connect attitudes to behaviors.

6. Equation 3.2 is the simplified version of the same equation (i.e., Equation 1.1) presented in Chapter 1.

7. The symbol R represents the multiple correlation coefficient. The multiple correlation coefficient represents the correlation between more than one predictor variable (in this case, attitude toward the behavior and subjective norms) and a single outcome variable (i.e., behavioral intentions).

8. Considerable controversy surrounds the cognitive measures employed by Delia and his colleagues. Some critics have argued that the cognitive differentiation measure is confounded with a person's verbosity and lexical diversity: the greater a person's command of the language, the more constructs he or she is likely to include in a description (Allen, Mabry, Banski, Stoneman, & Carter, 1990; Beatty, 1987; Beatty & Payne, 1984, 1985; Powers, Jordan, & Street, 1979). Such criticisms have not gone unnoticed by constructivist researchers who have attempted to demonstrate that lexical diversity and verbosity are unrelated to the measure of cognitive differentiation (Burleson, Applegate, & Newwirth, 1981; Burleson, Waltman, & Samter, 1987).

9. One limitation of this study stems from the measure of behavior intention, which may be little more than another measure of the participant's attitude toward his or her classmate. If this criticism is valid, then analysis of the situational, descriptive, and questionnaire measures of attitude demonstrated that attitudinal consistency was greater among subjects with lower cognitive differentiation scores. Though consistent with their reasoning, such a conclusion is not informative about the relationship between attitudes and behaviors.

4

The Effects of Behavior
on Attitudes

LOOKING AHEAD ...

Though in the previous chapter attitudes were viewed as the
causal antecedents to behavior, it is equally plausible that
behaviors influence people's attitudes. This chapter investigates
the causal influences of behavior on subsequent attitude
change. This discussion begins with a review of Cognitive
Dissonance Theory and the counterattitudinal advocacy
research paradigm. Following this, several modifications to
the original theory and alternative explanations for research
findings are discussed. One rival explanation, Self-Perception
Theory, has been particularly troublesome for Dissonance
Theory advocates. Theoretical differences between these
rival explanations and corresponding investigations of these
explanations are reviewed. Finally, we will discuss some
practical applications of Cognitive Dissonance Theory that
have recently been employed with regard to issues like
condom use.

Can changes in behavior affect subsequent attitudes? The answer is most
definitely yes, under certain circumstances. Advertisers have long recognized the role of behavior in the formation and reinforcement of attitudes. Automobile salespeople encourage potential customers to "test
drive" a particular car early in the sales process. A 1970s advertising tag
line for a breakfast cereal, "Try it, you'll like it," echoed similar convictions. Religious leaders encourage regular participation in organized religious ceremonies by their flocks to reinforce their beliefs and strengthen

their commitments. Few persuasion scholars would quarrel with the claim that behavior influences the formation and reinforcement of attitudes. However, the causal influence of behavior on subsequent *attitude change* is less straightforward.

Investigations of this issue have traditionally employed counter-attitudinal advocacy (CAA) procedures to investigate the effects of behavior on attitude change. CAA requires people to advocate a position that is inconsistent with their existing attitude. This research paradigm was initially developed in the early 1950s and was employed in several investigations of active and passive persuasive message processing (Janis & King, 1954; B. T. King & Janis, 1956). A decade later it had become a staple in attitude change research.

THE CAA RESEARCH PARADIGM

The CAA research procedure is relatively straightforward. However, it does require investigator knowledge of research participants' attitudes toward a particular issue, object, or situation. Sometimes investigators will conduct attitude pretests several weeks prior to the experiment in order to assess participant attitudes. More frequently, a topic is selected because most participants hold similar known attitudes about the issue. For example, most Americans are opposed to tax increases. Though not everyone opposes them, few people openly advocate tax increases. Similarly, college students are almost uniformly opposed to tuition increases. Thus, for most students, advocating a tuition increase represents CAA.

Once a topic has been selected, investigators ask research participants to advocate a position that is *opposite* to the attitude they hold. Participants are usually asked to write an essay, present a speech, or talk with another person in order to advocate the counterattitudinal position. Thus, for the topic of tax increases, CAA might involve writing an essay supporting a tax increase.

CAA poses an interesting dilemma. People engaging in CAA knowingly articulate a position that is inconsistent with their personal beliefs and convictions. They believe "*x*" but they advocate "not-*x*." What effect does such advocacy have on a person's attitude toward an issue? For example, if the campus president of a local chapter of college Young Republicans was opposed to tax increases, but advocated an income tax increase to reduce the budget deficit, would this CAA influence his or her attitude toward tax increases?

The answer to such questions is somewhat complicated, but a qualified generalization can be offered. Provided that certain situational conditions are present, CAA will produce attitude change in the direction of the position advocated within the message. It bears mentioning that CAA emphasizes attitude change in the advocate, not in an audience or target person. That is, CAA is a technique for inducing self-persuasion, not for persuading target audiences. The amount of attitude change that advocates experience following CAA is dependent on several situational factors, including perceived justification, freedom of choice, and the consequences of the CAA.

It is relatively uncommon for people in natural communicative interactions to freely engage in CAA without sufficient external justification. Thus, the pragmatic utility of CAA to induce attitude change may be limited. The studies and theories discussed in this chapter represent a good example of how researchers address theoretical issues (i.e., basic, as opposed to applied, science) with a variety of research designs. We will conclude this chapter, however, by reviewing some recent practical applications of the CAA paradigm. Regardless, the CAA paradigm has important theoretical implications for persuasion because it allows researchers to distinguish attitude-reinforcement and attitude-formation processes from attitude-change processes.

There has been little disagreement about the effectiveness of CAA for changing an advocate's position. However, considerable controversy has surrounded several theoretical explanations of this effect. The most extensively investigated explanation is Cognitive Dissonance Theory (Festinger, 1957). The original theory, along with its subsequent modifications and extensions, is discussed in the next section of this chapter. Following this is a discussion of several alternative explanations of the CAA effect.

A THEORY OF COGNITIVE DISSONANCE

In 1957, Leon Festinger described his Theory of Cognitive Dissonance (or, more simply, Dissonance Theory), which became the most widely investigated social psychological theory of its era. Evolving from basic consistency principles (Heider, 1946; Newcomb, 1953), Dissonance Theory postulated three basic assumptions about human cognition: (1) people have a need for cognitive consistency; (2) when cognitive inconsistency exists, people experience psychological discomfort; and (3) psychological discomfort motivates people to resolve the inconsistency and restore cognitive balance. Though it can be situated in a larger family of consistency theories, Dissonance Theory differs from other consistency models in that it is a postdecisional theory. Festinger was interested in explaining how people resolve the internal psychological conflict they often experience after making an important decision.

Basic Components of Dissonance Theory

Festinger (1957) argued that not all cognitive elements (e.g., thoughts, ideas, values, etc.) are relevant to one another. For example, the belief that one is an honest person is probably unrelated to one's preference for the color blue. Hence, Festinger stipulated that his theory only explained cognitions that were perceived to be relevant, or related to one another, by the attitude holder. Festinger then proposed two cognitive states to describe the relations among relevant cognitive elements. Though he employed somewhat different language, Festinger argued that a state of *consonance* was said to exist when two or more cognitions were consistent with one another. An example might be a person who is a registered Democrat and who voted for Al Gore in the 2000 presidential election. The cognitive elements in this case, one's party affiliation and knowledge of one's voting behavior, are consistent with one another. A state of *dissonance* was said to exist when two or more cognitions were inconsistent with one another. For example, a registered Democrat might experience dissonance after voting for Ralph Nader and the Green Party in the 2000 presidential election, given the cognition that George Bush won the election because Ralph Nader siphoned votes away from Al Gore in several key states.

Dissonance occurs in varying degrees. Some cognitive elements may be inconsistent with one another, yet produce a negligible amount of dissonance. For example, if a person believes in the merits of recycling, but disposes of a soft drink can in a wastebasket instead of recycling the can, he or she should experience cognitive dissonance. However, the extent of this dissonance and the person's subsequent motivation to reduce it will likely be quite small. If this same person failed to make the effort to vote for a proposition to institute a local recycling program and the proposition was defeated by a single vote, however, the magnitude of his or her resulting cognitive dissonance would be considerably larger.

Festinger (1957) stated that dissonance is an aversive state, that is, something that we try to avoid. Festinger also argued that dissonance creates psychological discomfort. If we do experience dissonance, we will try to reduce it. The greater the dissonance, the greater the psychological discomfort, and the greater the motivation there is to reduce it. The magnitude of dissonance is determined by two factors: (1) the importance of the dissonant elements, and (2) the proportion of consonant to dissonant relations among relevant elements in the cognitive system.

Implications of Cognitive Dissonance

Dissonance is an inevitable consequence of making decisions because decisions involve choosing one option and not another. When people

choose among two or more competing alternatives, the amount of dissonance (and psychological discomfort) experienced is dependent on the
importance of the decision and the relative attractiveness of the unchosen alternative.

Each year, college seniors interview for jobs in their chosen fields
of interest. The fortunate ones receive multiple offers and are placed in
the enviable position of having the freedom to choose among alternative employment opportunities. If the alternatives are quite dissimilar—
for example, a choice between a $20,000-a-year job in Otis, Kansas,
and a $50,000-a-year job in Minneapolis—the amount of dissonance
produced by the decision should be minimal because one option is
likely to be evaluated much more positively than the other. However, if
the alternatives are equally attractive—for example, a choice between
a $50,000-a-year job in Minneapolis and a $47,000-a-year job in
Chicago—the amount of dissonance experienced may be substantial,
and the decision maker will attempt to reduce it once the choice is
made.

Festinger (1957) described three ways a person can reduce cognitive
dissonance following a decision. First, the person can change the *cognitive element related to the behavior*. Thus, if our college senior's decision
to accept a job in Minneapolis instead of Chicago produces cognitive
dissonance, he or she might change the cognitive elements related to the
decision to reduce dissonance. He or she might attempt to change the decision itself, but might be more likely to change the cognitive elements
related to the decision by distorting information about the decision or
denying that there was much of a choice to begin with. For example, the
person might conclude, "I made the best decision that I could at the
time."

A second method of reducing dissonance is to change the *cognitive
element or elements related to the attitude*. That is, if the decision is inconsistent with the person's existing attitude, a common method of dissonance reduction is modification of the attitude. Indeed, most investigations of the theory have employed measures of attitude change to
document the existence and reduction of cognitive dissonance. Thus, another way for the college senior to reduce dissonance stemming from his
or her decision to accept the job in Minneapolis is to form a more negative attitude about living or working in Chicago, a more positive attitude
about living or working in Minneapolis, or both.

Finally, Festinger (1957) specified that *adding new cognitive elements* may reduce dissonance. Selective exposure to new information
(Freedman & Sears, 1965) often occurs after a decision has been made.
People intentionally expose themselves to information that will reinforce
the merits of their decision, and they intentionally avoid information

that may be critical of the decision. This new information can force a realignment of the cognitions and reduce dissonance. Extending the example about accepting the job in Minneapolis, the college senior might reduce dissonance after making the decision by paying special attention to reports that favorably compare Minneapolis to Chicago. For example, our student might seek out news reports of crimes committed in Chicago and cultural opportunities available in Minneapolis.

The Festinger and Carlsmith Study

Festinger and Carlsmith (1959) conducted the initial test of Dissonance Theory. In this study, participants arrived one at a time at the experimental laboratory and were asked to turn pegs on a board for a long period of time. This task was unmistakably dull. After completing this task, participants were told that the experiment was designed to examine the effects of expectations on performance. Participants were told that they were in a control condition where there were no prior expectations and that other participants would be in a condition where they would be told that the task was very exciting and interesting. Then the experimenter indicated that the assistant who had been hired to provide positive expectations for subjects in the expectancy condition had just called to say he would be unable to work that day. The experimenter then asked the subject if he or she would be willing to introduce the experiment to the next research participant and to be on call for performing this task in the future. The experimenter indicated that this procedure required the participant to indicate that the study was fun and exciting, and that the participant would be paid (either $1 or $20, depending on the experimental condition) for this assistance. Once the participant agreed to serve as the assistant, he or she was asked to introduce the experiment to the next participant (actually a confederate of the experimenter, who played the role of a subject). The participant introduced the task and described it as fun and exciting.

After introducing the experiment, the participant engaged in a previously arranged interview with another person in the psychology department who was conducting a separate survey on departmental research. Respondents were told that the survey was being administered to students who had participated in any type of research project sponsored by the department. Participants were asked how much they liked the experiment, how much they felt they had learned by participating in the experiment, and how likely they would be to participate in similar research projects. Actually, this interview was created to assess participant reactions to the experimental task (i.e., represented the study's dependent variables).

The Creation of Cognitive Dissonance

Because the procedure was dull and uninteresting, Festinger and Carl-smith (1959) hypothesized that people would experience dissonance after introducing the study as interesting and exciting. Because participants had clearly been deceptive when introducing the study, it was difficult for them to deny or distort the CAA behavior. Moreover, it was unlikely that participants could anticipate seeing the confederate again to alter the consequences of their decision or to provide an explanation for their behavior. There were also no sources of external information about the experiment readily available to participants. Hence, selective exposure to information was unlikely.

Thus, these procedures restricted two of the three methods outlined by Festinger (1957) for reducing dissonance—that is, changing the cognitive element related to the behavior or adding new cognitive elements. Hence, the easiest method for reducing dissonance created by the CAA was attitude change.

Effects of Cognitive Dissonance

To the extent that their procedures induced cognitive dissonance, Festinger and Carlsmith (1959) hypothesized that participants would change their attitudes, because other methods of reducing dissonance had been effectively blocked. Recall that there were two payment conditions in the investigation. Some participants received $1 and others were paid $20 for their CAA introduction of the experiment (roughly equivalent to $6 and $125 in today's dollars). The payment served as a source of justification for the CAA. Participants receiving $1 had little external justification for their behavior, whereas those receiving $20 could easily justify their CAA. Participants receiving $20 could easily say to themselves, "Why did I say the task was interesting? Because I received $20 for it." Because the CAA of participants in the $20 condition was easily justified, the possibility of cognitive dissonance and subsequent attitude change was reduced. In the $1 condition, however, participants had less external justification for their behavior, and hence would experience more cognitive dissonance. Thus, Festinger and Carlsmith hypothesized that to reduce their dissonance, participants who received $1 (low justification) would change their attitudes more than participants who were paid $20 (high justification).

Findings were consistent with these expectations. Participants in the $1 condition reported attitudes indicating that the experimental task was significantly more enjoyable than did participants in the $20 condition. However, there were no differences between these two groups on three additional questions regarding "desire to participate in a similar experiment," "the scientific importance of the experiment," and "the educational value of the experiment." Nevertheless, Festinger and Carlsmith concluded that difference between the attitudes of participants in the low and the high justification conditions "strongly corroborated the theory that was tested."

Though there was reason to question the strength of their convictions at the time they drew this conclusion, the pattern of attitudes emerging from the Festinger and Carlsmith (1959) study has been replicated in many subsequent investigations of Dissonance Theory (for reviews, see Cooper & Fazio, 1984; Greenwald & Ronis, 1978; Harmon-Jones, 2002; Harmon-Jones & Mills, 1999; G. R. Miller, 1973). Today, there remains little doubt about the persuasive effects of CAA. However, the "correct" theoretical explanation of these effects remains a source of considerable controversy.

Limitations of Cognitive Dissonance Theory

Although many investigations provided support for Dissonance Theory, it is difficult to imagine a set of research findings that could not be explained by Festinger's original explication of Dissonance Theory. Festinger's writing was conceptually vague and sufficiently general to prevent falsification of the theory. For example, Dissonance Theory fails to articulate when people will use each of the three methods for reducing cognitive dissonance. Instead, Festinger stated that dissonance is reduced by modifying the cognitive element that is least resistant to change. Because no suggestions are provided about how one might assess the resistance of various cognitive elements, it is difficult to predict a priori whether dissonance will produce behavior change, attitude change, or selective exposure to new information. In particular, the notion of adding new cognitive elements is vague and nearly impossible to assess.

The ambiguity in Cognitive Dissonance Theory is important because following CAA, a person may exhibit no observable signs of psychological discomfort or dissonance reduction, yet dissonance and its subsequent reduction may have occurred. Because thinking fulfills the requirement of adding new cognitive elements, a person may reduce dissonance by generating new thoughts or by recalling information stored in memory. Consider the earlier example of a campus Young Republican who had publicly supported a "no new taxes" position, only to find herself advocating a tax increase to reduce an unexpected deficit. Though no observable signs of dissonance reduction may occur, our Young Republican may internally rationalize her counterattitudinal behavior by recalling a similar move by the first President Bush, who initially stated

"Read my lips . . . no new taxes," but later raised taxes when economic conditions changed. Though investigators may never have access to this private internal rationalization, dissonance and its subsequent reduction may nevertheless have occurred.

Because two of the three methods for reducing dissonance, attitude change and adding new cognitive elements, are not directly observable, the original version of Dissonance Theory was virtually impossible to disprove. If observable changes follow CAA, Dissonance Theory may account for these changes. However, the absence of observable change does not mean that dissonance did not occur and was not reduced internally. It simply means that researchers did not observe dissonance reduction if it occurred. In an effort to resolve this limitation, researchers have suggested several modifications and extensions of the original theory. For the most part, these suggestions were intended to limit the scope of the theory.

Modifications and Extensions of Cognitive Dissonance Theory

The evolution of Cognitive Dissonance Theory has been impressive. Harmon-Jones and Mills (1999) recently summarized several modifications that have been suggested to clarify Festinger's original articulation of the theory. Brehm and Cohen (1962) suggested two of the earliest modifications as they conducted a series of investigations testing the theory. Brehm and Cohen introduced the notion of *commitment* to Dissonance Theory. Though Festinger originally argued that dissonance resulted from decision making, Brehm and Cohen argued that dissonance will only occur when people experience a state of psychological commitment to the decision they have made. In essence, if a decision can be easily reversed, then the decision maker should experience little dissonance. If the decision is not reversible, then cognitive dissonance should occur and the extent of this dissonance will be a function of the importance of the decision and the relative attractiveness of the unchosen alternative.

The importance of Brehm and Cohen's suggestion is apparent in consumer purchasing decisions. If you go to a shopping mall and buy $800's worth of clothes for your wardrobe, should you experience cognitive dissonance? According to Festinger's version of the theory, the answer is yes, and the amount of dissonance will be a function of the importance of the $800 and your evaluation of alternative uses you might have for the $800. If we consider Brehm and Cohen's notion of commitment, however, dissonance will only occur if you feel psychologically committed to your purchase. Because most clothing stores permit shoppers to return unwanted merchandise, often there is no *legal* commitment to the purchase. However, the act of returning clothes is psychologically easier for some people than it is for others. While Jim was growing up, one of his sisters made a hobby out of purchasing clothes and returning them a week later. She was rarely committed to her purchasing decisions. On the other hand, Jim often feels uncomfortable returning unwanted merchandise. Consequently, there is more psychological commitment associated with his purchasing decisions. Indeed, marketing experts understand the force of psychological commitment. Television ads routinely promise a 30-day, money-back guarantee for their products. Such guarantees serve to temporarily reduce the commitment consumers experience when they call to purchase a product. Once the product arrives, however, perceptions of commitment may return, the 30-day period passes, and the decision is no longer reversible. Such guarantees underscore the importance of psychological commitment in the postdecision dissonance reduction process.

In addition to commitment, Brehm and Cohen (1962) argued that *volition* (free choice) is essential to the onset of cognitive dissonance. If people perceive that their options were limited, or that someone else had heavily influenced their decision, then they may feel as though they had little choice in the decision they made. If people do not feel personal responsibility for a decision, then dissonance should not occur (Wicklund & Brehm, 1976).

The concept of volition highlights a major criticism of the *forced-compliance* research paradigm. If research participants engage in CAA in the course of fulfilling a research requirement, or to assist an experimenter, they may perceive limited choice in their behavior, and hence may experience limited dissonance. Thus, one explanation for the limited effects of earlier research may be the lack of free choice associated with the counterattitudinal behaviors of participants.

In addition to the stipulations offered by Brehm and Cohen, Aronson (1968) offered another modification of the original theory. Aronson's version of the theory argued that the source of dissonance following CAA was not the knowledge that cognitions were inconsistent with one another, but rather the belief that a person is sensible combined with the knowledge that he or she behaved in a nonsensible manner.

Sometimes referred to as Later Dissonance Theory, this modification casts the inconsistency at a higher level of abstraction that underscores the role of personality factors on cognitive dissonance. Aronson argued that people with positive self-concepts should experience greater dissonance following willful CAA than those with negative self-concepts. Presumably, people with more positive self-concepts can tolerate fewer inconsistencies than those with negative self-concepts. Since people with negative self-concepts do not have the expectation that they will always be sensible, they will experience limited dissonance when their behavior is inconsistent with their attitude—for example, when they write a CAA essay. The key to the modifications made by Brehm and Cohen (1962) and Aronson (1968) is the realization that not all people experience the same levels of dissonance.

Together, the modifications suggested by Brehm and Cohen (1962) and Aronson (1968) produced versions of Dissonance Theory that had greater precision and were more limited in scope. Although additional modifications have been suggested (Harmon-Jones & Mills, 1999), the issues discussed above represent the types of concerns dissonance theorists raised about the original version of the theory.

ALTERNATIVE THEORETICAL EXPLANATIONS

In addition to these modifications, two rival theoretical explanations have been developed to account for the findings produced by many dissonance experiments. Both Self-Perception Theory (Bem, 1967, 1972) and Impression Management Theory (Tedeschi, Schlenker, & Bonoma, 1971) questioned the viability of the cognitive dissonance construct. Bem's self-perception process represented a serious challenge for dissonance theorists and received considerable conceptual and empirical scrutiny (Cooper & Fazio, 1984). However, considerably less attention has been focused on the impression management explanation, which is no longer considered a viable explanation for the findings emerging from dissonance experiments (Cooper & Fazio, 1984). Thus, only Self-Perception Theory is examined below.

Self-Perception Theory

From 1957 to 1965, most Cognitive Dissonance Theory experiments served to provide empirical support for, or to clarify the scope of, the theory. In 1965, and later in 1967, Bem introduced Self-Perception Theory, which rejected the major assumptions of Dissonance Theory while accounting for the findings of prior dissonance experiments. In a short time, Self-Perception Theory emerged as a major theoretical roadblock for dissonance theorists. In the decade that followed, an intense rivalry evolved between the proponents of these two competing theories. The basic assumption of Self-Perception Theory is that:

> Individuals come to know their own attitudes, emotions, and other internal states partially from inferring them from observations of their own overt behavior and/or circumstances in which this behavior occurs. Thus, to the

extent that external cues are weak, ambiguous, or uninterpretable, the individual is functionally in the same position as an outside observer, an observer who must rely upon those same external cues to infer the individual's internal states. (Bem, 1972, p. 2)

In short, there are circumstances when a person is forced to infer his or her own attitudes in the same way that others' attitudes are inferred—from overt behavior. Bem (1972) reported findings from several investigations that corroborated his assumptions about the inference-making process. In each of these investigations, people's evaluations of experimental stimuli were guided by their overt behavior toward the stimuli.

Explaining Attitude Change

Bem employed this self-perception process to explain attitude change following CAA. Absent any external justification, Bem argued, people modify their attitudes following CAA because they have observed a change in their own overt behavior. Applied to the Festinger and Carlsmith (1959) experiment, Bem's explanation holds that participants receiving $1 for their CAA changed their attitudes because they observed a change in their overt behavior, the advocacy itself. The $1 that participants received, however, was not sufficient to be considered an external justification for doing so. Participants who received $20 for their CAA exhibited less attitude change because the monetary reward served as an external justification for their behavior. The $20 payment invalidated the inference-making process and provided a compelling explanation for their change in behavior. In short, Bem's alternative explanation accounted for the findings of Festinger and Carlsmith's (1959) seminal investigation without having to invoke either dissonance or psychological discomfort.

The concepts of volition and justification are equally important to Bem's explanation of attitude change. According to Self-Perception Theory, CAA will not produce attitude change when people perceive that their behavior was not volitional, or when they conclude that some external justification can explain their behavior. In these instances, people conclude that observation of their own behavior is not a valid indicator of the underlying attitude.

Self-Perception Theory versus Cognitive Dissonance Theory

The most compelling aspect of Bem's argument is his ability to account for the findings of most prior dissonance experiments without using either dissonance or psychological discomfort. Because the amount of attitude change predicted by the two theories is almost identical, Dissonance Theory and Self-Perception Theory are extremely difficult to separate empirically.

Nevertheless, the theoretical differences between Self-Perception Theory and Dissonance Theory are significant. The fundamental disagreement between these two explanations stems from assumptions about the underlying causes of attitude change. According to Dissonance Theory, CAA creates a feeling of psychological discomfort, which motivates people to reduce the cognitive inconsistency, often by changing their attitudes. Bem makes no mention of internal motivational pressures such as discomfort or arousal. Instead, Self-Perception Theory postulates that attitude change following CAA is produced by an attempt to explain the counterattitudinal behavior (i.e., the advocacy). When behavior is inconsistent with prior attitudes, and when no external justification is available to explain the behavior, people conclude that the underlying attitude that produced the behavior must have also changed.

Because the fundamental difference between these two theoretical processes is not directly observable, early tests of the relative merits of these theories produced equivocal findings (Greenwald, 1975). By the mid-1970s, most dissonance theorists had redefined Festinger's concept of psychological discomfort to mean *physiological arousal*. Arousal is manifested in increases in heart rate, blood pressure, respiration rate, and sweating. Because discomfort or arousal was the most important element of Cognitive Dissonance Theory that was absent in Self-Perception Theory, subsequent critical tests between these two competing explanations focused on the emergence of arousal following CAA.

AROUSAL, CAA, AND ATTITUDE CHANGE

Because arousal plays an important role in Cognitive Dissonance Theory but not in Self-Perception Theory, several studies have investigated the precise role of arousal in the attitude-change process. For the most part, studies investigating the effects of CAA on arousal and subsequent attitude change have employed a *misattribution* research procedure developed by Schachter and Singer (1962). This procedure does not involve the direct measurement of arousal, but it provides research participants with an external cue (e.g., taking a stimulant) to explain any arousal they might experience. Though the external cue is not the cause of the arousal, its presence allows people to misattribute the arousal as being created by the external cue.

Applied in dissonance experiments, an external cue provides a clear explanation for the arousal that participants experience following CAA.

If arousal is misattributed to the external cue, instead of being attributed to the CAA, then little or no attitude change should result. On the other hand, participants who experience arousal in the absence of an external cue should attribute their arousal to the CAA and subsequently change their attitude in order to reduce it.

The Zanna and Cooper Study

Zanna and Cooper (1974) used a misattribution procedure to determine whether arousal associated with CAA was sufficient to produce attitude change. Participants in the study either volunteered (free choice, dissonance arousal condition) or were induced to comply (forced choice, no dissonance arousal condition) with a request to write a counterattitudinal essay. Recall that Brehm and Cohen (1962) argued that free choice (volition) was necessary to produce dissonance following CAA.

In addition to the free-choice versus forced-choice manipulation, Zanna and Cooper gave all participants in their study a placebo (i.e., a pill that had no actual physiological effects). Half of the participants in the free-choice and forced-choice conditions were told that the placebo was a mild tranquilizer and that it would have a relaxing effect on them. The remaining participants in each condition were told that the placebo was a stimulant that would lead to physiological arousal.

As expected, participants in the forced-choice (no dissonance) conditions exhibited little attitude change after writing their CAA essay. Among participants who freely chose to write the CAA essay (dissonance condition), those who were told that the placebo was a stimulant exhibited little attitude change. Presumably, these participants attributed their arousal to the drug, not to the CAA. Thus, attitude change was unnecessary to reduce their arousal. Conversely, participants in the free-choice condition who were told that they had received a tranquilizer exhibited significant attitude change. These participants had no external cue to explain their arousal. Presumably, these participants attributed their arousal to the CAA and changed their attitude in an effort to reduce arousal.

Thus, in conditions where the arousal following CAA can be misattributed to an external cue (i.e., the alleged stimulant), no attitude change is necessary to reduce arousal. When arousal is attributed to CAA, attitude change occurs to reduce arousal. In sum, this study suggests that arousal attributed to CAA is sufficient to produce attitude change.

The Cooper, Zanna, and Taves Study

The conclusion that arousal is sufficient for attitude change does not imply that arousal is necessary for attitude change following CAA. To investigate this latter issue, Cooper, Zanna, and Taves (1978) conducted another study using the misattribution research procedure.

In this study, however, all participants were told that they had been placed in the placebo condition and that the pill they were to ingest would have no effect on them. Although this was true for one-third of the participants, one-third were actually given a tranquilizer that had a relaxing effect, and one-third were given an amphetamine that heightened their physiological arousal. Participants wrote CAA essays about Richard Nixon. Half of the participants were in the high-choice (dissonance) condition and half were in the low-choice (no dissonance) condition.

By manipulating arousal physiologically, the experimenters were able to hold constant participants' attributions for their physiological arousal. Participants experiencing heightened arousal had no external cue to explain their arousal and would be likely to attribute it to the CAA. Moreover, participants in the high-choice tranquilizer condition probably did not experience the arousal that they normally would because the drug physiologically relaxed them.

The attitudes of research participants after writing the counterattitudinal essay are summarized in Table 4.1. Inspection of this table reveals a number of interesting findings. First, attitudes toward Nixon were more favorable in the high-choice placebo condition than in the low-choice placebo condition. This difference represents the classic dissonance effect found in prior research. Moreover, the attitudes of participants in the three high-choice (dissonance) conditions suggest that as arousal increases, attitude change increases. This finding is consistent with Dissonance Theory's assertion that arousal motivates attitude

TABLE 4.1. Summary of Attitudes in the Cooper, Zanna, and Taves (1978) Study

	Type of drug administered		
	Tranquilizer	Placebo	Amphetamine
High-choice CAA (dissonance)	8.6	14.7	20.2
Low-choice CAA (no dissonance)	8.0	8.3	13.9

Note. Larger numbers reflect favorable attitudes toward Richard Nixon after writing the counterattitudinal essay. From "Arousal as a necessary condition for attitude change following induced compliance" by J. Cooper, M. P. Zanna, & P. A. Taves, 1978, *Journal of Personality and Social Psychology, 36*, 1101–1106. Copyright 1978 by the American Psychological Association. Reprinted by permission.

change following CAA. There was no difference in attitudes between the high- and low-choice tranquilizer conditions. The relaxing effects of the tranquilizer most likely offset heightened arousal that might have been associated with volitional CAA. As a result, participants in the high-choice tranquilizer condition exhibited little attitude change. Thus, volitional CAA was not sufficient to produce attitude change; it must be associated with a heightened level of arousal. This finding suggests that arousal may be necessary for attitude change following CAA.

The difference between the attitudes of the low-choice placebo and amphetamine conditions suggests that physiological arousal is sufficient to produce attitude change if it is misattributed. In the low-choice amphetamine condition, individuals probably misattributed the cause of their arousal to the CAA. Individuals in this condition, after experiencing an unexplained high level of arousal, may have perceived that they had more of a free choice than they actually did when they wrote the CAA essay. In fact, analysis of the measures of *perceived choice* in writing the CAA revealed that participants in the low-choice amphetamine condition reported significantly higher perceived choice than participants in the other two low-choice conditions and had perceptions of choice similar to participants in the three high-choice conditions. If individuals in the low-choice amphetamine condition attributed their arousal to the CAA—and there is good evidence to suggest that they did—then we should expect the same levels of attitude change as we observed in the high-choice placebo condition. This, in fact, was the case. After feeling aroused, the participants apparently deduced that they were in some way responsible for writing the CAA essay.

The Croyle and Cooper Studies

One limitation of the Zanna and Cooper (1974) and the Cooper, Zanna, and Taves (1978) experiments is their reliance on misattribution procedures to make inferences about arousal. Although these studies provided compelling support for Dissonance Theory explanations of attitude change, they employed indirect assessments of physiological arousal.

To address this limitation, Croyle and Cooper (1983) conducted two experiments that demonstrated the effects of CAA on attitudes and measured the physiological level of arousal induced by CAA. In the first experiment they found the traditional pattern of attitude change predicted by Dissonance Theory. Participants in the high-choice condition reported significantly more attitude change after writing a counterattitudinal essay than participants in the low-choice condition.

The second experiment employed the same design and used physiological measures to directly record participants' arousal after they wrote the counterattitudinal essay. Consistent with Dissonance Theory, participants in the high-choice CAA condition exhibited significantly greater levels of physiological arousal than participants in the low-choice CAA condition.[1] Taken together, these studies provide strong support for the dissonance arousal explanation for attitude change following CAA; the first study demonstrated the effects of CAA on attitude change and the second study demonstrated that willful CAA heightened physiological arousal, which is the hypothesized cause of the attitude change.

Summary of Arousal Studies

Findings from the arousal studies provide clear and compelling evidence for Later Dissonance Theory explanations of attitude change following CAA. Investigations using either the misattribution research procedure or direct measurement of arousal provide consistent evidence linking CAA to arousal and, in turn, linking arousal to attitude change. Two specific conclusions can be drawn from this research.

First, CAA is not sufficient to produce attitude change. For attitude change to occur, CAA must be both volitional and associated with physiological arousal. Cooper and Fazio (1984) argued that people must perceive that their counterattitudinal behavior will produce aversive consequences before they experience physiological arousal. If no aversive consequences are perceived, then dissonance arousal will not occur (though see Harmon-Jones, 2002, for another view). Zanna and Cooper (1974) and Cooper and colleagues (1978) provided support for this conclusion when they demonstrated that arousal attributed to CAA is necessary for attitude change. When arousal following CAA was misattributed, attitude change did not occur.

Second, the amount of physiological arousal experienced following CAA appears to determine the extent of attitude change. Croyle and Cooper (1983) provided a direct link between physiological arousal and attitude change, while Cooper and colleagues (1978) found that the amount of arousal attributed to CAA was positively related to the amount of attitude change exhibited by participants.

INTEGRATION OF COGNITIVE
DISSONANCE AND SELF-PERCEPTION THEORIES

Research examining the physiological arousal associated with CAA provides strong support for dissonance explanations of attitude change. Research establishing a link between arousal and attitude change is clearly incompatible with Self-Perception Theory. But does this research invalidate the self-perception explanation?

In an effort to reconcile the different theoretical positions advanced by self-perception and dissonance theorists, Fazio and his colleagues proposed that perhaps both theories were correct explanations of attitude change following CAA, but that each theory had its own domain (Fazio et al., 1977). That is, Fazio and his colleagues suggested that once the "scope" of each theory is clearly defined by specifying its boundary conditions, the apparent contradiction between dissonance and self-perception explanations of attitude change following CAA can be resolved.

Fazio and his colleagues argued that attitudes and behaviors are neither consistent nor inconsistent, but consistent or inconsistent to some degree. That is, some behaviors can be counterattitudinal, but only marginally discrepant from a person's attitude, whereas other counterattitudinal behaviors are largely discrepant from the relevant attitude. For example, if a student who was opposed to tuition increases wrote an essay advocating a 20% increase in tuition, the CAA would be greatly discrepant from the student's position on the issue. However, if the student wrote an essay advocating only a 5% increase in tuition, the CAA would be slightly discrepant from the student's position.

Fazio and colleagues (1977) argued that when the discrepancy between a person's attitude and a counterattitudinal behavior is relatively small, there should be little physiological arousal. However, when the discrepancy is quite large, physiological arousal should occur. In short, they proposed that because there is little or no arousal with mildly discrepant CAA, Self-Perception Theory could explain the subsequent attitude change. However, when the attitude–behavior discrepancy is quite large, physiological arousal is likely to occur and Dissonance Theory is needed to explain the subsequent attitude change (Fazio et al., 1977). Fazio and his colleagues proposed *boundary conditions* to limit the scope of each theory: Self-Perception Theory explains attitude change following mildly discrepant CAA and Cognitive Dissonance Theory explains attitude change following highly discrepant CAA.

To test this explanation, Fazio and colleagues (1977) conducted an experiment in which participants were given the option to write a counterattitudinal essay (high-choice condition) or were told to write the essay (low-choice condition). Based on the results of an attitude pretest, the counterattitudinal position was slightly discrepant or greatly discrepant from their position on the issue. In addition, the high-choice participants were asked to write their essays in a small soundproof booth during the experiment. They were told that the booths were new and that the psychology department was interested in people's reactions to them. Half of the high-choice participants were then asked if the booth made them feel tense or uncomfortable. This induction provided them with an external cue to misattribute any arousal they might have experienced to the booth instead of attributing it to writing the counterattitudinal essay. The other half of the high-choice participants were not asked about their reactions to the booth, and thus were not provided with a misattribution cue.

Both Self-Perception Theory and Dissonance Theory predict no attitude change in the low-choice conditions (Table 4.2). In the high-choice, no-misattribution-cue conditions, attitude change was expected to occur. In fact, attitudes in these two conditions were predicted to be significantly more favorable than attitudes in the two no-choice conditions. Thus far, the hypotheses were consistent with traditional dissonance and self-perception experiments.

The high-choice, misattribution-cue conditions provided the critical test of the study. According to the theoretical integration proposed by Fazio and his colleagues, participants in the high-choice, misattribution-cue condition who wrote a highly discrepant counterattitudinal essay were likely to experience dissonance-induced arousal. However, the presence of the misattribution cue would lead these participants to attribute their arousal to the booth and not to writing the counterattitudinal essay. Because their arousal would not be associated with the CAA, Dissonance Theory would predict no attitude change. Conversely, participants in the high-choice, misattribution-cue condition who wrote counterattitudinal essays that were less discrepant should not have experienced arousal, and would not have used the booth as a misattribution cue. Nevertheless, these participants should have observed a discrepancy between their behavior and their attitude, and according to Self-Perception Theory, should have adjusted their attitudes to match

TABLE 4.2. Predicted Pattern of Attitude Change in the Fazio, Zanna, and Cooper (1978) Study

Discrepancy level of CAA	Low choice	High choice, no misattribution cue	High choice, misattribution cue
Small	No attitude change	Attitude change	Attitude change
Large	No attitude change	Attitude change	No attitude change

their behavior. If this occurred, then attitude change of participants who wrote the slightly discrepant counterattitudinal essays in the high-choice, misattribution-cue condition would mirror the attitude change of participants writing slightly discrepant counterattitudinal essay in the high-choice, no-misattribution-cue condition. Moreover, the attitude change of participants who wrote the mildly discrepant essays in the misattribution-cue condition would be greater than the attitude change of participants who wrote the highly discrepant essays in the misattribution-cue condition. This predicted pattern of attitude change in this study is reflected in Table 4.2.

Findings of this study were generally consistent with the predicted pattern of attitudes and hence consistent with the boundary conditions that Fazio and his colleagues proposed for limiting the scope of these two theories. Given their proposed boundaries, both Self-Perception Theory and Dissonance Theory are viable accounts of attitude change following CAA. When CAA is only mildly discrepant and does not heighten arousal, Self-Perception Theory can explain subsequent attitude change. When CAA is highly discrepant and heightens a person's physiological arousal, Dissonance Theory can explain subsequent attitude change.

Although the Fazio and colleagues (1977) integration of dissonance and self-perception processes is compelling, it remains at odds with research finding that arousal is both necessary and sufficient for attitude change to occur following CAA (Cooper et al., 1978; Zanna & Cooper, 1974). However, neither of these studies examined the effect of the level of discrepancy in the counterattitudinal message and measured its influence on arousal. Thus, although arousal remains an important factor in the explanation of attitude change following CAA, it is possible that many of the counterattitudinal behaviors we engage in are only minimally discrepant from our position on an issue and unlikely to induce arousal. In these cases, Self-Perception Theory appears to be the better theoretical explanation for attitude change.

Finally, Fazio (1987) argued that Self-Perception Theory is a better explanation for *attitude formation* than it is for *attitude change*. Working from the functional perspective of attitudes (Chapter 1), Fazio argued that when people are forced to create an attitude, they look to their own past relevant behavior to determine what their attitude should be. The new attitudes serve to organize information that the individual has about the attitude object (i.e., serves the knowledge function of attitudes). When attitudes already exist (particularly when *strong* attitudes exist), on the other hand, the consideration of past behavior may be a relatively unimportant determinant of attitude change.

Summarizing Cognitive Dissonance Theory

Social scientific theories have a surprisingly short "shelf life." There tends to be a short time period between when a theory is developed and when it is abandoned for a newer theory. Bucking this trend, Cognitive Dissonance Theory is producing research over 40 years following its inception, in part, fueled by several theoretical modifications suggested by a number of scholars (see Eagly & Chaiken, 1993; Harmon-Jones, 2002; Harmon-Jones & Mills, 1999, for detailed recent reviews).

While much of the research discussed in this chapter is basic research that tested a theoretical concept or perspective, several recent studies have attempted to place Cognitive Dissonance Theory in a more applied context (Dickerson, Thibodeau, Aronson, & Miller, 1992; Stone, Aronson, Crain, Winslow, & Fried, 1994). For example, Stone and colleagues (1994) investigated the extent to which cognitive dissonance could influence college students' purchases of condoms. Half of the participants in the Stone and colleagues experiment wrote a persuasive speech advocating condom use and presented it before a video camera. These participants were told that the best of these speeches would be shown to local high school students as part of a safe-sex campaign (i.e., high commitment to the position). The remaining students simply wrote a message but did not present it (i.e., low commitment). Crossed with this commitment manipulation was a mindfulness manipulation. Half of the students in the high- and the low-commitment conditions were asked to recall and explain the circumstances where they engaged in intercourse without using a condom (i.e., high mindfulness). The other half of the participants did not recall these circumstances.

Participants who had publicly committed to a position advocating condom use *and* who had recalled their past unsafe sexual behavior were in what Stone et al. labeled the "hypocrisy condition" because they advocated a position that was inconsistent with their past behavior. This hypocrisy created cognitive dissonance "because although their public commitment about the importance of safe sex was consistent with their beliefs, the advocacy was inconsistent with their past risky sexual behavior" (Stone et al., 1994, pp. 121–122). After the study was over, participants were given an opportunity to purchase condoms with the money they had earned for participating in the experiment. Participants in the hypocrisy condition were more likely to purchase condoms and bought more condoms than participants in the other conditions. Stone and colleagues concluded that those in the hypocrisy condition experienced dissonance and that as a means of reducing that dissonance decided to engage in more consistent safe-sex practices, including the purchase of condoms.[2]

SUMMARY

Chapter 3 examined the attitude–behavior relationship, and concluded that under certain circumstances attitude change will result in behavior change. The present chapter examined the effects of behavior change on attitude change. Most studies investigating the behavior–attitude relationship employed a CAA research paradigm. Though few people willfully engage in CAA without some external justification for doing so, the CAA research paradigm has proven effective for investigating the effects of behavior change on subsequent attitude change.

Several theories have been proposed to explain the effects of CAA on subsequent attitudes. Among them, Dissonance Theory has received the most attention. Though the original version of Dissonance Theory (Festinger, 1957) was sufficiently vague to prevent falsification, the theory has undergone a remarkable evolution (Greenwald & Ronis, 1978; Harmon-Jones, 2002; Harmon-Jones & Mills, 1999; Ronis & Greenwald, 1979) and continues to receive considerable scholarly interest. Instead of its original description as "psychological discomfort," cognitive dissonance is presently defined as a state of "physiological arousal" Physiological arousal associated with CAA has been linked to attitude change in several investigations.

Self-Perception Theory (Bem, 1967) posed a serious challenge to Dissonance Theory. Many studies attempted to examine the relative merits of each theory. Although research linking physiological arousal to highly discrepant, counterattitudinal behavior is incompatible with Self-Perception Theory, other research has shown that minimally discrepant, counterattitudinal behaviors are likely to produce little arousal. In these cases, Self-Perception Theory remains a viable explanation for attitude change and perhaps an even better explanation for attitude formation.

Together, the studies reviewed in this chapter provide strong evidence that behavior change can produce attitude change. Although there is some debate about the best theoretical explanation for this effect, the relationship between behaviors and subsequent attitudes is clear. Although the scope of Dissonance Theory has been narrowed over the years, the theory remains a viable tool for persuasion in a variety of influence situations (Harmon-Jones & Mills, 1999; Wicklund & Brehm, 1976).

Dissonance Theory also provides a good example of how theories work in the social sciences. Rather than remaining the property of its developers, theories belong to all interested scholars. These scholars, in turn, can use the theory (and in many cases extend or expand the theory) to increase understanding of the particular phenomenon under consideration. In the case of Dissonance Theory (and many other theories in this book), it is the sustained inquiry performed by many scholars over the course of many years that increases our understanding of persuasive communication.

NOTES

1. There was no difference across conditions in the amount of attitude change in Study 2, but Croyle and Cooper attributed this finding to a misattribution of arousal. Participants in the high-choice condition could easily have attributed their heightened arousal to the devices that were used to measure arousal. If this misattribution occurred, then attitude change would be unlikely for these participants.
2. Not only does the Stone and colleagues study provide an applied use for Cognitive Dissonance Theory, it shows how cognitive dissonance can be created even if a message is pro-attitudinal. In this case it was the pro-attitudinal message combined with the recall of the counterattitudinal behavior that caused the dissonance.

Part II

Components of
Persuasive Transactions

This part of the book explores essential characteristics of persuasive transactions. Chapter 5 reviews research on characteristics of persuasive sources. Chapters 6 and 7 summarize research on persuasive message characteristics: Chapter 6 focuses on research on "rational" message appeals, while Chapter 7 focuses on "emotional" message appeals. Chapter 8 identifies features of message receivers that affect the effectiveness of a persuasive appeal. Finally, Chapter 9 describes characteristics of persuasive situations that influence the persuasion process.

5

Source Characteristics in Persuasive Communication

Looking ahead ...

This chapter examines characteristics of message sources that enhance the effectiveness of persuasive messages. We begin by identifying two dimensions of source credibility: expertise and trustworthiness. We then examine how people form judgments about these factors and how these judgments affect attitudes and behavior. The chapter concludes with a discussion of two related source characteristics, perceived similarity and physical attractiveness, and the effects of these factors on persuasion.

Are characteristics of message sources important factors in persuasive communication? Is the credibility or attractiveness of a message source more persuasive than the content of the message itself? Although there are no simple answers to these questions, source characteristics are often critical. Indeed, sometimes they are the most important features of persuasive communication. Public hearings, courtroom testimony, and political campaigns are situations in which effective communication skills and personal demeanor are essential for persuasive communication.

The Senate confirmation hearings of then Supreme Court nominee Clarence Thomas underscore the persuasive effects of source credibility. During the hearings, a national television audience was confronted with conflicting accounts of personal behavior, and there was scant physical evidence to directly substantiate either account. Ultimately, judgments about the validity of Anita Hill's complaint of sexual harassment and the suitability of Clarence Thomas as a Supreme Court justice were based on viewers' assessments of the believability of Professor Hill and Judge Thomas.

Shortly thereafter, a televised court case presented viewers with a similar set of judgments. Patricia Bowman accused William Kennedy Smith of sexual battery on the grounds of the Kennedy estate in West Palm Beach. There was little direct evidence to substantiate Ms. Bowman's accusation. Instead, judgments made by jurors and television viewers were based largely on the credibility of testimony provided by Ms. Bowman and Mr. Smith.

These high-profile examples provide compelling evidence for the importance of source features in persuasion. However, source factors are equally important in mundane persuasive transactions. Consumers prefer honest and likeable salespeople and voters often cast their ballots for candidates who demonstrate competence and trustworthiness.

This chapter examines the influence of source characteristics in persuasive communication. Because much of the prior research investigating source characteristics has focused on source credibility, much of the chapter will be devoted to this issue. Following this, the persuasive influence of additional source characteristics, such as likeability and perceived similarity, will be examined.

SOURCE CREDIBILITY

The roots of the source credibility construct can be traced to Aristotle, a fourth-century B.C. Greek philosopher. In his seminal work *The Rhetoric*, Aristotle claims that *ethos* (i.e., the character of the speaker) "is the most potent of all the means to persuasion" (1932/1960, p. 10). In the early 1950s, Hovland and colleagues (1953) conducted the first social science research on the characteristics and effects of source credibility.[1] Hovland and colleagues claimed that source credibility (how believable the source is) is likely to be an important determinant of persuasion across cultures; however, the particular characteristics that underlie credibility will likely differ across cultures. For example, Whittaker and Meade (1967) found that a source's sex was a component of credibility (i.e., male sources were found to be more credible than female sources) in Brazil, Hong Kong, and India, but not in Jordan or Rhodesia.

Over the past half-century, research in the United States has helped to identify areas of agreement and disagreement among scholars as to the nature of source credibility. First, while scholars generally agree that source credibility is multidimensional (i.e., is composed of more than one dimension or component), there has been considerable disagreement as to the number and nature of the dimensions. Second, there is general agreement that source credibility is a *perceptual* variable. Specifically, source credibility is the audience's *perception* of the source rather than a commodity that the source brings to a particular persuasive context. The dimensionality and perceptual nature of source credibility are issues that we will turn to next.

Dimensions of Credibility

One of the early empirical debates in the scientific study of persuasive communication focused on the definition and measurement of source credibility. Hovland and colleagues (1953) initially defined source credibility as a combination of two factors: *source expertise* and *source trustworthiness*. Hovland and colleagues defined expertise as "the extent to which a communicator is perceived to be a source of valid assertions" (p. 21). In short, expertise is the extent to which an audience member perceives the source as being well informed on the topic of the communication. Source trustworthiness, on the other hand, is an audience member's "degree of confidence in the communicator's intent to communicate the assertions he considers most valid" (Hovland et al., 1953, p. 21). In short, trustworthiness represents an audience member's perceptions that the source will tell the truth as he or she knows it.

Later, Berlo, Lemert, and Mertz (1969) conducted two studies that examined the dimensions people used to make judgments about a source's credibility. Using factor-analytic procedures,[2] they found three dimensions—safety, qualification, and dynamism—that explained most of the variance in people's ratings of a source's credibility. The qualification dimension found by Berlo and colleagues was similar to the expertise dimension identified by Hovland and colleagues (1953). However, the safety dimension identified by Berlo and his colleagues was much broader in scope than the trustworthiness dimension identified by Hovland and his colleagues. In addition to truthfulness (the important component in Hovland and colleagues' definition), safety in the Berlo and colleagues study included such concepts as "calm, safe, patient, friendly, kind, congenial, gentle, hospitable, and warm" (1969, p. 574). The third dimension identified by Berlo and his colleagues, dynamism (i.e., how animated and outgoing the source was seen as being), was previously unidentified in the literature.

The Berlo and colleagues paper had been circulated in unpublished form for nearly a decade before it appeared in print in 1969 (Cronkhite & Liska, 1980). During that period, McCroskey (1966) examined the dimensions of source credibility in a series of investigations. Though he included items to measure the dynamism dimension, McCroskey consistently found only two dimensions of source credibility, authoritativeness and character, which corresponded to the dimensions found in prior research. McCroskey's authoritativeness dimension (Table 5.1) was consistent with Hovland and colleagues' (1953) expertise dimension and accounted for a large amount of the variation (47%) in people's responses. The character dimension (Table 5.2) was consistent with Hovland and colleagues' trustworthiness dimension and accounted for a smaller (though still important) amount of the variation (29%) in responses to items in the credibility measure.

In summary, these three reports suggest that two factors, trustworthiness and expertise, adequately represent people's judgments about a source's credibility. Though the factor-analytic procedures employed in these investigations have been criticized, and though other dimensions of credibility have been suggested (Cronkhite & Liska, 1976, 1980), most persuasion scholars now describe credibility as a combination of a source's perceived expertise and trustworthiness.

TABLE 5.1. McCroskey's (1966) Authoritativeness Scale

1. I respect this person's opinion on the topic.
2. The speaker is *not* of very high intelligence.
3. This speaker is a reliable source of information on the topic.
4. I have confidence in this speaker.
5. This speaker lacks information on the subject.
6. This speaker has high status in our society.
7. I would consider this speaker to be an expert on the topic.
8. This speaker's opinion on the topic is of little value.
9. I believe that the speaker is quite intelligent.
10. The speaker is an unreliable source of information on the topic.
11. I have little confidence in this speaker.
12. The speaker is well-informed on this subject.
13. The speaker has low status in our society.
14. I would *not* consider this speaker to be an expert on this topic.
15. This speaker is an authority on the topic.
16. This speaker has very little experience with this subject.
17. This speaker has considerable knowledge of the factors involved with this subject.
18. Few speakers are as qualified to speak on this topic as the speaker.
19. This speaker is *not* an authority on the topic.
20. This speaker has very little knowledge of the factors involved with the subject.
21. The speaker has had substantial experience with this subject.
22. Many people are much more qualified to speak on this topic than this speaker.

Note. Recommended response options are Strongly Agree, Agree, Undecided, Disagree, and Strongly Disagree. From "Scales for the measurement of ethos" by J. C. McCroskey, 1966, *Speech Monographs, 33,* 65–72. Copyright 1966 by the National Communication Association. Reprinted by permission.

TABLE 5.2. McCroskey's (1966) Character Scale

1. I deplore this speaker's background.
2. This speaker is basically honest.
3. I would consider it desirable to be like this speaker.
4. This speaker is *not* an honorable person.
5. This speaker is a reputable person.
6. This speaker is *not* concerned with my well-being.
7. I trust this speaker to tell the truth about the topic.
8. This speaker is a scoundrel.
9. I would prefer to have nothing at all to do with this speaker.
10. Under most circumstances I would be likely to believe what this speaker says about the topic.
11. I admire the speaker's background.
12. This speaker is basically honest.
13. The reputation of this speaker is low.
14. I believe that this speaker is concerned with my well-being.
15. The speaker is an honorable person.
16. I would *not* prefer to be like this person.
17. I do *not* trust the speaker to tell the truth on this topic.
18. Under most circumstances I would *not* be likely to believe what this speaker says about the topic.
19. I would like to have this speaker as a personal friend.
20. The character of the speaker is good.

Note. Recommended response options are Strongly Agree, Agree, Undecided, Disagree, and Strongly Disagree. From "Scales for the measurement of ethos" by J. C. McCroskey, 1966, *Speech Monographs, 33,* 65–72. Copyright 1966 by the National Communication Association. Reprinted by permission.

Defining Credibility as a Receiver Perception

Perhaps the greatest source of agreement about the credibility construct lies in the definition of credibility as a perception held by message recipients. Eschewing a source-oriented approach to credibility, Hovland and his colleagues defined credibility as a perceptual state, not a characteristic of message sources (Hovland et al., 1953). Cronkhite and Liska echoed this sentiment when they wrote that "it is not merely the needs/goals of sources which must be assessed" (1980, p. 105). Instead, assessments of source credibility must focus on the attributions made by receivers of persuasive messages. This receiver-oriented focus has led persuasion scholars to define credibility in terms of the perceptions message recipients hold about a source's expertise and trustworthiness. Thus, credibility is not a commodity that message sources possess. Rather, it is the perception of trustworthiness and expertise that sources are able to engender in a target audience.

McCroskey's measures of authoritativeness (i.e., expertise; see Table

5.1) and character (i.e., trustworthiness; see Table 5.2) were intended to capture the audience members' perceptions of a source. These scales can capture people with different views of a source. For example, a person who has a favorable impression of President George W. Bush as a speaker on foreign policy would likely agree or strongly agree with statement number 1 on the authoritativeness scale, while a person with a negative view of his ability would disagree or strongly disagree with that statement.

McCroskey used many items to measure the authoritativeness and character dimensions of credibility (22 items and 21 items, respectively) in order to improve both the reliability and the validity of the scales. As we discussed in Chapter 2, the more items or statements that are used to measure a particular concept, the more reliable the measure will be. Moreover, in order to attain content validity, multiple items must be used to measure the entire breadth of the authoritativeness and character constructs.

The perceived trustworthiness and expertise dimensions are generally considered to be separate, but related, constructs. Although these perceptions are often related to one another, it is possible for a message source to engender the perception of expertise without creating the perception of trustworthiness. For example, Richard Nixon was generally believed to possess considerable expertise in foreign policy. However, in the aftermath of Watergate, most Americans no longer thought him to be worthy of their trust. Conversely, message sources can create the perception of trustworthiness without the perception of expertise. At the end of his political career, Jimmy Carter was regarded as highly trustworthy, but many voters no longer believed he possessed the expertise to run the country. As a result, the general factor credibility lacks the precision necessary for effective persuasion research. Instead of describing a source's credibility, persuasion scholars have relied on the more precise constructs of expertise and trustworthiness.

Variations in Perceived Expertise and Trustworthiness

Because trustworthiness and expertise are perceptions held by message recipients, judgments made about a message source's expertise or trustworthiness are likely to differ between audiences, to differ among members of the same audience, and to change over time. First, it is likely that perceptions of credibility will vary considerably from one target audience to another. As a result, a high school physics teacher may be perceived as highly expert when talking to students in a physics class, but may lack this same level of perceived expertise when presenting a paper before an audience of esteemed scholars at an international conference on nuclear physics. Similarly, an inmate at a federal penitentiary might be considered relatively trustworthy by other inmates but not by citizens who live outside the prison walls.

Second, perceptions of a single source's credibility will likely vary from person to person in the same audience. For example, it is likely that President George W. Bush is a more credible source for a lifetime Republican than for a person who is affiliated with the Socialist Workers Party.

In addition, the perceived expertise and trustworthiness of a message source can change over time. During the 1980s, this fact was evident throughout international politics. In the Philippines, the Marcos regime was toppled when citizens lost trust in their leaders. At the same time, Mikhail Gorbachov was rapidly gaining the confidence of the Russian people. In the span of only a few years, he rose from relative obscurity to become the leader of the Soviet Union. However, by 1991, it became clear that his economic reforms were unsuccessful, and soon thereafter his popularity declined and his political career was over.

In much the same fashion, perceived expertise may change from topic to topic. Although perceptions of trustworthiness are likely to be relatively stable across topics, an audience's judgment of a source's expertise may be topic-dependent. It makes sense that a known economist will be perceived by many people to have expertise when talking about deficit-reduction options. However, the same person may lack expertise to speak persuasively about child development.

Source Credibility and Attitude Change

There are ample data to suggest that source credibility influences attitude change. In one of the early investigations, Hovland and Weiss (1951) measured college students' attitudes toward a wide variety of topics. Five days later, under the guise of a guest lectureship, students in a college history class were exposed to messages on four of the topics measured earlier (i.e., over-the-counter sale of antihistamines, the feasibility of building nuclear-powered submarines, a steel shortage, and the future of movie theaters). Each message was attributed to either a high-credibility source or a low-credibility source. For example, the message on the future of movie theaters was attributed to either *Fortune* magazine (high-credibility source) or a movie gossip columnist (low-credibility source). After reading each message, participants indicated their opinion in addition to a number of other measures.

For three of the four topics (and for the overall results combined across topics), Hovland and Weiss (1951) reported that messages attributed to the high-credibility source created much more attitude change toward message recommendations when compared to the low-credibility source. In addition, the highly credible source was judged to have presented the facts more fairly and to have provided more justifiable conclusions when compared to the low-credibility source (Hovland & Weiss, 1951). This is an interesting result because the messages were *exactly* the same across the credibility conditions.

Source credibility, however, does not always influence attitude change. In his meta-analysis, Stiff (1986) reported that the correlation between source credibility and attitude change varied dramatically across studies. Some studies have found that low-credibility sources can be more persuasive than highly credible sources, particularly when presenting messages that receivers initially disagree with (Bochner & Insko, 1966). We will have more to say about the inconsistency with which source credibility influences attitudes when we discuss cognitive models of persuasion in Chapter 10.

Another factor that influences the persuasive effectiveness of credibility is the timing of the identification of the source. The question under consideration here is the extent to which source credibility effects depend on whether the source is identified before or following the persuasive message. In these studies, receivers hear a persuasive message (and we presume that the message is, at the very least, moderately compelling) that is attributed to either a low- or a high-credibility source (depending on the experimental condition). The source identification occurs either before or following the message presentation. Within a particular study, the same message is used across all credibility and timing conditions. Only the credibility of the source and the timing of the identification vary.

D. J. O'Keefe (1987) performed a meta-analysis of several studies that examined the timing of source identification on the persuasiveness of the source's credibility. He found that low-credibility sources tend to be more persuasive when they are identified following the message presentation compared to when they are introduced before the message. In contrast, high-credibility sources are somewhat more persuasive when they are introduced prior to the message compared to when they are introduced following the message.

D. J. O'Keefe (1987) also investigated the persuasive differences between high- and low-credibility sources when they are introduced before and after the message. He concluded that "delaying communicator identification substantially reduced the differential effectiveness of high- and low-credibility communicators" (p. 68). When sources were identified before the message, high-credibility sources had a strong advantage over low-credibility sources.

When sources were identified following message presentation, on the other hand, the persuasive impact of source credibility declines dramatically because the message (which is moderately strong and presented first) likely has a greater influence on attitudes. High credibility is not going to afford much of a persuasive advantage in these conditions because the source just sent a message containing moderately strong arguments. The low-credibility source benefits from this arrangement, however, because the persuasive effect of the message is greater than that of the negative source identification. In conclusion, if source credibility is going to influence receivers' responses, it is most likely to happen if the source is identified before the message is presented.

The emphasis on receiver perceptions, central to the definition of source expertise and trustworthiness, highlights the importance of factors that affect the perceptual judgments people make about message sources. The next section examines this perceptual process.

Attributions about Message Sources

After reaching agreement on the definition and measurement of credibility, researchers turned their attention to understanding how people make initial judgments about a source's expertise and trustworthiness. Because message sources rarely enter a persuasive situation with a blank slate, the expectations message recipients have about the source and the positions the source might advocate are essential to understanding perceptions of source expertise and trustworthiness.

Indeed, the notion of "creating expectations" was a hallmark of several recent presidential campaigns. Before his 1988 debate with Michael Dukakis, then vice president Bush's media specialists spread the message that although Dukakis was a polished debater, Bush lacked formal debate experience. The media specialists created the expectation that Dukakis would perform well during the debates, whereas expectations concerning George Bush's performance were significantly lower. Though both candidates performed well during the debates, Bush's performance was a "surprise" and received considerable media attention, while the Dukakis performance simply met expectations and was less newsworthy. George W. Bush's campaign handlers repeated this strategy effectively as he prepared for debates with Al Gore during the 2000 presidential campaign.

In a series of studies, Eagly and her colleagues investigated the influence of receiver expectancies on perceptions of source expertise and trustworthiness (Eagly & Chaiken, 1976; Eagly, Chaiken, & Wood, 1981; Eagly, Wood, & Chaiken, 1978). These investigations employed Kelley's (1967) Attribution Theory to explain how message recipients make causal inferences about message sources.

Attribution Theory

Kelley (1967) argued that people behave like naive psychologists as they attempt to form explanations for events that occur around them, particularly for others' behaviors. Attribution Theory is specifically concerned with understanding how people identify what caused other people to act the way they did. Two major categories of causal inferences exist. A person's behavior can be attributed to *dispositional* (personal) characteristics or to *environmental* (situational) characteristics.

When dispositional attributions are made, the inference is that the behavior is due to some characteristic of the person him- or herself. For example, you are waiting to go to a concert with a friend and he is 45 minutes late. If your friend is always late for class, appointments, and work, you might well conclude that the person is not punctual. That is, some characteristic of the person him- or herself causes the consistent tardiness.

When we make a situational attribution for someone's behavior, on the other hand, we suggest that situational constraints caused the behavior. If your friend is always punctual, but is late for the concert, you are much more likely to infer that a situational factor led to the person's tardiness.

Expectancies and Credibility Assessments

Eagly and colleagues (1981) argued that message recipients initiate this type of causal analysis when they evaluate the credibility of a message source. By using existing information about the source, message recipients generate expectations about the position the speaker will advocate. For example, during the 1960s, Americans heard a great number of political speeches about civil rights. Audiences anticipating speeches by Hubert Humphrey or Martin Luther King Jr. used information available to them to form expectations about the position these speakers were most likely to advocate. Indeed, people may have gone to hear Senator Humphrey or Reverend King speak at a political rally *because* they wanted to hear someone speak in favor of civil rights.

When we don't know the source very well, Eagly and colleagues (1981) claim that we will create expectations about the position the source will advocate. Two types of biases that people form about the positions a speaker will advocate can characterize these expectations. *Knowledge bias* refers to the judgment, based on available information about the source, that the source does not possess accurate information about the message topic. The source, because of his or her background or occupation is likely to have information that biases him or her toward a particular position. For example, the knowledge that a scientist works in the tobacco industry might lead you to expect him or her to speak favorably of the industry and against further restrictions in tobacco marketing and sales. This represents a *knowledge bias* because the person's background and position likely leads him or her to have biased information on the health effects of tobacco. In this case, the presumption is that the source is telling the truth as he or she knows it, but the information that he or she has is biased toward a particular position.

Reporting bias reflects the belief that the source is unwilling to report accurate or full information about the message topic (Eagly et al., 1978). For example, if all that you know is that a consultant is speaking on tobacco before executives of the large tobacco firms, you might expect him or her to take a position opposing restricting the availability of all tobacco products. This would be an example of a reporting bias because the position of the audience is well known and a source might be unwilling to take a position that runs counter to the audience's attitudes. The source, in this example, has accurate information but is not telling the whole truth, as he or she knows it.

Although Eagly and her colleagues (1978) distinguish between knowledge bias and source expertise, the two concepts are quite similar. In addition, reporting bias corresponds to perceived trustworthiness.

Expectancy Violations and Attitude Change

The premessage expectations of message receivers are based on available information about the source's personal preferences or background (e.g., his or her job or employer) and the situational pressures (e.g., the nature of the audience). These message expectations take the form of a "minitheory" as to why the source took the position that he or she did. These "minitheories" are either confirmed or disconfirmed by the position the communicator actually takes in the message (Eagly et al., 1981). When premessage expectations are confirmed, receivers may attribute the views advocated by the speaker to personal preferences of the speaker, the speaker's background, or to pressures of the situation. These causal attributions lead to the perception that the speaker is biased. Because communicator bias compromises the validity of the message as an accurate representation of the issue being discussed, the message has little persuasive impact (Eagly et al., 1978, 1981).

When a source *disconfirms* premessage expectations, message recipients generate a new minitheory to explain why the speaker advocated the position he or she did. Generally, this new minitheory suggests that especially compelling evidence made the communicator overcome the bias that was expected to influence the message content. Such explanations lead to perceptions that the source is unbiased and enhance the persuasive effect of the message.

Several investigations by Eagly and her colleagues (Eagly & Chaiken, 1976; Eagly et al., 1978; W. Wood & Eagly, 1981) examined the persuasive effects of expectancy disconfirmations. In one study, participants were exposed to a pro-environment message that was attributed to a source described as having either a pro-business or a pro-environment background (Eagly et al., 1978). The background attributed to the source created knowledge bias, the perception that the source would possess either pro-business or pro-environment information. Participants exposed to the message advocating a pro-environment position and attributed to the pro-environment source had their premessage expectancies confirmed. Those exposed to the pro-environment message attributed to a pro-business source experienced a disconfirmation of their premessage expectancies.

In order to create reporting bias expectancies, experimenters told participants that the message (pro-environment) was presented to either a pro-environment audience or to a pro-business audience. When presented to the pro-environment audience, the message confirmed the reporting bias expectancy. However, when the audience was pro-business, the pro-environment message disconfirmed the reporting bias expectancy.

When an audience's premessage expectancies were disconfirmed by the position advocated in the message, the message source was judged to be less biased and was more persuasive. Apparently, following expectancy disconfirmation, audience members concluded that factual evidence must have been overwhelming to cause the message source to sincerely advocate a new position. When premessage expectancies were confirmed, message recipients attributed the position advocated to the source's background characteristics or to situational constraints. Such attributions led to a perception of source bias and limited the persuasive effect of the message (Eagly et al., 1978). This process is depicted in the model in Figure 5.1.

These findings are consistent with the attribution analysis advanced by Eagly and her colleagues and suggest that the expectancies that message recipients bring to persuasive situations influence their judgment about the message source. This psychological approach to studying source characteristics is consistent with the definition of credibility as a perception held by message recipients that can change over time.

Persistence of Credibility Effects

The long-term persuasive effects of source credibility factors have been of interest to persuasion scholars since the early 1950s. Although most

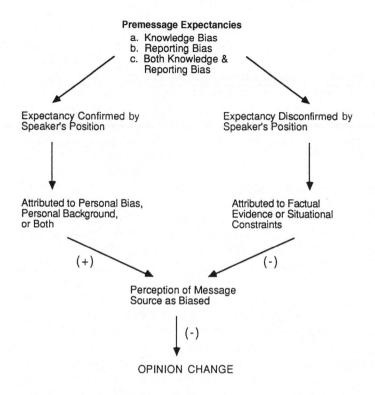

FIGURE 5.1. An expectancy model of opinion change.

scholars agree that the expertise and trustworthiness dimensions of source credibility are persuasive, the persistence of these persuasive effects has been questioned. Earlier in this chapter, we discussed the study by Hovland and Weiss (1951) that found that immediately following message exposure, messages attributed to a high-credibility source were more persuasive than messages attributed to a low-credibility source. When they measured attitudes 4 weeks later, they discovered something interesting. Attitude change declined over time for the message attributed to the high-credibility sources. Messages attributed to the low-credibility sources, however, were more persuasive after 4 weeks than they were immediately following the message. This unexpected finding was given an unusual but appropriate name, the *sleeper effect*.

Over the past 50 years, a number of researchers have attempted to replicate these early findings, but they have met with limited success (Gruder et al., 1978; Pratkanis, Greenwald, Leippe, & Baumgardner, 1988). Several alternative definitions of the sleeper effect have emerged to account for the contradictory findings in this body of research. Allen and Stiff (1989) meta-analyzed this body of research and summarized the differences among three different interpretations of the sleeper effect and evaluated the evidence supporting each of these models.

Before we discuss the three models developed to explain the workings of the sleeper effect, it is important to discuss what the sleeper effect studies actually found. First, across 20 tests of the sleeper effect, Allen and Stiff (1989) found that immediately following message presentation, the high-credibility source was more persuasive than the low-credibility source in all 20 cases (and the difference in attitudes across source credibility is statistically significant in 17 of the 20 cases). Second, Allen and Stiff reported that the impact of the high-credibility source decayed over time in 19 of the 20 cases. Third, changes in attitude over time in the low-credibility conditions were not so consistent. Participants in low-credibility conditions indicated greater levels of persuasion at the delayed attitude measure in only nine of 20 cases (and in only four of these cases was the difference statistically significant) (Allen & Stiff, 1989).

The first explanation of the sleeper effect, the *Traditional Model*, assumes that persuasion is a function of both source credibility and message content and that the evaluation of a source's credibility is separate from the evaluation of message content. The model further assumes that attention to speaker characteristics distracts message receivers from attending to message content (Hovland et al., 1949; Hovland & Weiss, 1951). Hence, persuasive effects are due primarily to message recipients' knowledge of the speaker's general position and their assessments of his or her credibility. Over time, the credibility of the source is forgotten, and recipients are left with a recommendation that has little support. Over time the persuasive effects of the highly credible source and the inhibiting effects of the less credible source are not remembered. Initial attitude change produced by the highly credible source decays, or becomes smaller. Meanwhile, the removal of the inhibiting effects of the low-credibility source causes an increase in attitude change over time. At the delayed posttest, the Traditional Model predicts that attitude change produced by the low-credibility source will exceed attitude change produced by the highly credible source (Matice, 1978).

It bears mentioning that the Traditional Model was developed as a post-hoc explanation for the findings in the Hovland and colleagues (1949) study. Thus, although this model is consistent with their findings, there is no theoretical explanation for the prediction that a low-credibility source will produce more attitude change over time than a high-credibility source. Indeed, Allen and Stiff's meta-analytic review of this literature found that only five of 20 studies investigating the sleeper effect produced a pattern of findings consistent with the Traditional Model.

Second, because early research failed to replicate the Traditional Model, later researchers offered a revised version that has been labeled the *Forgetting Model* (Gillig & Greenwald, 1974). The Forgetting Model predicts that immediately following message exposure, the message attributed to the high-credibility source will produce more attitude change than the same message attributed to the low-credibility source. However, as the message source is forgotten, attitude change decays over time, regardless of the credibility of the source. Message receivers remember message information that was persuasive, but they forget characteristics of the source. This process is evident in phrases such as, "I don't remember who told me this, but. . . . " Eventually, attitudes of people exposed to high- and low-credibility sources should converge, or become similar. Because initial attitude change produced by the highly credible source is greater, people exposed to this source will experience greater attitude decay once the source is forgotten. Thus, over time, there is a relative, but not absolute, increase in effectiveness of the low-credibility source.

Of the 20 experiments included in Allen and Stiff's review of this literature, only 10 were consistent with the predictions of the Forgetting Model. Though this model fared better in the review than the Traditional Model, half of the findings from prior research are inconsistent with this model.

One major problem for the Forgetting Model was data that indicated that people could remember the source of the message over time (Hovland & Weiss, 1951). This led scholars to develop a third model called the *Disassociation Model*. This model assumes that persuasion is a function of both message and source factors (T. Cook, Gruder, Hennigan, & Flay, 1979). Like the Forgetting Model, the Disassociation Model argues that attitude change produced by the highly credible source decays over time. In this case, attitude decay occurs because the characteristics of the message source are disassociated from the message content. In this case, the source is not forgotten, but over time the source is no longer associated with the message.

For people exposed to a persuasive message from a low-credibility source, the persuasive effects of message content are offset by the negative characteristics of the message source. Over time, when the source is disassociated from the message, these message recipients are influenced by the persuasive content recalled in the message. Thus, the Disassociation Model predicts no initial change for recipients of messages from low-credibility sources, but increased attitude change once the source is disassociated from the message, assuming that the message content is persuasive.

Unfortunately, only five of 20 studies included in Allen and Stiff's review met methodological requirements. However, four of these studies produced a pattern of immediate and delayed attitude change that was consistent with this model. Although there have been few tests of the Disassociation Model, relevant findings suggest it may be the best representation of the sleeper effect.

About the same time that Allen and Stiff reported their analyses, Pratkanis and colleagues (1988) presented an advanced analysis of the sleeper effect. They performed 17 separate experiments involving 29 separate tests of the sleeper effect. In half of these tests, they found some evidence of the sleeper effect (i.e., the persuasive impact of the low-credibility source increasing over time). In just four of these cases, however, was the increase in attitude change over time large enough to be considered statistically significant.

Producing the Sleeper Effect

It appears that several things have to occur to produce the sleeper effect. First, participants must process both the persuasive message and the message source. That is, recipients must pay attention to the message, its arguments, and the credibility of the source. Second, the message must be persuasive. The arguments in the message must be strong and compelling.

Pratkanis and colleagues (1988) present their *differential decay sleeper effect* to explain their own and others' results. To generate a sleeper effect, the persuasive effects of the message (i.e., an increase in attitude change) and the effects of a low-credibility source (i.e., a reduction in attitude change) must be separate, equal, and offset one another. Over time, the inhibiting impact of the low-credibility source decays faster than the facilitating impact of the message itself. As the effect of the source decays, the effect of the messages takes over and increases attitude change in the direction of message recommendations.

Implications of the Sleeper Effect

A number of theoretical and practical implications have emerged from this literature. First, the persuasive effects of source expertise and trustworthiness are short-lived. Though only a few studies have investigated the short- and long-term effects of credibility, these investigations have demonstrated that initial persuasive effects of source expertise and trustworthiness decay over time.

Second, these findings suggest that long-term effects of single message presentations are a function of message content and not source characteristics. Once the influence of the source decays, the effects of source credibility diminish, and the effects of message content take over. The persuasive effects of the message are not permanent either; they will eventually decay as well. The decay in the message effect, however, is slower than the decay in the source effect, producing the sleeper effect.

This literature has important implications for persuasion practitioners. Applied in natural persuasive settings, the Differential Decay Model suggests that if short-term attitude change is desired, then the credibility of the message source is likely an important consideration. However, if persisting attitude change is the goal, then the credibility of the message source is less important. In such persuasive situations, evidence and message arguments are likely to be most influential. Of course, one caveat bears mentioning. Investigations of the sleeper effect have employed a single message presentation. Advertising, health promotion, and political campaigns all rely heavily on the use of source credibility factors. However, they also generally involve the use of repeated message presentations. Though the influence of source characteristics may be temporary, repeated exposure to these factors during a persuasive campaign may create persisting attitude change. Unfortunately, research on the sleeper effect has not investigated the long-term effects of repeated exposure to highly credible message sources.

RELATED SOURCE CHARACTERISTICS

Although researchers have expended considerable effort to understand the persuasive effects of source expertise and trustworthiness, additional source characteristics have received somewhat less attention. Nevertheless, a sufficient number of investigations have examined the effects of source similarity and attractiveness to permit speculation about the influence of these factors in persuasive transactions.

Perceived Similarity

Practitioners have long believed that effective persuasion begins by establishing a personal connection between the message source and the target audience. Salespeople often spend a few minutes trying to build or maintain a good rapport with clients by claiming some degree of similarity in interests or background before focusing the discussion on the sale itself. Before the Iowa caucuses, presidential candidates often arrange for photo opportunities in which they are depicted helping farmers with their chores. Television advertisements for movies sometimes include testimonials from viewers as they leave a theater. The underlying goal of

these persuasive activities is to create the perception of similarity between the source and the target audience.

A number of psychological theories inform us that people should be
more susceptible to the persuasive appeals of similar, as opposed to dissimilar, others. Early investigations of similarity effects (Berscheid, 1966;
Brock, 1965) led authors of textbooks to conclude that perceived similarity may be an important characteristic of persuasive message sources
(Bettinghaus & Cody, 1987; Petty & Cacioppo, 1981). In a thorough review of the literature, however, Simons, Berkowitz, and Moyer (1970)
concluded that the persuasive effects of perceived similarity are less
straightforward.

Simons and his colleagues identified two dimensions of a message
source's similarity. They first distinguished between *membership similarity*
and *attitudinal similarity*. Sources create membership similarity through
references to demographic and social characteristics, personal experiences, and affiliations with groups and organizations that they share in
common with the target audience. Politicians will often refer to their association with whatever city, state, or region they might be in to create a sense
of similarity with the audience. Though less pronounced, college students
often establish membership similarity during initial interactions. For example, sorority and fraternity members will often describe themselves in
terms of membership in their particular organization and wear clothing
with Greek letters on them to advertise that membership.

Attitudinal similarity is established when speakers express opinions
and values that are shared by members of the target audience. Television
evangelists, for example, enhance their perceived trustworthiness by
continuously expressing values and opinions that are deeply held by
their target audience. The credibility enjoyed by those in the electronic
ministry is persuasive when requests for financial contributions are
made. Though indirect, the influence of attitude similarity on perceived
trustworthiness can enhance the persuasiveness of message sources.

There are times where membership similarity and attitude similarity
overlap. Politicians often emphasize their membership (or lack thereof)
in national organizations to build a sense of rapport and trust with the
target audience. For example, in the 1988 presidential campaign George
Bush "accused" Michael Dukakis of being a member of the American
Civil Liberties Union (ACLU). Aware of the negative attitude that many
conservative Republicans held toward the ACLU, Bush strategically associated Dukakis with the values of the ACLU, while at the same time
aligning himself with conservatives who were not members of the organization. In this case (and no doubt innumerable others), membership in
an organization implies (implicitly or explicitly) a particular set of beliefs, attitudes, and/or values.

In addition to the distinction between membership and attitudinal similarity, Simons and colleagues (1970) described similarities in terms of their relevance to the persuasive context. Irrelevant similarities, they argued, are offered simply to build rapport and lack persuasive influence. Relevant similarities, on the other hand, may lead to greater perceptions of source trustworthiness or expertise and thus indirectly influence attitudes. After reviewing research on the persuasive effects of similarity, Simons and colleagues concluded that perceived similarity is not always a persuasive cue. In fact, Goethals and Nelson (1973) argued convincingly that agreement from dissimilar others was sometimes more compelling than agreement from similar others. They found that when the issue was a statement of fact, that is, a verifiable position, agreement from dissimilar others increased the confidence with which people held beliefs. Apparently, agreement from similar others leads people to question whether their assessment of the issue is the correct one or whether it is subject to personal biases and the predispositions they share with a similar other. However, when agreement comes from a dissimilar other (i.e., a person who does not share the same biases and predispositions), people are more confident about the position they hold because the agreement is not likely due to similarity in opinions or personal biases. Although Goethals and Nelson focused on judgmental confidence, as opposed to attitudes, their finding is consistent with the following proposition about the persuasive influence of source similarity: "Attitude change toward the position advocated by the source depends on the extent to which interpersonal similarities or dissimilarities are perceived as having instrumental value for the receiver" (Simons et al., 1970, p. 12).

Applied to the Goethals and Nelson (1973) findings, this proposition suggests that agreement from similar others about a statement of fact had little informational value for people. However, agreement from a dissimilar other was more informative, because the other was not influenced by the same biases and predispositions. In much the same fashion, Simons and colleagues concluded that source similarity was not informative when it lacked relevance to the issue under consideration.

Relatively little has been learned about the effects of source similarity since the Simons and colleagues (1970) review. Presently, it is safe to advance two conclusions about its role in persuasive communication:

1. Source similarity does not always serve as a persuasive cue; in many situations it is unrelated to the persuasion process.
2. When similarity serves as a persuasive cue, it has a direct effect on source trustworthiness and a smaller, indirect effect on attitudes.

Physical Attractiveness

Laboratory and field investigations of the persuasive effects of physical attractiveness produced findings similar to those found in studies of source similarity. For example, in one of the seminal studies on the influence of physical attractiveness on attitude and behavior change, Chaiken (1979) asked attractive or unattractive participants to approach other students and read a script advocating the elimination of meat in both breakfast and lunch menus in all campus dining halls. Receivers of this appeal were asked to indicate their agreement with, and to sign a petition supporting, the position advocated in the message.

In the Chaiken (1979) study, attractive message sources generated more agreement with their position, generated somewhat more petition signing, and were judged as friendlier by message receivers. Attractive sources were also more fluent speakers, spoke marginally faster, reported higher GRE scores, and were more optimistic about their future when compared with unattractive sources.

In a review of this literature, Chaiken (1986) concluded that, like perceived similarity, source attractiveness is not always a persuasive cue. Instead, physical attractiveness seems to have its greatest influence in persuasive situations that are relatively unimportant. Unlike the effects of source similarity, however, the persuasive effects of source attractiveness are unrelated to evaluations of source expertise (Chaiken, 1979) and source trustworthiness (R. Norman, 1976). That is to say, the persuasive effects of source attractiveness are direct and not mediated by judgments of credibility.

Three different explanations have been advanced to account for the influence of source attractiveness (Chaiken, 1979, 1986). The *social reinforcement* explanation argues that the persuasive effects of physical attractiveness stem from the social rewards attractive people provide.

It is well established that we find attractive people to be socially rewarding, and when given a choice, we select attractive acquaintances over unattractive ones (Berscheid & Walster, 1974). Kelman (1961) argued that the process of *identification* increases susceptibility to influence from attractive sources. Thus, the social reinforcement explanation suggests that our desire to associate with attractive people leads us to accept influence from them. This is similar to the instrumental function of attitudes (as discussed in Chapter 1). Using this functional perspective, we agree more with attractive sources because they are more likely to provide us with rewards than unattractive sources.

A *cognitive-processing* explanation has also been advanced to account for the persuasive effects of source attractiveness (Chaiken, 1980,

1987). Chaiken argues that people often rely on simple decision rules to make judgments about message recommendations. These decision rules, called "heuristics," substitute for careful thinking about the persuasive message. Chaiken argues that heuristics are cognitive shortcuts that eliminate the need for effortful thinking about the message (see discussion of the Heuristic Model of Persuasion, Chapter 10, this volume). For example, one heuristic, the "likeability-agreement heuristic" suggests that we tend to agree with people we like. Because physical attractiveness has been associated with likeability (Chaiken, 1986), the likeability-agreement heuristic may be the basis for agreement with attractive sources.

Another cognitive explanation of the persuasive advantage of physically attractive people is called the *halo effect* (sometimes called the "what is beautiful is good" stereotype; Dion, Berscheid, & Walster, 1972). Physically attractive individuals are generally considered to have a number of other, positively evaluated, characteristics. Attractive individuals are generally evaluated as being more likely to be successful, more sociable, more popular, and more competent (Dion et al., 1972; Hatfield & Sprecher, 1986). This stereotype acts as a heuristic in which attractive individuals are often evaluated as being more expert and trustworthy when compared to their less attractive counterparts. These increased perceptions of credibility might be one indirect way that attractive individuals are more persuasive.

Finally, the *social skills* explanation suggests that physically attractive people are more persuasive because they have better social skills than less attractive people. Remember that in the Chaiken (1979) study attractive sources were significantly more fluent, spoke slightly faster, reported higher SAT scores and more favorable self-impressions, and were more confident of their persuasive skills than less attractive communicators. Although no specific test of the relationship between these communication factors and attitude change was made, it is likely that these factors contribute to the persuasive successes of attractive sources. Thus, the social skills explanation argues that attractive sources are more persuasive because they are more confident and skilled communicators than unattractive sources.

Regardless of the underlying explanations, the persuasive effects of physical attractiveness are clear. In situations where message recipients consider source characteristics, attractive sources enjoy a persuasive advantage over their less attractive counterparts. It bears mentioning that the three explanations for this effect are not mutually exclusive. More likely, some combination of the three explanations accounts for the persuasive effects of source attractiveness.

These explanations underscore the importance of understanding the influence of individual difference variables in persuasion research. The finding that attractive people have a persuasive advantage over unattractive people has significant predictive utility for persuasion practitioners, and it is equally important for persuasion theorists. Isolating the correct theoretical explanations for this effect will contribute to a broader understanding of how people process persuasive messages.

DeBono (2000) recently used the functional perspective to identify how one such individual difference characteristic, self-monitoring, influences the persuasive impact of a source's physical attractiveness. According to Snyder (1986), high self-monitors are individuals who are concerned with the image that they project in social situations. Essentially, high self-monitors want to fit in the social contexts they find themselves in and have the ability to modify their behavior to do just that. High self-monitors, then, typically utilize an instrumental (what DeBono calls "social-adjustive") function to attitudes because adjusting their behavior allows them to receive social rewards in various contexts. Low self-monitors, on the other hand, are concerned with acting in a way that is consistent with their own interpretation of the social situation. Low self-monitors want their own behavior to be a reflection of their own beliefs, moods, attitudes, and values. DeBono claims, then, that low self-monitors utilize primarily a value-expressive function of attitude because their behaviors reflect important values and attitudes that they hold.

DeBono, Ruggeri, and Foster (1997, cited in DeBono, 2000) investigated this relationship between self-monitoring and attitude functions in a study on evaluations of a consumer product. They claimed that high self-monitors (i.e., those utilizing an instrumental function) will respond to the image presented in an advertisement to a greater extent than the actual characteristics of the product. Low self-monitors (i.e., those utilizing a value-expressive function) will respond to the characteristics of the product itself more than to the image projected in an advertisement. In their study, DeBono and colleagues had high and low self-monitors look at one of two forms of a print advertisement for a new brand of chocolate. The two versions differed only in the physical attractiveness of the person depicted in the ad. Participants were then asked to sample one of two chocolate candies where one tasted significantly better than the other.

Consistent with their predictions, high self-monitors evaluated the chocolate associated with the attractive source more positively than the chocolate associated with the less attractive source. This was true regardless of the actual quality of the chocolate they sampled. Evaluations made by low self-monitors, on the other hand, were influenced by the nature of the chocolate sampled. The attractiveness of the person depicted in the advertisement did not influenced low-self monitors' ratings of the chocolate.

In summary, results of the DeBono and colleagues (1997, cited in DeBono, 2000) study indicated that the physical attractiveness of the source would be influential for some, but not for all, people. Individuals working from primarily instrumental attitude functions (high self-monitors in their study) will be influenced to a greater extent by physically attractive sources. Individuals working from a value-expressive function will be uninfluenced by an attractive source because they are careful to make their behavior consistent with their own values and beliefs.

SUMMARY

This chapter examined several characteristics of message sources that affect the persuasion process. We began by discussing two dimensions of source credibility, source expertise and source trustworthiness, and argued that although they are often related, these are separate dimensions that people typically use to evaluate a source. Next we discussed the expectations people have about message sources and the positions the sources are likely to advocate. We argued that when these expectations are confirmed, people perceive the source to be biased, and hence less convincing. However, when these expectations are disconfirmed, the source is perceived as less biased and more persuasive. We concluded the discussion of source credibility effects by reviewing research on the sleeper effect. Here, we argued that source credibility has its greatest persuasive influence in the short term and that, over time, people disassociate the source of a message from the message content. Thus, in the long term, message content features are much more persuasive than source characteristics.

Source similarity and physical attractiveness are two other factors that may affect the persuasion process. When characteristics of a message source that are relevant to the persuasive message are similar to characteristics of the audience, the trustworthiness of the source may be enhanced. In addition, research has shown that source attractiveness is only persuasive in some situations. Specifically, when the message is relatively unimportant to receivers, they are likely to be affected by the attractiveness of the source. Several possible explanations for these effects were discussed.

NOTES

1. Hovland and colleagues' work broke ground in several areas of persuasion; we will return to their work several times in this book.
2. Factor analysis is a statistical technique where responses to a number of questionnaire items are grouped together by how consistently (or inconsistently) participants respond to them.

6

Persuasive Message Characteristics

Rational Appeals

L OOKING AHEAD ...

The next two chapters examine features of messages that are influential in the persuasion process. In this chapter, we begin with a discussion of rational appeals and discuss how message receivers process evidence and when it is likely to be most effective. Then we examine the effectiveness of one- and two-sided messages. In the next chapter, we examine the use of emotional appeals. In particular, we review the broad area of research on fear appeals and the relatively new research on guilt-arousing appeals.

The decade of the 1960s was witness to a proliferation of persuasion research that attempted to catalog the characteristics of persuasive messages. These investigations culminated in several avenues of research that are generally referred to as "message effects research," which helped to inform most of our classic and contemporary theories of persuasion. We will spend the next two chapters reviewing some of this theory and research. Unfortunately, a thorough review of each of these research programs is beyond the scope of this book, let alone a pair of chapters.

In discussing the means of persuasion, Aristotle (1932/1960) claimed that there are three primary means of persuasion: *ethos*, *logos*, and *pathos*. We discussed *ethos* (i.e., the character of the speaker) in the previous chapter. Aristotle's other means of persuasion have to do with the message. Specifically, *logos* refers to the use of logic or the rational appeal in a persuasive message. This chapter examines the findings from message effects research that focus on rational appeals. Aristotle's third means of persuasion, *pathos*, concerns messages that persuade by creating emotions within audience members. The next chapter focuses on emotional appeals. The topics chosen for these chapters were selected because they made significant contributions to the understanding of persuasive communication, and because they continue to motivate persuasion research 40 years after the genesis of the message effects research paradigm.

This chapter begins with a review of the research on the persuasive effects of evidence. Following this, the chapter examines several models of rational argumentation. The chapter concludes with a discussion of the effectiveness of one- and two-sided message presentations.

A NOTE ABOUT RATIONAL
AND EMOTIONAL APPEALS

Before we begin, we feel compelled to admit the relatively arbitrary nature of our organizational scheme in these chapters. Specifically, textbooks continue to make a distinction between rational and emotional appeals that reflects a Western tradition of separating reason from emotion. Several scholars have noted that separating rational from emotional appeals is a false dichotomy (S. L. Becker, 1963; Gass & Seiter, 1999). Few messages are either purely rational or purely emotional. Instead, most messages generate some degree of both rational and emotional processes.

For example, some messages designed to be rational appeals can create any number of emotional reactions in recipients. An otherwise rational message on critical food shortages in third-world countries might foster fear, pity, guilt, and probably other emotions in receivers. Moreover, as we will discuss in the next chapter, explanations for the persuasive effectiveness of fear appeals (e.g., R. W. Rogers, 1975; Witte, 1992) have clearly become more cognitive (i.e., rational) and less emotion-based over time. As a consequence, while the distinction between rational and emotional appeals might be useful for organizing topics in a textbook, drawing a clear conceptual distinction between the two is a much more difficult task.

RATIONAL PERSUASIVE APPEALS

Persuasive messages that contain rational arguments are based on the assumptions that people have an implicit understanding of formal rules of logic and that they apply these rules when they make judgments about a source's recommendations. Rational arguments derive their influence from sound reasoning and the quality of evidence that is offered in support of the conclusion. Though there are many types of rational appeals, the most basic form of an argument contains three components: a claim, data to support that claim, and a warrant that provides a logical connection between the data and the claim (Toulmin, 1964).

In Toulmin's terms, a *claim* is the conclusion of the argument, the position implied by reasoning and supporting information. Typically, the claim is the position a source is advocating in a message. *Data* are evidence that provide support for the claim. McCroskey defined evidence as "factual statements originating from a source other than the speaker, objects not created by the speaker, and opinions of persons other than the speaker that are offered in support of the speaker's claims" (1969, p. 170). Finally, a *warrant* is a propositional statement that connects the data to the claim. Its specific form may vary, but a warrant always provides the logical connection between the data and the claim. It is the justification for the claim, given the data provided.

For example, consider the following argument: "Recent tuition increases at most state universities make it increasingly difficult for people from lower- and middle-income families to obtain a college degree. Thus, we should cap tuition increases in order to make public education accessible to students from all economic backgrounds." In this argument, the claim is that we should cap tuition increases. Support for this claim comes from the first sentence, which states that tuition increases make it difficult for students in lower socioeconomic groups to attend college. However, this evidence is not relevant to the claim unless we also consider our long-standing national commitment to make public education accessible to everyone. Hence, the warrant that connects the data to the claim is the statement that we must maintain our commitment to make public education accessible to everyone.

In our example above, the warrant was included as part of the argument (i.e., the warrant was explicit). This is not true of all arguments. Some messages include an implicit warrant. Consider a version of the tuition cap argument we presented above: "We should cap tuition increases at most state universities because they make it difficult for people from lower- and middle-income families to obtain a college degree." In this case, the claim and the data are the same as in the previous example; however, the warrant (i.e., that it is important to keep a college education available to everyone) is left unstated.

Toulmin's model of argument specifies an important role for evidence in the persuasion process and suggests two important questions for persuasion scholars. First, how persuasive is the evidence contained in rational appeals? Second, how do rational appeals influence the attitudes and beliefs of targets? In the next sections of this chapter we examine each of these questions. We begin with a discussion of the persuasive effects of evidence and then review studies that have modeled the effectiveness of rational appeals.

Persuasive Effects of Evidence

There are few notions in persuasive communication that are more intuitive than the hypothesis that the presence of high-quality evidence will increase the persuasiveness of a message. For example, although their terminologies vary, public speaking textbooks strongly suggest that persuasive speeches contain data, evidence, or supporting materials (e.g., German, Gronbeck, Ehninger, & Monroe, 2001). Several early reviews of evidence research, however, painted a picture far murkier than our intuitive notion would suggest. Early research on the use of evidence consisted of a plethora of variable-analytic studies.[1] Without a relevant theory to guide them, early reviewers had difficulty summarizing this literature (e.g., Kellermann, 1980; McCroskey, 1967, 1969).

It was not until the 1980s that a clearer picture emerged concerning the persuasive impact of evidence (see Reinard, 1988; Reynolds & Burgoon, 1983). Reinard (1988) argued that past inconsistencies in research on the persuasive impact of evidence were caused by different ways of manipulating (or controlling) evidence as well as by differences in the terminology used to describe these manipulations (see also Kellermann, 1980; Reynolds & Burgoon, 1983). For example, while several studies compared the persuasive effects of messages containing "evidence" and "no evidence," they differed strongly in what those two terms meant. One study might define evidence as statistical information while another study might define evidence as statements made by individuals other than the message source. To make matters even more difficult, what might count as "no evidence" messages differed across studies as well (Hample, 1978).

When John Reinard (1988) grouped studies by how evidence was manipulated (rather than according to the terminology used), he saw a much clearer picture of the effect of evidence. He concluded that different forms of evidence have different effects on attitude and behavior change. His conclusion was that "evidence appears to produce general persuasive effects that appear surprisingly stable" (p. 46). Reinard also suggested that not only does evidence influence attitude and belief change, but it influences a source's credibility (see also Reynolds & Burgoon, 1983; Reynolds & Reynolds, 2002).

Following Reinard's lead, scholars who have since addressed the issue of the persuasive impact of evidence have been much more optimistic than scholars of 20 or 30 years ago (Reynolds & Reynolds, 2002). But we need to be careful not to paint too rosy a picture of the experimental evidence. The persuasive impact of various forms of evidence depends on a variety of intervening and moderating variables (Kellermann, 1980). For example, Reinard (1988) noted that a number of source (e.g., source credibility), message (e.g., media of presentation), and receiver (e.g., prior attitude and knowledge) factors influence how persuasive a particular piece of evidence might be. Unfortunately, a comprehensive review of the persuasiveness of various evidence forms (with a discussion of all the accompanying intervening and moderating variables) is well beyond the scope of this book. Reinard (1988), Reynolds and Burgoon (1983), and Reynolds and Reynolds (2002) provide good overall reviews of the evidence literatures. In addition, several recent reviews of specific evidence forms are also available (e.g., D. J. O'Keefe, 1998; Reinard, 1998).

Our review of the evidence literature will focus on two central questions. First, what is the impact of message processing on the persuasiveness of evidence? Second, can and do receivers evaluate compelling evidence as compelling?

Evidence and Persuasive Message Processing

One of the most important factors that determines whether evidence is persuasive is the extent to which message recipients receive and cognitively process the persuasive messages containing the evidence (Reinard, 1988; Reynolds & Burgoon, 1983; Reynolds & Reynolds, 2002). Reynolds and Reynolds (2002) claim that in order for evidence to influence attitude change, recipients must cognitively process (i.e., think about and evaluate) it. The Elaboration Likelihood Model (ELM) of persuasion (Petty & Cacioppo, 1981, 1986) provides a theoretical perspective from which to discuss how message processing influences the effectiveness of evidence. A thorough discussion of this model and the controversies surrounding it appears in Chapter 10. For now, we will consider only the portion of the model that is relevant to the effectiveness of evidence. In the ELM, whether or not recipients cognitively process a message is determined, in part, by the audience's *motivation* to do so.

Petty and Cacioppo (1981, 1986) hypothesized that one factor that affects people's willingness to scrutinize the content of a persuasive message is their involvement with the message topic. According to the ELM, when recipients are highly involved in a message topic, they are motivated to scrutinize the message content because the topic is relevant to their lives and they are concerned about the outcome of the persuasive attempt. Thus, when message receivers are highly involved with the message topic, message characteristics such as the strength of supporting evidence and argument quality should influence attitude change. Conversely, when targets are relatively uninvolved with the topic of the persuasive appeal, they will be less motivated to scrutinize message content. In these cases, evidence and argument quality will go relatively unnoticed by message recipients, and their persuasive effects will be minimal. In short, the higher the audience's involvement with the message topic, the more strongly evidence should influence attitude change.

A meta-analytic review of the evidence literature provided support for this general hypothesis (Stiff, 1986). When the findings of 30 investigations were cumulated, Stiff (1986) found an overall positive correlation between the use of evidence and attitude change ($r = .18$). However, as predicted by the ELM, there was an interaction between message recipient involvement and the effectiveness of evidence. That is, there was a direct linear relationship between the level of message recipient involvement and the persuasiveness of message evidence. Specifically, when the message topic was relatively uninvolving for recipients, evidence was least persuasive ($r = .12$). For moderately involving topics, the correlation between the amount or quality of evidence and attitude change was somewhat stronger ($r = .18$). Finally, the correlation was strongest when the topic was highly involving ($r = .30$). Although small in size, the differences among these effect sizes were statistically significant. Thus, the meta-analysis of the effects of supporting information on attitudes was consistent with the effects predicted by the ELM.

The investigations included in this meta-analytic review contained a variety of different evidence manipulations. Some studies manipulated the amount of evidence contained in the message, other studies varied the presence or absence of evidence in the message, and still others manipulated evidence by varying the quality of arguments contained in the message. Petty and his colleagues (Petty et al., 1987) criticized the decision to collapse these different types of evidence manipulations into a single evidence category. They argued that the different types of evidence manipulations would produce different persuasive effects. However, subsequent analysis of these studies produced the same pattern of effects for each type of evidence manipulation (Stiff & Boster, 1987).

Thus, the pattern of findings that emerged from Stiff's (1986) meta-analysis appears to be quite robust. Across many studies employing a variety of operational definitions, the persuasive effects of evidence seem dependent on the motivation of recipients to scrutinize message content. When they are motivated to consider its content, persuasive targets are likely to be influenced by the quality of supporting evidence in the message.

Evaluating Evidence

Just because evidence is cognitively processed does not imply that it will influence attitude change. Reynolds and Reynolds (2002) claimed that in order for evidence to influence attitude change, audience members must evaluate it as being compelling. Most studies tacitly assume that persuasive targets are capable of effectively judging the logical validity of message arguments. However, prior research has documented several errors in reasoning that people frequently commit.

In an early study, Janis and Frick (1943) hypothesized that people make two types of systematic errors when judging the logical validity of arguments. First, Janis and Frick hypothesized that when people agree with the conclusion of an argument, they are more likely to judge invalid arguments that support the conclusion as valid and to judge valid arguments against the conclusion to be invalid. Conversely, Janis and Frick hypothesized that when people disagree with the conclusion of an argument, they are more likely to judge invalid arguments opposing the conclusion as valid and to judge valid arguments favoring the conclusion as invalid. In short, Janis and Frick speculated that people are likely to let their preferences about the argument's conclusion affect their judgments concerning the logical validity of the evidence.

To test these hypotheses, Janis and Frick presented college students with a series of arguments that were logically valid or logically invalid. A pretest revealed the arguments participants agreed with and those they opposed. Janis and Frick's analyses provided clear support for their hypotheses. When students made errors in reasoning, they tended to judge an invalid argument as valid if they agreed with the conclusion and a valid argument as invalid if they disagreed with its conclusion.

Bettinghaus and his colleagues extended this analysis, but argued that people are not equally likely to make errors in judging the logical validity of arguments (Bettinghaus, Miller, & Steinfatt, 1970). Instead, they argued that highly dogmatic people are more likely to let their preferences influence their judgments of argument validity. *Dogmatism* is a personality trait that reflects the extent to which a person is closed-minded. For example, a highly dogmatic person would most likely agree with statements such as "Of all the different philosophies that exist in this world there is probably only one that is correct," and "There are two kinds of people in this world; those who are for truth and those who are against truth" (Trodahl & Powell, 1965). Bettinghaus and colleagues (1970) hypothesized that because of their rigid cognitive style, highly dogmatic people would be more likely to let their preference for an argument's conclusion influence their judgment of the argument's validity. Using the measure of dogmatism developed by Trodahl and Powell

(1965), they replicated Janis and Frick's findings and also found support for their hypothesis. Specifically, they found that highly dogmatic people were more likely to judge an argument as valid if it came from a positive source than if it came from a negative source (Bettinghaus et al., 1973).

Together these studies suggest that people tend to make systematic errors when they judge the validity of arguments. Though the accuracy rates in studies like these are generally quite high, it bears mentioning that people can and do make errors in reasoning when processing persuasive messages.

Combined with the research on motivation, these findings challenge the tacit assumption that messages containing well-reasoned arguments with ample supporting information will be persuasive. In fact, in many instances people are unmotivated or unable to effectively scrutinize the content of persuasive messages. If message recipients are capable and sufficiently motivated, however, messages containing quality arguments and strong evidence are an effective means of persuasion.

Modeling the Effects of Rational Appeals

The preceding discussion of the limitations of rational appeals was not intended to create the impression that logical arguments and supporting information are ineffective for creating, changing, and reinforcing attitudes and behavior. Rather, it was intended to provide readers with a better understanding of the situations in which the influence of rational appeals is likely to be limited. Given that rational appeals are effective in a large majority of persuasive contexts, we should understand *how* they work to persuade targets.

Mathematical models of belief formation and change provide some insights into the effectiveness of rational persuasive appeals (Hample, 1977, 1978, 1979; McGuire, 1960; Wyer, 1970; Wyer & Goldberg, 1970). These models are derived from the logical syllogism as a form of rational argument, and they assume that humans are rational beings.

McGuire's Probabilistic Model

Belief in the conclusion of an argument is not always an all-or-nothing proposition. That is, people believe claims with a certain probability. Sometimes, people believe with a high degree of probability that a persuasive claim is true. Beliefs about abortion rights, for example, tend to be held with a high degree of certainty. Abortion rights advocates and their anti-abortion adversaries often express all-or-nothing beliefs about abortion. The battle lines have been clearly drawn, and for many people on opposite sides of this continuing debate there is no gray area, no common ground.

On the other hand, most of our beliefs about issues are held with less certainty. For example, we may believe that Al Gore or Ralph Nader would have been an effective president, or that the collapse of the former Yugoslavia has led to increased ethnic tensions in the Balkan states, but we may be less certain of these beliefs than we are about our beliefs surrounding the abortion issue. That is, we may hold these beliefs with a probability of less than 1.00.

To accommodate the variation in the extent to which people hold beliefs, McGuire (1960) developed a probabilistic model of beliefs. The foundation of this model is a form of argument known as a logical syllogism. Logical syllogisms have three components: a major premise, a minor premise, and a conclusion. If an argument is valid, its conclusion can be deduced from the major and the minor premises, providing they are true. Consider the following example:

Major premise: If I attend class and study 3 hours a week, I will receive an "A" in my persuasion course.
Minor premise: I will attend class and study 3 hours a week.
Conclusion: I will receive an "A" in my persuasion course.

In this example, if the major premise is true and if the minor premise is true, then the conclusion is true by definition. Thus, if attending class and studying 3 hours a week is sufficient to receive an "A" in your persuasion course, then you should expect an "A" if you attend class and study 3 hours a week. However, McGuire (1960) argued you may be less than certain about the major or the minor premise, yet still believe them. That is, you may believe with a high probability, say 80%, that the major premise is true, and believe with somewhat less probability, say 70%, that the minor premise is true. According to McGuire's model, if either the major or the minor premise is held with less-than-certain probability, then the conclusion will also be held with a less-than-certain probability.

McGuire's model is actually quite simple, and can be easily represented in the following equation:

$$p(B) = p(B/A)\,p(A) \tag{6.1}$$

where $p(B)$ (read: the probability of B) is the probability that the conclusion is true; $p(B/A)$ (read: the probability of B given A) is the probability that the major premise is true; and $p(A)$ (read: the probability of A) is the probability that the minor premise is true.

Thus, to estimate your belief in the conclusion of an argument, you simply multiply the probability that you believe the major premise is true by the probability that you believe the minor premise is true. Applying this model to the earlier syllogism about receiving an "A" in your persuasion course is one way to examine the effects of probabilistic beliefs. Assume that you believe the probability of the major premise to be .80 and the probability of the minor premise to be .70. Then the probability that you believe the conclusion, that is, that you will receive an "A" in the course, should be .56 (i.e., .80 multiplied by .70). Conversely, the probability that you will receive something other than an "A" is .44 (1.00 − .56).

It bears mentioning that like any other model or theory of persuasion, McGuire's model is simply a hypothesis, one that describes how the components of logical syllogisms determine people's beliefs about an argument's conclusion. Tests of this hypothesis were relatively straightforward. People were asked to indicate the probability that a number of belief statements were true. Embedded in this list of belief statements were minor premises, major premises, and conclusions from syllogistic arguments. By multiplying a person's belief probability for the major premise of an argument by that person's belief probability of the minor premise, researchers could obtain a predicted value for the person's belief in the conclusion. To specifically test McGuire's model, the person's reported belief in the conclusion is compared with the predicted belief in the conclusion. A strong positive correlation between the predicted and reported probabilities of belief in the conclusion indicates the extent to which the model describes how people form beliefs about an argument's conclusion. Several tests of McGuire's model produced the anticipated positive correlations between predicted and observed belief probabilities, thus providing support for this model (McGuire, 1960).

McGuire's (1960) probabilistic model presumes that people are being entirely logical when judging the validity of an argument's conclusion. This represents what he called the "logical consistency" of beliefs and attitudes. McGuire recognized, however, that people are not always logically consistent. He suggested that *hedonic consistency* (or wishful thinking) also influences judgments of an argument's validity. McGuire also reported that in addition to exhibiting logical consistency, people were also likely to report conclusions that represented favorable outcomes to be valid (even if they were entirely illogical). As a consequence, while the probabilistic model is useful in understanding how audience members cognitively construct arguments, there will always be more to the story than logic.

Wyer's Extension of McGuire's Model

Although evidence existed to support McGuire's model, correlations between predicted and observed belief probabilities were far less than perfect. In an effort to improve its predictive value, Wyer (1970) and Wyer and Goldberg (1970) proposed an extension of McGuire's original model. They hypothesized that factors other than those included in an argument influenced the probability with which people believe the argument's conclusion. In fact, Wyer hypothesized that people could believe the conclusion of a syllogism even if they did not believe the major and minor premises. For example, you may believe you will receive an "A" in your persuasion class even if you don't go to class and study. Instead, you may believe that you will receive an "A" because you are brilliant, cheat well, or believe the class is remarkably easy. Wyer's extension can be represented in the following equation:

$$p(B) = p(B/A)\, p(A) + p(B/\bar{A})\, p(\bar{A}) \qquad (6.2)$$

where the first part of the equation is identical to McGuire's model. Specifically, $p(B)$, $p(B/A)$, and $p(A)$ are identical to Equation 6.1. Wyer's extension appears after the addition sign. In this part of the model, $p(B/\bar{A})$ (read: the probability of B given *not* A) is the probability that the conclusion is true even if the minor premise is false; and $p(\bar{A})$ (read: the probability of *not* A) is the probability that the minor premise is false. By definition, the value of $p(\bar{A})$ is $1 - p(A)$.

Thus, Wyer's (1970) model suggests that a person's belief in the conclusion is determined by his or her belief in the major and minor premises *plus* the effects of factors not included in the syllogism. Extending our syllogism about the grade you believe you will receive, recall that your belief in the major premise is .80, your belief in the minor premise is .70, and the product of these two belief probabilities is .56. So far Wyer's equation works the same as McGuire's.

Wyer's model (1970) requires that you also consider your belief that you will receive an "A" even if you do not attend class and study 3 hours a week, $p(B/\bar{A})$. In Wyer's extension, the value of $p(B/\bar{A})$, or the probability that you will receive an "A" even if you do not attend class and study 3 hours a week, is multiplied by $p(\bar{A})$, or the probability that you will not attend class and study 3 hours a week.

Assume that you believe the probability that you will receive an "A" even if you do not attend class and study 3 hours a week is .40. Because $p(\bar{A})$ equals $1 - p(A)$, you believe the probability that you will not attend class and study 3 hours a week is .30. Multiplying these latter two values produces a belief in the conclusion (i.e., that you will receive an "A" even if you don't attend class and study 3 hours a week) of .12

due to factors other than those contained in the original argument. Combined with the probability that the conclusion is true because the major and minor premises are true (.56), the overall belief probability in the conclusion is .68 (i.e., .56 + .12).

Thus, in this example, Wyer's (1970) model predicts that you believe there is a .68 probability of getting an "A" in your persuasion class compared to the .56 probability predicted by the McGuire model. As does the previous model, Wyer's probabilistic model represents a hypothesis about the structure of people's beliefs. Tests of this hypothesis, however, produced disappointing results. In comparative tests of the two models, Hample (1979) found that the McGuire model predicted beliefs much better than the Wyer model.

Hample's Refinement of Wyer's Model

Hample (1979) found that when added together, the two components in the Wyer model tended to offset one another. Because the $p(A)$ is inversely related to $p(\bar{A})$—recall that $p(\bar{A}) = 1 - p(A)$—the values for the first multiplicative term (i.e., before the "+") in Wyer's equation were negatively correlated with the values of the second multiplicative term (i.e., following the "+") in the equation. The result was a model with less predictive validity than the original model offered by McGuire.

To alleviate this problem, Hample suggested applying a weight to each of the multiplicative components in the Wyer model. We discussed the concept of weights in Chapter 3 when we discussed the Theory of Reasoned Action. Weights in this case represent the relative importance of the two parts of Wyer's model. By applying weights, these two components can vary independently of one another, rather than being negatively related.

Using regression analyses, Hample (1979) demonstrated that applying weights to both parts of the Wyer model allowed each to work independently to predict people's belief in the conclusion of an argument (p. 144). That is, the weights allow the two components in Wyer's model to both contribute without having them cancel each other out. In short, Hample applied a statistical solution to the problems associated with Wyer's model. Hample further demonstrated that his weighted version of Wyer's model produced uniformly strong correlations between people's predicted and reported beliefs in the conclusions of various arguments. Hample's revision of the Wyer model provided a better explanation of people's beliefs in a conclusion than either the Wyer (1970) or the McGuire (1960) models.

Why These Models Are Important

Students often question the value of these mathematical models for persuasion practitioners. We frequently field inquiries about the relevance of probabilistic models for everyday interaction, or even for the development of persuasive campaigns. Although their value may not be intuitively obvious, these models provide considerable insight into the role that evidence plays in persuasion.

Recall the earlier discussion of Toulmin's (1964) model of argument. A valid argument contains a claim, data to support that claim, and a warrant that connects the data to the claim. Hample argued that whatever verbal form an argument may ultimately take, its warrant must serve the logical function of asserting "if D then C, where D represents the data and C represents the claim" (1978, p. 220). In a logical syllogism, the argument's warrant is the major premise of the syllogism. The data are represented in the minor premise, and the argument's claim is represented in the conclusion. Thus, the probabilistic models describe the effect of an argument's evidence and warrant on adherence to its claim. Hample's (1979) revision of Wyer's (1970) model accurately predicted people's acceptance of an argument's conclusion and thus provides insights into the operation of evidence in the persuasion process.

Hample's model underscores the importance of evidence in the success of a logical appeal. Furthermore, the model implies that belief in the argument's warrant is as important as the acceptance of supporting evidence. Given the importance of the warrant to the overall acceptance of the argument, sources may gain a persuasive advantage by explicitly stating the connection between the data and the claim and avoiding the use of implicit warrants. Because they are unstated, implicit warrants allow targets to provide their own connection between the data and the claim or to leave the evidence logically unconnected. Indeed, M. Burgoon cautioned against the use of implicit conclusions for the same reason. He argued that "persuaders must be cautious in assuming that the audience will draw the *correct* conclusion from the data" (1989, p. 144). Arguments with explicit warrants also require less cognitive participation from targets who may be content to adopt the logic, and hence the conclusion, of a source's argument.

One- and Two-Sided Rational Appeals

One characteristic of rational persuasion is that two or more opposing positions can be advocated for any persuasive topic. Because there are at least two sides to every persuasive story, persuaders must decide how much recognition they should direct toward opposing viewpoints. The extent to which messages recognize and attempt to refute those opposing viewpoints is called *message sidedness*. Messages can be crafted to focus exclusively on arguments in favor of a source's position, or they can be expanded to acknowledge the existence of opposing arguments. Messages that contain only supporting arguments are labeled *one-sided messages*; those that also address opposing viewpoints are labeled *two-sided messages*.

One familiar two-sided message is the negative political advertisement. In such an advertisement, the records of two candidates for the same political office are contrasted. Such a message might compare two candidates' voting records on issues like protecting Social Security or tax increases. Two positions are compared and one (i.e., the one held by the candidate sponsoring the ad, of course) is argued to be superior. A one-sided political advertisement might simply extol an incumbent's experience in office and his or her position as a community leader without mentioning the challenger's name or record.

As is true with several research topics in persuasive communication, Hovland and his colleagues (1949) were the first to investigate the relative persuasiveness of one- and two-sided messages. Like most variable analytic researchers of their day, Hovland and colleagues were motivated by a practical concern: they wanted to determine which type of message structure would enjoy the greatest persuasive success.

Initial investigations of this issue found that premessage agreement with the position advocated in the message and the education level of message recipients influence the relative persuasiveness of one- and two-sided messages. Participants who already agreed with the position advocated in a message were persuaded more by one-sided messages, whereas two-sided messages were more effective for targets who initially disagreed with the source's position (Lumsdaine & Janis, 1953). Moreover, two-sided messages proved more successful for targets with some high school education, whereas one-sided messages were more successful for less educated targets (Hovland et al., 1949).

These early research efforts sparked a considerable amount of interest in the structure of persuasive messages. At issue in this literature was the extent to which one- and two-sided messages influenced credibility assessments of the speaker. Presumably, well-informed audiences and audiences that disagree with the speaker's position are cognizant of opposing viewpoints and expect the source to address both sides of the issue. One-sided message presentations to these types of audiences were hypothesized to produce lower judgments of source expertise and trustworthiness and to limit the effectiveness of the message.

Unfortunately, subsequent investigations of message sidedness produced an array of conflicting findings. Some studies found two-sided messages to be more persuasive, some found one-sided messages more persuasive, and some revealed no effects for message sidedness. Moreover, the pattern of findings in these investigations did not support the anticipated effects of audience characteristics (for a review, see Allen, 1991).

Extending their review of this literature, Allen and his colleagues (Allen et al., 1990; Jackson & Allen, 1987) noted widespread differences in the message-sidedness manipulations of prior research. Although defining a one-sided message is relatively straightforward, defining a two-sided message is conceptually more difficult. For example, some investigations constructed two-sided messages that acknowledged, but did not refute, opposing arguments. Allen and his colleagues labeled these as "two-sided, nonrefutational messages." Other researchers developed two-sided messages that not only recognized opposing viewpoints, but also refuted them. These were labeled as "two-sided, refutational messages"

Allen and his colleagues (1990) hypothesized that the apparently conflicting findings in this literature may have resulted from a failure to recognize the operational differences of two-sided messages in prior research. They hypothesized that sources who recognize the existence of opposing viewpoints, but do not refute them, are likely to be viewed as having less expertise than sources who recognize and refute opposing viewpoints. In fact, they speculated that two-sided, nonrefutational messages would be less persuasive than one-sided messages.

To test their hypothesis, Allen and colleagues (1990) conducted three studies involving 17 topics, 51 messages, and over 1,000 research participants. For each of the 17 topics, they developed, or had students develop, three persuasive messages: a one-sided message, a two-sided refutational message, and a two-sided nonrefutational message. These messages were presented to research participants, and then their attitudes following the message were measured. A consistent pattern of findings emerged from their analyses. Two-sided refutational messages were more persuasive than one-sided messages, and one-sided messages were more persuasive than two-sided nonrefutational messages. The pattern for source credibility assessments was consistent with the attitude data. Targets who read the two-sided refutational messages provided the most favorable assessments of source credibility, followed by targets who read the one-sided messages and the two-sided nonrefutational messages, respectively (Allen et al., 1990).

A subsequent meta-analytic review of the literature confirmed the importance of the distinction drawn by Allen and his colleagues. Allen (1991) divided prior investigations into two categories, those that employed two-sided refutational messages and those that employed two-sided nonrefutational messages. His analyses revealed that two-sided refutational messages were more persuasive than one-sided messages, and that two-sided nonrefutational messages were less persuasive than their one-sided counterparts. Although the size of these persuasive effects were not large, Allen noted that the two-sided refutational messages were significantly more persuasive than two-sided nonrefutational messages. Moreover, the effect sizes he observed indicated that two-sided refutational messages were about *20% more effective* than one-sided messages, whereas two-sided nonrefutational messages were about *20% less effective* than one-sided messages (p. 400). It also bears mentioning that early predictions of the relative effectiveness of one-sided messages for favorable and less-educated audiences and two-sided messages for unfavorable and more-educated audiences were not confirmed in Allen's review. He found that audience favorability toward the topic was unrelated to message effectiveness.[2]

Hale, Mongeau, and Thomas (1991) employed cognitive response measures to explain the enhanced persuasiveness of two-sided refutational messages. They found that two-sided refutational messages produced more favorable thoughts about the message recommendation, which led to more favorable evaluation of the message and greater attitude change. Although this same causal process was found for both types of two-sided messages, the effect of the refutational message on positive cognitions ($B = .18$) was almost twice as strong as the effect of nonrefutational message ($B = .10$). Thus, one explanation for the effectiveness of two-sided refutational messages is that they engender more favorable thoughts about the message recommendation. In combination, the findings of Allen's (1991) meta-analysis and the Hale and colleagues study suggest that two-sided refutational messages are more persuasive because they produce more favorable thoughts about the message recommendation and more favorable evaluations of the source's credibility.

"FILLING IN THE BLANKS"

There are several findings in the preceding sections that suggest that making message arguments explicit will increase attitude change. First, we argued that an important implication of Hample's attitude change models is that both an argument's data and its warrant should be explicitly stated. Second, two-sided refutational messages may be superior to two-sided nonrefutational messages because they clearly show why one position is superior to another. In both these cases, message sources gain a persuasive advantage by making their arguments as complete as is possible. Receivers are not left to "fill in the blanks" left by an incomplete message.

Two recent meta-analyses speak to the issue of "filling in the blanks" in persuasive messages. First, D. J. O'Keefe (1997) meta-analyzed the effect of implicit versus explicit message conclusions. The issue he studied was the extent to which messages are more persuasive when they contain an explicit statement of the message's conclusion (as compared with messages that simply allow message receivers to "fill in" that information). D. J. O'Keefe found that messages that explicitly described the message's conclusions (i.e., "filled in the blanks" in our parlance) were more persuasive than messages that left such information implicit.

In the second meta-analysis, D. J. O'Keefe (1998) investigated the persuasive impact of the extent to which the *evidence* supplied in the message is explicitly stated. The explicitness of evidence was operationalized differently across studies (e.g., statement of the source of evidence, the completeness of arguments, and the specificity of arguments). Not surprisingly, given our discussion of evidence above, D. J. O' Keefe concluded that message sources "have little to fear from making their argumentative support explicit" (p. 68).

D. J. O'Keefe (1998) argued that leaving recipients to "fill in the blanks" by using implicit warrants or conclusions might make recipients work harder to draw their conclusions about the message. There is a tendency for audience members to consider their own thoughts to be stronger than message arguments (what Perloff and Brock [1980] call the "ownness bias"). While audience members' thoughts will influence their attitudes, they may not "fill in the blanks" the way the source intends them to. If message or argument elements are implicit, the audience might take what information is available to them and come to a conclusion that is consistent with their initial attitudes rather than the conclusion intended by the source (Bettinghaus et al., 1970; Janis & Frick, 1943).

SUMMARY

This chapter examined the use of rational appeals in persuasive messages. We began by examining the structure of rational appeals and how they functioned to influence attitudes and behavior. We concluded that when people are motivated and able to process the content of a persuasive message, rational appeals are an effective persuasive technique, and the quality of supporting information in these appeals determines the persuasiveness of the message. Although we are often accurate judges of the logical validity of a rational appeal, when we make errors, they tend to be systematic and to reflect our agreement or disagreement with the argument's conclusion. We also considered the relative merits of one- and two-sided rational appeals and concluded that two-sided refutational messages were more effective than both one-sided messages and two-sided nonrefutational messages.

NOTES

1. Variable analytic studies are not generated by an underlying theory or based upon previous research. Instead, researchers investigate how one variable (in the present case, evidence) relates to one or a small number of other variables with little link to the research that came before it.

2. D. J. O'Keefe (1993) questioned Allen's meta-analytic conclusions based on the classification of studies as two-sided refutational or two-sided nonrefutational as well as the adequacy of the literature analyzed. After changing six studies from two-sided refutational to two-sided nonrefutational, D. J. O'Keefe concluded that two-sided refutational messages were more persuasive than either one-sided or two-sided nonrefutational messages. In Allen's (1993) response, though not totally satisfactory, he stands by his original conclusions that two-sided refutational messages are more persuasive than one-sided messages, which are, in turn, more persuasive than two-sided nonrefutational messages. Other results consistent with Allen's conclusions (Allen et al., 1990; Hale, Mongeau, & Thomas, 1991) bolster our confidence in Allen's conclusions in the face of D. J. O'Keefe's concerns.

7

Persuasive Message Characteristics

Emotional Appeals

LOOKING AHEAD ...

In this chapter we continue our consideration of the characteristics of persuasive messages. In the previous chapter, we covered several topics relevant to logical appeals. Here we review theory and research that examine two types of emotional message appeals: fear appeals and guilt appeals. We discuss the long history of studying fear appeals and the explanations that have been developed to explain their effectiveness. We also discuss the research associated with changing attitudes and behaviors through the creation of guilt. While guilt appeals have not generated the research or theorizing that fear appeals have, creating attitude and behavior change through guilt appears to be an interesting and complex phenomenon.

Emotions have been the focus of scholars from a number of disciplines from philosophy to biology. Even within the study of communication, scholars look at emotions in a number of ways and in a number of contexts (e.g., Andersen & Guerrero, 1998). As a consequence, "defining emotion is a tricky proposition" (Guerrero, Andersen, & Trost, 1998, p. 5). Spearheading a recent resurgence in the study of emotion in communication scholarship, Dillard (1998) argues that human beings, as a species, "have evolved to meet adaptive challenges posed by the environment" (p. xvii). Thus humans, like other organisms, need to be aware of changes that occur in their environment. When these changes occur, people have to decide whether that change is good or bad for them. From this perspective, emotions represent the reactions that occur in response to these environmental changes.

Consider an example. While hiking in the Rocky Mountain wilderness outside Missoula, Montana, you suddenly confront a large bear. This represents a drastic change in your environment from appreciating awesome natural beauty to a confrontation with a wild animal that may be bent on making you his lunch. Given such an environmental change, many people would report experiencing an emotion that they describe as fear.

However, emotions like "fear" include several components (Guerrero et al., 1998). First, emotions have a cognitive component representing a person's interpretation of the environmental changes. You might interpret the large hungry-looking bear as a threat to your health and well-being. Dillard and Meijnders (2002) make an important point when they say that the bear, per se, does not create the fear. Rather, the interpretation of the bear as a large, likely hungry, carnivore causes the emotion. More relevant to the present context, it isn't the fear appeal that is persuasive but rather the audience's interpretation of the appeal that creates persuasion.

Second, emotions have a positive or a negative feeling component (generally called *affect*; see Guerrero et al., 1998). Most individuals' affective reaction to the bear is likely to be negative. Unexpectedly seeing a rare and endangered bird in the wilderness is likely to create a positive affective response in a birdwatcher. Generally speaking, if the change is evaluated as being positive for us, the affective reaction will be positive. However, if the environmental change is evaluated as being bad for us, the affective reaction will be negative.

Third, emotions have a physiological component. Encountering a bear in the woods (which elicits certain cognitive and affective reactions) is likely to generate a high degree of physiological arousal. This arousal might include increases in heart rate, respiration, and blood pressure; pupil dilation; and the release of adrenaline into the bloodstream.

Most relevant to the study of persuasive communication, the final component of emotions is behavioral. "The primary function of emotion is to guide behavior" (Dillard & Meijnders, 2002, p. 318). The cognitive (i.e., this is a dangerous animal), affective (i.e., this is not good), and physiological (i.e., arousal) reactions to the bear all function to create a behavioral response: Run!

It is the behavioral component of emotions that make them particularly well suited to persuasive communication in a variety of settings. If particular emotions generate a characteristic behavioral response, then persuasive messages may be able to exploit this effect.

Recent research and theorizing indicates that there are a relatively small number of discrete emotions (though the exact number and nature of emotions differs across scholars; see Guerrero et al., 1998, p. 6; Nabi, 2002). For example, Fehr and Russell (1984) reported that participants' reports of words reflecting emotions most consistently included joy, hate, fear, love, sadness, anger, and happiness. Moreover, recent theorizing (see, e.g., Dillard & Meijnders, 2002; Nabi, 2002) suggests that these emotions are discrete. By referring to them as *discrete*, we mean that emotions are considered to be separate and distinct in terms of the four components of emotions described above. Thus, a particular emotion, like fear, is the result of an environmental change (i.e., a threat) that creates a certain pattern of cognitive, affective, physiological, and behavioral reactions. The pattern of reactions for fear will be different from the pattern for other emotions.

The success of rational persuasive appeals rests on the assumption that persuasive targets behave as rational human beings. However, in many persuasive contexts, persuaders turn to emotional persuasive appeals.

Although there are many types of emotional appeals, ranging from humor to sympathy, fear appeals have received the most attention from persuasion scholars and practitioners. As a consequence, the greater part of this chapter will review fear appeals research and the various explanations that have been developed to explain their effectiveness. In addition, we will discuss the effectiveness of changing responses through the creation of guilt.

FEAR APPEALS

Fear appeals are frequently employed in prevention and safety campaigns directed at adolescents. "Don't drink and drive" campaigns, for example, routinely rely on the use of fear-arousing messages to attract the attention of teenagers and motivate them to change their attitudes and driving behavior. While many public health campaigns utilize fear as a persuasive tool, there are those who claim that such efforts will "backfire" (Witte & Allen, 2000, p. 591; see also Geller, 1989). These concerns about fear appeals lead to questions about their utility. Are these types of messages persuasive? The answer to this question is a qualified yes: given certain message and audience characteristics, fear-appeal messages can be persuasive. In this section of the chapter we examine the fear-appeal literature. We begin by defining a fear appeal and identifying models that describe how fear appeals work. Then we summarize some of the important findings from previous studies of this genre of persuasive messages.

Defining Fear Appeals

Over the years, a number of definitions have been used to separate fear appeals from other types of persuasive messages. For the most part, these definitions focus on message content and/or audience reactions to a message (D. J. O'Keefe, 1990). For example, a definition emphasizing message content would describe a fear appeal as a message that contains "gruesome content" (Leventhal, 1970). The gory films of crash victims we all watched during high school driver education classes reflect this type of definition. A second approach defines a fear appeal as a message that invokes considerable fear in message recipients. Studies adopting this definitional approach use manipulation checks to assess the amount of fear people report after their exposure to a message. Messages that produce significant levels of self-reported fear in message recipients are defined as fear-arousing (or high-fear) messages. Though some studies adopt one of these two approaches, many investigations incorporate features of both definitions. That is, many studies have defined a fear appeal in terms of message content, but have also employed manipulation checks to assess audience perceptions of fear. For our purposes, a fear appeal can be defined as a persuasive message that arouses fear by depicting a personally relevant and significant threat, followed by a description of feasible recommendations for deterring the threat (Witte, 1992).

Embedded in this definition are three concepts—*fear, perceived threat*, and *perceived efficacy*—that have guided thinking about fear appeals for nearly 50 years. Fear is a negatively valenced emotion that is usually accompanied by heightened physiological arousal. Perceived threat is an external stimulus that creates a perception in message receivers that they are susceptible to some negative situation or outcome. For example, a message that links cigarette smoking to lung cancer is likely to be perceived as threatening by many smokers because it links their behavior with a negative outcome. Finally, perceived efficacy is similar to the concept of perceived behavioral control that we discussed in Chapter 3. As applied in the fear-appeal literature, perceived efficacy is a person's belief that message recommendations can be implemented and will effectively reduce the threat depicted in the message (R. W. Rogers, 1975, 1983; Witte, 1992; Witte & Allen, 2000).

Even though these concepts have been around for decades, they are consistent with the modern theory of discrete emotions (Dillard & Meijnders, 2002; Nabi, 2002). Fear appeals depict a threat to audience members' health and well-being. From the discrete emotions perspective, the depicted threat represents the environmental change that starts the appraisal and emotional process. Perceived threat and perceived efficacy represent the outcomes of the cognitive appraisal of the persuasive message (i.e., the environmental change). The perception of a significant threat is likely to create physiological arousal. Finally, fear motivates individuals to avoid the threat (e.g., Witte, 1992). A fear appeal depicts a threat and recommends a coping response (generally some form of attitude and/or behavior change) as a means of avoiding the threat. Thus, the message developers hope that audience members will adopt the recommended attitude and behavior change, though other methods of avoiding the threat are possible.

The conceptual importance of these concepts is reflected in the three families of models—*drive theories, parallel response models,* and *subjective expected utility models*—that have been proposed to explain the persuasive effects of fear appeals (Dillard, 1994; Witte, 1992; Witte & Allen, 2000). Each of these models is described below.

Modeling the Effects of Fear Appeals

Humble Beginnings

One of the first investigations of the effects of fear-arousing persuasive messages speculated about the possibility of a curvilinear (inverted-U) relationship between the amount of fear-arousing content and acceptance of message recommendations. Janis and Feshbach hypothesized that "when emotional tension is aroused, the audience will become more highly motivated to accept the reassuring beliefs or recommendations advocated by the communicator" (1953, p. 78). However, they cautioned that the arousal of extreme emotional tension could activate defensive mechanisms that may thwart the persuasive effects of the message. Under conditions of high fear, for example, they speculated that persuasive targets might stop paying attention to message content in hopes of alleviating their anxiety. In their view, a moderate level of fear should produce the greatest levels of attitude change.

To test their speculation, Janis and Feshbach (1953) exposed 200 high school students to messages advocating better dental hygiene. The strong-fear message contained several references to the painful consequences of tooth decay, gum disease, and trips to the dentist that result from poor dental hygiene. The moderate-fear message contained the same information, but was less graphic in its depiction of the effects of poor dental hygiene. Finally, the minimal-fear message contained the same hygiene information, but rarely described the negative effects of poor hygiene. Each message was accompanied by a series of slides that corresponded to the amount of fear in the verbal message. Both 1 week before and 1 week after exposure to the persuasive messages, participants in the study completed a questionnaire describing their dental hygiene practices.

Janis and Feshbach's (1953) findings disconfirmed their expectations: they found no support for the curvilinear relationship they had hypothesized. Instead, they found that the minimal-fear message induced the most compliance with the message recommendations and the strong-fear message produced the least amount of compliance. In other words, they hypothesized a curvilinear (inverted-U) relationship between fear and attitude change, but they found a negative linear relationship.

Although their study found no evidence for the effectiveness of fear-arousing messages, the counterintuitive nature of Janis and Feshbach's (1953) results ignited considerable research and theorizing about the persuasive effects of fear appeals. Specifically, this early research laid the conceptual groundwork for the family of fear-appeal models known as drive models.

Drive Models

The first theoretical explanation for the effects of fear-arousing messages conceptualized fear as an acquired drive (Janis, 1967; Janis & Feshbach, 1953; McGuire, 1968; G. R. Miller, 1963). *Drive* is a psychological term for an unpleasant state that people strive to reduce or eliminate. These bodily states initiate activity and are frequently experienced as feelings of tension or restlessness (Newcomb, Turner, & Converse, 1965, p. 23).

As applied to the study of fear appeals, fear is conceptualized as a drive state that is usually initiated by a graphic description of negative consequences that message receivers are likely to experience if they do not adopt the message recommendations. Consider again the gory films that are part of many high school driver education courses. These films depict the consequences of drinking and driving and are designed to create fear as a drive state. Whatever reduces the drive is reinforced and is found to be rewarding. To effectively reduce this fear, these films also contain recommendations for safe driving. "When a response reduces fear, it is reinforced and becomes part of one's permanent response repertory" (Leventhal, 1970, p. 123).

Thus, the drive model suggests a sequence in which a fear appeal arouses fear in message receivers that acts as a drive. Acceptance of message recommendations reduces this fear and the corresponding drive state and that attitude or behavior change is reinforced. However, message receivers might also reduce fear by denying that the negative consequences of drinking and driving are likely to occur. This denial, if it reduces drive, is also rewarding, but is unlikely to produce attitude and behavior change in recipients. Denial of the threat is particularly relevant for adolescents, who sometimes feel invulnerable. The mechanism that reduces this fear, whether adaptive (e.g., behavioral change) or maladaptive (e.g., denial), is reinforced and becomes the preferred response to the threat (Janis, 1967; Witte, 1994; Witte & Allen, 2000). This process is depicted in Figure 7.1 and implies that "a fear appeal should have two components: a part of the message that instills fear and another that assuages it" (Dillard, 1994).

Drive models posit a curvilinear (inverted-U-shaped) relationship between the level of fear aroused by a message and message acceptance (Janis, 1967; McGuire, 1968). According to these models, messages that arouse very little fear are ineffective because people are relatively unaffected by mild warnings (Janis, 1967). That is, low levels of fear do not produce the drive necessary to motivate acceptance of message recommendations. Moderate levels of fear produce the drive that causes people to accept the message recommendations. Finally, messages that arouse high levels of fear may cause a defensive avoidance process in which people ignore or deny the threat contained in the message (G. R. Miller, 1963). Thus, the drive models predict that messages that arouse moderate levels of fear will be more effective than those that arouse very low or extremely high levels of fear (Figure 7.2).

Little evidence has been garnered to support drive models of fear appeals. Beginning with the Janis and Feshbach (1953) experiment, researchers have consistently failed to observe the curvilinear relationship between fear and message acceptance. Multiple meta-analytic reviews of this literature produced no evidence of a curvilinear relationship (Boster & Mongeau, 1984; Sutton, 1982; Witte & Allen, 2000). Indeed, by 1970, the lack of empirical support and growing concerns about the specification of variables that moderate the relationship between fear and message acceptance led Leventhal (1970) to propose an alternative model, the Parallel Response Model, to explain the persuasive effects of fear appeals.

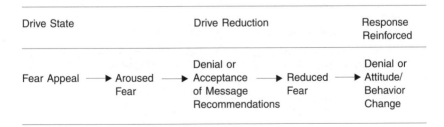

FIGURE 7.1. A drive model of fear appeals.

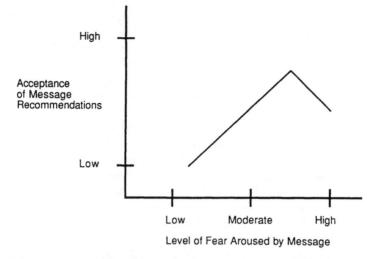

FIGURE 7.2. The relationship between aroused fear and message acceptance predicted by the drive model.

The Parallel Response Model

The findings from early research on the effectiveness of fear appeals (i.e., those performed in the 1950s and 1960s) were inconsistent. A few studies found low-fear messages to be most persuasive (e.g., Janis & Feshbach, 1953). In other studies, however, high-fear messages were found to be more persuasive than low-fear messages (e.g., Hewgill & Miller, 1965). Still other studies found that level of fear had no effect on attitude or behavior change (e.g., Wheatley & Oshikawa, 1970).

Leventhal's (1970) solution to the mixed findings in the fear-appeal literature was to propose two separate, but parallel, responses in message recipients. *Fear control* is one response people have to fear-arousing messages. This process involves the "initiation of responses in an attempt to reduce the unpleasant feeling of fear, and is guided by internal cues" (Sutton, 1982, p. 324). As such, this response is consistent with the process depicted by the drive models, as it functions to reduce the fear and leads to attitude and behavior change. A second, parallel, response to fear appeals is *danger control*. Danger control involves the evaluation and selection of responses that will avert the danger depicted in the message.

Perhaps the clearest distinction between these two responses stems from their focus on emotion and cognition. Fear control is basically an emotional response, whereas danger control is a cognitive process that is dependent on the information available to message receivers. Outcomes of the fear control process include avoidance of the situation and denial of the threat contained in the message. Outcomes of the danger control process include attitude and behavior change (Figure 7.3). Thus, adaptive behavior results from the danger control process, while maladaptive behavior is attributed to the fear control process.

Leventhal's (1970) distinction between fear control and danger control was a significant shift in theorizing about fear appeals. "The importance of the parallel response model lies largely in its movement away from the notion of fear as the central explanatory concept . . . " (Sutton, 1982, p. 324). Dillard (1994) put it differently when he noted:

> During the heyday of drive theories, fear was at the center of the theoretical stage. With the coming of the Parallel Response Model, it was forced to share the limelight with the cognitive machinations of the danger control process. (p. 301)

Since its introduction, research has failed to support the predictions of the Parallel Response Model. Failure to find empirical support stems largely from a lack of precision. Most important, the model fails to specify when recipients will engage in fear or danger control (Beck & Frankel, 1981; R. W. Rogers, 1975; Sutton, 1982). Although it lacked empirical support, the model drew an important distinction between emotional and cognitive reactions to fear appeals, and it provided the conceptual framework for a third family of fear appeal models: subjective expected utility models.

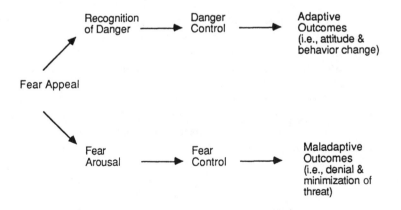

FIGURE 7.3. The Parallel Response Model of fear appeals.

Subjective Expected Utility Models

Subjective expected utility models have been developed to explain a variety of human behaviors. For example, in Chapter 3 we discussed two models, Fishbein and Ajzen's (1975) Theory of Reasoned Action and Ajzen's (1985) Theory of Planned Behavior, that are part of the family of subjective expected utility (SEU) models. The Health Belief Model (M. H. Becker, 1974) is an SEU model that includes elements of fear appeals that have been applied in many public health settings. This family of models adopts a rational view of humans and posits that people choose behaviors that maximize rewards and minimize punishments (W. Edwards, 1961; Lewin, 1935). According to these models, a person faced with two or more alternative courses of action will choose the one with the greatest *subjective expected utility* (SEU). The SEU for a course of action is a function of the *subjective value* (or utility) of the outcome associated with a course of action and the *subjective probability* (expectation) that the course of action will produce the outcome (Sutton, 1982, p. 325). Thus, the basic structure of these models is a simple equation in which the dependent variable is a multiplicative function (the product) of two or more independent variables (Dillard, 1994).

Protection Motivation Theory (R. W. Rogers, 1975, 1983) is an application of an SEU model to the study of fear appeals. R. W. Rogers argued that the effectiveness of a fear appeal was dependent on its ability to create three perceptions in message receivers: the perceived severity or noxiousness of the threat contained in the message, the perception of susceptibility to the threat contained in the message, and the perception that the recommended response will effectively reduce or eliminate the threat.

The original formulation of this model (R. W. Rogers, 1975) proposed that all three components were necessary ingredients in an effective fear appeal. That is, the model proposed that a person's intention to adopt a recommended behavior was a multiplicative function of *perceived noxiousness, perceived susceptibility,* and *perceived efficacy of the response* (Figure 7.4).

By the 1980s, several studies had failed to find evidence of the multiplicative relationship (i.e., the predicted three-way interaction) among these three variables and raised doubts about the validity of R. W. Rogers's model. In response, alternative SEU models were introduced (Sutton & Eiser, 1984), and modifications of the original model were suggested. For example, Beck and Frankel (1981) distinguished the concepts of *response efficacy* (i.e., the perception that a recommended response will effectively reduce the threat) and *self-efficacy* (i.e., the per-

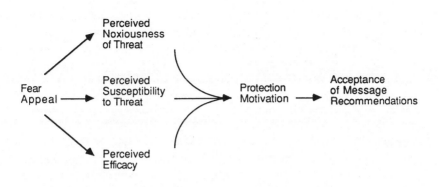

FIGURE 7.4. The Protection Motivation Model of fear appeals.

ception that one can personally execute the response), and they suggested that both dimensions of efficacy were important features of fear appeals. By 1983, R. W. Rogers revised his Protection Motivation Theory by incorporating the concept of self-efficacy and altering the predictions concerning the separate and combined effects of the four predictor variables.[1]

Tests of these models produced mixed findings regarding the specific effects of perceived noxiousness of the threat, of perceived susceptibility to the threat, and of the efficacy of the recommended responses on the intentions to adopt the action recommended in the fear appeal. Nevertheless, two important implications emerged from investigations of these models. First, these perceptual variables are "important sources of information for individuals attempting to determine what response to make to a potential threat" (Dillard, 1994). Second, the emergence of this family of fear-appeal models virtually excluded the concept of fear as an emotion from the study of fear appeals (Dillard, 1994). Instead of describing emotional reactions to a fear-arousing message, the SEU models emphasize cognitive, or rational, reactions to these messages. Indeed, over a 30-year period, beginning with Janis and Feshbach's (1953) seminal study, theorizing about fear appeals had evolved to the point where fear was no longer an essential construct.

Extended Parallel Processing Model

The most recent attempt at explaining the persuasive successes and failures of fear appeals is the Extended Parallel Processing Model (EPPM; Witte, 1992, 1994; Witte & Allen, 2000). Kim Witte attempted to combine the other fear-appeal models mentioned above into one comprehensive and testable package. The EPPM borrows the concepts of fear control and danger control from Leventhal's (1970) Parallel Response Model and the threat and efficacy components of fear-arousing messages from R. W. Rogers's (1983) Protection Motivation Theory.

Witte argued that the threat component of a message motivates recipients to respond, while the efficacy component of the message determines the nature of that response. The EPPM predicts that if a message depicts a minor threat, recipients will be unmotivated to respond and no attitude and behavior change should occur. When the message depicts both a significant threat and an effective coping response, the model predicts that recipients will engage in danger control and significant attitude and behavior change should result. If the message depicts a strong threat but the recommended response is ineffective, recipients are predicted to engage in fear control (i.e., denial, defensive avoidance, and/or reactance; Witte & Allen, 2000). If recipients engage in fear control, no attitude or behavior change is expected.

The most recent meta-analysis of the fear-appeal literature (Witte & Allen, 2000) provided mixed support for the EPPM. The EPPM's central prediction, like the Parallel Response Model, is that threat and efficacy combine multiplicatively to produce attitude change. In other words, only the high-threat–high-efficacy condition is predicted to produce strong levels of attitude and behavioral change. The other combinations of threat and efficacy should each produce no change (though for different reasons). Meta-analytic results, however, are not consistent with these predictions. Witte and Allen's (2000) meta-analytic results are most consistent with an additive model where threat and efficacy contribute separately to the production of attitude and behavior change.

While results are not entirely consistent with either model, R. W. Rogers's Protection Motivation Theory and Witte's EPPM highlight the importance of efficacy in the fear-appeal process. Results of the Witte and Allen (2000) meta-analysis clearly indicate that messages that create high levels of perceived threat and efficacy are maximally effective. Conversely, when a message lacks both threat and efficacy, attitude and behavioral change are unlikely to occur. This finding suggests that effective fear appeals must include information that poses a threat to message receivers and then prescribes effective action for alleviating the threat. Fear appeals that fail to accomplish *both* objectives are unlikely to be very persuasive. Thus, fear appeals that warn teenagers about their susceptibility to the AIDS virus without also providing workable recommendations for prevention (e.g., using a latex condom or abstinence) are unlikely to be persuasive.

Summarizing the Research Findings

While none of the theoretical perspectives can fully explain the fear-appeal results, research for the most part has found the strength of fear appeals to be positively correlated with attitudes, behavioral intentions, and behaviors (for reviews, see Boster & Mongeau, 1984; Dillard, 1994; R. W. Rogers, 1975; Sutton, 1982; Witte & Allen, 2000). Specifically, Witte and Allen (2000) assert that "the stronger the fear aroused by a fear appeal, the more persuasive it is" (p. 601). Although there are a few exceptions, there is little evidence that strong fear messages will backfire. In particular, there is no evidence in any of the reviews for the curvilinear (i.e., inverted-U-shaped pattern) predicted by the drive model.

While the strength of fear appeals is positively related to attitudes and behaviors, these relationships are rather weak. Across meta-analyses, the average fear–attitude correlations have ranged from .14 to .21, while the average fear–behavior correlation ranged from .10 to .17. As we suggested in Chapter 2, one reason for these weak relationships is that the manipulations of fear appeals have not been terribly effective. In fact, the average fear–perceived fear correlations across meta-analyses have ranged from only .30 to .36. While manipulations appear to be getting stronger over time (Witte & Allen, 2000), differences in recipients' levels of experienced fear across the low- and high-fear appeals are not terribly large. If fear manipulations are not strong, then the correlation between the strength of a fear appeal and attitudes or behaviors will not strong either (Boster & Mongeau, 1984).

Fear Appeals and the Creation of Other Emotions

One of the complexities involved in studying emotional appeals is that while emotions are discrete (i.e., separate and distinct), the same message can produce several emotions. While evaluating a fear appeal, an audience member might experience a number of emotions (e.g., fear, anger, sadness, surprise, etc.). So, as Dillard and colleagues (1996) suggest, "fear appeals do more than scare people" (p. 44). This complicates the persuasive process because each aroused emotion has a unique combination of cognitive, affective, physiological, and behavioral components. Some of these emotions might facilitate attitude and behavior change while others might inhibit it.

Dillard and colleagues (1996) investigated the extent to which fear appeals created emotional reactions beyond fear and how these multiple reactions influenced the persuasiveness of messages. In their study they used 31 public service announcements (PSAs) that had previously been identified as fear appeals. College students viewed a number of these messages and indicated their emotional reactions (i.e., fear, anger, puzzlement, happiness, sadness, and surprise) as well as their ratings of the persuasiveness of the messages.

Results of the Dillard and colleagues (1996) investigation indicated that all but one of the 31 PSAs produced statistically significant changes in two or more emotions (and over half generated changes in three or more emotions). So it is clear that fear appeals do more than simply create fear. Equally important, Dillard et al. report that these emotions varied considerably in how they influenced judgments of the messages' persuasiveness. Fear, surprise, and sadness were positively related to persuasiveness judgments, while puzzlement and anger were negatively related to the same judgments. Only happiness was unrelated to judgments of message persuasiveness.

The Dillard and colleagues (1996) results are important because they reinforce the meta-analytic data that indicates that fear appeals are persuasive. Strong fear appeals generate the emotion of fear in audience members and are positively related to the effectiveness the message. Fear appeals, however, do more than just create fear. Fear appeals create a number of emotional and affective reactions (e.g., anger, puzzlement, sadness) that likely have different impacts on the persuasiveness of the message. We don't know, however, which aspects of fear appeals create the different emotional reactions. However, the finding that fear appeals create different patterns of emotional and affective reactions might explain why correlations between fear appeals and attitude and behavior change vary so much from study to study.

Directions for Future Research

There appears to be a rekindled interest in the study of fear appeals. This interest may be due in part to the continued evolution of fear-appeal explanations and in part to the continued application of fear appeals in everyday persuasive campaigns. Recent conceptual developments have revived an interest in studying the "fear" component of fear-arousing messages. In a thoughtful review of the fear-appeal literature, Dillard (1994) chronicles the decreasing emphasis on fear in fear-appeal models and suggests that a reinstatement of the fear construct, and a renewed interest in emotional reactions to fear appeals, may be essential to our better understanding of their effects. Witte (1992) echoed this concern and introduced the Extended Parallel Processing Model (EPPM) to explain the effects of fear appeals. At this point, it seems clear that we know more about the cognitive evaluations inherent in danger control than we do about the far messier, emotionally driven, fear-control processes. A more complete explanation of fear appeals will have to fully explain the interconnected nature of these processes.

Compared to the amount of research and theorizing about fear appeals, relatively little research has been performed on other types of emotional appeals. However, there has been a recent interest in the persuasive implications of creating guilt (D. J. O'Keefe, 2000, 2002). The following section discusses research on the effects of guilt on persuasion.

GUILT AND PERSUASION

Scholars have proffered a number of different definitions for the concept of guilt (Baumeister, Stillwell, & Heaterton, 1994; Mongeau, Hale, & Alles, 1994; D. J. O'Keefe, 2000, 2002). For example, D. J. O'Keefe (2002) defined guilt as "a negative emotional state aroused when an actor's conduct is at variance with an actor's own standards" (p. 329). While various definitions have different foci, they also share several features in common. First, these definitions propose that guilt is a negative affective state. We don't enjoy feeling guilt. We try to avoid feeling guilt if we can; if we cannot avoid it, we will try to do something to reduce or eliminate it. Second, these definitions maintain that guilt is aroused through observing a difference between how one *should have behaved* and how one *actually behaved.*

Nabi (2002) asserts that guilt arises when an individual feels that he or she has done something wrong (i.e., broken some rule or violated a personal code of conduct). Like all emotions, guilt has an action tendency. Guilt's action tendency is to atone for one's mistake. Thus, in order to be persuasive, a guilt-appeal message needs to arouse guilt by pointing out that audience members' behavior has violated some personal standard. Next, guilt-appeal messages need to provide the audience members with a means of making up for their past behavior by changing their attitudes and behaviors. The effectiveness of a guilt appeal should depend on the extent to which guilt is successfully aroused and elicits an effective coping response.

Several studies have been performed on the persuasiveness of guilt appeals (see D. J. O'Keefe, 2000, 2002, for recent reviews of this literature). For example, Coulter and Pinto (1995) exposed working mothers to advertisements about one of two products (bread or dental floss). For each product, they created messages reflecting three levels of guilt (low, moderate, and high). After participants looked at the ads, they reported their levels of guilt, anger, and happiness; their attitudes toward the advertisement and the brand depicted; and their intentions to purchase the product.

Coulter and Pinto (1995) found that reports of felt guilt were greatest in the moderate-guilt message condition. Presumably, the participants who viewed the high-guilt messages evaluated a message as attacking their behavior and ability as a mother and, as a consequence, felt angry. Such an explanation is supported by the findings that levels of anger increased across the three guilt message conditions. Moreover, reports of guilt were strongly correlated with reports of anger. In addition, participants in the high-guilt message condition (when compared with the low-guilt message condition) evaluated the advertisement as more manipulative and felt that the company was simply out to make money.

Thus, like Dillard and colleagues (1996) in their study on fear appeals, Coulter and Pinto (1995) found that guilt appeals generate multiple emotions. In terms of persuasion outcomes, Coulter and Pinto reported that strong guilt appeals simply did not work. As guilt appeals became stronger, levels of all outcome variables (attitudes toward the advertisement, attitude toward the product being advertised, and intentions to purchase the products) became more negative. High-guilt appeals resulted in lower attitudes and behavioral intentions.

This pattern of results is, for the most part, consistent with a recent meta-analysis of the guilt-appeal literature. D. J. O'Keefe (2000) reports that, across studies, increasing guilt in messages increased the amount of guilt that respondents reported.[2] Moreover, he reports that, across studies, increasing guilt was associated with decreasing persuasiveness. In short, guilt appeals seem to be effective for producing guilt, but ineffective in producing attitude and behavior change in the direction of message recommendations.

Why Don't Guilt Appeals Work?

The accumulated literature reported in D. J. O'Keefe's (2000) meta-analysis clearly indicates that guilt appeals are ineffective in producing attitude and behavior change. Given our definitional discussion, it seemed that guilt was tailor-made for effective persuasive messages. If you can make someone feel guilt, then the preferred behavioral response should follow. To make matters even more mysterious, D. J. O'Keefe (2000, 2002) reports that inducing guilt is very effective in producing attitude and behavior change in other contexts. Before we attempt to explain why guilt appeals fail to work, we need to briefly discuss two contexts where guilt may influence attitudes and behaviors: the hypocrisy paradigm and the transgression–compliance paradigm.

First, in Chapter 4 we discussed a modern application of dissonance theory in the "hypocrisy" phenomenon. Specifically, we discussed the Stone and colleagues (1994) study, where participants in the hypocrisy condition were asked to record a message for high school students advocating safe-sex practices and then to privately recall those instances where they themselves did not engage in these behaviors. Compared to those participants who wrote a message (but did not present it) or who did not recall past behavior, participants in the hypocrisy condition were more likely to purchase condoms (and purchased more condoms) with the money they received for participating in the study.

Stone and colleagues (1994) concluded that purchasing condoms was motivated by, and was an effort to reduce, cognitive dissonance. D. J. O'Keefe (2000, 2002), on the other hand, argues that results from the hypocrisy paradigm could be explained just as well in terms of guilt. Specifically, engaging in unsafe sex practices represents a behavior that violates personal standards that are made particularly salient while recording the message. As a consequence, the hypocrisy condition could have created guilt instead of (or perhaps in addition to) dissonance. Purchasing condoms, then, could be interpreted as guilt reduction (trying to avoid making the same mistake in the future).

To date, there are insufficient data to choose between the guilt and dissonance explanation of the hypocrisy effect. A second area of research where guilt may clearly be involved is the "transgression–compliance" paradigm (D. J. O'Keefe, 2000, 2002). In transgression–compliance studies, participants engage in some transgression (e.g., knocking over a stack of papers, spilling a drink, etc.) and are later asked to do someone a favor. D. J. O'Keefe's (2000) meta-analytic investigation of research on this phenomenon provides clear findings. Participants who engaged in some transgression were much more likely to comply with a subsequent request than those who did not commit a prior transgression. This result is generally interpreted from a guilt perspective because participants have done something wrong and wish to make up for it (D. J. O'Keefe, 2000, 2002).

Given that guilt works as an effective persuasive tool in both the hypocrisy (apparently) and the transgression–compliance paradigms, why don't guilt appeals work to influence attitude and behavior change? One explanation might be that appeals that attempt to arouse strong levels of guilt also arouse other negative emotions that interfere with the persuasion process. As we noted above, Coulter and Pinto (1995) found that self-reports of guilt were strongly correlated with feelings of anger and irritation. Anger-irritation in the Coulter and Pinto study was more strongly and negatively related to both attitudes and behaviors than was guilt.

Our speculation is that negative reactions to guilt appeals are related to the source of the message. In both the hypocrisy and the transgression–compliance paradigms, there is no one trying to *make* participants feel guilty. Instead, in both cases, an internal consideration of personal behavior as it relates to personal standards creates the guilt. In this regard, no one may be quite as good at arousing guilt in a target person as the target him- or herself.

This is not to say that other people cannot make us feel guilty. Parents, close friends, and romantic partners may be best at getting us to feel guilty. Two studies (Baumeister et al., 1994; Vangelisti, Daly, & Rudnick, 1991) found that "one of the central issues in the elicitation of guilt was the transgressor's violation of relationship obligations or norms" (Vangelisti & Sprague, 1998, p. 138). This suggests that eliciting strong levels of guilt from a target will be difficult for those who are not in close relationships with that target.

Given this view of guilt, mass advertising may be at a disadvantage when trying to persuade consumers with guilt appeals. Because audience members do not have an existing relationship with the message source (e.g., a corporation, a faceless voice, or a celebrity spokesperson), there are likely to be no relational obligations or norms that can be violated. The very notion that a stranger might attempt to create guilt may create the anger and irritation that participants reported in the Coulter and Pinto (1995) study.

THE CHOICE BETWEEN RATIONAL AND EMOTIONAL APPEALS

Prior research has documented the effectiveness of both rational and emotional persuasive appeals. Although we seem to understand the process of rational argument more clearly than we do emotional appeals, research supports the persuasive value of both types of appeals. Given this finding, one might speculate about the merits of integrating rational and emotional appeals.

Though no research bears directly on this issue, investigations of heightened arousal on cognitive processing suggest that rational appeals may lose their effectiveness when combined with fear-arousing content. For example, investigations of short-term memory (Bacon, 1974; Mandler, 1984) suggest that heightened arousal may interfere with information processing. In fact, these investigations indicate that a variety of stressors can contribute to memory impairment. However, an investigation of college women found that arousal was unrelated to their learning and recall of contraceptive information (Goldfarb, Gerrard, Gibbons, & Plante, 1988). Thus, the relationship between arousal and cognitive processing appears unsettled. In addition, there may be some conceptual slippage between the arousal of fear and the physiological arousal induced in these studies. Nevertheless, these investigations provide little reason to expect that the arousal of fear or anxiety will facilitate the persuasive influence of rational appeals.

Because emotional and rational appeals appear to be incompatible persuasive companions, persuaders often rely on one or the other. An investigation provided information that may assist persuaders in choosing between these alternatives. M. B. Millar and Millar (1990) hypothesized that attitudes that are cognitively based—that is, formed through careful consideration of rational arguments—are more susceptible to affective appeals and that attitudes that are affectively based are more susceptible to rational appeals. Millar and Millar argued that when attitudes and arguments against them are based on the same class of information (rational/cognitive or emotional/affective), the argument threatens the way in which the person has thought about the object (p. 217). Because receivers often react defensively to threatening messages, such arguments may be ineffective. In the three investigations that provided support for their general hypothesis, when attitudes were formed through cognitive processes, affective appeals were more persuasive. Conversely, when attitudes were affectively based, rational appeals were more persuasive (M. G. Millar & Millar, 1990). Although the affective appeals in these studies were not fear appeals, these findings provide some recommendations for the use of rational and emotional persuasive appeals. Knowledge about the affective or cognitive basis of a target's attitude may be instructive in determining whether to construct a rational or an emotional appeal to alter that attitude.[3]

SUMMARY

Our review of emotional appeals focused primarily on the fear-appeal literature. The development of this literature, from the drive models to parallel response and SEU models, coincided with the reduced emphasis on the role of fear in these appeals. We concluded that all three families of models are instructive, but that none provides a satisfying description of the effects of fear appeals. Nevertheless, recent summaries of this literature provide a number of empirical conclusions that can safely be drawn about the effects of fear appeals. Recent theoretical developments provide important recommendations for future research. The chapter concluded with a discussion of the effectiveness of emotional and rational appeals for changing affectively based and cognitively based attitudes.

We also briefly reviewed the guilt-appeal literature. Several studies show that guilt appeals are ineffective in producing persuasion outcomes. However, guilt appears to be a powerful persuasive force in interpersonal situations. Further conceptual and theoretical work is necessary to explain when and how guilt is most effective in producing attitude and behavior change.

NOTES

1. Dillard (1994) provides a more complete discussion of these models and modifications.
2. Few researchers other than Coulter and Pinto (1995) have created three levels of guilt. It is much more typical to compare low-guilt appeals with high-guilt appeals.
3. K. Edwards (1990) argued that affect-based attitudes are most susceptible to affective appeals and that cognition-based attitudes are most susceptible to rational appeals. Three studies provide support for these predictions and appear to contradict the M. G. Millar and Millar (1990) findings. However, important differences exist between these investigations. For example, the manipulations employed in the K. Edwards studies appear to create a positive or negative mood state in participants. The stimuli used to create these mood states are unrelated to the attitude objects investigated in these studies. By comparison, the Millar and Millar studies assess the affective and cognitive dimensions of *existing* attitudes. Moreover, these dimensions were directly related to the attitude objects investigated in Millar and Millar's studies. Although the K. Edwards studies have important implications for the role of affect in persuasion, the Millar and Millar investigations are more relevant to the notion of affective-based and cognitive-based attitudes.

8

Receiver Characteristics

L OOKING AHEAD ...

A receiver-oriented approach to persuasion focuses attention on
those characteristics of message receivers that affect the
persuasion process. In this chapter we review the research on
these characteristics and discuss how they influence persuasion.
We begin with a discussion of gender and answer the question
"Are women more easily persuaded than men?" Then we look
at the message discrepancy literature and describe how the
difference between a receiver's opinion and the position
advocated in the message affects the persuasiveness of the
message. Finally, we look at the effects of receiver involvement
with the message topic. Three types of receiver involvement
will be identified; for each type, we describe its effect on the
persuasion process. Finally, we look at research on the concept
of function matching, which examines the persuasive impact of
messages whose arguments reflect the underlying functions of
message recipients' attitudes.

In the previous three chapters we focused on the characteristics of persuasive messages and persuasive message sources. Although carefully
crafted messages from highly trustworthy sources can promote response
formation, reinforcement, and change processes, persuasion scholars
have long recognized the importance of message receivers in the persuasion process. The persuasive effects of target characteristics were initially
investigated by Hovland and his colleagues (Hovland et al., 1953) and
gained prominence in the development of cognitive response theories in
the late 1960s and 1970s (Greenwald, Brock, & Ostrom, 1968; Petty,
Ostrom, & Brock, 1981).

This chapter examines the role of receiver characteristics in the persuasion process. Historically, persuasion scholars have paid considerable attention to four characteristics of persuasive targets: gender, message discrepancy, involvement, and function matching. In fact, these four characteristics continue to motivate contemporary programs of research on persuasive communication.

The chapter begins with a discussion of the effects of gender in persuasive communication, focusing on the question of gender differences in persuasibility. Following this is a discussion of message discrepancy research, which examines the persuasive effects of the discrepancy between the position advocated in a message and the position held by a message recipient. We then discuss the influence of receiver involvement on the processing and effectiveness of persuasive appeals. Researchers have traditionally employed a variety of conceptual definitions for the term *involvement*; as a result, investigations of the effects of involvement have produced apparently contradictory findings. Each of these definitional approaches, along with their related research findings, is examined in this chapter. Finally, we discuss the influence of function matching, or the extent to which attitude functions in persuasive messages match the underlying functions of receivers' attitudes.

SEX/GENDER DIFFERENCES IN PERSUASIBILITY

One colloquial truism about persuasive communication is that women are more easily persuaded than men. Indeed, for years social scientists argued that clear and convincing evidence existed to support such a proposition. Even today, we suspect that if you ask most communication scholars if men and women differ in persuasibility, many would indicate that the latter are easier persuasive targets. However, close scrutiny of research on this topic reveals that there is insufficient evidence to sustain this belief. This examination of research on the differences between men and women in social influence studies will conclude that the small differences that have been found are largely attributable to artifacts of the investigations rather than to inherent differences between men and women.

Eagly and her colleagues have been largely responsible for summarizing the research on differences between men and women into a cohesive set of defensible conclusions. Thus, the following discussion will draw heavily upon the findings of their reviews. Before we begin this review, however, two brief comments are in order.

The first comment centers on differentiating the variables of sex and gender. Specifically, *sex* refers to the biological differences between males and females. An individual's sex is indicated by anatomical and biological characteristics such as genitalia, chromosomes, and hormones. *Gender* (i.e., how masculine or feminine an individual is), on the other hand, is a psychological characteristic. Cultures determine which behaviors are considered *masculine* (i.e., expected of males) and which are considered *feminine* (i.e., expected of females) (J. T. Wood, 2001). In North America, for example, masculine behavior is to be "strong, ambitious, successful, rational, and emotionally controlled" (J. T. Wood, 2001, p. 22), while feminine behavior is to be "attractive, deferential, unaggressive, emotional, nurturing, and concerned with people and relationships" (J. T. Wood, 2001, p. 22). A person (either a man or a woman) who exhibits the former behavior set is considered masculine. A person (again, either a man or a woman) who exhibits the latter set of behaviors is considered feminine.

Biological definitions of sex (i.e., male and female) are most frequently employed in persuasion research; however, persuasion researchers are rarely interested in biological differences between men and women. Instead, researchers are more interested in gender, or the socialization and cultural differences between individuals. Although cultural and social (i.e., gender) differences are invoked to *explain* persuasive differences between men and women, they are rarely measured in persuasion research. The biological definition of sex that is frequently used in persuasion research is an imprecise way to measure social and cultural differences that exist among people, as a biological definition of sex inevitably miscategorizes people who have not experienced traditional sex-role socialization and do not identify with the social or cultural characteristics of their biological group. Nevertheless, because of its prevalent use in prior research, the following review of gender effects will employ this imprecise categorization of socialization differences between men and women as message recipients.[1]

Our second comment focuses on the nature of the differences that may exist between men and women. It has been quite popular recently to cast men and women as members of different cultures (or even different planets!) (Gray, 1992). But there are precious few data that support such an extreme view (e.g., Canary & Dindia, 1998). Instead, many scholars conclude that men and women are more similar than they are different (Canary & Hause, 1993). Applied to sex differences in social influence, this implies that men and women are likely to differ to some degree rather than being qualitatively different.

Eagly's Narrative Review

Eagly (1978) conducted a narrative review of research on gender differences in social influence. She noted several prior reviews of the persuasion and conformity literature that concluded that there were strong gender effects in prior research. She then examined two categories of prior investigations: traditional persuasion studies in which message receivers were individually exposed to a persuasive message, and conformity studies in which participants formed a small group and attempted to achieve consensus on an issue. Three types of findings were recorded for these studies: either women were more easily persuaded or conformed more than men; men were more easily persuaded or conformed more then women; or there were no differences in persuasability or conformity between men and women. Of the 62 persuasion studies included in her review, Eagly found that 51 (82%) revealed no gender difference in persuasability. Ten studies (16%) found that women were more easily persuaded than men, and one study (2%) found that men were more easily persuaded than women. The conformity studies yielded larger differences. Of the 61 group conformity studies, 38 (62%) found no gender differences, 21 (34%) found that women conformed more than men, and two studies (3%) found that men conformed more frequently than women. These findings clearly dampened the claims of strong gender effects that had been advanced in prior literature reviews.

Eagly speculated that the studies in her review that found significant gender differences may have been affected by cultural and experimental factors. She found that many of the studies finding significant gender differences were conducted prior to 1970 and the onset of the women's movement. In addition, she argued that many of these studies employed sex-biased persuasion topics. That is, studies finding that women conformed more readily, or were more easily persuaded, than men may have used male-oriented topics. At the risk of appearing sexist, examples of traditional female topics might include nutrition and child development. That is, women in traditional sex roles may have more knowledge and experience with these issues than men. Conversely, examples of traditional male topics might include auto mechanics and football. Eagly argued that the use of sex-biased topics prior to the women's movement may have made women more susceptible to influence in some studies. In fact, prior research has found that both men and women are more susceptible to influence when they lack knowledge of (McGuire & Papageorgis, 1961) or are uninterested in the persuasive topic (N. Miller, 1965). If these factors combined to influence susceptibility to persuasion in prior studies, then it is even less likely that gender is an important receiver characteristic in persuasive transactions.

Eagly and Carli's Meta-Analytic Review

Eagly's (1978) narrative review was limited by the use of a "counting procedure" for summarizing the findings of prior research. Because this review predated the development of more sophisticated meta-analytic procedures (see Chapter 2, this volume), a subsequent review of this literature was conducted to obtain more precise estimates of the effects of cultural and experimental factors in studies reporting gender effects (Eagly & Carli, 1981).

The primary advantage of the meta-analytic review is a precise estimate of the *size* of any gender difference in each study. Averaging these effect sizes across studies provides a much more precise estimate of gender differences in persuasion. Although the meta-analysis found that, for both persuasion and group conformity studies, women were more susceptible to influence than men, the size of this effect was quite small. Consistent with Eagly's (1977) narrative review, the effect sizes in group conformity studies were significantly stronger than those in the persuasion studies. Even with these larger effects in conformity studies, less than 1% of the variance in influenceability was attributed to subject gender. Eagly and Carli (1981) concluded that "a sex difference as small as this may have few implications for social interaction" (p. 11).[2]

In addition, their review failed to find evidence of gender bias in the topics employed in prior research. To examine this issue, they presented students with a list of topics from these studies and asked them to rate their interest and knowledge about the topics. Some topics were found to be biased in favor of men (e.g., football, soccer, the military, and automobiles), some were found to be biased in favor of women (e.g., cancer checkups and social work), and others were not biased toward either gender. Although many of the topics were gender-biased, there was no support for the position that male-oriented topics were overrepresented in prior studies. That is, the average gender difference on the interest and knowledge ratings for topics used in these studies was not significantly different from zero (Eagly & Carli, 1981). It should be emphasized that students made these interest and knowledge ratings some time before the meta-analysis was published in 1981; they were not made by the original participants in these studies. Given that the majority of the studies included in this review were conducted prior to 1970 (i.e., before the onset of the women's movement), it is possible that participants in many of these original studies may have had different knowledge and interest levels than the students who made the ratings for this review. Thus, the findings concerning the bias in message topics should be interpreted cautiously (Eagly & Carli, 1981).

Summary of Gender Effects Research

Together, these reviews provide little evidence to suggest that the sex of persuasive targets is an important feature of persuasive transactions. Although this belief has been widespread among the scholarly and lay community, the findings of these two reviews have nearly laid this issue to rest (for a recent contrasting view, however, see M. Burgoon & Klingle, 1998). No doubt, there are some persuasive situations in which women and men find themselves more susceptible to influence than members of the opposite sex (e.g., M. Burgoon & Klingle, 1998), but these situations are not sufficiently frequent to maintain the belief that important gender differences exist in persuasibility.

MESSAGE DISCREPANCY AND PERSUASION

The goal of many persuasive transactions is to change a target person's or an audience's attitudes or beliefs in a particular direction. When persuaders attempt to alter attitudes or behaviors, the position advocated in the persuasive message is likely to differ from the position held by message recipients. This difference is generally referred to as *message discrepancy*, that is, the extent to which a persuader's message recommendation differs from the position held by the target person or audience.

In Chapter 1 we defined *attitudes* as, in part, a positive, negative, or neutral evaluation of a target. As a consequence, a continuum can be constructed to represent the differing positions people hold for most attitude objects. At the risk of confounding legal and financial issues and appearing overly simplistic, let's consider the variety of positions people hold on the controversy over abortion rights. Some people oppose abortion under any circumstances; their position is represented on the right end of the continuum in Figure 8.1. However, there are a variety of people who globally oppose abortion, but who find it acceptable under certain extenuating circumstances. For example, some would advocate abortion only when the life of the mother is at risk or in cases of rape or

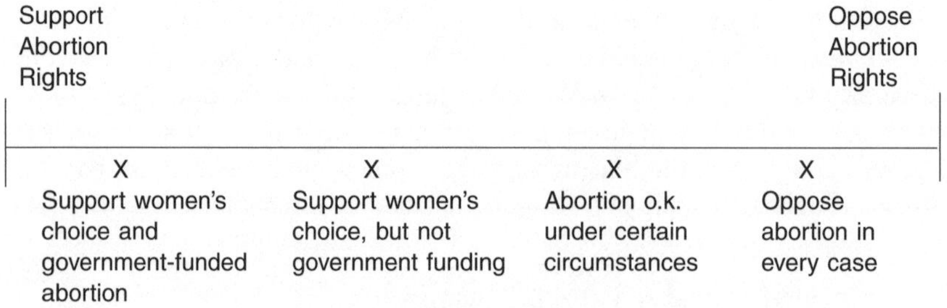

Support Abortion Rights			Oppose Abortion Rights
X	X	X	X
Support women's choice and government-funded abortion	Support women's choice, but not government funding	Abortion o.k. under certain circumstances	Oppose abortion in every case

FIGURE 8.1. Hypothetical attitude continuum.

incest. These positions are represented to the right of center on this continuum. At the other end of the continuum are people who support the right of every woman to have an abortion, even if it requires government assistance for women who are unable to afford the procedure. This position is represented at the extreme left end of the continuum. Less extreme, but still to the left of center on this continuum, are people who favor a woman's right to have an abortion, but oppose government funding of this procedure.

The diversity of viewpoints on the abortion issue is apparent in this example. As with many persuasive topics, people may hold similar global views about abortion, yet differ when more precise statements of their positions are outlined. As a result, persuaders who blindly assume that an audience's views on a topic are homogeneous may overlook subtle but important variations in the positions held. In other words, it is important to recognize that even when people generally agree on an issue, they are likely to differ somewhat in the specific positions they hold. Indeed, this may be one reason why politicians become "fuzzy" on some issues when speaking to diverse audiences. In their attempt to appeal to a wide spectrum of voters, politicians often attempt to minimize the perceived discrepancy between their own position and the positions held by their constituents.

Most persuasive messages advocate acceptance of a particular position. Combined with the fact that audience members are likely to hold a variety of positions on an issue, message discrepancy is likely to differ among message recipients. Extending the abortion rights example a bit further, we can conclude that a persuasive message advocating a ban on all abortions will be mildly discrepant for some people (e.g., those who favor abortion only under extenuating circumstances) and highly discrepant for others (e.g., those who believe that every woman should have the right to an abortion regardless of the circumstances). To the extent that message discrepancy affects attitude or behavior change, the persuasive effects of any message are likely to differ among message recipients.

The concept of message discrepancy raises two questions for persuaders. First, and most important, is message discrepancy an important factor in persuasive communication? If so, then effective persuaders should be interested in a second question: How does message discrepancy influence the attitudes and behaviors of message recipients? Two theories, Social Judgment Theory and Information Processing Theory, agree that message discrepancy is an important factor in the persuasion process; however, the two theories disagree on most everything else. Each of these theories, and the evidence supporting them, will be discussed next.

Social Judgment Theory

One of the first theories to address the issue of message discrepancy was Social Judgment Theory (M. Sherif & Hovland, 1961; C. W. Sherif et al., 1965). C. W. Sherif, M. Sherif, and their colleagues classified attitudes along a continuum that they divided into latitudes of acceptance and rejection.[3] The *latitude of acceptance* represents the positions on the attitude continuum that a person finds acceptable. By definition, a person's ideal or preferred position is centered within this latitude. Positions that are unacceptable to a message recipient constitute the *latitude of rejection*. People holding a moderate position on an issue may have a latitude of rejection on either side of their latitude of acceptance (Figure 8.2). However, when a person's attitude is extreme, then a single latitude of acceptance will be located on one end of the latitude continuum, and a latitude of rejection will be located on the other end (Figure 8.3). In both Figures 8.2 and 8.3, the ideal or preferred position is marked with an X.

Predicting Attitude Change

According the Social Judgment Theory, attitude change can be predicted succinctly from knowledge about the latitudes of acceptance and rejection: "Attitude change increases with [message] discrepancy as long as the message falls within the latitude of acceptance, but then it decreases if the discrepancy is so large that the message falls in the latitude of rejection" (Hunter, Danes, & Cohen, 1984, p. 57).

Underpinning the attitude change process are a series of perceptual judgments people make about message content and message sources. When people perceive that a message recommendation falls within their

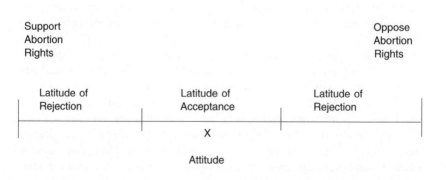
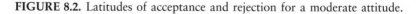

FIGURE 8.2. Latitudes of acceptance and rejection for a moderate attitude.

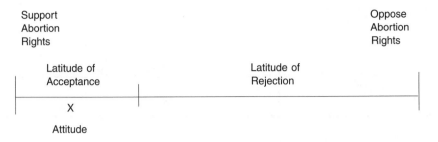

FIGURE 8.3. Latitudes of acceptance and rejection for an extreme attitude.

latitude of acceptance, *assimilation* is hypothesized to occur. That is, receivers judge the message recommendation as being closer to their own position than it actually is. However, when a message recommendation is perceived to fall within the latitude of rejection, *contrast effects* are hypothesized. A contrast effect causes receivers to judge the message as more discrepant from their own position than it actually is. In short, due to the latitudes of acceptance and rejection, as well as assimilation and contrast effects, Social Judgment Theory predicts a curvilinear (i.e., inverted-U-shaped) relationship between message discrepancy and attitude change (Figure 8.4).

Predicting Changes in Source Credibility

Social Judgment Theory did not offer specific predictions about the effects of message discrepancy on perceived source credibility. However, descriptions of the theory provide a clear set of expectations regarding this relationship. For example, M. Sherif and Sherif (1967) argued that source credibility was related to latitudes of acceptance and rejection, and hence to attitude change. Moreover, they identified source derogation as one outcome of extreme message discrepancy. They concluded that "when a communication is discrepant from a source's position on an issue, the source is dubbed as unreasonable, propagandistic, false, and even obnoxious. Conversely, when messages fall within the latitude of acceptance, the source is viewed as more truthful, factual, and less biased" (C. W. Sherif et al., 1965, p. 227).

This discussion of source derogation led Hunter and colleagues (1984) to argue that *if* predictions regarding message discrepancy and source credibility had been posited by social judgment theorists, the hypothesized relationship would mirror the message discrepancy–attitude change prediction. That is, when a message falls within the latitude of

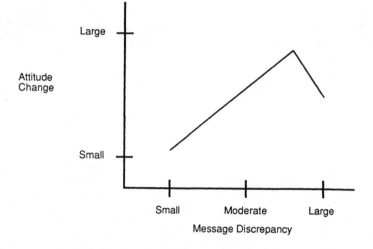

FIGURE 8.4. Curvilinear relationship between message discrepancy and attitude change as predicted by Social Judgment Theory.

acceptance, message discrepancy is positively related to changes in source credibility. When a message falls within the latitude of rejection, source derogation occurs, producing a negative relationship between message discrepancy and changes in source credibility (Figure 8.5). In short, Social Judgment Theory would predict a curvilinear (inverted-U-shaped) relationship between message discrepancy and source credibility change (Hunter et al., 1984).

Evidence Supporting Social Judgment Theory

A considerable number of studies have found evidence of the curvilinear relationship between message discrepancy and attitude change (Aronson, Turner, & Carlsmith, 1963; Bochner & Insko, 1966; C. W. Sherif et al., 1965; Whittaker, 1967). These studies provided evidence of a "discrepancy curve" reflecting a positive relationship between message discrepancy and attitude change up to a point, beyond which further increases in discrepancy decreased the amount of observed attitude change. These findings are consistent with the pattern of attitude change predicted by Social Judgment Theory.

Unfortunately, evidence for the predicted change in source credibility is less encouraging. In an extensive investigation of message discrepancy effects, Hunter and colleagues (1984) failed to find evidence of a curvilinear relationship between message discrepancy and source credibility change. Instead, they found that changes in source credibility were a positive linear function of message discrepancy. Moreover, prior message discrepancy studies that measured changes in source credibility (Bochner & Insko, 1966; Rhine & Severance, 1970; Tannenbaum, 1953) found the same positive linear relationship between message discrepancy and changes in source credibility.

In summary, the attitude change data suggest that discrepancy is positively related to attitude change until the message becomes sufficiently discrepant to fall within a receiver's latitude of rejection. In this regard, there is support for the theory. However, predictions concerning source credibility pose problems for the theory. Although C. W. Sherif, M. Sherif, and their colleagues did not specifically offer source credibility predictions, the curvilinear hypothesis advanced by Hunter et al. (Figure 8.5) is consistent with the theory. Studies measuring source credibility effects, however, failed to find evidence of this curvilinear relationship. An alternative explanation for the effects of message discrepancy stems from the predictions of Information Processing Theory.

Information Processing Theory

Information Processing Theory is a generic label for a family of persuasion models that maintain a common set of assumptions about the cognitive evaluation of persuasive messages (Anderson, 1959, 1971;

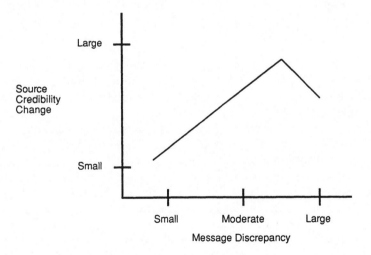

FIGURE 8.5. Curvilinear relationship between message discrepancy and changes in perceived source credibility as predicted by Social Judgment Theory.

Hovland & Pritzker, 1957; McGuire, 1968; Wyer, 1970). The fundamental assumption of Information Processing Theory is that messages have affective value. The value of a message can be represented along the same continuum that we developed to represent a person's attitude on a topic. The position of a message along the continuum is determined by the value of the attitude reflected in the message recommendation (Hunter et al., 1984). For example, the value of a message advocating a total ban on abortions would be represented on the right end of the continuum in Figure 8.1. Conversely, the value of a pro-choice message could be represented near the left end of this continuum.

According to the theory, message processing involves an internal comparison of one's own position to the position advocated in the message. The difference between these two positions is defined as message discrepancy, which stimulates attitude change. Several theorists propose a "distance-proportional" model in which attitude change is proportional to message discrepancy and is always in the direction advocated by the message (Anderson, 1959; Anderson & Hovland, 1957; Hunter et al., 1984, p. 36).

Linear Discrepancy Model

Hunter and colleagues (1984) demonstrate that the attitude change predictions of Information Processing Theory are formally equivalent to a simple Linear Discrepancy Model in which the amount of attitude change produced by a persuasive message will be a linear function of message discrepancy:

$$\Delta a = \alpha (m - a) \qquad (7.1)$$

where Δa represents attitude change, m is the value of the attitude reflected in the message, a is the receiver's premessage attitude, and α is the coefficient that represents the strength of the relationship between message discrepancy $(m - a)$ and attitude change.

There are two important differences between the predictions of Information Processing Theory and Social Judgment Theory. First, Social Judgment Theory predicts a curvilinear (inverted-U-shaped) relationship between message discrepancy and attitude change, whereas Information Processing Theory predicts a positive linear relationship between message discrepancy and attitude change (Figure 8.6). Second, Social Judgment Theory suggests that source derogation will occur when message discrepancy is large, producing a curvilinear relationship between message discrepancy and changes in perceived source credibility. Information Processing Theory, on the other hand, predicts that changes in perceived source credibility are a linear function of message value and premessage evaluations of source credibility (Figure 8.7).

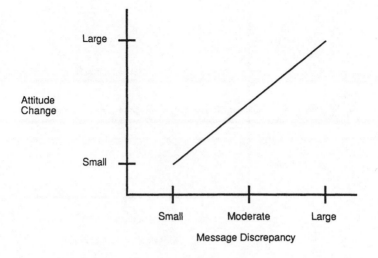

FIGURE 8.6. Linear relationship between message discrepancy and attitude change as predicted by Information Processing Theory.

Evidence Supporting Information Processing Theory

Several experiments provide support for the predictions of Information Processing Theory. First, there is considerable evidence of a linear relationship between message discrepancy and attitude change. Tests of Anderson's Information Integration Model (Anderson, 1971, 1981) and the Linear Discrepancy Model (Hunter et al., 1984) provide evidence of a positive linear relationship between message discrepancy and attitude change. That is, greater persuasive effects are associated with increased, not decreased, message discrepancy.

Perhaps the most compelling evidence for the information processing explanation of discrepancy effects stems from the source credibility data presented by Hunter and colleagues (1984). Consistent with the predictions of Information Processing Theory, the studies they reviewed and conducted all found a linear relationship between message discrepancy and changes in perceived source credibility.

Explaining the "Discrepancy Curves"

In summary, two different theories make contrasting predictions concerning the persuasive impact of message discrepancy. Social Judgment Theory predicts a curvilinear (i.e., inverted-U-shaped) relationship between message discrepancy and attitude change, while Information Processing Theory predicts a positive linear relationship. There are studies,

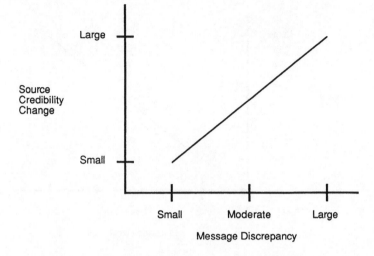

FIGURE 8.7. Linear relationship between message discrepancy and changes in perceived source credibility as predicted by Information Processing Theory.

moreover, that are consistent with both of these predictions. How do we make sense of these competing explanations and results? Which theory is right? It is very possible that both theories are right because they have different theoretical domains; however, on the whole, there is more support for Information Processing Theory than for Social Judgment Theory.

It is possible that both Social Judgment Theory and Information Processing Theory offer correct explanations of message discrepancy because each theory has a different set of conditions under which it works. In discussing Social Judgment Theory, C. W. Sherif et al. (1965) argue that in order to produce the curvilinear relationships between message discrepancy and attitude change (among other conditions), audience members must be ego-involved in the topic. Social Judgment theorists used the term *ego-involvement* to reflect a set of core values or beliefs that constitute a person's self-concept. Thus, ego-involving attitudes define a person's system of values. For example, gun control legislation is a highly involving topic for many National Rifle Association members because their attitudes on this topic define their core social and political values. Abortion rights is a highly involving topic because, for many people, this issue has come to symbolize fundamental characteristics of their religious and political self-concepts.

Studies finding a curvilinear relationship have tended to include highly ego-involved participants who already have a strong stand on an issue. Highly ego-involved persons have a small latitude of acceptance and a wide latitude of rejection. Messages falling in the latitude of rejection must be rejected if the person is to maintain his or her preexisting value structure.

Information Processing Theory studies, on the other hand, tend to use topics that are not closely linked to participants' values and self-concepts. Participants in these studies are unlikely to be ego-involved in the topic and have a wider latitude of acceptance. Participants can drastically change their attitudes without having to restructure their self-views.

In summary, curvilinear relationships between message discrepancy and attitude change are likely to occur under a specific set of circumstances. Information Processing Theory, then, presents a more general view of message discrepancy effects that works in a wider variety of circumstances. Of the two theories, Information Processing Theory is the preferred one because it can account for the curvilinear relationships found in early tests of Social Judgment Theory. Results from two studies described below suggest how Information Processing Theory can account for these nonlinear curves.

First, working from cognitive response models of persuasion. Brock (1967) found that highly discrepant messages generated more counterarguing from message recipients than less discrepant messages. This is important because counterarguing is consistent with the general position of Information Processing Theory. That is, to the extent that message processing includes counterarguing of highly discrepant appeals, the decrease in persuasiveness of highly discrepant messages is consistent with Information Processing Theory (Hunter et al., 1984, p. 176).

A second explanation for the discrepancy curves stems from investigations that have examined the effects of *positional* and *psychological* discrepancy (Fink, Kaplowitz, & Bauer, 1983). *Positional discrepancy* refers to the absolute difference between a receiver's attitude and the position advocated in the message. *Psychological discrepancy* refers to the difference a receiver perceives between his or her attitude and the position advocated by a message.

For example, consider the issue of capital punishment. Assume that a convention delegate who opposes the death penalty in all circumstances attended a panel discussion about the death penalty during a state political convention. If a candidate for the office of attorney general advocated limited use of the death penalty in certain types of cases (i.e., repeat violent offenders, murder of a law enforcement officer), the position advocated by this candidate would be discrepant from the delegate's position on the issue. The objective difference between the candidate's position and the delegate's position on the issue would be referred to as *positional discrepancy*. If a second candidate spoke and advocated widespread use of the death penalty, the second candidate's position would be even more discrepant from the delegate's attitude than the position advocated by the first candidate. However, if the two candidates spoke sequentially as part of the same panel discussion, the position advocated by the first candidate might be perceived as *psychologically* less discrepant by the delegate, because it would be compared with the more extreme position advocated by the second candidate.

In a test of the importance of positional and psychological discrepancy, Fink and colleagues (1983) found that positional discrepancy was associated with greater attitude change; however, they found that greater psychological discrepancy inhibited attitude change. Moreover, they found that surrounding messages influenced the psychological discrepancy of a message.

Applied to Information Processing Theory, these findings suggest that messages with extreme positional discrepancy may also serve to heighten psychological discrepancy in message recipients. If these two types of discrepancy are confounded, one would expect the nonlinear discrepancy curve observed in prior tests of Social Judgment Theory.

Summarizing Message Discrepancy Research

In summary, the body of existing evidence is more supportive of an information processing explanation than a social judgment explanation. However, it is possible that both theories work in their own domain. Information Processing Theory can explain both the linear and the nonlinear relationships between message discrepancy and attitude change found in prior studies. Moreover, the linear source credibility effects found in several studies can only be explained through Information Processing Theory.

It bears mentioning that social judgment theorists may claim that the source credibility prediction is a nonessential feature of the theory and discount the importance of the source credibility findings. Even if one discounts the theoretical importance of the source credibility data, however, Social Judgment Theory cannot explain the linear effects of message discrepancy on attitudes found in many investigations.

Regardless of the correct theoretical interpretation for these effects, the practical implications of message discrepancy research are clear. The discrepancy between the position held by a target audience and the one advocated in a message appears to enhance message persuasiveness. In many situations, highly discrepant messages will produce greater attitude change than less discrepant messages. However, when the message topic is linked to receivers' values, discrepant messages (those falling within a receiver's latitude of rejection) may cause receivers to discount the message, counterargue against it, and/or perceive it to be more psychologically discrepant than it objectively is. Any of these outcomes could limit the persuasiveness of the message.

The most confident practical recommendation is that message discrepancy enhances attitude change, but there are two limits to this advice. First, the message has to be realistic. Advocating spending $1 billion to elimmate crabgrass from national parks is unlikely to be effective. In such cases, the strategy of presenting highly discrepant messages may backfire. Second, message sources must be very careful if the message topic is linked to receivers' values.

RECEIVER INVOLVEMENT AND PERSUASION

A third characteristic of message receivers that has captured the attention of persuasion researchers is *involvement*. Over the years, receiver involvement has assumed a variety of different theoretical roles in the development of several persuasion theories. Beginning with the social judgment theorists in the early 1960s, *involvement* referred to the activation of ego-defensive mechanisms in message receivers that motivated them to reject persuasive appeals (C. W. Sherif et al., 1965). By the late 1960s social-cognitive theories of persuasion began to dominate persuasion research (Greenwald et al., 1968; Petty, Ostrom, & Brock, 1981). This theoretical shift led to the development of several social-cognitive theories in which involvement was hypothesized to stimulate thinking in message receivers (Chaiken, 1987; Petty & Cacioppo, 1981, 1986). In yet a third conceptual approach, Cialdini and his colleagues argued that receiver involvement can stimulate impression management behaviors and influence the persuasibility of message receivers (Cialdini, Levy, Herman, & Evenbeck, 1973; Cialdini, Levy, Herman, Kozlowski, & Petty, 1976).

The use of widely divergent definitions for the term *involvement* has produced a body of persuasion studies that appear contradictory. In their review of this literature Johnson and Eagly (1989) identified the different conceptual meanings underlying the use of this term and clarified the various roles of involvement in the persuasion process. They defined *involvement* as "the motivational state induced by an association between an activated attitude and some aspect of the self-concept" (p. 293).

Three research traditions of involvement—*value-relevant*, *outcome-relevant*, and *impression-relevant*—summarized in Johnson and Eagly's review reflect the different functions that involvement may serve in the persuasion process. Although Johnson and Eagly (1989) did not endorse a functional perspective for defining involvement, such a framework provides an excellent conceptual backdrop for understanding the essential characteristics of these research traditions. Four of the early psychological functions of attitudes—*ego-defensive, instrumental, value-expressive,* and *social-expressive* (Katz, 1960; Smith et al., 1956)—highlight differences among the three traditions of involvement research. These traditions and their psychological functions are reviewed in the following sections of this chapter.

Value-Relevant Involvement

This tradition of research on the persuasive effects of involvement evolved from investigations of Social Judgment Theory (C. W. Sherif et al., 1965; M. Sherif & Hovland, 1961; M. Sherif & Sherif, 1967). Earlier in this chapter we discussed the predicted effectiveness of messages falling within the latitudes of acceptance and rejection, as well as how ego-involvement determines the width of these latitudes. Social Judgment Theory posits that when message receivers are highly ego-involved in a message topic, their latitudes of rejection become wider, increasing the number of positions along the attitude evaluation continuum that are unacceptable. Conversely, when receivers are uninvolved, their latitudes of rejection become narrower, increasing the number of positions that receive an acceptable evaluation.

Johnson and Eagly (1989) labeled this type of involvement *value-relevant involvement* because it reflects a concern about values that define a person's self-concept. Regardless of the label, Levin, Nichols, and Johnson (2000) argue that this type of involvement serves either an ego-defensive or a value-expressive function as defined by Katz (1960). People become highly concerned about particular topics because these issues allows receivers to express their important values or defend their self-concepts from attack (Levin et al., 2000).

Given this function, the predicted relationship between this type of involvement and attitude change should be obvious. Value-relevant involvement should increase the number of unacceptable positions along the attitude-evaluation continuum and inhibit attitude change. Johnson and Eagly's (1989) meta-analytic review found a moderately strong negative correlation between value-relevant involvement and attitude change. In short, this type of involvement appears to inhibit attitude change.

Outcome-Relevant Involvement

Johnson and Eagly (1989) labeled a second category of involvement *outcome-relevant involvement*. This tradition of involvement research began with the social-cognitive approaches to persuasion. During the 1980s two related, yet distinct, models of persuasion identified an important role for outcome-relevant involvement. Both the Heuristic Model of Persuasion (Chaiken, 1987) and the Elaboration Likelihood Model (ELM; Petty & Cacioppo, 1986) posited that outcome-relevant involvement is one factor that motivates receivers to carefully scrutinize the content of persuasive messages (see Chapter 10, this volume).

In this research tradition, involvement serves an *instrumental function* similar to the one described by Katz (1960). This type of involvement reflects a concern about achieving particular positively evaluated outcomes (Levin et al., 2000). Typical investigations of the ELM, for example, manipulate outcome-relevant involvement by presenting college students with messages that warn of comprehensive exams for undergraduates or higher tuition rates. Both of these topics are central to the educational goals of the student participants in these studies but are unlikely to be linked to values or self-concept. Though only a handful of topics have been used in these investigations, people are likely to exhibit outcome-relevant involvement with a wide variety of persuasive topics. For example, a young couple preparing to purchase their first home may become highly interested in the Federal Reserve Board's policy decisions that ultimately influence home mortgage interest rates. However, after purchasing a home, this couple will likely become less concerned with the policy decisions that determine interest rates, especially if their mortgage has a fixed interest rate.

Outcome-relevant involvement with an issue is likely to rise as people work toward achieving an issue-related goal and decline once the goal has been achieved and the instrumental function of involvement declines. This characteristic distinguishes outcome-relevant involvement from value-relevant involvement. Value-relevant involvement is likely to be much more stable because of its connection to a person's core values (C. W. Sherif et al., 1965).

The persuasive effects of outcome-relevant involvement are somewhat complicated. Social-cognitive models of persuasion (see Chapter 10, this volume) posit that highly involved message recipients will scrutinize the content of persuasive messages more than less involved recipients will. Thus, the persuasive effects of this type of involvement are dependent on the quality of arguments and supporting material in the persuasive message. Consistent with this general prediction, Johnson and Eagly (1989) found that involvement enhanced the persuasive effects of strong persuasive messages and inhibited the effectiveness of weak persuasive messages.[4] Thus, when outcome-relevant involvement of message receivers is high, the quality of arguments and evidence in the persuasive message will determine the extent of attitude change.

Impression-Relevant Involvement

The third tradition of involvement research emphasizes *impression-relevant involvement*. Investigations by Cialdini and his colleagues (Cialdini et al., 1973, 1976; Cialdini & Petty, 1981) evolved from Zimbardo's (1960) concept of response involvement. Impression-relevant involvement occurs when individuals are concerned about the social consequences of expressing an attitude. Research on this type of involvement has consistently found that when people are concerned about the impressions they make on others, they may be reluctant to endorse positions that are incompatible with those of message sources. Cialdini's research found that when people are under public scrutiny, they tend to advocate more flexible and moderate attitudes compared to when their position is unlikely to be publicly evaluated.

Because concerns about impression management influence the attitudes people endorse, Johnson and Eagly prefer the label "impression-relevant involvement" to Zimbardo's "response involvement." Individuals high in impression-relevant involvement "employ their attitudes as a means of advancing interpersonally oriented goals" (Levin et al., 2000, p. 166). In this regard, Levin and colleagues (2000) argue that impression-relevant involvement serves what Smith and colleagues (1956) called a "social-adjustive function." In the social-adjustive function of attitudes, the expression of a particular attitude serves to "promote or preserve relationships with important others, or to break from those relationships no longer considered valuable to the attitude holder" (Hullett & Boster, 2001, p. 135).

For example, this concern is evident in the behavior of many job applicants who are cautious not to endorse extreme attitudes unless they are certain their potential employer endorses the same attitudes.

Given its social function, it should come as no surprise that impression-relevant involvement inhibits attitude change (Johnson & Eagly, 1989). Although the size of this effect was small, highly involved receivers were less likely to change their attitude or to endorse an extreme position when compared to receivers who were less concerned with impression management.

Summarizing the Effects of Involvement

Johnson and Eagly (1989) offer convincing evidence of the theoretical and empirical distinctions among these three research traditions of involvement research.[5] Although the pattern of effects for value-relevant and impression-relevant involvement is similar, the theoretical foundations for these traditions are clearly distinct. Whereas value-relevant involvement reflects concern about a set of core values, impression-relevant involvement stems from more superficial concerns about self-presentation. Although outcome-relevant involvement may be transient, the hypothesized effects of this type of involvement on the cognitive processes of message receivers distinguishes it from the other two types of involvement.

For scholars of persuasion, differences among the research traditions highlighted by Johnson and Eagly may help resolve many of the apparent inconsistencies among prior investigations of the persuasive effects of involvement. For persuasion practitioners, this analysis calls for considerable caution in the development and presentation of persuasive appeals. Because the specific type of receiver involvement is likely to influence the effectiveness of persuasive messages, persuaders are cautioned to carefully consider the values and goals that message receivers bring to each persuasive transaction.

Reconsidering Involvement

In recent critiques, Slater (1997, 2002) argued that while involvement is clearly related to important persuasion processes, it is also somewhat "problematic" (p. 126). As we discussed above, involvement is generally defined by a connection between a persuasive message and some aspect of the receiver's sense of self. That is to say, messages are involving because they are relevant to personal outcomes (Petty & Cacioppo, 1986), personal values (C. W. Sherif et al., 1965), or impressions others might generate (Cialdini et al., 1973). Each of these forms of involvement was created independently; no single theoretical explanation ties the three of them together.

As part of a theoretical reformulation, Slater (1997) argues that message processing, as is true with much human behavior, is goal-directed and that different goals have different implications for message processing. Thus, Slater is beginning with a single theoretical umbrella (goals) that can potentially explain different types of persuasive message processing. As the beginning point of this reformulation, Slater developed a typology of six message goals: entertainment, information/skill acquisition, surveillance, self-interest assessment, value-defense, and value-reinforcement. This goal typology includes the types of involvement discussed by Johnson and Eagly (1989). For example, self-interest assessment is similar to outcome-relevant involvement, while value-defense and value-reinforcement are related to value-relevant involvement.

According to Slater (1997), different receiver goals generate distinct message-processing strategies. Moreover, Slater suggests that each goal/processing strategy pair has a separate set of variables that influence the amount of message processing that receivers will perform. As a consequence, Slater's view provides a stronger base from which to consider involvement effects in persuasion. This view is quite new and to date no research has been published from this perspective, so Slater's view should be considered with caution.

FUNCTION MATCHING

The most recent receiver factor to be investigated by persuasion scholars is function matching (see, e.g., Hullett & Boster, 2001; Petty, Wheeler, & Bizer, 2000). One of the early predictions made by proponents of the functional approach to attitudes (Katz, 1960; Smith et al. 1956) was that persuasive messages are likely to be particularly successful when the arguments they contain match the functions that underlie audience members' attitudes. For example, an individual whose attitudes are based on the instrumental function (i.e., to gain rewards and avoid punishments) will likely positively evaluate, and be persuaded by, a message promising rewards or one that describes ways of avoiding punishments. These same individuals will be unpersuaded by an appeal to values.

Like much research on the functional approach, research was hindered by the lack of clear methods for identifying various attitude functions (Hullett & Boster, 2001). During the past decade, research on functional approaches (and function matching) has been facilitated by the development of either direct measures of attitude functions (Herek, 1988) or by personality measures that serve as indirect indicators of attitude functions. For example, several studies used the self-monitoring scale to identify value-expressive and social-adjustive functions (e.g., Snyder & DeBono, 1985).

Hullett and Boster (2001) investigated the extent to which functional matching influenced attitude change following exposure to a persuasive message on tuition increases. They developed measures to determine the extent to which participants valued conformity to others (i.e., a social-adjustive function) or self-direction and independence (i.e., a specific value-expressive function). Hullett and Boster measured conformity and self-direction values and then exposed participants to one of two versions of a message advocating a tuition increase. The "conformity" message indicated that the typical student in favor of tuition increases valued "politeness, self-restraint, and getting along with others" (Hullett & Boster, 2001, p. 142), while the "self-direction" message associated agreement with tuition increases with students exhibiting "self-sufficiency, self-reliance, ability to choose one's own goals, and independence" (p. 142).

Hullett and Boster's (2001) results were, for the most part, consistent with the functional matching hypothesis. Specifically, they found that the values students espoused were related to their evaluations of the persuasive messages. Students who strongly endorsed the conformity value found the conformity message to be of higher quality than students who did not espouse that value. In addition, students who strongly endorse the self-direction value found the self-reliance message to be of higher quality than students who did not espouse that value. In all cases, evaluation of message quality was positively related to agreement with the message's conclusions (i.e., to increase tuition).

SUMMARY

This chapter examined four characteristics of persuasive targets that have received considerable attention from persuasion scholars. We concluded that although some weak effects were found in prior research, the gender of message receivers is not an important feature in the effectiveness of persuasive messages. That is, there is scant evidence to suggest that women are more easily persuaded than men.

The discussion of message discrepancy effects was considerably more complicated. Social Judgment Theory and Information Processing Theory offered competing predictions about the persuasive effects of message discrepancy. Although some evidence supported both interpretations in different conditions, Information Processing Theory can more fully explain the findings of prior investigations. Regardless of the underlying theoretical mechanism, however, we concluded that message discrepancy appears to enhance attitude change unless the discrepancy is so large as to appear ridiculous or when audience members' values are involved in the message topic.

Involvement is an important characteristic of message receivers. We described three types of receiver involvement along with the functions they serve. The ego-defensive function served by value-relevant involvement has a moderately strong inhibiting effect on attitude change. Outcome-relevant involvement interacts with message quality to influence the effectiveness of message appeals, although there was some inconsistency among these research findings. Finally, impression-relevant involvement appears to have an inhibiting effect on attitude change, but this effect is much weaker than the one found for value-relevant involvement.

Finally, function matching appears to be another receiver factor that influences persuasion. Several studies have found that successful persuasive messages contain messages that match the functions underlying receivers' attitudes.

NOTES

1. This discussion leads us to one of the very few substantive issues upon which we (i.e., Jim and Paul) disagreed. Specifically, what do we *call* the differences between men and women? Jim argued that if differences between men and women in persuasibility do exist, they are almost certainly the result of differential socialization and, as a consequence, should be called *gender differences*. Paul, on the other hand, argued that while Jim is almost certainly correct, the data being reviewed focuses on biological sex, and as a consequence should be called *sex differences*. While there is no most correct answer to this issue, Jim is first author, so we will call them "gender differences."

2. M. Burgoon and Klingle (1998) take exception to this conclusion. Specifically, they conclude that Eagly and Carli's (1981) data indicate that between "20% and 25% of women tend to be more persuasible than the population of men. This is clearly neither a small nor trivial difference" (p. 273). Moreover, they suggest, contrary to the common misconception, that this gender difference is not due to women being easily influenced, but rather is due to a certain percentage of men refusing to change their attitudes and beliefs under any circumstances.

3. Some variations of the theory also include latitude of noncommitment that represents a range of positions that are neither acceptable nor unacceptable. Unfortunately, few testable hypotheses were ever offered about attitudes falling within this latitude.

4. This finding was not consistent across all studies. Johnson and Eagly (1989) found that researchers associated with Ohio State University (Petty, Cacioppo, and their colleagues) consistently found this pattern of effects, but that scholars with different research backgrounds were unable to replicate them. Johnson and Eagly were at a loss to explain these differences and suggested caution when interpreting them. Although this effect was not consistent across researchers, the overall pattern of findings suggests that the persuasive effects of outcome-relevant involvement differ from those of value-relevant involvement.

5. It bears mentioning that not everyone endorsed the conceptual distinctions drawn by Johnson and Eagly (1989). Petty and Cacioppo (1990) criticized the distinction between value-relevant and outcome-relevant involvement, opting instead for a broader concept they labeled "personal involvement." They also criticized the merits of the meta-analytic review that supported Johnson and Eagly's distinction. Interested readers are encouraged to carefully examine these arguments along with a comprehensive response provided by Johnson and Eagly (1990).

9

Characteristics of Persuasive Settings

LOOKING AHEAD ...

This chapter examines three situational characteristics that
influence the persuasion process. We begin with a discussion of
the relative effectiveness of various modes of presenting
persuasive appeals. After this, we examine the influence of
distracting stimuli on the persuasiveness of a message. The
chapter concludes with a discussion of group influences in the
persuasion process.

In the preceding four chapters, we discussed the effects of source, message, and receiver characteristics in persuasive transactions. The present
chapter concludes the discussion of the persuasive effects literature by
examining characteristics of persuasive situations. We begin with a discussion of modality research and review the relative effectiveness of
video, audio, and written modes of presenting persuasive messages.
Next, we review the distraction literature, which examines the influence
of distracting stimuli on the comprehension and effectiveness of persuasive messages. The final major section of this chapter is devoted to a discussion of the influence of others in the persuasion process. Though few
persuasion textbooks consider the persuasive effects of small groups, a
considerable portion of our persuasive activities occur in group settings.
We review two avenues of research that reflect important social and informational influences of groups on the attitudes and behaviors of individuals. Consideration of persuasion in interpersonal settings (generally
referred to as "compliance gaining") is taken up in chapters 11 and 12.

MODE OF MESSAGE PRESENTATION

Perhaps the most fundamental decision facing would-be persuaders is one about how best to present their persuasive appeals. With a larger variety of technological alternatives available to persuaders, this choice has become somewhat more difficult in recent years. Advertisers, politicians, business organizations, and relational partners routinely choose among several methods of message presentation. Sometimes these choices are based on research, but often they reflect personal preferences based on prior persuasive success. Since the mid-1970s, for example, television has been the media staple of politicians seeking to present their positions and cultivate their images. This trend was marked by the election of Ronald Reagan in 1980—Reagan was a former actor with a strong television persona. Recent campaigns have seen an increase in the use of the Internet and World Wide Web by candidates (e.g., Kaid & Bystrom, 1999). Advertisers employ a wide spectrum of media alternatives to establish and maintain brand loyalty, while relational partners frequently choose among face-to-face, telephone, and written forms of communication when attempting to influence one another.

Although these choices often become routine, one might question their effectiveness. Is television the most effective method for outlining the political positions of a candidate? When are various forms of media effective for achieving the particular goals of advertisers? Are face-to-face interactions the most effective method for making persuasive appeals to relational partners? Most likely, these questions require complex answers that depend on a variety of source, receiver, and message characteristics. Nevertheless, a growing body of research provides some preliminary insights about the persuasive merits of various modes of message presentation.

Research on the effects of message modality has found no simple effects for any mode of message presentation. That is, no overall persuasive advantage exists for live, video, audio, or written messages. Instead, message modality serves to influence other factors, including the salience of the source and message comprehension, which in turn determine the effectiveness of a persuasive message.

Message Modality and Source Salience

With respect to receiver involvement, two studies found that live and video messages were more likely to heighten the involvement of message receivers when compared to audio or written messages (Andreoli & Worchel, 1978; Worchel, Andreoli, & Eason, 1975). Involvement was conceptualized in these studies as attentiveness to the message and the message source. Live and video message presentations more effectively focused receiver attention on the characteristics of the message and its source than did written messages. When the source was perceived as trustworthy, this attention enhanced the persuasiveness of the message presentation. However, when the source was perceived as untrustworthy, this heightened attention decreased the persuasiveness of the message.

Chaiken and Eagly (1983) also investigated this issue and found similar effects. They argued that video presentations would make communicator-based cues more salient to message receivers than audio or written messages. Consistent with this hypothesis, they found that a video presentation presented by a likeable source was more effective than the same message presented in audio or written format. Conversely, for unlikeable sources, audio and written message presentations were more persuasive than video message presentations.

Taken together, these investigations provide a consistent pattern of effects. Live and video presentations focus more attention on the source of the message than audio and written presentations do. If the source's attributes are evaluated positively, this attention should enhance the effectiveness of the message. However, if the source lacks trustworthiness, or is for some reason unlikeable, then the use of a live or video presentation may inhibit the persuasiveness of the message. These findings provide a relatively straightforward set of recommendations for persuaders: live or video presentations should be most effective for favorable message sources, whereas sources who are viewed less favorably should be more persuasive when using written and audio presentations.

Modality and Message Comprehension

Message modality has also been related to message comprehension. Once again, however, the persuasive effects of this relationship are not straightforward. Chaiken and Eagly (1976) argued that the relative persuasiveness of video, audio, and written messages depends on the difficulty of the message content. In one study they manipulated message difficulty by creating one message that contained complicated language but was equivalent in all other respects to a more easily understood second message. They presented these difficult and simple messages in a video, an audio, and a written format.

Chaiken and Eagly (1976) found that *comprehension* of the simple message did not vary across video, audio, and written message presentations. However, the difficult message was best comprehended when it was presented in a written format, as compared to the audio or video format. This finding should come as no surprise when one considers that messages presented in written format afford receivers the opportunity to reread portions of the message that are not initially understood (i.e., written messages have what is called high "ease of referability"). This opportunity is typically unavailable to receivers exposed to audio and video message presentations.

Chaiken and Eagly (1976) also found that simple messages were most persuasive when presented in a video presentation, and that difficult messages were more persuasive when presented in written format. Given the positive relationship between message comprehension and message acceptance, these findings regarding the difficult message are easy to interpret: the difficult message was more persuasive when presented in a written format because message comprehension was highest in that format. The finding that the video presentation was most effective for the simple message may reflect an increased salience of favorable source characteristics or increased attentiveness to the message when it was presented in a video format.

Summary of Modality Effects

In combination, research on source salience and message comprehension provides a clear description of the persuasive effects of message modality. When a source's attributes are favorable and likely to engender attitude change, video and live message presentations are an effective way to emphasize these characteristics. If a source's characteristics are unfavorable and likely to inhibit persuasion, written and audio message formats appear most effective because they do not accentuate these characteristics.

A similar interaction effect was found for message comprehension. Written messages aid comprehension, and consequently persuasion, when the message content is difficult to understand. However, when message content is simple and comprehension is less of a concern, live and video presentations appear to be more persuasive.

"On-Line" Persuasion

The past decade has seen the introduction of the Internet and the World Wide Web as mainstream communication modalities. These technological advances provide persuaders with an even wider array of media from which to attempt response shaping, reinforcing, and changing than were available even a few years ago. However, there has not been much research investigating the persuasive impact of "on-line" media. Moreover, the research that has been conducted is difficult to summarize as it focuses on many different questions relevant to persuasion in on-line settings (see, e.g., Hill & Monk, 2000; W. C. King, Dent, & Miles, 1991; see Fogg, Lee, & Marshall, 2002, for a recent review of the literature).

Our suspicion is that research on on-line persuasion will not generate straightforward effects. This is likely true in part because there are wide array of phenomenon that fall under the general rubric of on-line communication. For example, two or more individuals can interact via computer-mediated communication (CMC) as occurs in chat rooms, instant messaging, or e-mail. In other cases, an individual can interact not with another person but with a computer (i.e., human–computer communication, or HCC), as when an individual accesses a web site. Even these broad categories can be further subdivided. For example, CMC can be either synchronous, where individuals send and receive messages at the same time (e.g., instant messaging [ICQ-"I Seek You"] or chat rooms) or asynchronous, where messages are sent, read, and responded to at different times (e.g., e-mail). The nature of human–computer communication can also vary. Web sites might include exclusively text or also include graphics, sound files, and pictures and/or video clips that can either stand alone or accompany text.

As a consequence, there are a variety of communication media that fall under the "on-line" label. Given that on-line environments provide various forms of communication, the modality research reviewed above provides some suggestions for what might happen in on-line persuasion. Specifically there are on-line analogies to the print (i.e., text-only web sites), audio (sound files without accompanying text), and video (i.e., video clips) media discussed in the modality research. One important issue in on-line persuasion research, then, will likely be the extent to which the on-line media focus attention on the source of the message. Text-only presentations are unlikely to focus readers' attention on the source; however, video files where the sender can be seen presenting the message will. When the computer media focus attention on the source (e.g., a video clip of a source giving a speech), characteristics of message sources like source credibility will likely influence responses to the message.

As a consequence, there are likely important differences between forms of on-line persuasion. There will likely be modality effects in on-line persuasion just as we have reviewed above with traditional media. There are a number of differences between these forms of CMC and HCC that will likely have important influences on persuasion processes and outcomes. Perusing a web site for information on cancer prevention is likely to generate a different set of cognitive, emotional, and communication processes and persuasive outcomes when compared to interacting in a chat room with cancer survivors.

Another feature of some persuasive situations is the presence of distracting stimuli. The next section describes two types of distracting stimuli and examines this influence on persuasive outcomes.

PERSUASIVE EFFECTS OF DISTRACTING STIMULI

Many years ago, Jim went shopping for a waterbed and experienced firsthand the use of distraction as a persuasive strategy. He entered a waterbed store and was immediately approached by a slick salesperson who was eager to describe the line of waterbeds the store had to offer. After listening to his sales pitch for several minutes, Jim had some questions about the reliability of the mattress and heating element. Just as the salesperson stopped to ask if Jim had any questions about the beds, another salesperson came over and told us a joke that was in poor taste. After the second salesperson left, the first salesperson asked, "Well, are there any more questions I can answer before you make a decision?" When Jim reminded him that his partner's rude interruption prevented him from asking any questions at all, the salesperson looked somewhat disappointed. Luckily, Jim was able to recall the questions formulated prior to the interruption. At first, we were skeptical about whether the interruption was a planned distraction. After talking with several friends who were former salespeople, however, we became convinced that the distraction was indeed intentional. Most of these former salespeople indicated that planned interruptions were part of their sales pitches, and most believed these distractions facilitated their sales performance.

Fortunately, a large body of scientific research provides some insights about the practical application of distraction techniques. Since a seminal investigation by Festinger and Maccoby (1964), many persuasion scholars have examined the effects of a variety of distracting stimuli on the attitudes and behaviors of persuasive targets.

A cursory review of these investigations reveals that researchers have created a wide variety of stimuli that act as distractions in their studies. These various manipulations can be simplified by placing them into two relatively distinct categories of distraction research. One research tradition has conceptualized distractors as stimuli that are external to the message presentation. Many different *external distractors* have been manipulated in these studies, including using flashing lights (Osterhouse & Brock, 1970), playing audio feedback (Zimbardo & Ebbesen, 1970), and having receivers eat while they read a persuasive message (Janis, Kaye, & Kirschner, 1965). These distractors are hypothesized to divert attention away from the message presentation and toward the source of the distraction.

The second category of studies has conceptualized distractors as communicator-relevant behaviors. *Communicator-relevant distractors* are defined as behaviors that are intentionally manipulated by the speaker that cause receivers to shift attention away from the content of the message and toward characteristics of the speaker (Buller, 1986,

p. 109). Manipulations of this type of distractor include varying the synchrony of a source's nonverbal behaviors (Woodall & Burgoon, 1981), violating interpersonal distancing expectations (J. K. Burgoon, Stacks, & Burch, 1982), and using intense language (M. Burgoon, Cohen, Miller, & Montgomery, 1978).

Studies employing external and communicator-based distractors reflect researchers' fundamentally distinct questions about persuasive communication. Studies of external distractors are primarily concerned with the effect of distraction on message processing and subsequent attitude change. Conversely, studies of communicator-relevant distractors are primarily concerned with the effect of the distracting aspects of a source's communicative behavior on perceptions of source credibility and subsequent attitude change.

Examining the Effects of External Distraction

Researchers have developed a number of explanations for the persuasive effects of external distractions. However, two explanations, the *cognitive response* and the *information processing* theories of persuasion, have received the most attention. Cognitive response explanations were initially invoked to explain the findings of Festinger and Maccoby's (1964) seminal investigation. Shortly thereafter, McGuire (1966, 1969) applied information processing theories as an alternative explanation for distraction effects. The competing predictions offered by these two theoretical perspectives are considered in the following sections.

Cognitive Response Explanations

Cognitive response approaches to persuasion reflect a theoretical perspective that the cognitive responses (a fancy term for thoughts) generated by message receivers contribute significantly to the effectiveness of a persuasive appeal. These theorists argue that when receivers process a message, they generate favorable and/or unfavorable thoughts about the merits of the message recommendation. These self-generated thoughts combine with the message content itself to influence the postmessage attitudes and behaviors of receivers (see Chapter 10, this volume).

According to a cognitive response explanation, distracting stimuli interfere with the production of the predominant cognitive responses. That is, when the message recommendation is counterattitudinal, distraction is hypothesized to inhibit the production of the predominant cognitive response, that of counterarguments (Osterhouse & Brock, 1970; Zimbardo & Ebbesen, 1970). Recipients who are distracted will change their attitudes more (because they cannot generate the counterarguments that would inhibit attitude change) than recipients who are not distracted (and who are able to generate the full complement of counterarguments).

When the message recommendation is proattitudinal, distractors are hypothesized to limit a receiver's favorable thoughts about the message (Harkins & Petty, 1981; Insko, Turnbull, & Yandell, 1974; Petty, Wells, & Brock, 1976). Because they cannot generate as many positive cognitive responses as they would have without the distraction, recipients will exhibit less attitude change in response to a proattititudinal message when compared to recipients who are not distracted.

Thus, the number of positive cognitive responses and counterarguments produced by recipients are the important intervening variables between distraction and attitude change. Distraction should be negatively correlated with the number of positive cognitive responses, the number of counterarguments, and attitude change. While both positive cognitions and counterarguments are important components of the cognitive response explanations, most distraction studies only measure counterarguments, if they measure cognitive responses at all.

Information Processing Explanations

A second genre of explanations stems from Information Processing Theory. Information processing explanations suggest that in order for a message to be persuasive, the arguments and evidence contained in it must be received and understood by message recipients. Failure to learn the arguments supporting a recommendation should reduce the effectiveness of the persuasive appeal (McGuire, 1969).

According to information processing explanations, external distractors interfere with message comprehension and hence reduce the persuasiveness of the message. Because distractors divert attention away from the message, receivers have a more difficult time understanding the arguments and evidence supporting the message recommendations (Haaland & Venkatesen, 1968; Vohs & Garrett, 1968). Message comprehension, then, is the important intervening variable in information processing explanations of the persuasive effects of distraction. Specifically, both message recall and attitude change should be negatively correlated with distraction.

Specific Predictions and Supporting Evidence

In short, both the cognitive response and information processing explanations posit that distractors divert attention away from message processing and toward the distracting stimulus, but the hypothesized effects of this distraction differ. Cognitive response theorists argue that when the message is counterattitudinal, distraction inhibits counterargument generation, enhancing acceptance of the message recommendations. However, distraction interferes with the generation of favorable thoughts when the message recommendation is congruent with receiver attitudes, and thus inhibits the persuasive effects of the message.

Several investigations provide support for the first half of this prediction. For example, Osterhouse and Brock (1970) found that external distractors reduced the number of counterarguments generated by receivers and increased attitude change. However, evidence for the second half of the prediction has been limited. Petty and colleagues (1976) did find that distraction enhanced attitude change when the message presentation was counterattitudinal, and that it inhibited message acceptance when the message was proattitudinal. However, in this investigation, distraction was unrelated to the production of favorable thoughts and counterarguments, limiting confidence in the cognitive response explanation examined by the study.

Although investigations provided mixed support for the cognitive response explanation, other tests of distraction effects produced findings that are consistent with Information Processing Theory, which predicts that distraction interferes with message learning and reduces the effectiveness of persuasive messages. Studies supporting this explanation found that distraction reduced message recall (an indication of learning) and led to less acceptance of message recommendations (Haaland & Venkatesen, 1968; Vohs & Garrett, 1968).

Although the findings from these studies are contradictory, a meta-analytic review of this literature revealed some support for both explanations. However, support for the information processing hypothesis was somewhat stronger than for the cognitive response hypothesis (Buller, 1986). Across studies using a variety of different manipulations of external distraction, Buller (1986) consistently found that the number of counterarguments and message comprehension were both negatively correlated with attitude change. Across the types of distraction, however, Buller reported a consistently stronger negative relationship between distraction and message comprehension than between distraction and the generation of counterarguments. This finding provides stronger support for the information processing explanation than for the cognitive response explanation. A second finding from Buller's analysis—that, overall, distraction was negatively related to attitude change—provides additional support for the information processing explanation, although the relationships between distraction and attitude change varied across types of external distractions.

Thus, although some individual studies provide evidence for each of these explanations, a cumulative summary of these studies suggests that persuasive effects of an external distraction are mediated primarily by the distraction's negative effect on message comprehension. Several researchers have noted, however, that a significant distraction is needed to create the reduction in message comprehension necessary to reduce message effectiveness. That is, rather small distractors are unlikely to produce the significant reduction in comprehension necessary to reduce acceptance of message recommendations.

Examining the Effects of Communicator-Relevant Distraction

A second category of distraction studies has produced much more consistent findings. Investigations of communicator-relevant distraction hypothesize that the distraction diverts attention away from the content of the message presentation and toward the characteristics of the communicator. Information processing and cognitive responses are not central to this explanation. Instead, the persuasive effects of communicator-relevant distraction are dependent on features of the source that affect persuasion.

Studies of this type of distraction were analyzed separately in Buller's (1986) review. These analyses revealed that communicator-relevant distraction enhanced attitude change when the source was highly credible and decreased attitude change when the message source lacked credibility. The estimates for these effects were consistent across studies, though small in size. Nevertheless, the difference between the persuasive effect of communicator-relevant distraction among high-credibility ($r = .15$) and low-credibility ($r = -.10$) sources provides compelling support for the importance of this explanation. In addition, Buller found that communicator-relevant distraction was unrelated to counterarguing ($r = .00$) and message recall ($r = -.02$), providing further evidence of the distinction between source-based and external distractors.

Summary of Distraction Effects

Differences in the persuasive effects of external and communicator-based distraction underscore the importance of manipulations created by researchers in prior studies. More important, they provide a fuller understanding of situational features that affect the persuasion process. When a distraction that is external to the source occurs during a message presentation, it apparently shifts the attention of message receivers away from processing message content and toward the irrelevant distractor. The effect of this distraction appears to be a reduction in message comprehension and message effectiveness. It is important to note, however, that the different types of external distraction produced different relationships with attitude change, message comprehension, and counterarguments.

However, when distraction stems from the source of the message, the distractor shifts attention away from processing message content and toward the characteristics of the message source. The effectiveness of this type of distraction is dependent on the favorability of source characteristics. In this regard, the effects of communicator-relevant distractors mirror the modality effects discussed earlier in this chapter. In both cases, the effect is to increase the salience of source characteristics, which may enhance or restrict acceptance of the message recommendation.

PERSUASIVE INFLUENCES OF COLLECTIVES

Another important situational factor that influences persuasion is the presence of others. Every day, we spend a considerable amount of time working and socializing with other people. Whether we communicate in large organizations or small groups, we are rarely immune from the social influences of collectives (i.e., groups). Although communication scholars and social psychologists have sought to understand the persuasive effects of social and work collectives, these social effects are routinely neglected in persuasion textbooks. Though a complete discussion of these effects is beyond the scope of this book (see Boster & Cruz, 2002, for a recent review), the remainder of this chapter examines two types of influence that collectives have on their individual members. This section begins with a discussion of conformity effects and concludes with an examination of the persuasive effects of group discussion.

Conformity Effects

Most of the communicative messages that are exchanged in small groups and organizations are expressions of the values, beliefs, and goals of people in those small groups and organizations. Over time, these individual expressions are codified into a collective set of values, beliefs, and goals that establish a norm of acceptable behavior for individual group (or organization) members. Once these norms have been established, social pressure is exerted on individual members to adopt them. Pressures toward attitudinal and behavioral uniformity in collectives have been well documented (for a review, see Forsyth, 1999). *Conformity* is the general label for this genre of social influence processes and is commonly defined as "a change in attitude, belief, or behavior as a function of real or perceived group pressure" (Aronson, 1999, p. 17). People often conform because they perceive that the collective, or its individual members, exerts pressure on them to behave in a particular manner. However, overt pressure is not necessary to produce conforming behavior; all that is required is a *perception* of group pressure.

The Asch experiments provide a compelling example of the influence that collectives can have on their members. Solomon Asch (1955, 1956) was interested in the effect of apparent group consensus on the judgments of individuals. His experiment involved several confederates who played the role of research participants and an actual research participant who was naive about the purpose of the study. Asch presented the confederates and research participant with a series of card pairs. There were 18 pairs of cards in the series. For each pair, the first card contained three lines of different length. On the second card was a single line that was the same length as one of the lines on the first card. The task was to determine which line on the first card was the same length as the line on the second card.

When participants completed this task alone, they made correct judgments over 99% of the time. However, when they were placed in a group setting, their decisions were influenced by the choices of the confederates. Asch (1956) identified 12 of the 18 trials as critical trials. On the critical trials, confederates were instructed to choose the same wrong response. On the noncritical trials confederates were instructed to choose the correct response. The experimenter asked each of the confederates for their judgment before asking the naive research participant who was seated at the end of the row.

On each trial, the judgments of the confederates established a group norm. On the critical trials, this norm was obviously in error. Recall that participants who made these decisions alone were correct over 99% of the time, indicating that the correct response was obvious. Asch (1956) was interested in knowing how often research participants would choose the wrong response in order to conform with the group norm. The findings were remarkable. Asch found that more that 75% of the participants conformed to the group norm on at least one of the 12 critical trials. In fact, over 35% of the total judgments made on critical trials were in error! Although only a very small percentage of people conformed on all 12 critical trials, participants frequently conformed to the norm established by the group.

It bears mentioning that the confederates and participant in this study did not form a "group" in the everyday usage of the term. There was no group history, no group leader, and no anticipation of future group interaction. It also bears mentioning that the confederates exerted no overt pressure on the naive research participant: they simply established a norm by choosing the wrong response. As a consequence, conformity rates in the Asch (1956) studies are likely underestimates of what would be found in actual functioning groups. However, despite the fact that the participants in Asch's study had little commitment to the group and there was no overt pressure on them to conform, the pressures of an established group norm influenced them. Subsequent research has demonstrated that group norms can be quickly established, and that once established, members tend to maintain these norms even when group members are no longer present (M. Sherif & Sherif, 1956). These studies indicate the pervasive effect of conformity influences on individual behavior.

Conformity occurs in a variety of ways. Conformity occurs when an employee agrees with his or her boss's request to work late into the evening in order to complete an important project. Conformity also occurs when teenagers wear a particular brand of clothing or consume a particular soft drink because sports personalities and movie stars promote those products. Kelman (1958) provided a conceptual framework for categorizing conformity behavior by identifying *compliance, identification*, and *internalization* as three distinct types of conformity processes.

Compliance

When compliance occurs, people accept influence from a group or organization in hopes of attaining some reward or avoiding some punishment. Festinger (1953) defined this type of influence as "public conformity without private acceptance." That is, compliance does not require an actual change in attitude, only a change in observable behavior. People routinely engage in conforming behavior without changing their corresponding attitude or belief. For example, many drivers routinely exceed posted speed limits so long as they perceive they will not be caught. The sight of a highway patrol officer, however, triggers an immediate change in most people's driving behavior. The presence of the highway patrol officer increases the likelihood of sanctions for noncompliance and causes drivers to obey the speed limit or to exceed it only by an acceptable margin. The fact that many drivers routinely disobey posted speed limits suggests that they privately believe that the limits are unreasonable. In this case, surveillance and the threat of a fine are required to produce compliance with the law.

Compliance processes are not always motivated by a desire to avoid punishment. People often comply in order to gain rewards. A young professional may work overtime in hopes of impressing a supervisor and gaining consideration for an upcoming promotion. Hospital volunteers follow the rules and procedures of the hospital in order to enjoy emotionally rewarding work with patients. College students may agree to participate in a persuasion experiment in order to gain extra credit. Behaviors like these are motivated by the rewards they offer and not by the threat of reprisal.

Regardless of the motivation, however, the fundamental characteristic of compliance processes is that they are motivated by a desire to *avoid punishment* or to *gain a reward*. As a result, compliance is only effective so long as the controlling agent is likely to offer rewards for compliance or to apply sanctions for noncompliance. Although we have focused on the ways that collectives affect this type of conformity, compliance processes are also prominent in interpersonal interaction. In fact, Chapter 11 of this volume examines the large body of research that has investigated compliance processes in interpersonal settings.

Identification

A second type of conformity identified by Kelman is *identification*. When identification occurs, people accept influence from a controlling agent in order to "develop and maintain a favorable self-defining relationship with the controlling agent" (Kelman, 1958, p. 35). These self-defining relationships allow people to construct favorable self-images. Identification processes are often sufficiently subtle that they go unrecognized by sources and targets of influence. For example, college fraternity and sorority members often wear "Greek clothing" that identifies the organization to which they belong. Although the decision to purchase and wear clothing bearing an organization's label is clearly an identification process, few people would argue that this form of influence is a conscious effort to promote conformity among organization members. Nevertheless, these identification processes represent a type of conformity that facilitates the adoption of collective norms and values.

Though frequently subtle, identification processes can also be explicit. The "Be Like Mike" advertising campaign to promote a sports drink product is a prime example of an explicit identification appeal. The ad campaign, featuring basketball superstar Michael Jordan, encouraged people to "be like Mike" and drink the product. Though often less explicit, most ad campaigns that involve an endorsement by a sports figure derive their effectiveness from identification processes.

Kelman (1958) noted that the success of identification appeals is dependent on the maintenance of a favorable social relationship between the source of the influence and the target audience. As people grow, their attraction to reference groups changes, altering the effectiveness of persuasion agents who rely on identification processes. Because the social attractiveness of an individual, group, or organization is subject to rapid change, influence stemming from identification processes may not persist for extended periods of time.

Internalization

Kelman's (1958) third type of conformity was labeled *internalization*. Internalization processes are similar to traditional conceptions of attitude change. When people internalize a behavior, they do so after careful consideration of the reasons offered to adopt a particular behavior. This type of conformity is akin to Festinger's (1953) concept of public conformity with private acceptance. Thus, internalization involves changes in both behaviors and attitudes. In this regard, internalization reflects the use of rational message appeals (see Chapter 6, this volume) that are the cornerstone of Information Processing Theory (see Chapter 8, this volume).

Internalization is the type of conformity that is the most stable of Kelman's three types of conformity. Internalized behaviors stem from a person's beliefs and values, and thus are likely to persist in the absence of a controlling agent. Whereas behavior change created by compliance is dependent upon the presence of the controlling agent, behavior change created by internalization will endure so long as the attitudes, beliefs, and/or values last.

Summary of Conformity Effects

Regardless of their specific characteristics, conformity processes are a prominent form of social influence in collectives. Normative expectations emerge from interaction with other people, and once formed they exert pressure on people to conform with them. Although compliance, identification, and internalization are qualitatively distinct forms of conformity, they all stem from the desire of individuals in collectives to behave in a uniform fashion. Pressure toward uniformity is most apparent in group discussions that require a single decision. In the next section we extend the discussion of group influence by examining the effects of group discussion on the attitudes of individual members.

Polarization of Group Decisions

Another important influence of group interaction on the attitudes and behaviors of individual members is apparent from investigations of group decision-making processes. Beginning in the 1960s, social psychologists examined what was initially labeled the *risky shift phenomenon*, the tendency for groups to make more risky decisions than individuals. The discovery of the risky shift was a surprise because it was generally believed that groups are cautious and unwilling to make bold and risky decisions.

Investigations of the risky shift relied primarily on the methodology of a choice–dilemma item (Kogan & Wallach, 1967). This methodology presents research participants with a problem and two potential solutions. One solution is almost certain to resolve the dilemma and has a moderately rewarding outcome. The probability of success for the second alternative is less likely, but if successful it will provide a much more rewarding outcome. Perhaps the adage "A bird in the hand is worth two in the bush" represents the dilemma created by items like these. Respondents must choose between a certain, but less rewarding, alternative, and an uncertain, but potentially more rewarding, alternative. For example, financial planning often involves choosing between a safe investment that almost certainly will produce moderate profits and a risky investment that if successful will produce much greater returns, but if unsuccessful will lose money.

Researchers investigating this phenomenon typically ask research participants to read a choice–dilemma scenario and make an individual choice prior to participating in a group discussion of the dilemma. A risky shift is said to occur when the group decision, or average post-discussion choices of individual group members, is more risky than the average prediscussion decision of individual group members.

Using this methodology, several early investigations found that small-group discussions produced more risky choices than those made by individuals (Dion, Baron, & Miller, 1970; Kogan & Wallach, 1967). Subsequent research, however, found evidence that groups may also make more cautious decisions than individuals (Baron, Baron, & Roper, 1974; Stoner, 1968), leading researchers to relabel the risky shift phenomenon as the *polarity shift phenomenon*. That is, groups tend to make more extreme (or polar) decisions (either more risky or more cautious) than individuals. When the group is somewhat cautious to begin with, group discussion will generally produce cautious shifts. When groups are somewhat risky initially, discussion will generally produce a risky shift.

Since these initial investigations, several studies have provided evidence of a polarity shift phenomenon in group discussions (for reviews, see Boster, 1990; Lamm & Myers, 1978). How can these opinion shifts be explained? The most likely explanation stems from the influence of group interaction on the attitudes and judgments of individual group members. Two theoretical explanations that emphasize group communication have received most of the attention from researchers. Consistent with Deutsch and Gerard's (1955) distinction between normative and informational social influence, researchers have examined the merits of the *social comparison* and the *persuasive arguments* explanations of the polarity shift phenomenon.

Social Comparison Explanations

Social normative explanations of the polarity shift phenomenon evolved from Festinger's (1954) description of Social Comparison Theory and Deutsch and Gerard's (1955) concept of normative social influence. Social Comparison Theory posits that people are concerned about the correctness or appropriateness of positions they hold, and this concern motivates them to validate their positions through interaction with others. In highly ambiguous situations, people are less certain about the validity of their positions, so social comparison processes become more likely. Consistent with the earlier discussion of conformity effects, discussion about a particular issue creates a social norm. Once a norm has been established, normative social influence is exerted on group members to conform to the normative position.

Social comparison processes occur in daily interaction. For example, college students often engage in social comparison processes after an exam when they gather just outside the classroom to discuss their impressions about the test's difficulty, fairness, and so forth. Students engage in this comparison process to reduce their uncertainty about the exam. Social pressure to conform to a normative position about the perceived difficulty of the exam may be limited, but a normative position is likely to emerge during discussions like these. That is, students participating in these discussions may collectively conclude that the whole exam was difficult or that a particular question was unfair.

In much the same fashion, group discussions are social comparison processes that produce normative positions about the issue under consideration. The fundamental assumption of Social Comparison Theory is that people view themselves as a better than the average group member on abilities, traits, and attitudes that are valued by the group (Lamm & Myers, 1978, p. 176). Lamm and Myers (1978) provide a variety of evidence to support this assumption, including findings that most businesspeople view themselves as more ethical than the average businessperson (Baumhart, 1968) and research indicating that most people perceive they are less prejudiced than the average person (Lenihan, 1965). But, as Lamm and Myers point out, people's perceptions that they are superior to the average person are distorted (to say nothing of self-serving) because "the average person is not better than the average person" (p. 176).

Applied to the polarity shift phenomenon, a social comparison (or normative influence) explanation posits that our desire to view ourselves more favorably than we view the average person affects the extremity of the positions we advocate. That is, social comparison processes in group discussions disconfirm the average group member's belief that his or her position is more favorable (i.e., extreme in the right direction) than the group norm. If discussion reveals that the group favors a cautious position, then members striving to maintain the perception that they are more favorable than the average group member will advocate a position that is more cautious than the group norm. On the other hand, if group discussion reveals a risky norm, then members will endorse a position that is more risky than the group norm. The result of social comparison processes is to cause individuals to endorse a more extreme position, either more risky or more cautious, than the group norm. The result of these individual position shifts is a postdiscussion position that is more extreme than the prediscussion position of the group.

Persuasive Arguments Explanations

An alternative explanation of the polarity shift phenomenon is more straightforward. The persuasive arguments explanation posits that group discussions expose members to novel arguments that are persuasive. Consistent with Information Processing Theory, this explanation holds that if the group norm favors a cautious position, then the distribution of these novel arguments is likely to be skewed in the cautious direction, that is, a greater proportion of novel arguments will favor a cautious position than a risky one. On the other hand, if group members favor a risky position, then a greater proportion of novel arguments are likely to favor risk more than caution.

The informational influence of these novel arguments is hypothesized to produce the shifts in group discussions. Group discussions produce more reasons for advocating the normative group position than individual members could develop on their own. Armed with these additional new arguments, individual members become more confident in their judgments and advocate a more extreme position following group discussion. Thus, when the group norm favors caution, group discussion should produce a more cautious decision than the average prediscussion decision of individual group members. However, if the normative position is risky, group discussion should produce a decision that is more risky than the average prediscussion position of individual group members.

Testing Competing Explanations

Examining the validity of these two explanations is a difficult task. Social comparison explanations posit that all that is required to produce a group shift is knowledge of the positions held by group members. Persuasive arguments explanations argue that information content, and not the normative positions of individual members, is responsible for the polarity shift phenomenon.

Unfortunately, these two forms of information (i.e., the attitudes that members hold and the arguments supporting those attitudes) are confounded in naturally occurring group discussions. As Boster (1990) aptly noted, an argument offered during group discussion contains both types of information: it provides an indication of another member's position on the issue as well as his or her reasons for advocating that position. Thus, if the argument is persuasive, social comparison theorists might conclude that it was due to the statement of opinion contained in the argument and not to the argument itself. However, persuasive arguments theorists would contend that the argument itself was persuasive. Conversely, if a person offered an opinion statement with no explicit argument to support it, social comparison theorists would argue that any persuasive effects were caused by the normative information in the opinion statement. However, persuasive arguments theorists might conclude that opinion statements include implicit arguments, and that these arguments, rather than group pressure, are responsible for the persuasive effects of the message (Boster, 1990, p. 305).

To examine each of these explanations, researchers have employed a variety of experimental procedures that systematically control group composition and the number of risky and cautious arguments that emerge during group discussion. For example, one study created groups with either a risky or a cautious majority by selecting members on the basis of their prediscussion responses to a choice–dilemma item. These groups then discussed an issue that tended to produce either a risky or a cautious shift (Boster, Fryrear, Mongeau, & Hunter, 1982). These researchers argued that a group's composition and the type of choice–dilemma item they discussed would combine to influence the number of risky and cautious arguments that emerged in group discussion. Boster and Mayer (1984) employed a more direct manipulation of persuasive arguments and normative influences by having research participants observe videotaped discussions that varied both the number of arguments favoring a risky and a cautious position *and* the majority of group members with risky and cautious positions. Although this procedure did not involve research subjects in a group discussion, it more precisely controlled the social normative information and persuasive arguments to which they were exposed.

Investigations like these have examined the relative merits of the social comparison and persuasive arguments explanations (for reviews, see Lamm & Myers, 1978; Mayer, 1986). Support for the social comparison explanation has been found in studies where participants altered their positions after being exposed solely to the positions of others. Evidence of this *mere exposure effect* was found in a meta-analysis of group polarization experiments. Isenberg (1986) reported that the average effect of social comparison processes in these studies was substantial ($r = .44$).

Considerable support has also been found for the persuasive arguments explanation. In fact, Isenberg's review found the average effect of persuasive arguments processes was quite strong ($r = .75$). Indeed, further support for the persuasive arguments explanation has emerged from studies employing the Linear Discrepancy Model (see Chapter 8, this volume) to explain group polarization effects (Boster et al., 1982; Boster, Mayer, Hunter, & Hale, 1980).

Evidence supporting both explanations might cause one to question whether social comparison or persuasive arguments influences are responsible for the group polarization effects. Most likely, both social normative and informational influences affect polarity shifts in group discussions (Boster, 1990). One study that was designed to examine the relative importance of both processes found evidence supporting both explanations, although the persuasive arguments explanation accounted for more variance in polarity shifts than the social comparison explanation did (Mayer, 1986). This finding is consistent with Isenberg's (1986) meta-analytic review, which found a much stronger persuasive arguments effect, though the influence of social comparison processes was also large. Furthermore, a strong correlation between the persuasive arguments and social comparison effects led Isenberg to conclude that "at this point in time there is very good evidence that there are two conceptually independent processes even though outside of the laboratory they almost always co-occur" (p. 1149). Regardless of the relative contributions of these theoretical processes, investigations of the polarity shift phenomenon provide compelling evidence for the influence groups have on their individual members.

What Do Persuasive Arguments Look Like?

While there is a good deal of research consistent with the persuasive arguments explanation of polarization (Isenberg, 1986), relatively little of this research helps us to identify what aspects of group discussions that are persuasive. Renée Meyers and her associates have spent a considerable amount of time trying to understand the interactive processes that create persuasive arguments effects in group discussions (e.g., Meyers, 1989; Meyers, Brashers, & Hanner, 2000; Meyers & Seibold, 1990). In a recent study, Meyers and colleagues (2000) analyzed the arguments made by attitudinal majority and minority group factions and by the winners and losers in a decision-making context.

In the Meyers and colleagues (2000) study, 15 groups were asked to discuss and reach consensus on three issues. Myers and colleagues categorized group members as being in the attitudinal minority or in the attitudinal majority, based on their prediscussion opinions. Meyers et al. also identified the winning and losing factions by identifying the subgroup that held the attitude that was consistent with the group's final decision. Adapting the Conversational Argument Coding Scheme (Canary, Brossman, & Seibold, 1987), Meyers and colleagues investigated the arguments made by the winning and the losing factions on each issue.

Consistent with prior research, they found that the initial attitudinal majority "won" the discussion (i.e., the eventual group decision was consistent with their initial positions) nearly 80% of the time. They also found some important differences between the arguments made by the attitudinal majority and minority subgroups. Majority factions used more statements indicating agreement with other group members (i.e., bolstering; "That's a good point, Jim, I agree with you") and fewer statements of disagreement when compared to minority faction members. Statements of agreement reinforced the perception of majority faction unanimity (what they referred to as "tag-team arguing") because while just one person might present an argument, other faction members can validate it with bolstering comments. Tag-team arguing can also occur when one member extends the argument begun by another faction member. This bolstering and tag-team arguing is, in itself, persuasive.

Members of minority factions, on the other hand, were less likely to use agreements and spent more time disagreeing with the majority faction. If you are the lone dissenting voice in a group, you have no one to agree with and your only choice may be to disagree with the larger majority. This suggests that attitudinal minority factions will be more persuasive when they have at least two members. Minority factions with multiple members can use the same bolstering and tag-team arguing that is typical for majorities.

Meyers and colleagues (2000) also found differences in the arguments made by winning and losing factions. Their findings regarding winning minorities were particularly interesting. It has long been suggested that in order to be persuasive, attitudinal minorities have to be consistent in the way that they present their arguments (e.g., Moscovici, Lage, & Naffrechoux, 1969). Meyers and colleagues confirmed this general belief and reported that those attitudinal minorities that ended up convincing the initial majority were those who argued most consistently. In order to win the argument, however, a consistent minority had to be pitted against a less consistent majority. Moreover, the more consistent the arguments presented by a particular faction, the less likely those faction members were to change their attitudes during the discussion. This was particularly true for losing, as opposed to winning, subgroups.

SUMMARY

The present chapter examined characteristics of persuasive situations that influence the attitudes and behaviors of persuasive targets. Persuasive effects of the mode of message presentation appear to be moderated by characteristics of the message and the message source. Live and video presentations focus attention on message sources and enhance the persuasiveness of highly attractive and credible sources. Written presentations were found to be more effective for complex messages that are difficult to understand.

Distracting stimuli are a second category of situational factors that affect the persuasiveness of messages. Distractions that are external to the message source seem to interfere with message learning and restrict the persuasiveness of the message. However, the effect of communicator-based distractions is to direct attention toward the message source, enhancing the persuasiveness of highly credible sources and restricting the effectiveness of less credible sources.

Finally, investigations of conformity effects and the polarization of individual attitudes provided clear evidence of the influence that collectives have on their individual members. Conformity research suggests that social norms are developed in the presence of others. Once these norms are established, groups and organizations exert influence on their members to adopt them. Investigations of the polarity shift phenomenon reflect a different type of influence that groups have on individual members. These investigations found that group discussion causes individuals to advocate more extreme positions (either risky or cautious) than they did prior to group discussion. Social comparison effects and the influence of novel persuasive arguments are two prominent explanations that account for these effects.

Part III

Persuasion Models

This last part of the book describes persuasion models that incorporate the essential features of persuasive transactions discussed in Part II. This part is divided into four chapters. Chapter 10 reviews several models of persuasion that emphasize message recipients' cognitive processes and their influence on the persuasion process. Chapters 11 and 12 review research traditions on interpersonal influence: Chapter 11 focuses on the effectiveness (or ineffectiveness) of several compliance-gaining strategies, while Chapter 12 focuses on the research and theorizing on producing and resisting those strategies. Finally, Chapter 13 examines models of persuasive communication that are frequently employed in media campaigns.

10

Cognitive Models of Persuasion

LOOKING AHEAD ...

In this chapter we discuss cognitive models of persuasion. These models incorporate the essential elements of persuasive activity that we discussed in previous chapters into a set of cohesive predictions about persuasive communication. After discussing how people cognitively process messages, we describe and evaluate two dual-process models, the Elaboration Likelihood Model (ELM) and the Heuristic Model of Persuasion (HMP), which explain how people's cognitive responses influence the effectiveness of persuasive messages. Finally, we discuss the Unimodel, a recent rival to the dual-process models.

Early persuasion research largely examined the influence of source and message factors on the psychological processes that affect message recipients' attitudes and behaviors. By the early 1960s, however, persuasion scholars began to consider the importance of message receivers in the attitude change process. For example, Inoculation Theory (McGuire, 1964) described a technique for increasing people's resistance to persuasive attempts by providing them with counterarguments. Armed with such arguments, people are somewhat more effective at counterarguing a subsequent persuasive appeal. This focus on individual responses to persuasive appeals became more pronounced by the late 1960s and has since evolved into present-day cognitive theories of persuasion.

The concept of cognitive processing during message reception is not new. Early persuasion scholars sowed the seeds of this contemporary approach to persuasion. Indeed, one of the earliest programs of persuasion research suggested that an audience can protect itself against persuasion by going over its own arguments against the persuasion while hearing a presentation (Hovland et al., 1949).

The primary assumption of many cognitive theories of persuasion is that message receivers may play an active role in the formation, reinforcement, and change of their own attitudes and behaviors. According to this approach, when people are exposed to a persuasive message presentation, they attempt to integrate the message appeal with their existing attitudes and knowledge about the topic. In the course of this integration process, message recipients may generate additional arguments and information to support or oppose the message recommendation. These self-generated thoughts and arguments contribute in important ways to the overall persuasiveness of the message. To the extent that the communication evokes favorable thoughts in message recipients, receiver-generated cognitions should enhance the effectiveness of the persuasive appeal. If, however, the communication evokes counterarguing by message recipients, receivers' cognitive responses are likely to inhibit the persuasiveness of the appeal.

Two empirical issues are fundamental to the utility of this theoretical perspective. First, research must document that people generate favorable and unfavorable thoughts as they process persuasive messages and that these self-generated thoughts influence their attitudes about the message recommendation. Second, research must identify characteristics of persuasive situations that affect the production and valence of these cognitive responses.

This first issue was the focus of a program of research by Abraham Tesser and his colleagues (Sadler & Tesser, 1973; Tesser, 1978; Tesser & Conlee, 1975), who established a link between cognitive processes and attitudes. More recently, two models, the Elaboration Likelihood Model (ELM; Petty & Cacioppo, 1981, 1986; Petty & Wegener, 1999) and the Heuristic Model of Persuasion (HMP; Chaiken, 1987; Chen & Chaiken, 1999), have sought to address the second issue by identifying factors that motivate and guide the generation of these cognitive responses. Details of these research programs are presented in the following sections of the chapter.

THE PERSUASIVE EFFECTS OF "MERE THOUGHT"

A basic assumption of cognitive models of persuasion is that people are capable of recalling and evaluating previously held information about a particular issue as they process persuasive messages. These self-generated cognitions (thoughts) combine with message content and the persuasive characteristics of the communicator to affect a receiver's evaluation of the message recommendation. To demonstrate the existence and influence of these self-generated thoughts on subsequent evaluation of a stimulus object, Tesser and his colleagues conducted a series of investigations of the effects of "mere thought" on attitudes (Sadler & Tesser, 1973; Tesser, 1978; Tesser & Conlee, 1975).

In the first study, research participants were told that they were participating in a study of "first impressions" (Sadler & Tesser, 1973). Participants were told they were being matched with another person in an adjoining cubicle and asked to briefly introduce themselves. After giving their own self-descriptions, participants listened to a simulated self-description of their partner via a recorded message. Half of the participants heard a description of a likeable person and half heard a less favorable description. Following these introductions, half of the participants were asked to think about the person who had just been described and half were asked to complete an irrelevant task. The irrelevant task was designed to distract participants from thinking about the description they had just heard. Following the relevant or irrelevant thinking task, participants evaluated their partner.

As expected, participants evaluated the likeable partner more positively than the unlikable partner. More important, these differences were most pronounced among the participants who were given time to think about their partner before offering their impressions. That is, when offered a chance to think about their partner, people's reactions became more extreme, in either a positive or a negative direction, depending on the valence of the initial introduction (Sadler & Tesser, 1973).

A second study examined the effects of the amount of time spent thinking about a political issue on evaluation of that issue. In two experiments, Tesser and Conlee (1975) found a direct positive relationship between the amount of time participants spent thinking about an issue and the polarization of their attitudes about the issue. It is likely, however, that this positive linear relationship does not extend indefinitely. For example, Tesser (1978) found that the positive relationship between self-reported thought and attitude polarization diminished after a period of several minutes. As Tesser noted, "Thoughtful people simply don't walk around with more and more extreme attitudes" (p. 301). Indeed, there seem to be practical limits to the persuasive effects of the "mere thought" phenomenon.

Nevertheless, these studies document the influence of self-generated thoughts on the evaluation of stimulus objects. Whether the object under consideration is a political issue or another person, the opportunity to think about the stimulus object is likely to make favorable evaluations more favorable and unfavorable evaluations more unfavorable. This attitude polarization process is similar to the group polarization effects discussed in Chapter 9 of this volume. In the present case, however, *biased processing* (i.e., recalling either primarily favorable or primarily unfavorable thoughts) is the result of individual cognitive processes rather than of group interaction.

Tesser (1978) argued that the persuasive effects of "mere thought" were guided by individuals' cognitive structures. Cognitive schemas assist information processing by directing attention toward certain stimuli and away from others and by providing rules for making inferences about the stimuli under evaluation. In the case of the Sadler and Tesser (1973) study, the likeable (unlikeable) introduction served to activate favorable (unfavorable) cognitive structures that guided the generation of thoughts about the stimulus object. These cognitive structures result in biased processing by affecting the favorableness (unfavorableness) of self-generated thoughts and information recall. For example, evaluating an individual as "outgoing" (a positive trait) is likely to produce other positively evaluated characteristics (e.g., sociable, fun to be around, socially attractive). Thus, when given time to think about an issue, people who favorably evaluate the issue are likely to generate mostly favorable thoughts about the issue, while people with unfavorable evaluations are likely to generate mostly unfavorable thoughts. Combined with research on cognitive schemas, Tesser's investigations of the "mere thought" phenomenon establish an important link between individual cognitive responses toward a stimulus object and evaluations of that object.

Applied to persuasive transactions, this body of research suggests that message recipients' thought processes play a significant role in determining the effectiveness of a persuasive message. Investigations of several different persuasive phenomena have established that people are capable of generating their own arguments to support a message recommendation (Vinokur & Burnstein, 1974) or to oppose it (M. Burgoon et al., 1978; McGuire, 1961b; G. R. Miller & Burgoon, 1978). For example, Hample (1978) argued that if a persuasive message contained no evidence supporting the claim, receivers would add the missing information from information they have in memory. Given the potential persuasive influence of self-generated arguments, researchers have focused attention on the processes that guide the generation of these cognitive responses and determine their persuasive effects.

During the 1980s, two contemporaneous programs of research attempted to model factors that affect the production of cognitive responses to persuasive messages and explain the influence of these self-generated thoughts on individual attitudes. The Elaboration Likelihood Model (ELM) of persuasion (Petty & Cacioppo, 1981, 1986) has received the most attention from persuasion scholars and is most closely associated with traditional cognitive response approaches to persuasion (see Petty et al., 1981). A second model, the Heuristic Model of Persuasion (HMP; Chaiken, 1987), is more firmly rooted in theories of social cognition. Though the two models are similar in many respects, important differences exist between them. Because their differences are more subtle than their obvious similarities, students of persuasion often discuss these models as though their conceptual components are interchangeable. However, the theoretical differences between these two programs of research necessitate a separate discussion of the respective models.

THE ELABORATION LIKELIHOOD
MODEL OF PERSUASION

The ELM evolved from a dissatisfaction with the contradictory findings of various theoretical approaches to studying persuasive communication. Based on their review of prior persuasion research, Petty and Cacioppo (1981) argued that many of these approaches reflect one of two distinct routes to persuasion. The *central route* to persuasion is marked by a careful scrutiny of message content and posits that attitude change is a function of message content and recipients' self-generated thoughts (what Petty & Cacioppo [1981, 1986] called "elaboration"). A second general approach, the *peripheral route*, reflects an attitude change process that is marked by the association of message recommendations with positive or negative cues in the message environment (Petty & Cacioppo, 1981).

The ELM posits that when message receivers engage in central processing, characteristics of persuasive messages (particularly a variable called "argument quality") determine the extent and direction of attitude change. When people engage in peripheral processing, persuasive cues that are peripheral to the message itself (e.g., source expertise, source trustworthiness, source attractiveness, and message length) determine the extent and direction of attitude change.

Distinguishing between Central
and Peripheral Processing

Given the distinction between central and peripheral routes to persuasion, the primary goal of the ELM is to identify the conditions under which message receivers engage in central and peripheral processing. The ELM's first two postulates were derived to assist in this prediction process. The primary postulate of this model is that people are motivated to hold "correct" attitudes. Referring to Festinger's (1954) Social Comparison Theory, Petty and Cacioppo argued as follows: "Incorrect or improper attitudes are generally maladaptive and can have deleterious behavioral, affective, and cognitive consequences" (1986, p. 6). As a result, people are often motivated to actively process persuasive messages in an effort to adopt an appropriate or correct attitude about message recommendations. However, the ELM's second postulate recognizes that although people are often motivated to maintain correct attitudes, they simply cannot actively process every persuasive message in the environment. As a consequence, the ELM posits that the amount of cognitive effort people are willing or able to engage in to process persuasive appeals varies widely across people and situations (Petty & Cacioppo, 1986, p. 6).

To represent the range of processing activity available to message receivers, Petty and Cacioppo (1986) introduced the concept of an *elaboration likelihood continuum*. One end of this continuum represents highly active cognitive processing, in which message receivers scrutinize message content and generate their own cognitive responses to it. According to the ELM, when conditions are ripe for this type of message processing, elaboration likelihood is high and the central route to persuasion is most probable. Issue-relevant thoughts generated by receivers during message elaboration affect attitude change and contribute to the overall effectiveness of the message. If these thoughts are favorable toward the message recommendation, acceptance of the message recommendation is more likely. Conversely, thoughts opposing the message recommendation are likely to decrease acceptance.

The other end of the continuum represents message processing that requires very little cognitive effort. Instead of paying careful attention to message content, receivers rely on persuasive cues in the message environment to make decisions about message recommendations. When conditions are ripe for this type of processing, elaboration likelihood is low and the peripheral route to persuasion is most probable. When receivers use a peripheral route to persuasion, positive persuasion cues in the message environment (e.g., a highly attractive source) increase message acceptance, whereas negative persuasion cues decrease message acceptance.

Predicting Message Elaboration

The ELM's second postulate suggests that cognitive elaboration of persuasive messages varies across people and situations. Thus, the crux of this model is identifying the conditions under which message elaboration is likely to occur. Though a variety of situational and personal character-istics may affect elaboration likelihood, two factors, *motivation* and *ability*, have received the most attention from ELM researchers.

Motivation

Message receivers must be motivated to hold a socially appropriate or correct attitude on a particular issue before they will engage in effortful cognitive elaboration of a persuasive message on that issue. One factor that reflects the motivation of message recipients is the personal rele-vance of the issue. Accordingly, receivers who perceive a high degree of outcome-relevant involvement (see Chapter 8, this volume) should be motivated to carefully scrutinize message content in hopes of making the correct decision about the message recommendation. Though a variety of other factors, such as need for social approval and self-monitoring, may also influence a person's motivation to scrutinize a message, out-come-relevant involvement has been used most often to manipulate re-ceiver motivation in prior ELM research (see Petty & Cacioppo, 1986; Petty & Wegener, 1998, 1999).

One individual difference characteristic that affects a person's moti-vation, and perhaps his or her ability, to elaborate message content is *need for cognition* (A. Cohen, Stotland, & Wolfe, 1955). This personal-ity characteristic was developed to reflect differences among individuals in their "need to engage in and enjoy effortful cognitive endeavors" (Petty & Cacioppo, 1986, p. 48). Questionnaire measures of this con-struct were refined by Cacioppo and Petty (1982, 1984), and have been employed to represent another motivational factor that influences elabo-ration likelihood. Although this factor has been considered mainly to reflect a person's motivation to scrutinize persuasive messages, it may also reflect a person's ability to do so. If you have a high need for cogni-tion and routinely scrutinize persuasive message content, you are likely to develop the cognitive skills necessary to effectively scrutinize even very difficult messages. Thus, people with a strong need for cognition are probably better able to scrutinize message content than people with relatively little need for cognition.

Ability

A second factor that affects message elaboration is cognitive ability. Ac-cording to the ELM, recipients must be both willing *and* able to cognitively elaborate message content. ELM researchers have largely ig-nored this factor, although investigations of message comprehension un-derscore the importance of this variable. For example, distracting stimuli

(Buller, 1986), message distortion (Eagly, 1974; Eagly & Warren, 1976), and message difficulty (Chaiken & Eagly, 1976) have all been found to reduce message learning and comprehension, thereby affecting cognitive evaluation of message content. Though many persuasive situations involve message recipients who have the cognitive ability to elaborate message content, message presentations that are difficult to understand are less likely to result in cognitive elaboration.

In summary, the ELM posits that receivers must be willing and able to cognitively elaborate messages in order to travel the central route to persuasion. Outcome-relevant involvement is one factor that reflects motivation, message comprehensibility is one factor that affects ability, and need for cognition is an individual factor that probably affects both motivation and ability to scrutinize message content.

Message Elaboration and Attitude Change

The ELM's predictions regarding message processing are straightforward: "As motivation and/or ability to process arguments is decreased, peripheral cues become relatively more important determinants of persuasion. Conversely, as argument scrutiny is increased, peripheral cues become relatively less important determinants of persuasion" (Petty & Cacioppo, 1986, p. 5). That is, when central processing occurs, the quality of message arguments (i.e., argument quality) will influence attitudes more than peripheral cues in the persuasive situation. However, when peripheral processing is predominant, message arguments become relatively unimportant and persuasion cues external to the message itself affect attitude change. Thus, when people centrally process a message, its persuasiveness depends mostly on the quality of the arguments and their supporting evidence. When people engage in peripheral processing, the persuasive appeal's effectiveness depends mostly on the valence of persuasive cues, including source credibility and source attractiveness.

An impressive number of experiments have examined the validity of the ELM, though for the most part these investigations have employed the same experimental procedure. This general procedure evolved from original tests of the model that we discussed in Chapter 2 (Petty, Cacioppo, & Goldman, 1981). This procedure involves creating two persuasive messages that advocate the same position (typically a tuition increase or comprehensive exams for undergraduate students). One message contains strong arguments supporting the message recommendation and the other contains weak arguments. These messages are attributed to a highly or less expert source as they are presented to research participants (usually college students).

To control the motivation factor, experimenters usually tell half of the message recipients that the message is personally relevant to them, and tell the remaining participants that the message has little relevance for them. For example, when messages advocate a tuition increase or comprehensive exams, half of the student participants are told that the advocated action will begin the following year, while the remaining participants are told that the recommended action is not scheduled to occur for several years (or will occur at another university). When the recommended action is proposed for the recipients' school and for the following year, outcome-relevant involvement is high for students who are not in the final year of their degree program. When the recommended action is proposed for several years in the future (and/or at another school), the message has low outcome-relevant involvement for message recipients.

The three variables manipulated with this procedure reflect three important components of the ELM. Receiver motivation to scrutinize message content is manipulated by varying levels of outcome-relevant involvement.[1] Argument quality represents a central cue that may or may not be scrutinized by message recipients, and source expertise represents a peripheral cue that is external to the message content.[2] Consistent with ELM predictions, Petty and his colleagues have repeatedly found that under conditions of high outcome-relevant involvement, argument quality has a stronger effect on attitudes than source expertise. When receiver involvement is low, the source expertise manipulation routinely has a much stronger effect on attitudes than the argument quality manipulation (see Petty & Cacioppo, 1986). In statistical terms, two two-way interactions provide support for the ELM. In the first interaction, outcome-relevant involvement and argument quality combine to affect attitudes (Figure 10.1). In this case, argument quality has a stronger impact on attitudes when outcome-relevant involvement is high, compared to when outcome-relevant involvement is low. The second interaction reflects the combined effects of outcome-relevant involvement and source expertise on attitudes (Figure 10.2). Specifically, source credibility will have a stronger impact on attitudes when outcome-relevant involvement is low (compared to when it is high).

Evaluating the Utility of the ELM

The ELM is an important theory of persuasion. The metaphor of the central and peripheral routes of persuasion and the corresponding prediction that different variables are likely to influence responses at the extremes of the elaboration likelihood continuum are powerful ideas. For example, until the ELM came along, reviewers found it impossible to explain inconsistencies in the persuasive impact of evidence (see Chapter 6). More recent reviews all conclude that evidence influences

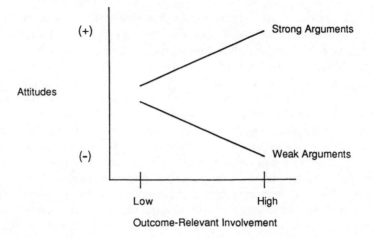

FIGURE 10.1. Combined effect of outcome-relevant involvement and argument quality on attitudes.

attitude change when receivers actively cognitively process the message (e.g., Reinard, 1988; Reynolds & Reynolds, 2002).

Although Petty and Cacioppo, and their colleagues, have mar-shaled considerable evidence in support of the ELM, several investiga-tions have raised a number of concerns about the logical validity and

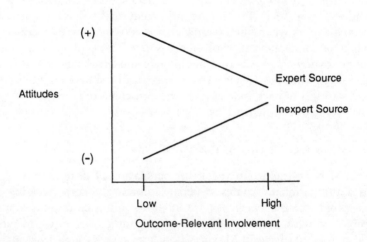

FIGURE 10.2. Combined effect of outcome-relevant involvement and source ex-pertise on attitudes.

practical utility of this model. These concerns stem from the theoretical specificity of the model and the quality of empirical support for the model.

Theoretical Limitations of the ELM

In the first published critique of the ELM, Jim questioned the extent to which it accurately reflected human information processing capacities (Stiff, 1986) and argued that the ELM depicted humans as single-channel information processors. Single-channel information processors can only deal with one stream of information at a time. Jim argued that this was inconsistent with theories of information processing that argue that humans are capable of parallel information processing (i.e., dealing with two simultaneous streams of data; see Kahneman, 1973; Stiff, 1986). At issue is whether people are able to engage in both central and peripheral processing of persuasive messages simultaneously. If message content and peripheral cues can be processed in parallel, then both types of information may simultaneously affect attitudes. However, as articulated by Petty and Cacioppo, the ELM postulates "a trade-off between argument elaboration and the operation of peripheral cues" (Petty & Cacioppo, 1986, p. 21). This postulate led to an interpretation of the ELM as a single-channel processing model (Stiff, 1986).

The practical implication of this debate centers on the persuasive effects of variables that are processed centrally and peripherally. That is, in many persuasive situations (but not all of them; see Petty & Wegener, 1999), message arguments are processed centrally and persuasive cues (e.g., source characteristics) are processed peripherally. In these situations, single-channel processing models would predict that either message arguments or persuasive cues are processed and subsequently influence attitudes. Conversely, parallel processing models predict the simultaneous evaluation of both message and source characteristics and specify that both types of processing may contribute independently or together to influence attitude change. Specifically, parallel processing models allow for equal contributions from both types of processing, a clear departure from the processing trade-off described by Petty and Cacioppo (1986, p. 21).

To reflect the persuasive effects of parallel processing, Jim (Stiff, 1986) proposed an alternative persuasion model derived from Kahneman's (1973) Elastic Capacity Model (ECM) of human information processing. Applied in persuasive settings, the ECM posits that message receivers are capable of parallel processing and specifies the conditions under which they engage in central and peripheral processing. Specifically, the ECM predicts that under conditions of low outcome-relevant involvement, receivers engage in *neither* central nor peripheral process-ing because they are unmotivated to do so. At moderate levels of involvement, receivers are motivated to engage in *both* central and peripheral (i.e., parallel) processing. At high levels of involvement, although the ECM admits that parallel processing is possible, the ECM specifies that receivers will focus attention on a single processing task. Given the importance of holding an appropriate position on the issue, Jim hypothesized that central processing of the message would receive the primary attention of highly involved receivers (Stiff, 1986).

The predictive differences between the ELM and Jim's application of the ECM are apparent. The ELM predicts a negative relationship be-tween a person's level of involvement and the influence of peripheral processing on attitudes and a positive relationship between involvement and the influence of central processing on attitudes (Figure 10.3). Con-versely, applied in persuasive settings, the ECM predicts a curvilinear (inverted-U-shaped) relationship between receiver involvement and the influence of peripheral processing on attitudes. Similar to the ELM, however, the ECM predicts a positive linear relationship between re-ceiver involvement and the influence of central processing on attitudes (Figure 10.4).

A meta-analytic review of the persuasion literature tested the pre-dictions of the ELM and the ECM (Stiff, 1986). Results of the meta-analysis that focused on central processing were consistent with both the ELM and the ECM. Specifically, Stiff (1986) reported a positive linear

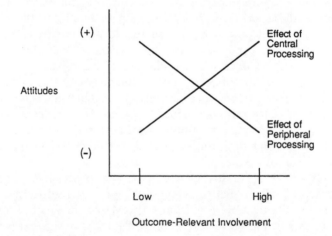

FIGURE 10.3. Effects of central and peripheral processing on attitudes across levels of outcome-relevant involvement as predicted by the ELM.

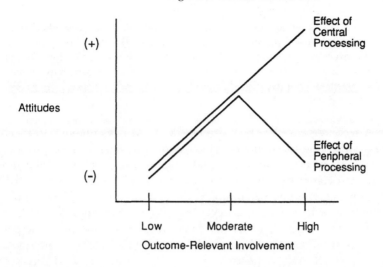

FIGURE 10.4. Effects of central and peripheral processing on attitudes across levels of outcome-relevant involvement as predicted by the ELM.

relationship between outcome-relevant involvement and the effects of supporting information on attitudes. In short, the higher the involvement, the stronger an impact supporting information had on attitudes (Stiff, 1986).

Jim's meta-analytic review also found a curvilinear relationship between receiver involvement and the effects of source credibility on attitudes. Source credibility influenced attitude change most strongly at moderate (when compared to both low and high) levels of outcome-relevant involvement. Assuming that source credibility effects reflected peripheral processing, this latter finding is consistent with the ECM and incompatible with the ELM (Stiff, 1986).

At the time, Petty and his associates rejected Stiff's model and the data supporting it (see Petty et al., 1987; Stiff & Boster, 1987). In response to the depiction of the ELM as a single-channel processing model, Petty and his colleagues argued that their description of the ELM "does not mean that people are incapable of processing *both* arguments and cues" (Petty et al., 1987, p. 238, emphasis in original). More recently, however, while stopping short of predicting the simultaneous impact of message arguments and persuasive cues, Petty and Wegener (1999) have argued that the relationship between peripheral processing (e.g., source credibility evaluations) and attitude change is curvilinear, as predicted by Stiff (1986) and presented in Figure 10.4. Specifically, Petty and Wegener argued,

When one is going from extremely low levels of elaboration likelihood to moderately low levels of elaboration likelihood, the impact of some peripheral processes . . . might be increased. Once one is past the minimal point on the continuum necessary to invoke the process, however, moving higher along the continuum should reduce the impact of the process on attitudes. (1999, p. 67)

A second theoretical limitation of the ELM is its inability to specify a priori the conditions under which particular cues will be processed centrally and peripherally. Original investigations of this model uniformly associated message content cues such as argument quality with central processing and persuasion cues such as source expertise and attractiveness with peripheral processing (Petty, Cacioppo, & Goldman, 1981). That is, under conditions of high receiver involvement, the positive relationship between argument quality and attitudes was interpreted as evidence of central processing. Under conditions of low receiver involvement, the positive relationship between source expertise and attitudes was interpreted as evidence of peripheral processing (Petty, Cacioppo, & Goldman, 1981). However, by 1986, Petty and Cacioppo had specified that the same variable can serve multiple persuasive roles. Recently, Petty and Wegener (1999) postulated that "a variable can influence attitudes in four ways: (1) by serving as an argument, (2) by serving as a cue, (3) by determining the extent of elaboration, and (4) by producing a bias in elaboration" (p. 51). For example, the beautiful scenery depicted in a vacation resort advertisement is likely a peripheral cue if the recipient is not thinking about the ad very much. As elaboration likelihood increases, however, that same scenery can act as a message argument because the scenery is relevant to the recipient's evaluation of the resort's quality (Petty & Wegener, 1999). If the same scenery appeared in an advertisement for an automobile, on the other hand, it is likely to be processed peripherally no matter how much elaboration occurs.

As M. Burgoon (1989) noted, classification of these cues is often

derived from inferring antecedents from consequents, or a teleological method of explanation. Thus, *if* specific outcomes occur (e.g., attitude change), then certain kinds of intrapsychic message processing had to have occurred. Such an explanatory mechanism is relatively unproductive for people interested in the social effects of strategy choices. The more appropriate approach is to specify a priori how message variables affect the persuasive process. (p. 157)

In other words, this conceptual flexibility clearly identifies the ELM as "primarily a descriptive, rather than explanatory, theory of persuasion" (Eagly & Chaiken, 1993, p. 321). According to the ELM, whether a recipient engages in central or peripheral processing depends on where he or she is on the elaboration likelihood continuum. "The actual placement of an individual along the continuum, of course, cannot be known until after the message or attitude object has been processed" (Petty & Wegener, 1999, p. 66). As a consequence, rather than predicting a priori whether central or peripheral processing will occur, the ELM looks at attitude and other study results to decide, after the fact, what persuasive process must have occurred. This practice "allows the ELM to explain all possible outcomes of an experimental study without predicting which will occur," making it practically impossible to falsify (Stiff & Boster, 1987, p. 251).

Empirical Limitations of the ELM

In addition to pointing out the theoretical shortcomings of the ELM, recent reviews of the persuasion literature have challenged the validity of empirical support for the model. Perhaps the most important revelation emerged from the meta-analysis of the involvement literature that we discussed in Chapter 8 (Johnson & Eagly, 1989). When cumulating the effects of outcome-relevant involvement on attitudes, Johnson and Eagly found evidence of an involvement by argument quality interaction as predicted by the ELM. However, there were significant differences among the findings of individual studies that contributed to this overall estimate. Some studies found robust interaction effects while others found none at all. Johnson and Eagly found one interesting moderator variable that helped to explain the variation: who performed the study. Specifically, studies authored by Petty, Cacioppo, and their colleagues obtained the predicted interaction between argument quality and involvement, whereas studies authored by other researchers found weak or no evidence of this same interaction (Johnson & Eagly, 1989, p. 304). That is, studies conducted by Petty, Cacioppo, and their colleagues consistently found a significant positive relationship between involvement and attitudes when receivers heard strong arguments and a significant negative relationship between involvement and attitudes when they heard messages containing weak arguments. However, these effects were small and not significantly different from zero when other researchers conducted similar studies.[3]

One possible explanation for this curious result stems from Petty and Cacioppo's operational definition of argument quality (i.e., how strong and weak arguments are created). Petty and Cacioppo (1986) arbitrarily defined a strong argument as information that, when scrutinized by message receivers, causes message receivers to generate 65% favorable or supportive cognitions and 35% unfavorable cognitions. They defined a weak argument as information that, when scrutinized by message receivers, produces only 35% favorable cognitions (pp. 54–55).

There are several important implications of this view of argument quality. First, although the variable is called "argument quality," we (Mongeau & Stiff, 1993) have argued that the variable being manipulated has little to do with the actual message arguments. Specifically, we questioned the validity of the argument quality construct in the ELM. In an important clarification, Petty, Wegener, Fabrigar, Priester, and Cacioppo (1994) responded that we misunderstood what they intended the argument quality manipulation to do.

> The ELM has never attempted to provide a theory of argument quality, cogency, or quality per se. Instead, argument strength [quality] manipulations have been used as a methodological tool for indexing the level of argument-based processing underlying post-communication attitudes. (p. 350)

In short, the argument quality manipulation, as defined in the ELM, is designed to influence the valence (i.e., positive or negative nature) of recipients' cognitions *if* they actively process the message. The argument quality variable in the ELM tells us nothing about the quality or strength of an argument (Petty & Cacioppo, 1986; Petty & Wegener, 1999). Thus, the practical value of argument quality (and the entire ELM) is very limited. The ELM provides no useful advice as to how to construct a persuasive message (aside from saying to produce a message that generates as many positive cognitions as possible).

The final implication of the argument quality operational definitions adopted by Petty and Cacioppo (1986) is that they may be responsible for their ability to consistently produce the argument quality by involvement interaction that had eluded many other researchers. The "proper" way of manipulating argument quality was first fully described in Petty and Cacioppo's review of the literature in 1986 (nearly a decade after ELM-like studies were first performed). Studies conducted by scholars other than Petty, Cacioppo, and colleagues employed more traditional definitions of argument quality—for example, definitions based on the structure or logical validity of arguments (cf. Reinard, 1988; Toulmin, 1964) and not the pattern of cognitions they produce. Consequently, their failure to replicate the argument quality by involvement interaction may stem from the use of a different operational definition of argument quality. Though speculative, careful examination of these methodological issues may resolve the conflicting findings of experiments conducted by Petty, Cacioppo, and their associates and those conducted by other researchers.

A second empirical limitation of many investigations of the ELM stems from the repeated use of a relatively small sample of message and source manipulations. Indeed, a large majority of investigations of the ELM have employed one of two topics: advocating tuition increases or recommending comprehensive exams for undergraduates. D. J. O'Keefe (1990) succinctly summarized this concern when he wrote:

> What is worrisome about this, of course, is that the ELM purports to be a theory of persuasion generally, not a theory of persuasion about comprehensive exams and tuition charges. One would naturally have reservations about a theory of persuasion resting on evidence from just a few human respondents, and one should similarly have reservations about a theory that rests on evidence from just a few message topics. (p. 109)

Of course, concerns about the importance of message diversity in persuasion research are not new (see Jackson & Jacobs, 1983). Although methods for message generalization have been vigorously debated (Jackson, O'Keefe, & Jacobs, 1988; Morley, 1988a, 1988b; D. J. O'Keefe, Jackson, & Jacobs, 1988), persuasion scholars generally agree about the importance of message diversity in establishing the breadth of theories.

Summary of ELM Limitations

For two decades, the ELM dominated thinking about the effects of cognitive responses in persuasion. Although the model has provoked significant research and considerable speculation about the persuasion process, several theoretical shortcomings call into question the theoretical validity and practical utility of the model. Specifically, researchers have questioned whether the ELM is compatible with the parallel information processing capacities of message receivers and whether it can in principle be falsified. Combined with these theoretical limitations, contradictory findings of prior studies limit the confidence some researchers have about the validity of the model.

Although questions remain about some aspects of the model, the ELM has provided evidence of two types of message processing and established an important relationship between receiver motivation, message scrutiny, cognitive responses, and attitudes. In addition, the ELM has spawned a considerable amount of research and renewed interest in the study of persuasive message processing. A second cognitive model of persuasion, the HMP (Chaiken, 1987; Chen & Chaiken, 1999), coincided with the development of the ELM. Although the two models share a number of conceptual similarities, they differ in several important respects.

THE HEURISTIC MODEL OF PERSUASION

Although Chaiken's (1987) HMP has received considerably less attention from persuasion scholars than the ELM, the HMP provides an attractive alternative to persuasion researchers seeking a cognitive model of persuasion (see Todorov, Chaiken, & Henderson, 2002, for a review). Like the ELM, the HMP posits that two distinct cognitive processes guide the evaluation of persuasive messages. One process, labeled *systematic processing*, involves the careful scrutiny of message content and is similar to Petty and Cacioppo's concept of central processing. A second type of processing, labeled *heuristic processing*, involves very little cognitive effort by message receivers.

Although Chaiken's (1987) "systematic processing" is similar to Petty and Cacioppo's (1986) "central processing," the concepts of "heuristic processing" and "peripheral processing" are distinct. Petty and Cacioppo's peripheral processing reflects a wide variety of theoretical associations with reactance theory (Brehm, 1966), identification processes (Kelman, 1961), and models of classical conditioning (Staats & Staats, 1957), among others. Chaiken argues that these theoretical perspectives "feature motivational orientations *other* than assessing the validity of persuasive messages" (p. 7, emphasis added). Conversely, heuristic processing reflects a single theoretical orientation about the evaluation of persuasive messages in which receivers employ cognitive heuristics to assess the validity of a persuasive message. *Heuristics* are simple decision rules that allow people to evaluate message recommendations without effortful scrutiny of message content. For example, the heuristic that "experts are usually correct" permits receivers to make a decision about a message recommendation based on a quick assessment of the source's expertise. Thus, peripheral processing reflects a variety of psychological motivations emphasizing the association of a speaker's position with rewarding or unrewarding persuasive cues. Conversely, heuristic processing reflects a single motivation, that is, evaluation of the message recommendation with minimal cognitive effort.[4]

The centerpiece of the HMP is the explicit recognition that people are often "minimalist information processors" who are unwilling to engage in highly active, conscious processing of persuasive message content. Applying prior investigations of cognitive heuristics (Kahneman & Tversky, 1973; Tversky & Kahneman, 1974, 1982), Chaiken argued that many distal persuasion cues are processed by means of simple schemas or decision rules that have been learned on the basis of past experiences and observations (1987, p. 4). For example, many people hold a cognitive schema that "taxes are bad," which leads to a simple decision rule that messages advocating tax increases should be rejected. Indeed, the political effectiveness of George H. W. Bush's 1988 campaign promise, "Read my lips, no new taxes," was derived from the assumption that voters would enact this simple heuristic and vote for him.

Other, more general, heuristics may guide the processing of a variety of different persuasive messages. For example, the heuristic that "expert sources are probably correct" is a decision rule that evolves over time as sources with expertise demonstrate a propensity for advocating correct positions on issues. Once established, this heuristic is available to people for use in evaluating the statements of both expert and inexpert sources. Applied in a persuasive situation, this heuristic may lead message receivers to accept the recommendations of an expert source without the need for careful examination of the reasons offered in support of such recommendations (or to reject recommendations of inexpert sources). In much the same fashion, the heuristic "more is better" may produce greater message acceptance of messages containing four supporting arguments than those messages containing a single supporting argument. In this case, the sheer number of arguments (regardless of how good they are) is the critical factor for attitude change.

Unlike the careful scrutiny of message content, the use of cognitive heuristics requires little cognitive effort. In general, all that is required is the application of a situation to the heuristic. If characteristics of the persuasive appeal under consideration are representative of a general, prototypical example of the heuristic, then the heuristic is likely to guide the evaluation of the persuasive appeal. Thus, the heuristic "experts are probably correct" may guide the evaluation of a speaker's recommendation once the level of the speaker's expertise has been established.

Once formed, these heuristics are available in message receiver's cognitive structures. The operation (accessibility) of these heuristics depends not only on their existence (availability), but also on the frequency and recency of their use (Fiske & Taylor, 1991; Higgins, 1996; Wyer & Srull, 1981). For example, Higgins, King, and Mavin (1982) concluded that the cognitive constructs that people frequently use to evaluate others are likely to become chronically accessible. Bargh and Pratto (1986) argued that the "frequency of use of a cognitive process results in its becoming more efficient, and eventually in its automation" (pp. 295–296). Thus, cognitive heuristics allow many persuasive cues to be processed automatically, requiring minimal cognitive effort from message receivers.

Predicting Systematic and Heuristic Processing

Although the HMP is a cognitive model of persuasion, it does not emphasize message receivers' cognitive responses. Instead, Chaiken (1987) describes how cognitive processes permit message receivers to evaluate persuasive messages without much conscious control or cognitive activity. As "cognitive misers" (Fiske & Taylor, 1991) people generally seek to minimize their cognitive activity, preferring less effortful methods of information processing. Thus, although systematic processing is one method of message evaluation, it is employed less often than cognitive heuristics.

The central predictions of the HMP describe the conditions that determine when message receivers will rely on cognitive heuristics and when they will engage in systematic processing to evaluate persuasive messages. A critical assumption of the HMP is that "heuristic and systematic processing of persuasion cues represent parallel, rather than mutually exclusive, modes of message processing" (Chaiken, 1987, p. 11). Thus, whereas the ELM posits "a trade-off between argument elaboration and the operation of peripheral cues" (Petty & Cacioppo, 1986, p. 21), the HMP clearly views systematic and heuristic processing as complementary forms of information processing. Given the minimal requirements of cognitive load necessary for heuristic processing, it is likely that most persuasive messages can be processed in this manner. Thus, people with minimal motivation to scrutinize a message can nevertheless process the appeal with cognitive heuristics. However, the systematic evaluation of persuasive messages is predicated on the ability of receivers to comprehend the message and their motivation to exert the cognitive effort required for systematic processing (Chaiken, 1987; Chen & Chaiken, 1999). Thus, although they are derived from separate theoretical perspectives, the HMP and the ELM hypothesize similar roles for motivation and ability in determining the extent of systematic (central) processing. As a result, the situational and individual difference factors that affect receiver ability and motivation are equally relevant to the HMP as to the ELM.

Comparison of the HMP and the ELM

Because it reflected a bold attempt to integrate the conflicting predictions and findings from a variety of different persuasion theories, the ELM has received considerably more attention from persuasion scholars than has the HMP. However, the HMP offers an attractive alternative to researchers and practitioners who have concerns about the theoretical and empirical limitations of the ELM.

Perhaps the single greatest asset of the HMP is that it was derived from a single theoretical perspective: a cognitive approach to information processing. Because the ELM is clearly aligned with cognitive response approaches to persuasion, it also represents a conglomeration of motivational and learning theory perspectives. Indeed, the theoretical breadth of the ELM is reflected in the claim that "many theories of attitude change could be roughly placed along an elaboration likelihood continuum" (Petty & Cacioppo, 1986, p. 8). However, the theoretical breadth of the ELM may be related to the lack of depth in its specification of the precise cognitive processes that mediate the effects of messages on attitudes.

The most important distinction between these two models stems from the HMP's explicit recognition of the parallel processing capacities of message receivers. Not only is this recognition consistent with current theories of human information processing (Eagly & Chaiken, 1993; Kruglanski & Thompson, 1999; Stiff, 1986), it alleviates the source of several limitations of the ELM. Because it posits a trade-off between central and peripheral processing, the ELM cannot explain findings that both types of processes contribute equally to a message's persuasiveness (cf. Stiff, 1986). Because the HMP posits that systematic and heuristic processing can occur in parallel, evidence of the effects of parallel processing is not a problem for this model.

Their shortcomings aside, these two models have made significant contributions to an understanding of speaker, message, and receiver factors that affect attitude change. Specific tests of these models produced an overwhelming volume of persuasion research during the past two decades. Though far from complete, these research programs reflect the dramatic shift from the source-centered approaches to persuasion that were prevalent in the 1960s and early 1970s to a receiver-centered focus, which is apparent in much of today's theorizing about persuasive communication. A recent rival to these models, the Unimodel, questions the assumptions of the dual-process models. We turn our attention to this model next.

THE UNIMODEL

While not uncontroversial, the ELM and the HMP have been the leading persuasion theories for nearly two decades. Recently, however, in the "Unimodel," Kruglanski argues that there is no need for two routes or modes of message processing because central and peripheral (or systematic and heuristic) processing are both examples of the same underlying process (Kruglanski & Thompson, 1999; Thompson, Kruglanski, & Spiegel, 2000).

According to the Unimodel, *persuasion* "is a process during which beliefs are formed on the basis of appropriate evidence" (Kruglanski & Thompson, 1999, p. 89). In turn, *evidence* is "information relevant to a conclusion" (Kruglanski & Thompson, 1999, p. 89). Given these definitions, both message arguments and persuasive (or heuristic) cues represent forms of evidence that are more similar than they are different.

> The distinction between heuristic (or peripheral) cues and message arguments is now assumed to represent a difference in contents of evidence relevant to a conclusion, rather than a qualitative difference in the persuasive process as such. (Kruglanski & Thompson, 1999, p. 90)

The primary difference between the Unimodel and the dual-process models (i.e., the ELM and the HMP) is that the Unimodel assumes that message arguments and heuristic/peripheral cues are processed in the same way. Therefore, in this reformulation, there is only one route to, or mode of, persuasion, instead of two. Previous ELM and HMP studies have generated evidence of what *looks like* two routes to (or modes of) persuasion because of the way the studies were performed rather than because of inherent differences between message arguments and persuasive cues. Results *appear* to support two routes to persuasion because, as presented in most studies, persuasive cues (e.g., a single-sentence description of a source to establish credibility) are presented before, and are considerably easier to process than, message arguments. There is no reason why this should be the case, though. Persuasive cues can be just as difficult to evaluate as message arguments. For example, having to evaluate Jim's résumé to determine his credentials as a persuasion scholar and trial consultant would likely entail considerable cognitive effort. Similarly, message arguments can be presented briefly and in a way that is very easy to process (e.g., "Don't judge a book by its cover" vs. "You must be careful not to evaluate and categorize a person or idea until you have an adequate chance to properly understand and appreciate them").

The Unimodel claims that if message receivers are motivated and able to do so, they will process whatever evidence is relevant to the conclusion being advocated, no matter whether this evidence is traditionally considered a persuasive cue or a message argument. Kruglanski and Thompson (1999) presented evidence supporting the Unimodel. For example, they report the results of several unpublished studies they have performed indicating that detailed information about a source (e.g., a page-long résumé) influenced attitudes more under conditions of high outcome-relevant involvement (or no distraction) than under conditions of low outcome-relevant involvement (or distraction) conditions.

The jury, as they say, has yet to return a verdict on the Unimodel.

Initial reactions to the Unimodel are quite varied; some are positive (e.g., Lavine, 1999; N. Miller & Pederson, 1999; Strack, 1999), others quite negative (e.g., Chaiken, Duckworth, & Darke, 1999; Petty et al., 1999; Wegener & Claypool, 1999), and still others are cautiously optimistic (Strahan & Zanna, 1999; Stroebe, 1999). Further theoretical development and empirical testing of the contrasting predictions, definitions, and assumptions underlying the Unimodel and dual-process models are likely to generate considerable research interest in the years to come.

SUMMARY

This chapter examined three cognitive models of persuasion. After reviewing research by Tesser and his colleagues that documented the effects of "mere thought" on the extremity of people's attitudes, the ELM was introduced as one model of persuasion that posits an important role for message receivers' cognitive responses. The ELM specified conditions that cause people to carefully consider the substance of persuasive messages and argued that when such conditions were met, message characteristics such as argument quality and supporting evidence would influence attitudes. According to the model, when people are unwilling or unable to carefully scrutinize message content, they base their message evaluation on persuasion cues that are peripheral to the message itself. Several concerns were raised about the theoretical validity and empirical support of the ELM. These theoretical and empirical limitations of the ELM call into question the validity of the model. The HMP was introduced as one alternative that is free of several of these limitations. Although they have many similarities, the HMP and the ELM represent distinct conceptualizations about the persuasion process. For example, the HMP reflects a single theoretical approach, rather than an attempt to integrate many different theoretical perspectives. In addition, the HMP explicitly accommodates the ability of message receivers to simultaneously conduct systematic and heuristic processing. Finally, the Unimodel was presented as an alternative to both the ELM and the HMP. The Unimodel predicts that there is only one way to process message information, including traditional conceptions of persuasive cues and message arguments.

In summary, these models reflect a recent movement among persuasion scholars to pay more attention to the contributions of message receivers in the persuasion process. Recent theorizing about this issue has stimulated scholarly inquiry and debate and promises to provide a more comprehensive understanding of persuasive communication.

NOTES

1. It bears mentioning that a number of other factors, including need for cognition, can motivate cognitive elaboration of messages (see Petty & Cacioppo, 1986; Petty & Wegener, 1998, 1999, for reviews of the literature).
2. Although early tests of the ELM uniformly associated the persuasive effects of argument quality with central processing and the persuasive effects of source expertise with peripheral processing, Petty and Cacioppo (1986) later specified that these variables can serve multiple roles. As is revealed later in the chapter, this conceptual flexibility raises serious concerns about whether the model can be falsified.
3. Petty and Cacioppo (1990) contested the conceptual and methodological decisions made by Johnson and Eagly (1989). However, the quality of Johnson and Eagly's (1990) response to this critique reaffirms the serious challenge their findings pose for proponents of the ELM.
4. In social influence situations, however, Chaiken, Liberman, and Eagly (1989) claimed that two other motives might operate. Specifically, they argue that with a defensive motivation, individuals are motivated to maintain a particular set of beliefs, attitudes, or values. An impression motivation occurs when an individual wants to express a belief or attitude because it is socially appropriate (Chaiken et al., 1989).

11

Models of Interpersonal Compliance

L OOKING AHEAD ...

The next two chapters review research on interpersonal influence. Chapter 11 focuses on the selection and effectiveness of compliance-gaining strategies and techniques. Chapter 12 reviews research that describes how people produce and resist influence messages in interpersonal contexts.

It bears mentioning that there are a number of conceptual frameworks that one could develop to organize and discuss the related research traditions that are reviewed in Chapters 11 and 12. For example, one might argue that the parallel development of research programs on compliance-gaining message selection (Chapter 11) and message design logics (Chapter 12) should be reviewed within a single chapter because both research traditions focus on single compliance-gaining messages, as opposed to more complex techniques involving sequential requests. However, we chose to distinguish between strategy selection and effectiveness (Chapter 11) and persuasive message production (Chapter 12) because questions surrounding the selection and effectiveness of various strategies are qualitatively distinct from questions surrounding the production of influence and influence-resisting messages. Nevertheless, we recognize that there are as many similarities as differences among the research traditions reviewed in these chapters.

In Chapter 10 we reviewed three models of persuasion that examined the cognitive responses people generate as they process persuasive messages. Our focus in that chapter was the contributions of message recipients to the overall effectiveness of a persuasive appeal. In the next two chapters, we shift attention to examining characteristics of messages in interpersonal persuasive transactions. This chapter focuses on two avenues of research that examine the evaluation, use, and effectiveness of messages designed to gain compliance in interpersonal settings. Chapter 12, in turn, focuses on the processes involved in producing and resisting compliance messages (see also Dillard, Anderson, & Knobloch, 2002; Wilson, 1997).

The first avenue is labeled *compliance-gaining message selection* research. Though advanced primarily by communication scholars, this research path originated in the field of sociology. In 1967, sociologists Marwell and Schmitt identified a typology of persuasive strategies that individuals might use to gain compliance from one another. This typology was subsequently adopted by communication scholars who examined situational factors that affect the evaluation of these strategies (G. R. Miller, Boster, Roloff, & Seibold, 1977). Together, these early investigations provided a research paradigm for examining compliance-gaining messages (for a review, see Seibold, Cantrill, & Meyers, 1985). Though these investigations were typically labeled as compliance-gaining "message selection" or "message use" studies, very few of these studies examined actual communicative behavior. Instead, researchers were content to rely on research participants' evaluations of the likelihood that they would use various strategies to gain compliance in a particular situation. This failure to investigate actual communicative behavior raised serious questions about the predictive utility of these evaluations and the generalizability of this research paradigm (Dillard, 1988; Seibold et al., 1985).

Concurrent with the efforts of communication scholars, a second avenue of research was instigated by social psychologists who studied the effectiveness of several sequential request strategies. Unlike compliance-gaining research in communication, many of these investigations observed actual communicative behavior and focused attention on persuasive outcomes rather than on the generation of interpersonal persuasive messages (for reviews, see Cialdini, 1987, 2001).

This chapter examines both of these traditions of interpersonal persuasion research. We examine the theoretical foundations of each tradition and empirical findings of representative investigations within each tradition. Along the way, we identify the shortcomings of each approach and attempt to integrate the findings across these research traditions. In the next chapter, we will focus on the research investigating how individuals produce and resist interpersonal influence messages.

COMPLIANCE-GAINING MESSAGE SELECTION

One important research tradition investigating interpersonal persuasion has been labeled "message selection research." Compliance gaining involves situations in which one person wants to convince a second person to do something for him or her. Given this definition, the term *compliance gaining* is a misnomer; a better term would be *compliance seeking*. However, we will use the established terminology. One consistent question in this research focused on identifying the strategies that people use when they attempt to gain compliance.

Relying primarily on French and Raven's (1960) review of power and influence literature, Marwell and Schmitt (1967) developed a list of 16 compliance-gaining strategies. To examine how people would evaluate each of these strategies, Marwell and Schmitt created hypothetical scenarios that described a source attempting to gain compliance from a target. For example, a father might attempt to persuade his son, Mike, to improve his study habits. Marwell and Schmitt developed 16 messages specific to the hypothetical situation to reflect each of the 16 compliance-gaining strategies. Research participants read the scenario and rated how likely they would be to use each of the 16 messages to gain compliance from the son described in the hypothetical situation. Factor analysis of these likelihood-of-use ratings produced five factors. That is, five clusters of messages emerged, which were interpreted as reflecting French and Raven's five bases of social power. These factors were labeled "Rewarding Activity," "Punishing Activity," "Expertise," "Activation of Interpersonal Commitments," and "Activation of Personal Commitments."

Concerns about the representativeness of Marwell and Schmitt's typology fostered the development of an alternative list of compliance-gaining strategies. Wiseman and Schenck-Hamlin (1981) provided students with hypothetical influence situations and asked them to generate descriptions of the messages they would send to gain compliance from the person depicted in each scenario. This procedure produced a typology of 14 strategies. Based primarily on its inductive (i.e., based on people's actual responses) rather than its deductive (i.e., based on theorizing) derivation, Wiseman and Schenck-Hamlin concluded that their typology was more generalizable, and hence superior, to the typology developed by Marwell and Schmitt.

Wiseman and Schenck-Hamlin's claim about the superiority of their inductively derived typology resides more on their philosophical approach to data collection than on any empirical differences observed from the use of these typologies. For example, Boster, Stiff, and Reynolds (1985) found that the structural qualities of these typologies, and people's responses to them, were quite similar. The complementary nature of these lists caused Boster and colleagues to conclude that "the 16 Marwell and Schmitt strategies could be combined with the 8 new strategies to form a 24 strategy list" (p. 186).

While Marwell and Schmitt and Wiseman and Schenck-Hamlin developed the two best-known typologies, Kellermann and Cole (1994) found 74 distinct classification systems containing 1,268 examples of strategies! In a conceptual reexamination of the various schemes, Kellermann and Cole concluded that an exhaustive list included 68 strategies. Individuals seeking compliance clearly have a wide array of tactics and strategies available to them.

Though questions about the structure and representativeness of these typologies are likely to remain, researchers have since followed the recommendations of G. R. Miller and his colleagues (1977) and examined aspects of compliance-gaining situations that affect people's evaluations of these strategies. Two models have been developed to explain how situational and individual-difference factors affect people's likelihood-of-use ratings as they respond to hypothetical compliance situations. These models are described below.

The Subjective Expected Utility Model

The first published model in this literature adopted a subjective expected utility (SEU) framework to explain strategy evaluation (Sillars, 1980). According to Sillars, when deciding whether to use a particular compliance-gaining strategy, people evaluate the acceptability of the strategy. This model posits that the acceptability of any persuasive strategy is a function of the perceived value of compliance (i.e., the importance of having the target perform the desired behavior); the perceived value of the relational costs and rewards associated with using the chosen strategy; and the expected probability that the strategy will be successful.

The SEU Model highlights several factors that affect the evaluation of persuasive messages. First, it suggests that situations influence people's judgments about the appropriateness of message strategies such that the more important it is to them to have the target comply in the situation, the more likely it is that people will find a strategy acceptable for use. The SEU Model also recognizes the importance of relational constraints on strategy selection. For example, the relational costs of coercive strategies may be sufficient to cause people in well-developed relationships to eschew coercion in favor of less costly or more rewarding strategies. However, people in less developed relationships may perceive that there are fewer costs associated with the use of coercive strategies, and thus may find them acceptable for use to gain compliance. Finally, the model emphasizes a critical feature of strategy evaluation: the likelihood that the strategy will produce compliance. Strategies that hold little promise for successful compliance are unlikely to be selected by persuaders.

To test the SEU Model, Sillars (1980) provided research participants with hypothetical scenarios in which the target of compliance was either a spouse or a new neighbor. In addition to standard likelihood-of-use ratings, Sillars asked respondents to rate the advantages and disadvantages of using particular strategies in terms of their persuasiveness and their likely effects on the relationship depicted in the scenario. Consistent with the SEU Model, results indicated that strategies that were perceived to be more persuasive and less likely to adversely affect the relationship were generally rated as more likely to be used than strategies that were perceived to be less persuasive and more costly to the relationship (see also Reardon, 1981).

The Ethical Threshold Model

Hunter and Boster developed an alternative model of message selection (1978, 1979, 1987). This model evolved out of a critical examination of previous factor-analytic studies of strategy selection ratings. Several prior investigations that explored the dimensions that underlie people's ratings of compliance-gaining strategies found that the number and nature of the dimensions varied across studies.

> Marwell and Schmitt (1967) identify five dimensions, one for each type of interpersonal power (French & Raven, 1960). G. R. Miller et al. (1977) report eight dimensions, which they interpret as showing that compliance-gaining messages are chosen largely on situational bases. Kaminski, McDermott, and Boster (1977) report two dimensions, labeled positive message strategies and negative message strategies. Roloff and Barnicott (1978, 1979) report two dimensions, labeled pro-social and anti-social strategies. (Hunter & Boster, 1987, p. 63)

Through a series of complex statistical arguments, Hunter and Boster (1987) demonstrated that the factor-analytic findings of these studies were incorrect. Reanalyzing data from several prior studies, Hunter and Boster argued that there was only one dimension underlying likelihood-of-use ratings.[1] The conceptual implication of their reanalysis was that strategies could be arrayed on a single continuum.

Hunter and Boster (1978) argued that positive, prosocial strategies typically receive higher use ratings than negative, antisocial strategies.

For example, messages reflecting a positive esteem strategy (i.e., you will feel better about yourself if you comply) should receive higher use ratings than messages that reflect a threatening strategy (i.e., if you don't comply, I will punish you). Thus, at one end of the strategy continuum are positive, prosocial strategies that receive high use ratings. Anchoring the other end of the continuum are negative, antisocial strategies that receive low use ratings (Figure 11.1).

Hunter and Boster (1978) argued that the dividing point on this continuum is a person's *ethical threshold*. Above the threshold are strategies that persuaders deem acceptable for use in a particular compliance-gaining situation. Strategies residing below the ethical threshold are sufficiently negative that persuaders deem them unacceptable for use to gain compliance. Given that a person's ethical threshold identifies which strategies are acceptable for use in compliance-gaining situations, an important concern is to identify the situational and individual difference factors that affect a person's ethical threshold. People with characteristically low ethical thresholds will rate more strategies as acceptable for use than people with higher ethical thresholds. Operationally, the ethical threshold is defined as the number of strategies a person finds acceptable for use in a particular situation. Hence, factors that affect strategy use determine the ethical threshold.

Situational Predictors of Strategy Selection

Several situational factors have been investigated as possible determinants of strategy selection (for reviews, see Boster & Stiff, 1984; Cody & McLaughlin, 1985). Two factors that have received the most attention are the level of relational intimacy between the source and the target of the compliance request and the perceived benefits from the compliance.

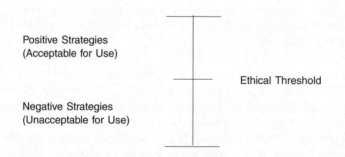

FIGURE 11.1. Ethical threshold continuum.

Relational intimacy has been the focus of many compliance-gaining investigations. Perhaps the most accurate summary of these findings is that intimacy is positively correlated with the use of prosocial strategies, but that the size of this relationship is small (Fitzpatrick & Winke, 1979; G. R. Miller et al., 1977; Sillars, 1980; D. L. Williams & Boster, 1981). That is, relational intimacy may serve to raise a persuader's ethical threshold, but not by much. In short, existing data provide limited support for intimacy as an important determinant of a persuader's ethical threshold.

A second situational factor that has been the focus of several investigations is *perceived benefit*. Boster and his colleagues (Boster & Stiff, 1984; D. L. Williams & Boster, 1981) were among the first researchers to investigate the predictive utility of this factor. They argued that situations vary in the degree to which compliance benefits the persuader and/ or the target of the compliance-gaining message. For example, if you were trying to convince your roommate to quit smoking, the perceived benefit may be high for your roommate, but moderate or low for yourself. However, if you are asking your roommate for a $100 loan, the situation has considerable benefit for you and no benefit for your roommate.

Research on perceived benefit has produced a consistent pattern of findings (Boster & Stiff, 1984; D. L. Williams & Boster, 1981). Both benefit to self and benefit to the target influence the likelihood of use of negative strategies. Thus, both types of perceived benefit serve to lower a persuader's ethical threshold, though the effect of benefit-other appears to be stronger than the effect of benefit-self (Boster & Stiff, 1984). These findings are also consistent with Sillars's (1980) Subjective Expected Utility Model, which specifies that the perceived value of gaining the target's compliance affects the evaluation of compliance-gaining strategies.

Personality Predictors of Strategy Selection

In addition to situational factors, Boster and Hunter (1978) argued that personality factors may also affect a person's ethical threshold. Two personality factors that have received the most attention are Machiavellianism and dogmatism (for reviews, see Boster & Stiff, 1984; Seibold et al., 1985).

Machiavellianism is a personality construct developed by Christie and Geis (1970) to assess the manner in which people view their interactions with others. People with highly Machiavellian belief systems are cynical and believe that most people are unscrupulous. A second personality variable that affects strategy selection is *dogmatism*: highly dogmatic people tend to be closed-minded and exhibit limited flexibility in communicative situations. Studies investigating Machiavellianism (Boster & Hunter, 1978; Roloff & Barnicott, 1978) and dogmatism (Roloff & Barnicott, 1979; D. L. Williams & Boster, 1981) found small but positive correlations with strategy selection. Thus Machiavellianism and dogmatism appear to have a small effect on the ethical thresholds of persuaders.

Studies have consistently found a small positive relationship between dogmatism and message selection. Like the Machiavellianism construct, dogmatism appears to lower a person's ethical threshold and results in greater selection of relatively negative compliance-gaining strategies. That is, highly dogmatic people desiring compliance are more willing to use negative, antisocial strategies than less dogmatic people.

Evaluation of Strategy Selection Research

In summary, several studies provide evidence of a unidimensional model of strategy selection. Hunter and Boster (1987) argued that a person's ethical threshold separates strategies that are acceptable from those that are deemed unacceptable for use to gain compliance. Two personality factors, Machiavellianism and dogmatism, and one situational factor, perceived benefit, suggest that ethical thresholds differ across people and situations. Though it has received less attention from persuasion scholars, Sillars's (1980) Subjective Expected Utility Model offers an explanation of situational factors that affect the selection of compliance-gaining messages.

Although the models developed by Sillars (1980) and Hunter and Boster (1978, 1987) provided theoretical frameworks for investigating compliance-gaining message selection, attempts to explain compliance-gaining behavior were few and far between (Dillard et al., 2002). Moreover, limitations of the message selection research paradigm raised concerns about the validity of this line of research. In a review of this literature, G. R. Miller, Boster, Roloff, and Seibold (1987) echoed these concerns and concluded that "most previous research on the selection of compliance-gaining strategies has used procedures that do not capture the interactive nature of compliance gaining" (p. 103).

To support this conclusion, they (G. R. Miller et al., 1987, pp. 103–104) identified several important differences between the hypothetical selection of compliance-gaining strategies and strategy use in naturally occurring compliance transactions. The argued that acting as a participant in a study was quite a different experience, cognitively and emotionally, from actually engaging in a real interaction.

Though several authors have questioned the external validity of Marwell and Schmitt's (1967) strategy selection research paradigm

(Boster et al., 1985; G. R. Miller et al., 1977), scant empirical evidence exists to assess the degree of correspondence between hypothetical message selection and actual message use. Boster and Stiff (1984) failed to find evidence of the complex message strategies identified by Marwell and Schmitt (1967) and Clark (1979). Along similar lines, Dillard (1988) found very little correspondence between the strategies selected in response to the hypothetical compliance scenarios and those used in role-play situations. Though far from conclusive, the Boster and Stiff and Dillard studies suggest that there is merit to prior concerns about the generalizability of findings from studies using the message selection procedure (for a contrasting position, however, see Boster, 1995).

As an alternative to the message selection research paradigm, constructivist researchers adopted message generation procedures to study compliance behavior. Instead of asking respondents to select the strategies they would use in particular situations, constructivist researchers ask respondents to write the types of things they would say to gain compliance in a hypothetical situation. These messages are evaluated and the strategies reflected in them are taken as evidence of compliance strategy use or message generation (e.g., see Clark, 1979; Delia & O'Keefe, 1979). There is evidence that this message generation procedure is more representative of actual compliance behavior than the message selection procedure. For example, Applegate (1982) found that the number of persuasive strategies people generated in response to a hypothetical situation was positively correlated with the number of strategies they employed in face-to-face persuasive situations ($r = .31$). In addition, the level of listener-adapted communication reflected in people's hypothetical messages was correlated with the level of listener-adapted communication in their face-to-face interaction ($r = .67$). Studies such as this (see also Applegate, 1980) provide evidence of the predictive validity of message generation procedures and alleviate some of the limitations inherent in message selection procedures. Nevertheless, the relative utility of message generation versus message production procedures has been the topic of considerable debate (for examples, see Boster, 1988; Burleson & Wilson, 1988; Burleson et al., 1988; Hunter, 1988; Seibold, 1988).

Whatever utility these perceptual judgments may have for persuasion scholars, they are no substitute for investigations of compliance-gaining behavior in naturally occurring persuasive situations. Indeed, "certain complex compliance gaining strategies (e.g., the bait and switch, low bailing, the method of relevant scenarios, etc.) are difficult to put into a questionnaire format" (Boster et al., 1985, p. 186).

Though more than 100 articles and convention papers employing hypothetical compliance-gaining scenarios have emerged since the G. R.

Miller and colleagues (1977) investigation, researchers concerned about external validity soon abandoned the message selection paradigm. Recently, the compliance-gaining message selection literature has become a conceptual ghost town, as researchers adopted alternative methods that promised findings with greater correspondence to behavior in naturally occurring compliance situations (e.g., Levine & Boster, 2001).

Several alternative avenues of research provide ample opportunity for scholars of interpersonal influence. One of these research traditions evolved contemporaneously with the message selection/message generation research. Studies of sequential request strategies emerged in social psychology in the mid-1970s and focus on compliance-gaining behavior. Recently, the study of sequential request strategies has captured the attention of communication scholars as well.

SEQUENTIAL REQUEST STRATEGIES

About the same time that Marwell and Schmitt (1967) published their seminal investigation of compliance-gaining message selection, Freedman and Fraser (1966) initiated a program of research on more complex compliance-gaining behaviors. Unlike studies that employed hypothetical scenarios to stimulate evaluations of compliance-gaining messages, this line of research examined the effectiveness of specific compliance strategies and emphasized the study of actual compliance behavior. Studies on compliance-gaining behavior have investigated techniques that employ either single or multiple messages that are easily applied in everyday persuasive encounters. Examples of single request strategies include the "every penny can help" technique (Cialdini & Schroeder, 1976) and the "that's not all" technique (Burger, 1986). For the remainder of this chapter, however, we will focus on sequential request strategies. Three types of sequential request techniques—the foot-in-the-door, the door-in-the-face, and the low-ball techniques—are representative of this body of literature.

The Foot-in-the-Door Technique

In 1966, Freedman and Fraser published their seminal investigation of an influence strategy known as the foot-in-the-door (FITD) technique. The FITD requires a persuader to send two sequential messages in order to gain compliance. The first message makes a request that is relatively innocuous and sufficiently small that most targets will agree to it. The second request, which often occurs several days after the initial request, can be made by another person and is much larger than the initial request. Persuaders using the FITD are interested in gaining compliance with the second, larger request. Presumably, persons agreeing to the initial small request will be more willing to comply with the second larger request.

The FITD gets its name from a strategy employed by door-to-door salespeople who ask for a glass of water or to come in from the rain (literally getting their "foot in the door") before attempting to sell their product. Salespeople in these situations may perceive that getting their persuasive target to do something for them may increase the likelihood that the target will comply with a subsequent request to purchase their product. People using this technique are only concerned with the initial request to the extent that it facilitates compliance with the second larger request.

Freedman and Fraser (1966) conducted two studies to assess the effect of compliance with an initial small request on compliance with a second larger request. In Study 1, they canvassed a residential neighborhood in Palo Alto, California, and asked housewives if they would answer a brief survey about household products they use. After 3 days, these same housewives (experimental group), along with others who were not contacted during the initial phase of the study (control group), were contacted and asked if they would allow a team of researchers to spend 2 hours in their home cataloging the types of household products they had in their home. The pattern of compliance with this larger request was remarkable. Of those who agreed to participate in the survey 3 days earlier, 55% agreed to the larger request to allow researchers in their home. Conversely, only 22% of the people who had not received the initial request agreed to the larger request.

In Study 2, Freedman and Fraser (1966) asked some people in a neighborhood to sign a petition or to place a small sign in the front window of their homes (experimental group). The topic of the petition and the sign was either safe driving or a "Keep California Beautiful" campaign. Once again, this initial request was sufficiently small that most people agreed to it. Other residences were bypassed during the initial phase of this study (control group). Different researchers canvassed the neighborhood 2 weeks later and now asked everyone—both those who had received the initial small request and those who had been bypassed—if they would be willing to place a large sign promoting safe driving in their front yard. Once again, Freedman and Fraser found that those who had complied with the initial small request were more likely to comply with the second larger request (54%) than control group participants who did not receive the initial small request (16%). Thus, in both studies, large compliance effects were obtained when participants were first asked to comply with a small initial request.

Evidence for the FITD

Over 50 published articles have examined the FITD since Freedman and Fraser's (1966) seminal investigation. Several meta-analytic reviews have synthesized the findings of these studies (Beaman, Cole, Preston, Klentz, & Steblay, 1983; Dillard, 1991; Dillard, Hunter, & Burgoon, 1984; Fern, Monroe, & Avila, 1986). Findings from these reviews paint a consistent picture of the effectiveness of this technique, though each review highlights separate subgroup analyses.

The overall effect of the FITD on compliance in prior studies was small; average effects range from $r = .09$ to $r = .12$ in the three meta-analyses (Table 11.1). However, subgroup analyses indicated that the FITD is more effective than one might conclude from these overall analyses. For example, two reviews included an analysis of "pure tests" of the FITD. Because the FITD requires an initial request that is sufficiently small that most people will comply with it, researchers have defined "pure tests" of this effect as those studies in which at least 80% of the participants complied with the initial request (Beaman et al., 1983; Fern et al., 1986). Among studies that met this 80% criterion, the FITD was somewhat more effective. The average effect was $r = .14$ in the Beaman and colleagues (1983) study and $r = .21$ in the Fern and colleagues (1986) study. In addition, Dillard et al. (1984) found that the FITD was only effective when the compliance request was prosocial and when targets were not offered incentives to comply ($r = .16$). A prosocial request is one that does not directly benefit the requestor (e.g., a charitable donation where the money goes to the organization rather than to the requestor). In studies where the request was self-oriented (i.e., directly benefiting the requestor) or targets were offered incentives for compliance, the FITD effect was trivial.

TABLE 11.1. Summary of FITD Effects from Meta-Analytic Reviews

	Meta-analytic review		
	Dillard et al. (1984)	Beaman et al. (1983)	Fern et al. (1986)
Overall effect (r)	.11	.12	.09
Number of estimates	37	77	120
Effect from "pure tests" (80%) compliance with initial request	—	.14	.21
Effect from tests using prosocial appeal and no incentive to comply	.16	—	—

These subgroup analyses suggest that when certain conditions are met, the FITD is an effective technique for gaining compliance. In summary, when the initial request is small enough to produce compliance from most targets, when the compliance requests are prosocial (vs. self-oriented), and when no incentives are provided for compliance, the FITD should increase compliance rates by about 20%.

Theoretical Basis of the FITD

The most frequently cited theoretical explanation of the FITD effect is Self-Perception Theory (Bem, 1967, 1972). Recall from Chapter 4 of this volume that Bem's theory hypothesized that people look to their own behaviors for evidence of their underlying attitudes and beliefs. Applied to FITD studies, Self-Perception Theory predicts that when people comply with an initial small request, they conclude that their attitude toward the issue or the source of the compliance request must be favorable. After inferring that their attitudes are favorable toward the issue, the requestor, or both, people are more likely to comply with a second larger request.

Though the general pattern of compliance behavior in prior FITD studies is consistent with this interpretation, most studies failed to test directly the self-perception explanation. A study by Dillard (1990b) is a rare exception. He argued that evidence of a self-perception explanation would be reflected in attitude change following compliance with the first request. He measured general attitudes toward the topic of the compliance request and toward several specific reasons for complying with the request. Analysis of the attitude data revealed that compliance with an initial request to support an environmental organization indicated more favorable attitudes toward the general issue of the environment, but less favorable attitudes toward several specific reasons for compliance (i.e., the source, emotional benefit, and appearances and obligations) (Dillard, 1990b).

Dillard (1990b) concluded that although a self-inference explanation was a viable account of his findings, the specific predictions of Self-Perception Theory were not supported. Specifically, neither the size of the initial request nor actual compliance with the initial request (vs. simply agreeing to comply) predicted compliance with the larger second request. Along a similar line, Gorassini and Olson (1995) also found that agreeing to a small request affected people's perceptions of their own helpfulness, but those perceptions did not predict agreement with the second request.

Thus, although self-inference processes account for the attitude data, they were not the specific processes hypothesized by Self-Perception Theory. Burger (1999) recently claimed that FITD techniques likely generate a number of psychological processes (including self-perception) that may combine to produce compliance to the second request. Together, Dillard's (1990b) and Gorassini and Olson's (1995) findings that FITD strengthened some attitudes and weakened others suggest that additional theorizing about these self-inference processes may be necessary to fully explain the FITD phenomenon.

The Door-in-the-Face Technique

A companion to the FITD technique is the door-in-the-face (DITF) technique. The DITF begins with an initial compliance request that is so large that it is rejected by most targets. After rejection of the initial request, the source proceeds with a second, smaller, request. The DITF is similar to the FITD in that both techniques are designed to increase compliance with the second of two sequential requests. However, instead of beginning with an initial small request and following it with a second larger request, the DITF begins with a very large initial request. Presumably, people who refuse an initial large request are more likely to comply with the more moderate second request than people who only receive the moderate request.

A variety of organizations attempt to use the DITF to generate sales or donations. For example, Paul is a regular donor to his alma maters (Arizona State and Michigan State) and is contacted annually by both institutions. Not long ago Paul received a call from one of the schools asking for alumni donations. This time, however, the student making the call suggested a $1,000 donation to enter an elite group of donors. This was a large request because Paul had never given more than $100 in any prior donation. When Paul refused the request to donate $1,000, the student asked it he would donate the same amount he gave the year before. Paul agreed, and even gave a little more than the previous year.

Cialdini and his colleagues (1975) were the first to investigate the effectiveness of the DITF. In the first of three studies, they asked some college students if they would be willing to work as counselors to juvenile delinquents for a period of at least 2 years. None of the students agreed to this initial request. Following their refusal, a second moderate request was made of these students: they were asked to act as chaperons for a group of juvenile delinquents on a 2-hour trip to the local zoo. Of the students who refused the large initial request, 50% agreed to the smaller second request. Conversely, less than 17% of the people in a control condition, who only received the moderate request, agreed to act as chaperons on the trip to the zoo (Cialdini et al., 1975). In this study, the DITF produced compliance rates that were three times higher than those obtained in the single request condition. Cialdini and his colleagues reported the findings from two additional studies that found the same patterns of compliance. They argued that the concession reflected in the difference in size of the first larger request and the second smaller request establishes an obligation among targets who refused the initial request to make a concession of their own and agree with the second moderate request. No concession was made to people in the control group. They received a single moderate request and felt little obligation to comply with it.

Cialdini (2001) recently suggested that there is another process facilitating the effectiveness of the DITF technique. Specifically, Cialdini argued that a perceptual contrast likely influences how targets perceive and evaluate the second request. Perceptual contrast "affects the way we see the difference between two things that are presented one after another" (pp. 12–13). Applied to the DITF, the second smaller request is likely to seem even smaller because it comes immediately following the first large request. To go back to our earlier example about giving to an alma mater, $100 did not seem like such a large donation to Paul because of its proximity to the initial $1,000 request.

Evidence of the DITF

Since the seminal investigations by Cialdini and his colleagues, at least 30 published articles have reported investigations of the DITF. Four meta-analytic reviews have synthesized the findings of these studies (Dillard et al. 1984; Fern et al., 1986; D. J. O'Keefe & Hale, 1998, 2001). Findings from these reviews paint a consistent picture of the effectiveness of this technique, though once again each review highlights separate subgroup analyses. For example, Fern and colleagues (1986) found that the overall correlation between the use of DITF and compliance was small ($r = .07$), but subsequent analysis revealed that the timing of the second request had a significant effect on compliance rates. When there was no delay between refusal of the initial request and the second request, DITF had a positive effect on compliance ($r = .09$). However, when there was a delay between the first and second requests, the DITF technique had a *negative* effect on compliance ($r = -.08$). These findings suggest that the DITF may only be effective when the two requests occur in the same interaction.

The Dillard and colleagues (1984) review found that two factors maximized the effectiveness of this technique. They too found that the DITF was most effective when there was no delay between the two requests, as well as when the request was prosocial in nature ($r = .15$). When these conditions are met, DITF increases compliance rates by about 17%.[2] However, DITF appears to be ineffective when a source's request is self-oriented, or when there is a delay between a target's refusal of the first request and the subsequent smaller request. D. J. O'Keefe and Hale's (1998, 2001) recent meta-analyses come to much the same conclusions; however, they also report that compliance with the second request increases when the same person makes both requests, both requests benefit the same person or group, and when requests are made face-to-face rather than over the telephone. Together these reviews provide evidence of the effectiveness of this strategy. Although the overall correlations are small in size, these findings suggest that DITF is a reliable technique for significantly increasing the likelihood of a target's compliance.

Theoretical Basis of the DITF

The primary theoretical explanation of the DITF stems from Gouldner's (1960) concept of the *norm of reciprocity*. This culturally accepted norm suggests that "you should give benefits to those who give you benefits" (Gouldner, 1960, p. 170). Cialdini and colleagues extended this discussion by identifying the concept of reciprocal concessions, that is, "you should make concessions to those who make concessions to you" (1975, p. 206).

Applied to the DITF phenomenon, this norm suggests that

> two conditions are necessary to activate the normative force that increases the likelihood of compliance to the second request . . . (1) the original appeal must be rejected and . . . (2) the target must perceive a concession on the part of the requestor. (Dillard et al., 1984, p. 464)

In two studies, Cialdini and colleagues (1975, Study 2 & Study 3) found that the success of the DITF technique requires that targets view the second smaller request as a concession from the source's original position. Consistent with this requirement, the meta-analytic reviews found that DITF is only effective when the second request follows immediately after a target's refusal of the initial request. Indeed, a long delay between the two requests reduces the connection between the two requests and the likelihood that the target will perceive the second request as a concession by the source. The size of the concession, however, appears to have little impact on compliance with the second request (D. J. O'Keefe & Hale, 1998, 2001).

A second, more recent explanation for DITF effects centers on the creation and reduction of guilt (D. J. O'Keefe, 2000, 2002; D. J. O'Keefe & Figgé, 1997). As we discussed in Chapter 7, D. J. O'Keefe (2000) defined guilt as "a negative emotional state aroused when an actor's conduct is at variance with an actor's own standards" (p. 329). Guilt can be a powerful influence tool. Applied to the DITF, rejecting the first large request creates guilt if it violates a personal standard (e.g., to help those in need). Agreeing to the second request, then, gives the target an opportunity to reduce his or her guilt (D. J. O'Keefe & Hale, 1998, 2001).

D. J. O'Keefe's (2000, 2002; D. J. O'Keefe & Figgé, 1997) guilt-based explanation is consistent with each of the moderating variables identified in the various meta-analyses. Remember that the meta-analyses suggested that DITF works best when the appeal is prosocial, when there is no delay between the two requests, when the requests are made by the same person, when the two requests benefit the same person/sponsor, and when the requests are made face-to-face (rather than over the telephone).

According to the guilt-based explanation of DITF, guilt arises when a particular behavior (or the lack of a behavior) violates some personal norm. This suggests that some rejections will generate more guilt than will others. The moderating effect of the nature of the source suggests that guilt is more likely to be created by refusing a request from a needy person or organization than a request from a salesperson. For example, ignoring a TV ad depicting starving third-world children might create more guilt than avoiding an appeal to buy a new car. Analysis of moderator variables also suggests that it might also be less guilt producing to hang up on a telephone solicitor (even for a recognized charity) than to walk away from a person in a face-to-face context.

The guilt-based explanation also suggests the conditions under which complying with the second request will help to reduce guilt. Guilt wanes over time, so compliance with a second request should be greatest when the second request immediately follows the initial request. Moreover, if rejecting the first request generated guilt, it might be easiest to reduce the guilt by agreeing to a smaller request from the same person and sponsoring agency.

The guilt-based explanation of the DITF phenomenon is interesting and worthy of further study. However, it is largely untested in the DITF arena.[3] Thus, while promising and consistent with the meta-analytic data, we remain skeptical about the explanation until studies are conducted to directly test the explanation.

Conceptual Integration of Sequential Request Techniques

Given the obvious similarities between these sequential request techniques, scholars have sought to find a single theoretical explanation of FITD and DITF phenomena. The separate explanations of the FITD and

DITF (described above) are incompatible with one another. For example, Self-Perception Theory, which is frequently invoked to explain FITD, cannot account for the DITF effects. According to Self-Perception Theory, refusal of the initial request should cause targets of the DITF to infer that their attitudes toward the issue or source of the request are unfavorable, decreasing the likelihood of compliance with the second request. Similarly, the norm of reciprocal concessions and the guilt-based explanation, which have been invoked to explain the DITF phenomenon, cannot account for the effects of the FITD. Recall that the FITD requires a small initial request that is accepted by a target before a second larger request can be made. However, because no concession is made in the FITD, the norm of reciprocal concessions cannot explain its effectiveness. In addition, agreeing to a small request should produce no guilt, so the guilt-based explanation cannot explain the FITD effects either.

Several researchers have attempted to identify a single theoretical process that will permit a conceptual integration of these techniques. One such explanation is the *availability hypothesis*, which suggested that availability of favorable information in a person's cognitive framework influences agreement with compliance requests (Tybout, Sternthal, & Calder, 1983). Applied to the FITD effect, the availability hypothesis suggests that compliance with an initial small request increases the amount of favorable information a target has available in memory to guide a response to the second larger request. This increased favorable information increases the likelihood of compliance with the second request. Applied to the DITF effect, the availability hypothesis suggests that the perception of a concession in the source's second smaller request is favorable information that targets use to make decisions about the compliance request. Thus, the greater the perceived concession, the more likely the target is to comply with the second request.

In assessing the viability of this explanation, Dillard (1991) concluded the following:

> Though conceptually elegant and empirically promising in its first tests (Tybout et al., 1983), the availability model does not comport well with the meta-analytic data. Fern et al. (1986) derive several hypotheses that are closely modeled on the reasoning of Tybout et al. (1983). . . . But, by my count only three of those seven hypotheses received support. . . . In short, despite its hopeful beginning, the information availability perspective does not appear adequate to the task of providing a unified theoretical account of sequential-request phenomena. (p. 286)

Thus far, scholars have been unsuccessful in their search for a unifying theoretical process to explain the FITD and the DITF. It may be time to conclude that DITF and FITD are separate phenomena. This suggestion is bolstered by several studies indicating that source factors such as power and legitimacy work differently in FITD and DITF contexts. For example, Stahelski and Patch (1993) report that people see a greater power differential between requestor and target in typical DITF situations when compared with typical FITD situations. K. D. Williams and Williams (1989) report that requestor power amplified the DITF effect but has no effect on FITD processes. Finally, Patch (1988) reports that when requests are made by sources low in legitimacy, FITD strategies are effective but DITF strategies are not.

That source variables such as power and legitimacy influence DITF and FITD processes differently suggests that they are fundamentally different (through structurally similar) persuasive processes. Although the search continues for a unifying process to explain the effectiveness of both strategies it is likely that, although they are similar, two theoretically distinct processes drive these two sequential request strategies.

DITF and FITD are just two examples of sequential request strategies for gaining compliance. Though these two techniques have received the most interest from persuasion scholars, other sequential request strategies, such as low-ball procedures (Cialdini, Cacioppo, Bassett, & Miller, 1978), have proven effective for gaining compliance.

The Low-Ball Technique

The low-ball technique involves initially securing compliance from a target and then increasing the cost of performing the behavior by changing the request. The low-ball technique is a staple of salespeople, and it is especially prevalent among new-car dealers (Cialdini et al., 1978). This technique can take a number of forms. For example, new-car dealers often negotiate the price of a new car in combination with an offer to purchase a customer's used car. In these situations, the sales price of the new car may not be very attractive, but a generous offer for the customer's trade-in makes the total cost of purchasing the new car attractive. After the customer agrees to the new car sales price and trade-in value, the salesperson leaves the negotiation to seek a supervisor's approval of deal. Upon returning, the low-ball technique is enacted when the salesperson indicates that he or she has offered too much for the trade-in and that the supervisor has rejected the deal. The salesperson indicates that the company "would lose money" on the original deal and attempts to renegotiate the value of the customer's trade-in. Typically, customers feel committed to their decision to purchase the new car and accept a lesser amount for the trade-in. Although the price of the new car has not changed, the total cost of the sale may be significantly greater than the original agreement.

Of course, there are a variety of ways to enact the low-ball technique. Several years ago Jim and his wife decided to buy a convertible sports car with a hardtop option. When they took delivery of the car several weeks later, they were told that the hardtop option had gone up in price. Although they had a written agreement, the salesman wanted them to pay an additional $700 for the car! Indeed, the salesman attempted to use a low-ball technique to increase his profit. He anticipated that after waiting several weeks for the car Jim and his wife would be so anxious to take delivery that they would agree to the price increase, or at least a portion of it. Although it was ultimately unsuccessful, this example reflects the variety of ways that a low-ball technique can be implemented.

Evidence for the Low-Ball Technique

Cialdini and his colleagues (1978) conducted three experiments that provided evidence of the effectiveness of the low-ball technique. In one study, undergraduate students were contacted by phone and asked if they were willing to participate in an experimental study in order to fulfill a requirement for their psychology class. Students in the control condition were told that the experiment was to take place at 7:00 A.M. before they were asked if they wanted to participate. Students in the low-ball condition were asked to participate, and if they said yes, only then were they told that the experiment was to take place at 7:00 A.M. and asked if they were still willing to participate.

Participants in the low-ball condition agreed to participate significantly more often (56%) than participants in the control condition (31%). More important, the behavioral commitment was similar across the two conditions: 95% of the participants in the low-ball condition and 79% in the control condition who agreed to participate actually showed up at 7:00 A.M. (Cialdini et al., 1978). Cialdini and colleagues (1978) reported the findings of two additional studies providing further evidence of the effectiveness of the low-ball technique.

Theoretical Basis for the Low-Ball Technique

In an attempt to explain the effectiveness of the low-ball technique, Cialdini and his colleagues (1978) tested the efficacy of dissonance, self-perception, and commitment explanations. In an experiment designed to separate these effects, Cialdini and colleagues found that the notion of *psychological commitment* was the most viable explanation for this effect. According to Kiesler (1971), committing to a particular decision makes it more difficult to change that decision. Applied to the low-ball technique, this formulation posits that once people agree to a request, they feel committed to their decision and are less likely to change it, even if the nature of the request changes. Applied in automobile sales situations, this explanation suggests that once people become psychologically committed to purchasing a car, they are unlikely to change their minds, even if the ultimate cost of the car is more than they originally agreed to pay.

We only applied the low-ball technique to automobile sales situations, but this technique has proven to be quite effective across a variety of compliance settings. There are similarities between the FITD and the low-ball technique, but Cialdini and colleagues (1978) drew important conceptual and empirical distinctions between these two sequential request strategies. Although the technical aspects and theoretical foundations of the FITD, the DITF, and the low-ball procedures differ, these techniques all reflect the influence that sequential compliance requests can have on the behavior of persuasive targets.

SUMMARY

This chapter reviewed two distinct traditions of research on interpersonal influence. The compliance-gaining message selection research examined situational and personality factors that affect the ways in which people evaluate strategies for gaining compliance. Though few studies in this tradition examined communicative behavior, these studies provided a framework for understanding how people approach persuasive situations. A second tradition of research on interpersonal influence paralleled the growth of the message selection tradition. Studies of compliance-gaining behavior focused on the relative effectiveness of sequential request strategies for gaining compliance. Specifically, we discussed three strategies (i.e., FITD, DITF, and low-ball) that attempt to gain compliance by sending multiple messages in a sequence. While similar in structure, the FITD, DITF, and low-ball strategies are distinct and appear to work from different persuasive processes.

NOTES

1. Essentially, Hunter and Boster (1987) argued that the nonlinear regression of strategy use ratings onto the total strategy use score invalidated the findings of *linear* factor-analytic models. They demonstrated that likelihood-of-use

ratings formed a Guttman (1955) simplex and actually reflected a uni-dimensional factor model.

2. While the average correlation may not seem terribly large, a 17% increase in compliance is important. Consider a sales situation where hundreds (or perhaps thousands) of sales calls are being made every day. Using the DITF strategy to increase compliance would generate a large number of people agreeing to the second request (and generate substantial amounts of money).

3. Part of what makes D. J. O'Keefe's (2002) guilt-based explanation so interesting is that he has extended it beyond the DITF context. For example, in Chapter 7, we noted that D. J. O'Keefe argues that some dissonance studies can be explained equally well through guilt processes (e.g., the Stone et al. [1994] study on increasing condom use through creating hypocrisy).

12

Producing and Resisting Influence Messages

L OOKING AHEAD ...

In this chapter, we take a more detailed look at the processes of producing and resisting influence messages. First, we investigate how goals and plans influence the production of influence messages. We focus specifically on the nature of influence goals and the role of plan complexity on message production. We also consider how influence agents deal with multiple simultaneous influence goals and the role of message design logics in interpersonal influence. Finally, we discuss how and why people resist influence attempts. After examining resistance in general, we examine these issues in the context of resisting drug and alcohol influence attempts.

The contemporaneous research traditions of compliance-gaining message selection and compliance-gaining behavior discussed in the previous chapter provided useful knowledge about how people evaluate and effectively employ strategies for gaining compliance in interpersonal situations. Although these research traditions have been informative on the issues of message evaluation and effectiveness, they have offered little information about factors that affect the *production* of compliance messages. Recently, a number of communication scholars have turned their attention toward understanding how these messages are produced. A discussion of these emerging traditions of research on message production is the initial focus of this chapter. After this discussion, we will examine recent research performed on compliance resistance.

Several recent investigations of message production have examined how people form persuasive goals (Dillard, Segrin, & Hardin, 1989; B. J. O'Keefe & Shepherd, 1987; Wilson, 1990, 1997), how these goals are translated into action, what the effects of these persuasive goals are (Dillard et al., 1989), and how the functions of communication (B. J. O'Keefe, 1988, 1990; B. J. O'Keefe & McCornack, 1987) produce interpersonal influence messages. We examine each of these lines of research below.

GOALS, PLANS, AND ACTION
IN INTERPERSONAL INFLUENCE

Cognitive theoretical frameworks have guided much of the recent research on message production (see Greene, 1997, for an overview of these perspectives). Many of these theoretical perspectives, in one way or another, focus on the concept of goals (Wilson, 1997). A number of scholars have used the goal concept (though they have used different names to describe them) to help explain interpersonal influence (e.g., Dillard, 1990a; Hample & Dallinger, 1987; Samp & Solomon, 1998). The approach that we will use as a guide to describe this research derives from a combination of James Dillard's Goals, Plans, Action (GPA) Model of interpersonal influence and Charles Berger's Theory of Planning. These frameworks posit that people in interpersonal influence situations develop interaction goals, which lead then to plan and select message strategies. Once developed, these plans are implemented as persuasive message appeals (Dillard, 1989, 1990b). Because message production processes appear to be guided by the goals of persuaders, knowledge of the nature of influence goals and how these goals are transferred into action is essential to our understanding of the message production process.

The Nature of Influence Goals

Dillard (1990a) defines goals as "future states of affairs which an individual is committed to achieving or maintaining" (p. 43). There are a number of different persuasive goals that people can bring to influence interactions (for descriptions, see Cody, Canary & Smith, 1994; Dillard, 1989; Rule, Bisanz, & Kohn, 1985). Some goals represent the particular outcome desired by the persuader. Dillard refers to these as *primary goals*: "In interpersonal influence attempts, the desire to bring about behavioral change in a target person is the primary goal" (Dillard et al., 1989, p. 20). For example, an influence situation may involve giving advice, asking for a date, or obtaining information.

Primary goals are important because they define the nature of the influence situation, direct behavior, and represent yardsticks for measuring the effectiveness of an influence attempt (Dillard, 1990a). Primary goals also help message sources identify and evaluate behavior that occurs in influence interactions. For example, if your primary influence goal is to get your roommate to quit smoking, then the success or failure of your influence attempt should be based upon whether or not he or she actually quits (or cuts down on) smoking.

Several studies (Cody et al., 1994; Dillard et al., 1989; Rule et al., 1985) provide compelling evidence that there are a relatively small number of primary influence goals. Despite using different research methods, these studies generated similar lists of goals. Primary influence goals include changing a relationship (whether by initiation, escalation, or deescalation), asking for a favor, giving advice, sharing activities, and changing responses (i.e., attitudes and behaviors) (Schrader & Dillard, 1998).

However, other goals, such as relational maintenance and impression management, are also apparent in interpersonal influence situations. Dillard (1987, 1990a) refers to these as *secondary goals*: "Rather than driving the influence episode, as does the primary goal, secondary goals act as a counterforce to it and as a set of dynamics that help to shape planning and message output" (1990b, p. 46). Perhaps the best evidence for these secondary goals is the fact that people often avoid using coercive influence strategies, especially when they judge more socially desirable strategies to be equally effective. If these secondary goals did not exist, then people would routinely use the most forceful compliance strategy available to them, regardless of its impact on the target or its reflection on the source. For example, you might really want your roommate to stop smoking in the room you share, but you do not want to criticize his or her behavior too harshly for fear of damaging your relationship with him or her.

Just as is true for primary goals, there are multiple secondary goals that may be operating in any particular influence situation. In one study Dillard and colleagues (1989) presented students with hypothetical compliance-gaining situations and Wiseman and Schenck-Hamlin's (1981) list of compliance-gaining strategies. These students were asked to imagine themselves in the compliance situation, indicate whether or not they would use each strategy in the situation, and provide a written justification for each decision. These written justifications were content-analyzed and provided the basis for establishing the goals that determine strategy use.

This analysis revealed that four secondary goals—*identity, interaction, resource,* and *arousal*—were reflected in people's reasons for rejecting a message strategy (Table 12.1) (Dillard et al., 1989). *Identity* goals reflect concerns about a person's internal moral standards (e.g., be honest) and appeared in 34% of the justifications offered by respondents. *Interaction* goals reflect concerns about social appropriateness and impression management. These goals were present in 9% of the justifications. For example, an aggressive strategy might be rejected because it may be socially inappropriate for a particular situation and may project an image that the persuader does not want to send. *Resource* goals are revealed through concerns about relational and personal costs/rewards associated with the compliance attempt. For example, threatening strategies may be avoided because they may damage the relationship and are incompatible with the resource goal of relational maintenance. These goals were apparent in 5% of the justifications. *Arousal* was the final secondary goal and focused on managing the anxiety or arousal that might be present in some influence situations. Arousal was least frequently cited (1%) as a reason for not selecting particular compliance-gaining strategies. In a second study, Dillard and his colleagues (1989) developed and validated self-report measures for each of these secondary goals.

Goal Formation

A Cognitive Rules Model has been introduced to describe the formation of interaction goals (Wilson, 1990). This model proposes that people

TABLE 12.1. Justifications for Rejecting Message Strategies

Goal category	Frequency	Proportion	Exemplar statements
Influence	865	44%	It won't work. It's irrelevant.
Identity	672	34%	It's immoral. Not my style.
Interaction	180	9%	That would make me look bad. This is inappropriate for the situation.
Resource	98	5%	This would cost me our friendship.
Arousal	8	1%	This would make me apprehensive. Makes me too nervous.
Uncodable	136	7%	This is stupid. You must be kidding.
Total	1,959	100%	

Note. From "Primary and secondary goals in the production of interpersonal influence messages" by J. P. Dillard, C. Segrin, & J. M. Hardin, 1989, *Communication Monographs, 56*, 19–38. Copyright 1989 by the National Communication Association. Reprinted by permission.

possess cognitive rules for developing goals. These rules are stored in long-term memory and are activated when there is a "match between the perceived features of the situation and the situational conditions represented in the rule" (Wilson, 1990, p. 82). The accessibility of a cognitive rule and its fit with the persuasive situation affect the production of persuasive goals. For example, Wilson (1990) found that "people were more willing to form supporting goals if a situational feature associated with those goals recently had been activated, making the relevant cognitive rules accessible" (p. 97). The activation process described in the Cognitive Rules Model depicts people as parallel information processors. This suggests that rules for forming multiple persuasive goals can be simultaneously activated. How people create these multiple goals represents an important theoretical issue.

Goals and Plans

Dillard's (1990a) discussion of primary and secondary goals suggests that persuaders will enter most influence situations with multiple goals (i.e., one or more primary goals linked with one or more secondary goals). For example, a person might attempt to achieve a primary goal of convincing his or her roommate not to smoke in their room while at the same time attempting to achieve the secondary goals of not looking foolish, not making the roommate look foolish (i.e., interaction goals), and not violating personal standards (i.e., identity goal). The fact that most influence situations involve multiple goals suggests that the production of influence messages is unlikely to be a simple process. Instead, the complexity of goal structures highlights the importance of the second stage of Dillard's GPA Model, that of planning.

In both Dillard's (1990a) GPA Model and Berger's (1997) Theory of Planning, the intermediate process between the production of an influence goal and the production of an influence message is *planning*. Planning represents the cognitive work that goes into realizing primary and secondary goals. The end result of the planning process is the development of one or more plans. Plans are "hierarchical cognitive representations of goal-directed action sequences" (Berger, 1997, p. 25). There are several aspects of this definition that require further consideration. First, this definition highlights the fact that plans are developed in an effort to reach goals. Second, plans are not behaviors, but rather the thoughts that are related to those behaviors. Third, plans are hierarchical because they can and do occur at varying levels of abstractness. If your goal is to get your roommate to stop smoking in your shared room, you might develop an abstract plan to "reward him or her." After considering different means of reward, a specific plan can be developed that fulfills the general one (e.g., promise to take him to dinner at his favorite restaurant if he doesn't smoke in the room for a week).

C. R. Berger (1997) assumes that people have a number of "canned plans" stored in long-term memory. "Canned plans" are those that individuals have been used before in goal-related influence situations and, because they were successful in the past, they might want to use again. Because people have limited information processing capacity and cannot generate an entirely new set of plans every time they enter an influence situation, they prefer to use these canned plans rather than plans that they have to develop from scratch. If the goal and situation closely match what is required for the plan to work, C. R. Berger assumes that the canned plan will be used. This is similar to the argument that S. R. Wilson (1990) made in discussing the production of goals.

According to C. R. Berger (1997), plans differ in how simple or complex they are. Plans can be called complex in either (or both) of two ways. First, plan complexity depends upon the level of detail a particular plan has. To continue the smoking example, a complex plan might involve developing and mentally rehearsing everything that you will say (down to the specific gestures you will use and when) to your rommate. If, on the other hand, you enter the interaction with only a vague sense of how to convince your roommate, then your plan is quite simple.

The second way that plans can differ in complexity has to do with the number of contingencies they contain. A *contingency* represents an attempt to deal with events that might interfere with the successful completion of your plan (C. R. Berger, 1997). For example, you might plan a primary means of attempting to get your roommate to stop smoking in the room. You expect, though, that your roommate might object to your primary plan by claiming that it is his or her room too and that he or she has the right to smoke there. A plan contingency would involve developing a "subplan" of how you might respond to that particular objection. In short, the greater number of contingencies in a plan, the more complex it is. For example, if you wanted to achieve a primary goal of relational initiation by asking someone out on a first date, developing a complex plan might include thinking about and plotting who you would ask, when you would ask them, what specifically you would say, what sort of response you expect, and how you might react to that response.

While developing a plan filled with a number of contingencies might be useful in making a message source feel prepared, it might also make presenting messages more difficult. A complex plan replete with contingencies likely requires message sources to closely monitor the recipient's response and decide the extent to which the influence attempt is going "according to plan." A complex plan might give the message source a lot of things to think about—and all this while presenting the influence message. It would seem, then, that complex plans might be more difficult to present smoothly.

Berger, Karol, and Jordan (1989) were interested in the role plan complexity might play in verbal fluency in producing influence messages. Berger and colleagues (Experiment 1) had college students in two experimental conditions write out a plan designed to convince another student that alcohol consumption should be banned in dormitories (an important campus issue at the time). In one condition (i.e., plan–question), the experimenter looked at the plan and asked the participant what he or she would do if four specific aspects of his or her plan were to fail. In the other condition (i.e., plan-only), participants were not questioned about their plans (Berger et al., 1989)

After the participants developed their plan (in the plan-only condition) or after the experimenter asked participants to reconsider their plan (i.e., the plan–question condition), the participants were taken to a different room and asked to convince another student of their position. Unbeknownst to the participants, the other student was a confederate. A *confederate* is a person who acts as if he or she is a participant in the study, but who is actually working for the experimenter and has been told to act in a particular way. In the Berger and colleagues (1989, Experiment 1) study, the confederate was instructed to act in a neutral fashion initially, but to become more skeptical of the source's position as the influence attempt went on.

Berger and colleagues (1989) presumed that facing the experimenter's questions about the plan would cause participants to become more aware of alternative plans and to increase the number of contingencies in their existing plans. Thus, participants in the plan–question condition should have had more complex plans than participants in the plan-only condition. Given the relatively little time participants had to rehearse the influence attempt, increased plan complexity was expected to reduce message fluency, particularly when the recipient asked questions.

Results of the Berger and colleagues (1989) study were consistent with their predictions. Participants in the plan–question condition (i.e., those who were asked to reconsider their plan before its presentation) were judged as being less fluent than participants in the plan-only condition. Berger and colleagues concluded that when the initial message is questioned, the more complex plans made it more difficult for participants to change the nature of their influence message. In summary, while increased plan complexity might make a person feel more prepared to make an influence attempt, it might also make it more difficult for that person to change the plan to meet unexpected circumstances.

Goals, Planning, and Message Production

In an effort to link primary and secondary goals with the production of plans and persuasive messages, Dillard and his colleagues asked research participants to recall and describe a recent interaction in which they attempted to influence someone with whom they were well acquainted. Participants were also asked to indicate how much planning and effort was involved in their influence attempt (Dillard et al., 1989, Study 3). Trained coders evaluated these influence descriptions to determine the level of directness, positiveness, and logic reflected in them. Participants also responded to measures of primary and secondary goals in influence situations (Dillard et al., 1989, Study 2). These scales assessed the influence, identity, interaction, relational resource, and arousal goals that people bring to interpersonal influence situations.

The goals that people reported in these influence situations were related to the characteristics of the messages they produced. Respondent concerns with the primary goal of influence were positively related to their level of planning of, and effort exerted in producing, persuasive messages, as well as to the level of logic and reasoning reflected in them. In addition, secondary goals were associated with planning and characteristics of persuasive messages. Identity goals were positively associated with both the level of planning and logic, and negatively related to the directness of the message. Interaction goals were positively related to planning and the level of positivity in the message. Relational resource goals were positively associated with message positivity. Finally, concerns about arousal management were negatively related to the directness, positivity, and logic of message appeals.

The overall pattern of effects in these findings suggests an important relationship between goals, planning, and message production. The strongest relationships were observed between the primary goal, influence, and message production. Moreover, greater degrees of planning went into messages that reflected primary influence goals and the secondary goals of identity and interaction concerns. However, significant relationships were also observed between secondary goals and characteristics of the persuasive messages. In addition, some goals created negative effects on message characteristics, whereas other goals created positive effects—a finding that underscores the problem of goal management and the complexity of interpersonal influence attempts. For example, identity and interaction goals were positively associated with message positivity, but arousal management goals were negatively related with message positivity. Also, the primary goal of influence was positively associated with the logic of message appeals, but arousal management was negatively associated with message logic. Dillard and his colleagues (1989) offered the following conclusion about the influence of primary and secondary goals on message production:

> The primary goal serves to initiate and maintain the social action, while the secondary goals act as a set of boundaries which delimit the verbal choices available to sources. (p. 32)

When secondary goals of impression management (i.e., presenting a positive image) are involved in an influence attempt, politeness is likely to be a very important concern. Influence messages that are perceived as impolite may be ineffective because they depict the message source as being rude. A message that is too polite, however, may be ineffective because it may be so indirect as to be easily avoided. As a consequence, Dillard, Wilson, Tusing, and Kinney (1997) recently attempted to identify those characteristics of influence messages that are related to judgments of politeness. According to Brown and Gilman (1989), "Politeness means putting things in such a way as to take account of the feelings of the hearer" (p. 161). Achieving persuasive goals may depend on finding the right balance between presenting the most effective message while at the same time being polite.

Dillard and colleagues (1997) were interested in the extent to which three message characteristics—directness, dominance, and logic—influenced judgments of politeness. They developed videotapes of 320 influence messages that were based on college students' actual influence experiences. Different groups of students rated the messages on dominance, argument, explicitness, and politeness. When they compared these various judgments, Dillard and colleagues found that dominance (i.e., the extent to which the source uses power to influence) was by far the factor most strongly related to politeness judgments. Dillard and colleagues report that messages containing high degrees of dominance were judged as very impolite. Moreover, they report that the dominance communicated in the verbal message (i.e., linguistic dominance) and the dominance communicated nonverbally combined to have the strongest effect on perceptions of impoliteness.

As Dillard and colleagues (1997) expected, messages judged to be high in logic (i.e., that provided a reason for the influence attempt) were judged as being more polite than messages that contained no reasons. Finally, they were surprised to find that directness was positively related to politeness (rather than negatively related, as they expected) and may be due to the generally close relationships participants recalled.

Multiple Goal Management

The preceding discussion clearly indicates that the development of influence goals and plans, and the presentation of an influence message, are not simple matters. One source of complexity in the goals–plans–action sequence occurs when primary and secondary goals are incompatible with one another. In many influence situations, management of these competing goals requires the use of complex tactics that enable sources to gain compliance without harming themselves or their relationships. In this regard, the management of multiple goals reflects Sillars's (1980) concern about the perceived value of the relational costs and rewards associated with strategy use.

B. J. O'Keefe and Shepherd (1987) describe three strategies people use to manage the conflict created by incompatible primary and secondary goals. Their first goal management strategy, *selection*, allows people to resolve this conflict by choosing between the conflicting goals. Applying the Dillard and colleagues (1989) distinction between primary and secondary goals, the selection strategy requires people to assign priority to either the primary goal of influence or to subsidiary goals such as relational maintenance and identity management. For example, if you wish to collect an overdue $50 loan from your roommate, your primary goal may be to reclaim the unpaid money. However, secondary goals of relational maintenance (you have to live with this person) and identity management (you don't want to appear cheap or petty) may affect the nature of your compliance request. To manage the apparent conflict between these primary and secondary goals, you might adopt the selection strategy and give priority to either the primary or the secondary goals. If priority is given to the primary goal, you might produce a compliance message that reflects little concern about your own image or your relationship with your roommate—for example, "You still haven't repaid the $50 loan I gave you, and I want the money today." However, maintaining a favorable relationship with your roommate may be a higher priority than reclaiming the money you are owed. If priority is given to the secondary goals of relational maintenance and identity management, you might construct a more tactful message, even if it is less likely to cause your roommate to repay the loan—for example, "Gee, I could really use some money to buy books for my English class."

The second strategy for managing conflicting goals is *separation*. B. J. O'Keefe and Shepherd (1987) argue that a separation strategy results in compliance messages that place priority on the primary goal and then address the secondary goals by elaborating messages with phrases that are designed to account for, minimize, or repair the negative characteristics of the primary message (p. 401). Applied to the hypothetical loan situation, a separation strategy might involve a direct, forceful request to achieve the primary goal of loan repayment and another statement or phrase that explains why the money is important to you—for example, "You haven't repaid the $50 I loaned you weeks ago, and I really need the money today. I'm sorry about being so direct, but I don't get paid until next week and I have to buy books for my English class."

Integration is a third strategy for managing competing goals. Integration strategies resolve the competing demands of primary and secondary goals by redefining the persuasive situation (B. J. O'Keefe & Shepherd, 1987). Returning again to the hypothetical loan scenario, an integrative strategy might cause you to generate a message that redefines the loan obligation as a willingness for roommates to help one another. Such a message might permit you to request payment of the loan from your roommate without threatening the relationship—for example, "I am happy that we have the type of friendship that allows us to ask each other for help when we need it. And right now, I really need to ask for the $50 I loaned you a couple weeks ago. You see, I need to buy books for my English class and don't get paid until next week"

In a study examining the use of these goal management strategies, B. J. O'Keefe and Shepherd (1987) found that the frequency of strategy use was unrelated to persuasive outcomes. However, greater use of integration strategies was associated with interpersonal success ratings. The more people used an integration management strategy, the more they were liked and perceived as competent by their interaction partners (p. 415). These findings, and others like them (Bingham & Burleson, 1989; B. J. O'Keefe & McCornack, 1987), suggest that although the three goal management strategies may be equally effective for achieving the primary persuasive goal, use of an integration goal management strategy appears most effective for achieving secondary goals such as identity management and relational maintenance.

Message Design Logics and Message Production

In contrast to the cognitive rules and planning approach to message production, B. J. O'Keefe has introduced an alternative description of the message production process. B. J. O'Keefe claims that message production research based on rational goals analysis (such as suggested by Dillard [1990a] and C. R. Berger [1997]) implies that people with similar goals will produce and enact similar persuasive messages. For example, if several people have the same primary and secondary influence goals, then they should generate similar-looking messages. However, the findings of prior studies also suggest that differences exist among the messages produced by people holding similar interaction goals. Results of the B. J. O'Keefe and Shepherd (1987) study and other studies suggested that people approach influence message generation in specific yet different ways. B. J. O'Keefe (1988) introduced the concept of *message design logics*, which reflect differences in fundamental premises people have about the nature and function of communication. Differences in these belief systems are reflected in three separate message design logics.

Expressive Design Logics

The most simple design logic one can possess is based on the premise that "language is a medium for expressing thoughts and feelings" (B. J. O'Keefe, 1988, p. 84). People using this design logic fail to separate their thoughts and feelings from the messages they produce. These people are described as "dumpers" who openly express their thoughts and feelings and assume that others interact in the same fashion (B. J. O'Keefe, 1990).

Individuals using the expressive design logic are unlikely to consider the context or the audience in generating their message. For such people, asking someone out on a date would entail identifying a likely person and directly asking her (or him) for a date. Individuals using the expressive design logic would devote little, if any, consideration to the issue of whether it is a good time to ask the other person out, or if the other person would even be interested in going out on a date.

Conventional Design Logics

People adopting conventional design logics view "communication as a game that is to be played cooperatively, according to socially conventional rules and procedures" (B. J. O'Keefe, 1988, p. 86). People who use conventional design logics view the characteristics of communicative situations as fixed parameters that define rules of appropriate interaction.

Individuals using conventional design logics, unlike expressives, are likely to make great use of elements of the context and the audience in generating influence messages. In a date-initiation context, the conventional individual is likely to follow the "rules" of courtship and will converse and flirt with the person chosen as a possible date before actually asking that person out because this is what he (or she) sees as the "game" of asking another person to go on a date.

Rhetorical Design Logics

People employing rhetorical design logics view communication as the "creation and negotiation of social selves and situations" (B. J. O'Keefe,

1988, p. 87). For this kind of person, the primary function of messages is negotiation of a consensus about the social reality people find themselves in. Rather than reacting to prior situations, or viewing the situation as a fixed set of parameters, rhetoricals attempt to define the situation in a manner that is beneficial to the achievement of their goals. Rather than ask another person on a date, then, the rhetorical individual would likely attempt to redefine the nature of his (or her) relationship with the other person through conversation using integrative messages.

Design Logics and Message Production

B. J. O'Keefe argues that these three design logics can be ordered on a developmental continuum. The expressive design logic is viewed as the least cognitively developed, while the rhetorical design logic is viewed as most cognitively developed. Using this developmental ranking, B. J. O'Keefe and McCornack (1987) assessed perceptions people have of messages that reflect these design logics. Their research participants rated messages with a rhetorical message design logic as more favorable and potentially more persuasive than messages that reflected conventional and expressive design logics. However, a subsequent study found that although messages with rhetorical design logics were perceived as more communicatively competent, they were not perceived as more effective than messages reflecting conventional and expressive design logics (Bingham & Burleson, 1989).

Together, these findings provide support for the preferential status given to rhetorical design logics. Presumably, people who employ these logics are likely to be judged as more competent communicators than people who use conventional and expressive design logics. These findings also suggest that persuaders who employ rhetorical design logics *may* be more influential in some persuasive situations.

Although these findings hold promise for the concept of message design logics, participants in all of these investigations were undergraduate students enrolled in communication courses. It should come as little surprise that students enrolled in courses designed to improve communication skills would perceive polished messages reflecting a rhetorical design logic to be more competent, satisfying, and successful than less developed messages indicative of an expressive design logic. Members of different social, cultural, and economic communities may place a higher value on messages that are more direct expressions of feelings and values. In other words, the perceptions of college students may differ considerably from the perceptions of people in other walks of life. Clearly, additional research on the robustness of these findings and the effects of message design logics is warranted.

All interpersonal influence situations involve two people, an influence agent (i.e., the personal trying to persuade) and the target (i.e., the person being persuaded). Our discussion to this point and in the previous chapter has focused on the influence agent. Comparatively speaking, relatively little research has focused on the *target* of these influence attempts. When research does focus on influence targets, it is generally to study how these individuals resist influence attempts. As a consequence, our discussion now turns to the research and theorizing on how people resist unwanted influence attempts.

RESISTING INFLUENCE ATTEMPTS

Research indicates that compliance-gaining strategies generally meet with success (Cody et al., 1994; Dillard et al., 2002). There are times, however, when targets of influence messages do not want to comply with the influence agent's request. Put simply, there are going to be times when targets of influence messages want to resist others' influence attempts.

Much of the compliance-gaining research focused on the messages that participants might send without consideration of the target's response. Compliance-resistance messages, on the other hand, are clearly part of an ongoing interaction. The study of compliance-*resistance* messages presumes that there was an earlier influence attempt that the persuasive target is responding to. Moreover, the structure and content of the resistance message is likely to have an important impact on subsequent influence message attempts (if any) that the agent generates.

Consider the following example. Imagine that you are back in high school "hanging out" at a friend's house with a group of several friends and acquaintances. Some of these people are good friends of yours while others are "friends of friends"—people that you don't know very well. You are having a good time when someone you don't know very well reaches into his or her backpack and produces a joint. The joint is lit, passed around, and handed to you. Assuming that you do not want to smoke pot, what do you do?

In situations where influence targets do not want to comply with a request, Ifert (2000) recently argued that there is a tension between a desire to comply and a desire to resist compliance. The desire to comply likely stems, in part at least, from relational concerns and obligations. Ifert argues that compliance research (on both compliance resisting and compliance gaining) "assumes that, for the most part, a fairly intimate relationship exists between requester and request target" (p. 127). In our smoking pot example, the forces pushing for compliance might include a desire to maintain a positive relationship with your friends and to be viewed favorably by everyone present. Relational forces pushing targets toward compliance are particularly important for influence messages related to drugs. As we will discuss in greater detail below, Alberts, Miller-Rassulo, and Hecht (1991) reported that drug offers from strangers are relatively rare and easily refused. A majority of drug offers (including offers of alcohol) come from friends and thus are much more difficult for targets to refuse.

On the other hand, the forces pulling influence targets toward resistance have generally been conceptualized in terms of obstacles to compliance (Ifert, 2000). Obstacles include not wanting to comply, not being able to comply, or not liking the person asking for the compliance. In our smoking pot example, the primary obstacle to compliance might be that you are proud of your ability to resist using alcohol and other drugs up to this point in your life and you do not want to begin now.[1] We will have more to say about obstacles to compliance later, but for now they can be considered the reasons why a person might not want to comply.

Our focus in this section will be on compliance-resistance research. To begin this discussion, then, we will focus on compliance-resistance strategies. We will follow this discussion with a consideration of obstacles to compliance and their relation to politeness. Finally, we will consider research performed on influence and resistance as it relates to adolescent drug use.

Compliance-Resisting Strategies

Following the lead of compliance-gaining researchers, scholars interested in compliance resistance initially developed several lists of verbal strategies that individuals could use to resist compliance (e.g., Alberts et al., 1991; McLaughlin, Cody, & Robey, 1980; see Ifert, 2000, for a detailed review of these typologies). As an example, consider the compliance-resistance strategy typology developed by McLaughlin and colleagues (1980). Based on previous research on conflict, they described five compliance-resistance strategies. *Nonnegotiation* refers to strategies where the target clearly and unequivocally refuses the influence attempt (e.g., "Just say no"). *Identity management* strategies involve manipulating the identity of either the target or the requester (e.g., by flattering the influencing agent or by acting incompetent). *Justifying* strategies involve attempting to explain the reason for noncompliance by focusing on the positive or negative outcomes that compliance would generate for the self, target, or others. *Negotiating* strategies involve the target suggesting an alternative activity to the one specified by the requestor. Finally, *emotional appeals* are those strategies that directly involve affect (e.g., pleading or playing with the requestor's affection) (McLaughlin et al., 1980).

While the various lists of compliance-resisting strategies differ in several important ways (Ifert, 2000), they also contain several over-lapping strategies. For example, strategies of deception, withdrawal, justification, negotiation, and nonnegotiation are included in multiple typologies (Ifert, 2000). These typologies are helpful in identifying some of the common ways that people resist compliance. However, they contain several of the same problems associated with compliance-gaining typologies (e.g., Marwell & Schmitt, 1967; Wiseman & Schenck-Hamlin, 1981). Concerns with compliance-resistance typologies include (among other things) how representative and generalizable they are. Ifert (2000) argues that it may be impossible to find a category scheme that truly includes all of the possible resistance strategies available to potential resistors in every situation (e.g., Kellermann & Cole, 1994).

Given that an "ideal" list of compliance-resisting strategies will likely never be agreed upon and that arguing about the merits of one typology over another rarely generates usable knowledge, several researchers have turned their attention from *how* people resist compliance toward the question of *why* people resist. As we noted above, many scholars consider this phenomenon under the label of *obstacles to compliance*.

Obstacles Inhibiting Compliance

In order for compliance to occur, an influence target must be both motivated and able to comply (Francik & Clark, 1985). In broad terms, then, people resist compliance because they lack motivation (i.e., they do not want to comply) and/or ability (i.e., they cannot comply).

When influence attempts are refused, the refuser is generally expected to provide a reason or reasons why he or she is not complying. Rather than creating lists of obstacles, recent research has attempted to identify the dimensions along which obstacles differ (Ifert, 2000). For example, Wilson, Cruz, Marshall, and Rao (1993) argued that obstacles vary along three dimensions: stability, locus, and controllability. *Stability* refers to how permanent or temporary an obstacle is. *Locus* refers to the extent to which the obstacle is internal (to the target) or external. Finally, *controllability* refers to the extent to which the obstacle is under the target's control. For example, refusing a date because you find the other person unattractive is likely to be a stable, internal, and uncontrollable obstacle. Refusing a date because you are busy on the particular night that the person asked about, on the other hand, is unstable (temporary), external, and uncontrollable.

Even though obstacles inhibiting compliance can and do vary independently along these three dimensions, the obstacles that are actually expressed (i.e., reasons or excuses) tend not to use the full range of these continua. For example, in a study of date refusals, Folkes (1982) found that the reasons stated for refusing a date differed significantly from the real reasons for the rejection. Folkes reported that stated obstacles tended to be unstable ("I'm sorry, but I'm busy that night"), while unstated obstacles tended to be internal and stable ("I don't find you physically attractive"). Along a similar line, Ifert and Roloff (1994) found that students reported inability obstacles to a greater extent than they reported unwillingness obstacles.

Obstacles and Politeness

In resisting influence attempts, people are more likely to provide some obstacles as stated reasons (or excuses) for refusals than they are to provide other reasons or excuses. Why might this be? One likely explanation for this finding is that some ways of refusing are seen as more polite than others. We argued above that in making requests, there is generally a preference for developing influence messages that are polite. The same is true of resistance messages. Being polite while refusing a request is one way of managing the tension between the forces pushing toward compliance and the forces pulling toward refusal (Ifert, 2000). For example, Besson, Roloff, and Paulson (1998) recently reported that even when a request for a date is directly refused, stated refusals contained apologies, statements of concern for the requester's feelings, and statements of appreciation. Thus, even though the date (i.e., influence attempt) is refused, the stated obstacles allow both parties to maintain face (i.e., positive identities).

While polite refusals may be easy to give (and to receive), they are somewhat problematic because they may be so indirect and take the requester's feelings into account to such an extent that they become ineffective (Ifert, 2000). For example, Metts, Cupach, and Imahori (1992) found that one of the more polite sexual rejection messages indicated that the target was not ready to engage in sexual activity. This strategy was seen as being polite because it was comfortable to give and took the target's feelings into account. This same strategy, however, was ineffective because it suggested that the obstacle was unstable ("I'm not ready *right now*") and left the requester with the mistaken expectation that sexual activity would occur in the future (Metts et al., 1992).

One of the important contexts where resisting influence messages have been applied is that of adolescent drug and alcohol use. As a consequence, it is important to consider one such research program.

Resisting Drug Influence Messages

Consider the smoking pot example we used earlier in this chapter. As we noted, this example represents a difficult situation because the target of the influence is likely caught between competing demands. On the one hand, the obstacles to compliance are that the target may be proud of his or her ability to resist using alcohol and other drugs to this point in his or her life and does not want to start using them now. At the same time, the target doesn't want to alienate him- or herself from a group of friends and doesn't want to be evaluated negatively by them or by the people that he or she doesn't know very well. What does the target person do? How do individuals resist the peer pressure to take drugs while at the same time maintaining positive relationships with those around them?

The drug resistance dilemma highlighted in the smoking pot example represents the heart of a series of research projects performed by several researchers at Arizona State University and Penn State University (see M. A. Miller, Alberts, Hecht, Trost, & Krizek, 2000, for a detailed review of this research). These researchers are spearheading the *Drug Resistance Strategies Project*, a series of survey and interview studies investigating how adolescents (i.e., from middle school through college) can effectively resist unwanted offers of alcohol, tobacco, and other drugs.[2] These studies have been performed in various geographic regions of the United States and have included individuals from a variety of racial/ethnic and socioeconomic groups.

Situations such as our smoking pot example are important because M. A. Miller and colleagues (2000) suggest that in many cases adolescents say no to a drug offer (either to themselves or to the offerer) and then use the drug anyway (Trost, Langan, & Kellar-Guenther, 1999). Refusing a drug offer is a particularly difficult for middle school and high school students who may not have developed the cognitive complexity to develop and use effective resistance strategies. Thus, developing effective resistance strategies can help adolescents more confidently refuse drug offers.

There are similarities between producing compliance messages and resisting them. First, both are communication phenomenon (McLaughlin et al., 1980). In the drug scenario, it would be impossible to effectively refuse the drug offer without sending some message (even if it is to "Just say no"). Second, as we suggested above, resisting influence messages can be described using the same primary and secondary goals used to describe message production (Dillard, 1990a; McLaughlin et al., 1980; M. A. Miller et al., 2000). Applying Dillard's (1990a) terminology to the smoking pot example above, the primary goal might be to resist the influence attempt (i.e., not to smoke pot). The secondary resistance goals in the example above may be to maintain a positive relationship with those others in the situation (particularly your good friends) and to maintain your identity as a non–drug user. Dillard would refer to these secondary goals as resource and identity goals, respectively.

Reaching both the primary goal of resistance *and* the secondary goals of maintaining one's identity and relationships requires a delicate balancing act (Harrington, 1995; McLaughlin et al., 1980). According to M. A. Miller and colleagues (2000, p. 43), "Competently maintaining relationships and sustaining a nonuse identity, while meeting one's instrumental goal of refusal, is a difficult task to assume." Strategies that are most direct and effective in resisting the influence attempt might harm the relationship, while indirect and "relationship-friendly" strategies may be ineffective in maintaining resistance.

Maintaining relationships is likely to be an important secondary resistance goal because most drug and alcohol use among adolescents are social activities—that is, something done with friends and romantic partners (M. A. Miller et al., 2000). Moreover, counter to stereotypes, very few drug offers come from strangers (Alberts et al., 1991; Hecht, Trost, Bator, & MacKinnon, 1997; Trost et al., 1999). Same-sex friends were more likely to offer drugs than any other group (e.g., relatives, acquaintances, family members, or strangers). Friends are also more likely to exert social pressure in making drug offers. Indeed, the drug offer is most likely to occur in a social setting (e.g., at a party or other informal gathering) when several friends and acquaintances are around (Alberts et al., 1991; Hecht et al., 1997). Finally, a majority of respondents who indicated that they took drugs even though they did not want to indicated that they did so because of peer pressure or the acceptance of those who were around at the time (M. A. Miller et al., 2000).

The Nature of Drug Offers

Consideration of compliance resistance must begin with consideration of how the compliance was sought in the first place. Thus, to better understand the nature of drug resistance strategies, we need to consider how drug offers are made.

Most drug offers are initially simple; they generally involve either a simple request (e.g., "Want some [beer, pot, tobacco, etc.]?") or a nonverbal pass (e.g., being passed a joint without a corresponding verbal offer). These simple initial requests tend to contain very little overt social pressure. Even though they apply at best very little social pressure, "a direct request challenges the target to construct a message that not only effectively resists the influence attempt, but pacifies the interaction partner as well" (M. A. Miller et al., 2000, p. 54).

Refusing an initial simple offer rarely ends the episode (except in samples from junior high schools where more complex offers are relatively rare; see Alberts et al., 1991). Following the initial refusal, the offerer is likely to respond with multiple counteroffers. Trost and colleagues (1999) indicated that drug offer interactions contained multiple types of offers. Overt social pressure to take drugs generally comes *after* the first offer is refused. After the first offer is refused, the offerer is likely to come back with a more complex offer that contains more overt social pressure (particularly in high-school- and college-age samples; Alberts, Hecht, Miller-Rassulo, & Krizek, 1992).[3]

The escalating nature of multiple drug offers clearly indicates that the advice given to adolescents to "just say no" is likely going to be ineffective because it leaves them unprepared to resist the more complex and potentially persuasive subsequent counteroffers. Thus, it is important to consider how adolescents can develop relatively complex drug resistance strategies.

Drug Resistance Messages

Most refusals begin with a simple "no" (Alberts et al. 1991; Hecht et al., 1997). This makes sense because the simple initial drug offer ("Want some?") is met with an equally simple initial refusal ("No"). Just saying "no," however, is likely to be inadequate because, as we noted, many people initially refused the drug offer but ended up taking the drug anyway. Part of the reason for this is that refusals are likely met with more sophisticated and pressure-laden offers (particularly for those in high school and college) that the refuser may be unprepared to overcome. The more complex and pressure-laden messages need to be met with equally complex refusal messages that explain a person's reasons for refusing. These more complex strategies are particularly difficult for middle school students (who likely lack the cognitive development) to effectively resist.

Thus, an effective resistance strategy must include an explanation that appeases the offerer. Some strategies are likely to be ineffective because they do not directly focus on the secondary goals of relationship maintenance or nonuse identity. For example, explaining that the refuser does not like drugs may generate a negative reaction in the offerer, who is being painted in a negative light. Indicating that a refuser doesn't want to take the drug "may simply be seen as a weak response and an invitation for encouragement" (M. A. Miller et al., 2000, p. 59).

So what is an effective drug resistance strategy? It is overly optimistic and simplistic to maintain a belief that a single message (or strategy type) will be effective in all resistance situations. Instead, what will be an effective resistance message almost certainly depends on the nature of the refuser, the nature of the offerer, and their relationship. Moreover, the context within which the refusal is given (including what drug is being offered and how many others are around) also likely influences the effectiveness of a given strategy.

There are individuals who can effectively refuse drug offers while at the same time maintain friendship with the offerer (Alberts et al., 1999). Given participants' own stories of successful refusals, M. A. Miller and colleagues (2000) discuss the REAL system of refusing drug offers. The REAL system presents a series of escalating resistance messages. The four steps in the REAL system are *R*efuse (a simple "no"), *E*xplain ("no" with an explanation), *A*void (avoid exposure to situations where drugs might be present), and *L*eave (leave the situation).

Thus, the first step in an effective refusal is to *refuse* (i.e., "Just say no"). If the simple refusal works, then the episode is over. However, simple refusals rarely end the episode. In such a case, targets need to move on to the next step.

If the offerer persists, the refuser should then provide an *explanation* for his or her refusal. M. A. Miller and colleagues (2000) claim that "nonuse identity ('I'm not that kind of person') and fear of consequences were most common among White students, whereas nonuse identity and anti-drug attitudes were the most common among the African-American students" (p. 57). Again, if the offerer accepts the explanation, then the episode is over. Explanations that reach both resistance and relational goals are most likely to be accepted.

If the offerer continues to exert pressure following the explanation, the third step in the REAL system involves *avoiding* the situation. Avoidance might include "not exposing oneself to situations where drugs are present" (M. A. Miller et al., 2000, p. 57). Not attending parties at a drug user's house would be an example of avoidance. Avoidance also includes deception—for example, holding a glass of beer but not drinking from it. Deception may not be an honest response, but it continues interaction, involvement, and positive evaluations of the social group that is partaking.

The final step in the REAL system is to *leave* (M. A. Miller et al., 2000). If all else fails, get away from the situation. This does not necessarily imply abandoning the relationship with the offerer, but does involve refusing to interact with those friends while they are doing drugs.

There are some data to indicate that the REAL program does help adolescents avoid drugs (at least for the short term). Hecht and colleagues (1993) developed both a video and a live presentation of the REAL program where the screenplay was developed directly from interviews performed by Alberts and colleagues (1991). When these presentations were paired with a group discussion on drug resistance, participants reported that they were significantly less likely to have used drugs 1 month later (when compared to participants in a control group who did not see the presentation).

One key to producing an effective resistance strategy is to plan ahead. Alberts and colleagues (1991) found that individuals who were more motivated to resist drug offers were more likely to plan their resistance behaviors. Moreover, the extent to which individuals planned was related to how effective their messages were. This is consistent with Dillard's GPA Model of compliance messages and suggests that waiting until a drug offer is made to develop a resistance strategy will make it more difficult to develop an effective resistance strategy.

SUMMARY

This chapter focused on the production and resistance of interpersonal influence messages. Using Dillard's theory of Goals, Plans, and Action, we first discussed the nature of social influence goals. Dillard asserts that primary goals (e.g., asking for a favor) define the nature of the influence attempt while secondary goals serve to limit a source's options in message generation. Plans are produced in an effort to reach goals. Plan complexity is an important aspect of plans. Research indicates that while complex plans are more complete, they are also more difficult to present (particularly when the message source is uncooperative). Message presentation, in turn, depends upon the goals and plans previously developed, including the impression that the message source wants to provide.

We also focused on resisting compliance messages. In this section we focused primarily on the recent research performed on refusing offers of alcohol and other drugs. The same primary and secondary goals outlined by Dillard (1990a) can be invoked in resistance situations as well. In this case, however, the primary goal is resistance while the secondary goals (particularly identity and relationship management) limit the number of viable resistance strategies. M. A. Miller and colleagues (2000) reported that while initial drug offers were simple and direct (e.g., "Wanna beer?"), subsequent offers following a refusal were more complex. Refusing the more complex counteroffers required a more complex explanation of why the offer is being refused. The more successful explanations included claiming a nonuse identity (e.g., "I'm not the sort of person who does that") and noting a fear of consequences (e.g., fearing the high or getting into trouble). The nature of the transaction between offers, counteroffers, and refusals highlights the importance of the relationship between offerer and refuser.

NOTES

1. This discussion of competing forces toward and away from compliance can also be cast in terms of goals as discussed in the compliance-gaining section. In Dillard's terms, the primary goal in the smoking pot example would be to resist compliance (i.e., to *not* smoke pot). The secondary resistance goals in the smoking pot example are likely relational (i.e., maintain a positive relationship) and identity (i.e., maintain your identify as a non–drug user).
2. While offers can involve tobacco, alcohol, or other drugs, we will use the generic term "drugs" from this point forward.
3. That the second drug offer contains more overt social pressure than does the first is consistent with what Hample and Dallinger (1998) refer to as the *rebuff phenomenon*: "when an initial persuasive effort is rebuffed, follow-up persuasive messages are ruder, more aggressive, and more forceful than the first one" (p. 305; see also Dillard et al., 2002).

13

Persuasive Communication Campaigns

LOOKING AHEAD ...

This chapter reviews two theories of persuasion that can effectively serve as the foundation for persuasion campaigns designed to affect political, health, and social behavior. We begin with a discussion of persuasive communication campaigns. Next we review McGuire's (1964, 1999) Inoculation Theory, which has provided the foundation for many political and public health campaigns. Finally, we discuss the implications of Social Cognitive Theory (Akers, Krohn, Lanza-Kaduci, & Radosevich, 1979; Bandura, 1977, 1986), which has been used to mold prosocial behavior in adolescents.

Much of the research we have discussed in this book is essentially composed of "one-shot" studies where a number of people (usually college students) come to a laboratory and are exposed to a single presentation of a single persuasive message (e.g., Janis & Feshbach's seminal 1953 study on fear appeals). In many applied settings, persuasion occurs quite differently. In persuasive communication campaigns, receivers are exposed to multiple presentations of multiple messages. These multiple messages, moreover, are not haphazardly put together, but are part of a planned set of activities designed to accomplish a set of persuasive goals.

PERSUASIVE COMMUNICATION CAMPAIGNS

Simons, Morreale, and Gronbeck (2001) define *persuasive communication campaigns* as "organized sustained attempts at influencing groups or masses of people through a series of messages" (p. 211). Jimmy Carter's 1976 presidential campaign (which we briefly discussed in Chapter 1) represents a good example of a successful persuasive communication campaign. Jimmy Carter was an obscure (from a national perspective at least) former southern governor when he announced his candidacy for president in December 1974. Less than 2 years following this announcement, he was elected president of the United States. Between the campaign announcement late in 1974 and the general election in November 1976, several dramatic changes occurred in voters' beliefs, attitudes, behavioral intentions, and behaviors. These changes were the result, in large part, of the persuasive communication campaign generated by the Carter campaign organization.

The Carter campaign highlights several important characteristics of successful persuasive campaigns. First, like all persuasive interactions, persuasion communication campaigns are goal-driven. Goals for persuasive communication campaigns might include persuading people to vote for a particular political candidate (e.g., Jimmy Carter in 1976), to engage in health-related behavior (e.g., wear a condom while having sex), or to support a particular issue (e.g., the National Rifle Association campaign against gun control). Second, unlike simple one-shot persuasive contexts, persuasive communication campaigns generally have *multiple* goals. The Carter organization's initial goal was simply to raise voters' awareness of who Jimmy Carter was and what he stood for. Without this initial persuasive work, reaching subsequent goals (e.g., attempting to convince voters to vote for him) would have been impossible.

Third, while many one-shot persuasion studies tend to generate small effects (S. L. Becker, 1971), persuasion campaigns can and often do generate dramatic changes in receivers' responses (Pfau & Parrott, 1993). The fourth implication of the Carter example is that persuasion created by campaigns occurs over time. Unlike one-shot studies, this change is created by a carefully crafted and orchestrated series of messages that have the ultimate goal of shaping, changing, or reinforcing recipients' responses. Once they develop goals, campaign strategists then produce a plan that they believe will help them to accomplish each of their goals. The creation of these plans generally results in the development of a series of messages, each building on the one that preceded it, designed to produce the desired outcome or outcomes (Pfau & Parrott, 1993). In the Carter campaign, the goals changed over time (from creating a favorable image of Carter for potential voters to convincing actual voters to choose Carter in the general election) and the messages designed to meet these goals changed as well.

As the Carter example suggests, the political arena is one place where persuasive campaigns are frequently used. During the past 40 years, the mass media, and television in particular, have become an essential conduit for the communicative messages of broad-based political campaigns. For example, Ross Perot's 1992 campaign for the presidency involved very few personal appearances or speeches before live audiences. Instead, he relied on television newscasts, talk shows, and paid commercial announcements to explain his economic proposals to U.S. voters.

Health promotion campaigns have also found that mass media-based campaigns are an effective form of persuasion. Anti-smoking, AIDS education, and driver safety campaigns routinely involve the heavy use of mass media to disseminate informational and motivational messages. Slogans such as "Be a designated driver" and "Friends don't let friends drive drunk" have become etched in our memories as we have been repeatedly exposed to them over the course of several years.

Finally, of course, advertisers frequently utilize persuasive communication campaigns. From the Tidy Bowl man piloting his motorboat through a giant toilet tank to the lonely Maytag repairman, to Mr. Whipple admonishing shoppers "Please don't squeeze the Charmin," television ads have long been a staple of advertising persuasion campaigns. The fact that many people can sing advertising jingles from 20 or more years ago highlights the power of these persuasive campaigns.

Stages of Persuasive Communication Campaigns

We noted above that persuasive communication campaigns involve developing and sending a series of messages over time that are designed to meet multiple persuasive goals. That persuasive goals (and the messages that are designed to meet them) change over time suggests that persuasive communication campaigns go through a number of identifiable stages. The number and nature of these stages likely depends on the type of campaign under consideration (Larson, 2001). For example, the stages in a presidential political campaign (Trent & Friedenberg, 2000) are different from those in a campaign to introduce and sell a new communications technology (e.g., digital cellular phones) (E. M. Rogers, 1985).

Larson (2001) argues that a five-stage model of international politics developed by Binder (1971) can be usefully applied in the context of persuasive communication campaigns. Larson argues that these stages, in one form or another, occur in all types of campaigns. In the first stage, *identification*, campaigns must "develop an identity in the minds of voters, and potential converts or donors" (Larson, 2000, p. 242). Jimmy

Carter's 1976 presidential campaign depended strongly on the identification stage since voters had little previous knowledge about who he was or what he stood for. In political campaigns, identifying key campaign themes is an important part of the identification phase. In public health campaigns, identification likely involves generating awareness of a particular health hazard (e.g., communicating the hazards of smoking to junior high school students).

The second stage in Larson's model is establishing *legitimacy*. In political campaigns, establishing legitimacy involves winning primary elections, gaining important endorsements, fundraising, and gaining the attention of the media. In advertising campaigns, legitimacy is established by promoting the effectiveness of the product (e.g., the Good Housekeeping seal of approval or a positive review in *Consumer Reports* magazine). In public health campaigns, legitimacy is generated by establishing the effectiveness of the recommended behavior (e.g., quitting smoking or eating more fruits and vegetables).

The third stage in Larson's model is *participation*. In political contexts, participation can occur at large rallies where supporters yell slogans or go door-to-door as a means of participating in the campaign. In product campaigns, participation might involve giving away coupons or free samples of the product at the grocery store.

In the fourth stage of campaigns, *penetration*, the person or product being promoted can be described as having "made it" (Larson, 2000, p. 247). At this stage, many people use the product or support the candidate. In presidential politics, this might involve winning (or doing better than expected in) early primaries. This energizes the campaign, generates contributions, and gains converts in states with later primaries. In advertising a product, this stage might involve giving a product an advantage over its competition (e.g., a longer car warranty or a larger rebate).

The final stage in Larson's model, *distribution*, occurs "when the campaign or movement succeeds and becomes institutionalized" (Larson, 2000, p. 247). In political campaigns this might involve engaging in activities that fulfill earlier promises. While this stage may not occur for advertising campaigns, rebates or incentives for storeowners might occur in the distribution stage.

Social influence campaigns are familiar to mass media consumers and persuasion scholars alike. Beginning with the propaganda research of half a century ago (e.g., Doob, 1950; Lasswell, 1950), persuasion research has examined the effectiveness of several theories that have been applied in mass media campaigns. In this chapter we describe two of these theories and examine their effectiveness in media campaigns. Although they are not "mass media" models, per se, each of these theories has been effectively employed in mediated persuasion campaigns.

INOCULATION THEORY

In the early 1960s, William McGuire developed a program of research that investigated resistance to persuasive messages. He was interested in understanding the psychological and cognitive processes that affect a person's willingness and motivation to resist arguments that attack widely held beliefs. McGuire called these types of beliefs *cultural truisms* or beliefs that are thought to be true among a vast majority of members of a particular culture (e.g., "You should brush your teeth at least twice a day" and "Mental illness is not contagious"). Cultural truisms are interesting to study because they are rarely challenged or given much thought.

A Biological Metaphor

McGuire (1961a, 1961b, 1964, 1999) described a technique for inducing resistance to persuasive attacks against cultural truisms. Inoculation Theory posits that promoting resistance to persuasion is analogous to inoculating the body against a virus. When people are inoculated against a virus, such as smallpox or the flu, the vaccine they receive contains a weak dosage of the virus itself. In response to the inoculation, the body's immune system creates antibodies to fight the virus. If the body's immune system is functioning properly, the initial attack of the weak virus leaves the body better prepared to attack stronger, naturally occurring, infections from the same virus type.

Applied in persuasive situations, the inoculation metaphor suggests that because cultural truisms are widely believed, they are rarely scrutinized or given much attention. Such beliefs are often vulnerable to persuasive attacks because people "have had little motivation or practice in developing supporting arguments to bolster [them] or in preparing refutations for the unsuspected counterarguments" (McGuire & Papageorgis, 1961, p. 327). McGuire's inoculation technique was designed to prepare people to resist attacks against cultural truisms. Similar to the biological process of inoculation, inoculation against persuasive arguments involves presenting people with weak arguments against a cultural belief and allowing receivers to develop stronger arguments to refute these attacks. McGuire and Papageorgis proposed that "the 'supportive therapy' approach of pre-exposing a person to arguments in support of

[a] belief has less immunizing effectiveness than the 'inoculation' procedure of pre-exposing them to weakened, defense stimulating forms of the counterarguments" (1961, p. 327). Presumably, after receiving weak counterarguments and developing a refutational defense of the cultural truism, people are better able and more motivated to counterargue future, stronger, attacks on their belief systems.

Persuasive Inoculation

The basic procedure for inoculating people against persuasive attacks involves providing them with an attack message containing weak arguments that oppose a particular belief. People are then given the opportunity to generate arguments that refute the arguments contained in the attack message. Sometimes, inoculation procedures involve presenting people with the refutational arguments (passive refutation) instead of asking them to generate their own refutational arguments (active refutation). For example, if you wanted to inoculate schoolchildren against likely persuasive appeals to try drugs, you might present them with a series of weak arguments supporting drug use, and then ask them to write an essay (active refutation) refuting the arguments advocating drug use that they had just heard. You could also inoculate students by presenting them with a weak message advocating drug use and then asking them to read a second message that refuted the arguments advocating drug use (passive refutation).

Once the inoculation procedure has been performed, people who have been inoculated should be less susceptible to future arguments attacking their beliefs than people who did not experience the inoculation procedure. To test the effectiveness of this technique, researchers usually conduct an experiment in which an inoculation treatment (attack message followed by refutation message) is presented to people in the experimental group, while people in the control condition receive a message supportive of the cultural truism (or no message at all). Some time after receiving these initial messages, people in the experimental and control groups are exposed to a message containing stronger arguments that attacks their beliefs about the issue in question. Following this second attack message, the attitudes or beliefs of experimental and control group participants are measured. If the attitudes or beliefs about the issue in question are more favorable among the experimental group than among the control group, then the inoculation treatment is deemed effective for promoting resistance to a persuasive attack. Extending the example of promoting resistance to drugs, if children who receive the inoculation treatment are better able to resist subsequent invitations to use drugs than children who do not receive the inoculation treatment, then we can conclude that the inoculation treatment was effective.

Supporting Evidence

In an initial test of this technique, McGuire and Papageorgis (1961) examined beliefs about a number of cultural truisms such as "Everyone should brush his teeth after every meal if possible" and "The effects of penicillin have been, almost without exception, of great benefit to mankind." For one belief, participants either read or generated a message supporting the belief statement (supportive message condition). For a second belief, participants read a weak attack against the belief statement and then were asked to read (passive refutation condition) or write (active refutation condition) a message that refuted the attack on their belief.

Two days after these initial treatments, participants read essays that attacked the cultural truisms they had defended in the prior experimental session. After reading the stronger attack essays, participants indicated the extent to which the truism was true or false. Findings revealed that the inoculation treatment was more effective than the supportive message in promoting resistance to persuasion. People who received the supportive message treatment, followed by the persuasive attack, were uncertain about whether the cultural truism was true or false. However, when they received the inoculation treatment, people were more resistant to the subsequent persuasive attack and indicated greater agreement that the cultural truism in question was indeed true.

In addition, McGuire and Papageorgis (1961) compared active and passive refutation inoculation procedures. When people read the refutational statement, they were more resistant to subsequent persuasive attacks than when they generated their own refutational arguments. One explanation for this finding may be that students in this study had difficulty developing refutational arguments that were as strong as the arguments created by the experimenter in the passive refutation condition. But McGuire (1999) claimed that the superiority of the passive refutation message was due to the recipients' lack of practice in coming up with their own counterarguments in active refutation condition.

While it could be due to a lack of practice, that passive refutation is superior to active refutation is also consistent with our discussion of "connecting the dots" in Chapter 6. In that chapter, we argued that leaving parts of the message implicit for recipients to "fill in" (e.g., implicit conclusions or warrants) was a relatively ineffective persuasive choice. McGuire and Papageorgis's (1961) results were consistent with this hypothesis because people who were asked to develop their own counterarguments were less resistant to counterpersuasion than participants who read the passive refutation message. In this sense, McGuire's biological metaphor breaks down because it does not appear that providing a weak attack message "naturally" provides receivers with the ammunition to counter future attacks.

In addition to offering further evidence of the effectiveness of this technique (McGuire, 1961b), subsequent studies have extended the influence of inoculation treatments. For example, the combination of supportive and refutational treatments has been found to produce more resistance to persuasive attacks than the refutational treatment alone (McGuire, 1961a). Papageorgis and McGuire (1961) found that in addition to promoting resistance to attacks against the cultural belief that was the focus of the inoculation treatment, inoculation procedures also enhanced resistance for other, related beliefs.

In recent years, Inoculation Theory has been employed to strengthen attitudes and promote resistance to counterpersuasion for beliefs that are not culturally accepted (Pfau, 1995; see Szabo & Pfau, 2002, for a recent review of this literature). However, a review of the literature concluded that inoculation treatments appear to be less effective for controversial topics than they are for cultural truisms (D. J. O'Keefe, 1990). Pfau (1992) argued that one difference between traditional inoculation studies and more recent investigations of supportive and refutational messages that involve more controversial topics is that traditional inoculation studies involved the use of *threat*, or the "forewarning against an impending challenge to existing attitudes" (Pfau, Van Bockern, & Kang, 1992, p. 201). According to Pfau (1992, 1995), threat is required for successful inoculation (see also, McGuire, 1999). Pfau and his colleagues argued that "inoculation promotes resistance through the use of the impending attack, *employed in conjunction with* refutational preemption. The warning of an impending attack is designed to threaten the individual, triggering the motivation to bolster arguments supporting attitudes" (Pfau, Kenski, Nitz, & Sorenson, 1990, p. 28). Message treatments that do not threaten a person's belief system are unlikely to motivate people to generate arguments against the attack. Thus, the relatively small differences in effectiveness between supportive and refutational messages in many recent investigations may be due to the fact that the forewarning contained in these studies' messages failed to threaten the belief systems of message receivers.

Applications of Inoculation Theory

Although most investigations of Inoculation Theory have been conducted in laboratory environments, inoculation treatments have recently become a central component in many persuasive campaigns. Extending the analysis that threat is an essential feature of effective inoculation treatments, Pfau and his colleagues have revitalized interest in Inoculation Theory by examining the effectiveness of inoculation treatments in political campaigns (Pfau & Burgoon, 1988; Pfau & Kenski, 1990; Pfau et al., 1990), comparative advertising (Pfau, 1992), and campaigns designed to prevent the onset of smoking among adolescents (Pfau et al., 1992). In this section we examine how Inoculation Theory has been employed effectively in political and public health campaigns (see also Szabo & Pfau, 2002).

Inoculation against Political Attacks

Recent political campaigns for national, state, and local offices have become increasingly negative. Political campaigns must provide reasons for voting *for* a particular candidate, but they must also present reasons for voting *against* the opponent. As a result, the negative campaign, or *attack politics*, has become an essential feature of many campaign operations (Devlin, 2001). Pfau and Kenski (1990) offer several reasons for the increased use of negative campaign advertising. For example, negative messages can be more influential than supportive messages. Negative messages are also cheaper to produce and can be aired effectively on radio, a low-cost medium. In addition, negative messages are often viewed as a counterweight against the influence of incumbency (p. 4).

The rapid growth of attack politics has sent candidates and campaign coordinators scrambling for effective defenses against negative campaign messages. Inoculation techniques provide an effective means for defending against the attacks of political candidates. Effective inoculation messages in political campaigns have two essential components. First, inoculation messages must contain a threat, a warning that an opponent is likely to launch a persuasive attack. The threat of an impending attack serves to motivate receivers to defend against the persuasive attack. Second, inoculation messages must contain a preemptive refutation. That is, they must respond in advance to counterarguments that an opponent is likely to produce. Thus, effective inoculation (refutational) pretreatments warn of an impending threat that motivates receivers to develop arguments to bolster their position against subsequent attacks on their candidate (Pfau & Kenski, 1990, p. 75). Audience members' bolstering of their position in the face of attack messages is facilitated by the preemptive refutation provided in the inoculation message.

Two studies provide evidence of the effectiveness of inoculation techniques in political campaigns. Pfau and colleagues (1990) performed a study of attitudes toward Bush and Dukakis in the 1988 presidential campaign that involved direct mailing of political campaign messages and measured voters' candidate preferences and voting intentions through interview procedures. Three experimental conditions were created. Several days after responding to a telephone survey about their voting preferences, Bush and Dukakis supporters in the *inoculation condition* received an inoculation message in the mail. These messages warned that potentially persuasive attacks on their candidate were likely to occur (threat component) and provided a refutation to these attacks (refutational component).

People in the *inoculation-plus-reinforcement condition* responded to the telephone survey, received an inoculation message (containing both the threat and preemptive refutation components), and a week later received another mailing that reinforced their candidate preference. Finally, people in the *post-hoc-refutation condition* responded to the telephone survey and later received a message that attacked the candidate whom they supported. A week later, these people were mailed a refutational message that responded to attacks against their candidate. Because this refutation occurred after the original attack message, it was labeled a *post-hoc refutation*.

Several days after the reinforcement and post-hoc refutations were mailed, researchers conducted interviews in the homes of the research participants. During these interviews, people in the inoculation and inoculation-plus-reinforcement conditions were presented with a message that attacked their candidate's position. Following this, participants completed a survey of their attitudes toward the candidate and indicated their likelihood of voting for the candidate. People in the post-hoc refutation condition had already received the attack message in the mail. These participants simply completed the attitude and voting preference survey.

Although party affiliation and treatment conditions interacted to affect posttest attitude and voting intentions, the general pattern of findings indicated strong support for the inoculation techniques. The effects for people with weak party affiliations were somewhat mixed, but the effects among people who clearly identified with one of the two political parties and among those with no party affiliation were consistently clear: the inoculation and inoculation-plus-reinforcement treatments were superior in deflecting the influence of an attack message to the post-hoc refutation treatment (Pfau et al., 1990).

A similar study found additional evidence of the effectiveness of inoculation treatments. Studying a campaign for a U.S. Senate seat, Pfau and Burgoon (1988) found that inoculation treatments increased resistance to attitude change following a persuasive attack. In discussing the implications of their findings, they concluded that "inoculation deflects the persuasiveness of subsequent political attacks in a number of ways: undermining the potential influence of the source of political attacks, deflecting the specific content of political attacks, and reducing the likelihood that political attacks will influence receiver voting intention" (Pfau & Burgoon, 1988, pp. 105–106).

Inoculation against Smoking

Based on the success of these earlier studies, Pfau and colleagues (1992) endeavored to study inoculation's effectiveness in an adolescent smoking prevention program. Students in seventh-grade health education classes were exposed to a videotaped message that was designed to help them resist peer pressure to smoke. This is a particularly important group to target because students generally leave elementary school with negative attitudes toward smoking and smokers. This negative view, however, tends to erode through the junior high school years when many long-term smokers begin their smoking habit. Thus, inoculation theory seems an obvious choice for preventing attitude slippage among the junior high school age group.

As a consequence, Pfau and colleagues (1992) expected seventh-grade students who were exposed to the typical inoculation series of messages to exhibit more negative attitudes toward smoking and be more likely to resist smoking initiation when compared with students in the control condition. They were also interested in the extent to which self-esteem (a person's positive, neutral, or negative view of themselves) influenced the effectiveness of the inoculation messages. Self-esteem is important because of the significant role of peer pressure in smoking onset. Individuals with low self-esteem are likely to be particularly susceptible to peer pressure and may be most helped by inoculation.

During the first week of October in 1990, over 1,000 seventh-grade students in Sioux Falls, South Dakota, were randomly assigned to either the inoculation or the control conditions. Students in the inoculation condition watched a video presentation that included, first, a threat component warning students of oncoming peer pressure to get them to smoke; second, inoculation messages that challenged anti-smoking attitudes (e.g., "Smoking is cool"; Pfau et al., 1992, p. 219); and third, messages that contained direct refutations of the attacking arguments. This study did not include a subsequent attack message because the researchers expected such messages to occur naturally in the form of peer pressure.

In both February and May of 1991 (19 and 33 weeks following message exposure, respectively), four dependent variables (attitudes toward smoking, attitudes toward smokers, likelihood of smoking, and the chance of resisting smoking) were measured. These same variables had also been measured 1 month *before* message exposure in order to gain baseline levels of attitudes and likely behaviors.

Pfau and colleagues' (1992) results indicated that students reported negative attitudes toward smoking and few behavioral intentions to smoke at the beginning of the school year. These attitudes and intentions, however, eroded as the school year went on. Results also indicated that inoculation did help to slow this erosion, but only for low-self-esteem participants. Low-self-esteem participants in the inoculation condition exhibited more negative attitudes following message exposure when compared to low-self-esteem participants in the control condition. Inoculation had no impact for moderate- and high-self-esteem participants.

Pfau and Van Bockern (1994) reported data from the study's second year (the participants' eighth-grade year). These follow-up results indicated, first, that the erosion of attitudes and intentions in the first year continued over the course of the eighth grade. Second, in both September and May of that second year, inoculation was effective in forestalling that attitudinal erosion (but not likelihood of smoking or the chances of resisting). The finding that inoculation was effective only for low-self-esteem participants was only evident (and barely so) in September and only for attitudes. The inoculation effect for low-self-esteem participants had completely disappeared by May of the second year.

Summarizing Inoculation Findings

Early investigations of Inoculation Theory conducted by McGuire and his colleagues demonstrated the effectiveness of inoculation treatments in promoting resistance to persuasion. These investigations occurred in controlled laboratory settings and involved the use of cultural truisms, issues that are so widely believed that they are rarely questioned (e.g., "Capitalism is good" or "Patriotism is important"). Recently, inoculation treatments have also proved effective in promoting resistance to persuasion in naturally occurring persuasive campaigns. Through studies involving political, advertising, and public health campaigns, Pfau and his colleagues demonstrated that inoculation treatments that warn of an impending persuasive attack motivate receivers to resist a subsequent persuasive appeal (K. I. Miller, 2002).

The breadth of this theory is evident in the variety of mass media persuasive campaigns that have effectively employed inoculation treatments. Inoculation can be an effective technique once people have established an attitude for a particular candidate, product, or idea. This suggests that inoculation will be put to best use in the legitimization, participation, and penetration campaign stages. Pfau and colleagues (1992) attempted to legitimize nonsmoking attitudes and behaviors. The early stages of the "Just say no" campaigns performed a similar function by attempting to portray not taking drugs as "cool."

Along a similar line, a nonsmoking campaign can be seen as working at the participation stage. As Pfau and colleagues (1992) found, students generally leave elementary school with negative feelings toward smoking. Inoculation campaigns such as those reported in Pfau and colleagues are attempts to maintain a participation stage where adolescents refrain from smoking.

In the political arena, inoculation strategies come at the crossroads of two competing persuasive communication campaigns (one for the candidate and one for the opponent). For example, in recent political campaigns, there has been effective use of both positive and negative campaign messages. Thus, a prospective voter with an established attitude is likely to have that attitude challenged by the opponent's negative ads. Forewarning of threat and providing counterarguments are likely to be effective means for maintaining voters' support and represents one persuasive communication campaign trying to defuse another persuasive communication campaign.

It is important to point out that inoculation message strategies do not have to provide the actual attack message in order to work. In several contexts (as in the Pfau et al. [1992] study on smoking), the attack messages will occur naturally. While persuaders may not be able to predict the specific nature of an attack message, they should be able to predict what issues or positions might be attacked.

Inoculation works because it arms individuals with counterarguments to fend off future persuasive attacks. There are times, however, when providing individuals with possible counterarguments is not enough. Sometimes people not only need the proper arguments, but the knowledge that others share their attitudes and practice in using them as well.

SOCIAL COGNITIVE THEORY

The other theory that we will discuss in this chapter, Social Cognitive Theory, is "not specifically an account of learning from exposure to mass communication, but rather is a general explanation of how people acquire new forms of behavior" (DeFleur & Ball-Rokeach, 1989, p. 212). Thus, like Inoculation Theory, Social Cognitive Theory (Bandura, 1977, 1986) was not developed as a mass media model of persuasion. Instead, it was developed as a general model of behavior acquisition (initially called Social Learning Theory) and has expanded into a more general theory of human functioning (Bandura, 2001). Social learning remains an important component of the theory, and, as a consequence, remains an important model from which to develop persuasive communication campaigns (Bandura, 2000).

Social Cognitive Theory, like its predecessor Social Learning Theory, has been particularly relevant to the study of social influence via the mass media. Bandura noted that "an influential source of social learning is the abundant and varied symbolic modeling provided by television, films, and other visual media" (1977, p. 39). This modeling can have positive or negative consequences. For example, there are those who argue that media depictions of violence produce aggressive behavior (see, e.g., Gunter, 1994).

An example of inappropriate modeling might be the "backyard wrestling" phenomenon, where teens establish wrestling federations and carry out matches in their backyards (where they imitate the stars they see on television). This modeling is inappropriate because the backyard matches are not as carefully choreographed as their professional counterparts, frequently leading to injuries to either or both of the backyard combatants.

On the positive side, Social Cognitive Theory has become a staple of health-related persuasive communication campaigns. We begin the discussion of this theory by describing its major assumptions. Then, we examine tests of the theory and describe persuasive campaigns in which it has been effectively applied.

Social Learning

Before discussing the application of this theory in social influence campaigns, it is important to understand the fundamental assumptions of the theory and the predictions it makes about learning behavior. Many early learning theories posited that behavior acquisition or change in an individual is a function of positive reinforcements provided when a desired behavior is produced and punishments provided following undesirable behavior (e.g., Skinner, 1938). Given this perspective, humans and animals learn behavior by pairing performance of a particular behavior with the rewards or punishments that it generates. For example, when parents teach their children to read, they routinely provide verbal praise when a word, phrase, or sound is properly pronounced. When a word, phrase, or sound is incorrectly pronounced, the error is noted and assistance is provided to help the child pronounce it correctly. Over time, the child learns the correct pronunciation because it has been associated with positive reinforcement. This learning process takes time and occurs "over a number of 'trials' in which the link between the stimuli and the response to be learned is reinforced" (DeFleur & Ball-Rokeach, 1989, p. 216).

Social Cognitive Theory (Bandura, 1977, 1986) differs from other learning theories in that it emphasizes the capacity of humans to learn through *observation*, instead of through direct experience of the positive and negative outcomes of trial and error.

> Observational learning is vital for both development and survival. Because mistakes can produce costly, or even fatal consequences, the prospects for survival would be slim indeed if one could learn only by suffering the consequences of trial and error. For this reason, one does not teach children to swim, adolescents to drive automobiles, and novice medical students to perform surgery by having them discover the appropriate behavior through the consequences of their successes and failures. The more costly and hazardous the possible mistakes, the heavier is the reliance on observational learning from competent examples. (Bandura, 1977, p. 12)

In addition to the advantages of observational learning over trial-and-error experience, some behaviors cannot be learned through trial and error alone. For example, adults and older children who constantly provide a model of developed communicative behavior for children to mimic serve to facilitate a child's language acquisition and development. In other cases, observational learning provides the benefit of experience that cannot be acquired through trial and error. For example, high-risk activities such as sky diving and bungee-cord jumping may not afford participants the chance to recover from the negative effect of an error. In this regard, Social Cognitive Theory is tailor-made for persuasive campaigns that promote resistance to high-risk behaviors such as drug use and drunk driving.

Social Cognitive Theory and Social Influence

The fundamental assumption of Social Cognitive Theory is that by observing others, an individual forms an idea of how new behaviors are performed as well as how those new behaviors are rewarded or punished. On later occasions this information serves as a guide for his or her own behavior (Bandura, 1977, p. 22). Observing the positive and negative consequences of a model's behavior serves several functions in the social cognitive process.[1] First, this observation provides information about the consequences that are associated with particular behaviors. Thus, the *information function* allows people to develop and test hypotheses about which responses are most appropriate and most likely to be rewarded in particular situations. Second, observation of a model's behavior serves a *motivation function* by establishing a value (either positive or negative) for the desired behavior and an incentive (or disincentive) to enact the behavior. Finally, observation serves a *reinforcement function* by strengthening the connection between behaviors and outcomes that have already been learned (Bandura, 1977, p. 17).[2] Observational learning is effective to the extent that it causes people to anticipate the consequences of a particular behavior and establishes an incentive for learners to receive the positive consequences of behavior and a disincentive to avoid the negative ones.

There are several stages of effective observational learning in mass media contexts. First, a target person *observes* a model engaging in a particular behavior. Second, the observer *identifies* with the model. Third, the observer *realizes* that the observed behavior will produce a desired result. Fourth, the observer *remembers* the actions of the model and *reproduces* the relevant behavior in appropriate situations. Fifth, the modeled behavior is *reinforced*. Reinforcement increases the probability that the behavior will be repeated (DeFleur & Ball-Rokeach, 1989, pp. 216–217).

Consistent with these stages of modeling, Bandura (1977) identified several factors that affect the extent to which people learn behavior through observation. For example, the rate and amount of observational learning is determined in part by the nature of the modeled behaviors: the more complex the behavior, the less likely it will be modeled effectively. In this regard, applications of Social Cognitive Theory in persuasive campaigns often include a skills training component. That many campaigns based on Social Cognitive Theory involve developing new skills highlights the importance of self-efficacy in observational learning. We addressed self-efficacy in our discussion of fear appeals in Chapter 7. Fear-appeal theorists borrowed Bandura's concept of self-efficacy because they found it useful in explaining the cognitive processing of fear appeals (e.g., R. W. Rogers, 1983; Witte, 1992). Bandura (2000) defined *self-efficacy* as "beliefs in one's capabilities to organise and execute the courses of action required to promote given levels of attainment" (p. 300). For example, when applied to safe-sex behaviors, a person with high self-efficacy is more likely to talk to his or her sexual partners about engaging in safe-sex practices and take control of behavior that leads to condom usage. Individuals low in self-efficacy about engaging in safe-sex behaviors, on the other hand, are unlikely to be successful in using a condom if their partner complains about doing so (Perloff, 2001). Consistent with this view of self-efficacy, researchers have found that skills training is an essential component of effective drug resistance campaigns targeted at adolescents (M. A. Miller et al., 2000; Rohrbach, Graham, Hensen, & Flay, 1987). While self-efficacy generally focuses on behavior, it might involve focusing on an individual's motivations, thoughts, feelings, and/or environment, depending on what is being managed (Bandura, 2000).

In addition to observing and learning to perform a desired behavior, *differential reinforcement* serves to motivate people to enact the behavior they have learned. Differential reinforcement occurs when models are rewarded for performing desired behaviors and when they are punished or left unrewarded for performing undesired behaviors. Over time, observers learn to match the performance of desired behaviors with the positive reinforcements and undesired behaviors with less favorable outcomes. This matching process motivates observers to enact desired behaviors once they have been acquired. In adolescent drug resistance campaigns, differential reinforcement increases the likelihood that teens will produce the resistance messages they have learned through modeling and practice. Bandura argued that the anticipated benefits of a particular behavior can strengthen what has been learned observationally by motivating people to rehearse modeled behavior that they value highly (1977, p. 37).

Supporting Evidence

Research has repeatedly found that children and adults acquire attitudes, emotional responses, and new styles of conduct through film and televised modeling (Bandura, 1973, 1977, 2000; Liebert, Neale, & Davidson, 1973). Recently, the Social Cognitive Model has been applied to investigations of adolescent drinking and driving (DiBlasio, 1986, 1987) and to adolescent sexual behavior (DiBlasio & Benda, 1990), among many others (Bandura, 2000). Based on a Social Cognitive Model of deviant behavior (Akers et al., 1979), DiBlasio argued that "social behavior is understood through studying the impact of differential association with adults and peers, internalization of group norms (normative definitions), modeling, and the combination of positive and negative reinforcement (differential reinforcement)" (1986, p. 175).

Akers and his colleagues (1979) defined *differential association* as the approval levels of adults and peers for a particular behavior. For example, in his study of adolescent drunk driving, DiBlasio (1986) defined *peer association* as the frequency, duration, and intensity of interactions with peers who drive under the influence of alcohol (DUI), or who ride with someone who is under the influence of alcohol. *Group norms* reflect adherence to laws or a willingness to adhere to laws. In a study of adolescent drunk driving, group norms might reflect on the social group's attitudes toward DUI laws and justification for occasional violation of DUI laws. Differential reinforcement actually reflects two theoretical factors. *Combined differential reinforcement* reflects the rewards, such as group acceptance and good feelings, derived from a particular behavior compared to the costs of performing the behavior. Adolescents may perceive that drinking and driving is fun and one way to gain acceptance from peers, but these benefits might be offset by the consequences of an accident or anticipated feelings of guilt. When perceived rewards outweigh anticipated costs, the behavior is more likely to be performed, and vice versa. *Differential social reinforcement* reflects the social praise and negative reactions of others. For adolescent drivers, praise from parents and peers for avoiding DUI combined with the negative reactions of peers and parents to DUI serves to reinforce adolescent decisions to abstain from drinking and driving. Finally, *modeling* occurs by observing others who either engage in or abstain from a particular behavior. In the case of adolescent drunk driving, television personalities who participate in DUI campaigns may serve as positive role models for adolescents. However, parents, relatives, and attractive friends also serve as important role models for adolescent drivers.

These five theoretical factors were hypothesized to affect the learning and performance of adolescent behavior (Akers et al., 1979). Several studies have examined their ability to predict the behavior of adolescents (DiBlasio, 1986, 1987; DiBlasio & Benda, 1990). A consistent pattern of findings emerges from investigations of this model (Table 13.1). For example, in a study of adolescent drinking and driving, DiBlasio (1986)

TABLE 13.1. Multiple Correlation Coefficients for the Theoretical Factors in the Social Learning Model

| | Adolescent behavior | | |
| | Study 1 | | Study 2 |
Theoretical predictors	DUI	Riding	Sex
1. Differential association	.66	.62	.54
2. Group norms	.52	.50	.41
3. Combined differential reinforcement	.44	.33	.50
4. Differential social reinforcement	.35	.30	NA
5. Modeling	.37	.44	.28
Total variance explained by theoretical factors	.56	.52	.40

Note. DUI = driving under the influence of alcohol; Riding = riding with person operating vehicle under the influence of alcohol; Sex = sexual intercourse; Study 1 = DiBlasio (1986); Study 2 = DiBlasio and Benda (1990); NA = not available.

found that all five of the theoretical factors in the Akers and colleagues (1979) Social Learning Model were significantly related to DUI and riding with drivers under the influence. Combined, these five theoretical factors accounted for 56% of the variance in adolescent DUI and 52% of the variance in riding with drivers under the influence. A subsequent study of adolescent sexual behavior produced similar results (DiBlasio & Benda, 1990). In this study, four theoretical factors were employed, and each factor was significantly related to sexual activity. Combined, these four factors accounted for 40% of the variance in the frequency of adolescent sexual intercourse.

These results clearly indicate that the constructs developed from Social Cognitive Theory are an accurate depiction of the forces that influence behavioral intentions. Moreover, DiBlasio concluded that these findings were consistent with prior studies that found peer groups are most influential for adolescents (Alexander & Campbell, 1966; Jessor & Jessor, 1977); that reinforcement is an important determinant of behavior (Bandura, 1969; Wodarski & Bagarozzi, 1979); and that observation of adult and peer models contributes to DUI and riding with drivers under the influence (DiBlasio, 1986, p. 186). Findings from these studies provide strong evidence of social learning and its significant influence on behavior. Unlike learning by doing, which requires repeated experience by individuals, social learning occurs by observing others and recognizing the positive and negative reinforcements associated with their behavior (Bandura, 1977).

Application of Social Cognitive Theory

Regression models such as the ones developed by DiBlasio established the influence of processes described in Social Cognitive Theory on the individual behavior of adolescents. The explanatory success of these models suggests that Social Cognitive Theory may provide an excellent foundation for persuasive campaigns targeted at adolescents. Rather than focus on each theoretical predictor (and there are a lot of them), research projects attempt to determine the effectiveness of an overall program that is based on Social Cognitive Theory.

As we have noted, one important problem that adolescents experience is peer pressure to smoke. Adolescent smoking is a social phenomenon. More than one-third of the cigarettes smoked by adolescents are smoked in the presence of another teen, and over one-half are smoked in the presence of another teen or an adult (Biglan, McConnell, Severson, Bavry, & Ary, 1984). Over the years, a number of persuasive campaigns have been implemented to promote resistance to smoking. For the most part, these campaigns rely on school-based educational programs and mass media to affect adolescent smoking behavior (Flay, 1986, 1987). Given the social nature of adolescent smoking and the important influence of peer pressure, group norms, and social reinforcement in the regression models described above, Social Cognitive Theory has served as a foundation for many smoking prevention campaigns.

One campaign tested the effectiveness of a refusal-skills training program for over 1,500 junior high and high school students. Mirroring the essential elements of Social Cognitive Theory, this program included instruction on specific skills for refusing cigarettes, modeling of effective refusals, behavioral rehearsal, teacher and peer reinforcement for refusal behavior, and practice (Biglan et al., 1987, p. 618). Videotaped presentations were used extensively to provide instruction on refusal skills and examples of effective refusals. Nine months after the intervention, adolescent smokers who received the refusal-skills program reported significantly less smoking and had significantly lower biological readings of smoking (carbon monoxide in saliva) than smokers in the control condition. However, students who were originally *nonsmokers* and who received the refusal-skills training reported significantly higher levels of smoking on the posttest than nonsmokers in the control condition, although the biochemical measures revealed no significant differences between these groups. Despite this finding, the overall results of this investigation indicate that a refusal-skills training program consistent with Social Cognitive Theory was effective in reducing smoking among adolescents. Other skills training programs have proved equally effective in promoting long-term resistance to smoking among adolescents (Leupker, Johnson, Murray, & Pechacek, 1983; Schinke & Gilchrist, 1984).

As another example, Domel and colleagues (1993) reported on the effectiveness of a program designed to get fourth- and fifth-grade students to consume five servings per day of fruits and vegetables. They developed a curriculum program based on the tenets of Social Cognitive Theory. The program was designed to improve the availability of fruits and vegetables at school and at home, increase students' liking of fruits and vegetables, establish behavior change, and create social support. Modeling, role playing, and entertaining activities such as raps, games, mock newspaper columns, comic strips, and rhymes were included in the program (Domel et al., 1993).

During and after the month-long program, students were asked to keep a diary of their food consumption. At the completion of the program they were asked questions concerning their food preferences and knowledge. Results indicated that participants in the experimental condition reported greater fruit consumption (but not vegetable consumption), more knowledge about fruits and vegetables, and greater preferences for fruits in general and for fruits and vegetables as snacks. While consumption did not reach the recommended level of five servings per day, these results also indicate that Social Cognitive Theory is useful for the creation of effective health promotion campaigns.

Social Cognitive Theory underscores the human capacity to learn through observation and describes how people acquire integrated patterns of behavior without having to form them gradually by tedious trial and error (Bandura, 1977, p. 12). However, some behaviors, such as communicative strategies for refusing drugs, alcohol, and cigarettes, are sufficiently complex that they can only be acquired through modeling and rehearsal.

Research has demonstrated the powerful influence of behavioral models portrayed in the mass media. When combined with interpersonal skills training, these models can effectively promote resistance to unwanted behavior. As a consequence, such behavioral models are an important focus for scholars who study and develop persuasive communication campaigns.

It seems likely that social learning processes can be used at several points in the campaign process. For example, an important part of Larson's (2001) legitimacy stage, when applied to political campaigns, involves gaining important endorsements (frequently from celebrities, newspapers, and political and religious groups). Social cognitive factors are at work during the legitimacy state because attractive social models help to create social norms about a particular candidate.

College campus campaigns that focus on reducing binge drinking have used similar social cognitive processes. One popular advertisement indicates the percentage of students who do *not* engage in binge drinking. This helps to create accurate social norms because college students frequently overestimate the extent to which their peers engage in unhealthy behaviors (e.g., binge drink, engage in unsafe sex, etc.). Alcohol-free campus events also serve to reinforce anti-drinking norms and provide attractive abstaining models.

Persuasive communication campaigns can also directly focus on several aspects of social cognitive processes. For example, anti-smoking campaigns have focused both on negative peer reaction (differential reinforcement) and parental disapproval (differential social reinforcement).

RECONSIDERING HEALTH PROMOTION CAMPAIGNS

Persuasion theories have been useful in guiding the development of persuasive communication campaigns. The theories that we discussed in this chapter as well as some described earlier (e.g., Theory of Reasoned

Action, etc.) have been successfully utilized in promoting healthy behavior and lifestyles (e.g., DiClemente & Peterson, 1994; P. Norman, Abraham, & Conner, 2000). While several of the models we have discussed have been used quite successfully, Bandura (2000) characterizes such persuasive communication campaigns as "costly, cumbersome, and minimally effective" (p. 316). One common element to these theories and campaigns is that they take an individual perspective from which to attempt health behavior change. While such an assumption seems reasonable (after all, it's an individual person doing the changing), Bandura (2000) notes several fundamental flaws with the individualized focus. We will discuss two of these concerns.

"One Size Fits All"

One of the problems facing those developing health promotion communication campaigns, according to Bandura (2000), is that the individuals being targeted differ on a wide variety of factors (e.g., demographics, needs, risk factors, current health status, etc.). If a single set of messages is developed to serve these vastly different individuals, the campaign developers are essentially using a "one size fits all" perspective. Put simply, a single set of messages cannot effectively serve the needs of a diverse audience. It is no wonder, then, that campaigns based on Inoculation Theory (Pfau et al., 1992) and Social Cognitive Theory (Biglan et al., 1987) were more effective for some people than for others. What is needed instead is a campaign where messages can be varied to fit the audience's unique situation and needs. Given a program that fits individual needs and condition, Bandura argues, receivers will be better able to manage their own health promotion.

DeBusk and colleagues (1994) discuss just such a program. This program focused on helping hospital patients recover from a heart attack. While still in the hospital, participants were given detailed training on how to change their diet, develop an exercise program, and reduce their weight and cholesterol levels. Using a computer-based system, DeBusk and colleagues allowed participants to focus on the particular outcomes they felt were important and to set their own short-term, attainable, goals. A single program administrator kept in contact with participants via telephone and mail. These contacts provided participants with detailed feedback on the outcomes that they had chosen and "individually-tailored guides for self-directed change" (Bandura, 2000, p. 316).

Results of the Debusk and colleagues (1994) study indicated that participants in the individualized promotion program, based on Social Cognitive Theory, had more positive health outcomes than participants in the control condition (who received typical, physician-based, care).

Participants in the individualized promotion condition were more likely to have stopped smoking, had lower cholesterol levels, and had more efficient heart functioning than participants in the control condition.

One major advantage of the individualized program is that patients self-manage their recovery from major illness. "The self-management approach, therefore, serves as a generic model that can be adapted to different chronic diseases" (Bandura, 2000, p. 324). Informing patients about the benefits of health-related behaviors and allowing them to choose which outcomes and behaviors to focus on helps to provide them with the motivation and self-efficacy necessary for effective behavior change. Bandura (2000) provides several examples of such focused persuasive communication campaigns that have been successfully implemented.

Persuasive Communication Campaigns and the Social Environment

Bandura's second concern about the individual focus of many typical health promotion persuasive campaigns is that people do not live in isolation. Human functioning, according to Social Cognitive Theory, is a function of the reciprocal causal relationships among "(1) personal determinants in the form of cognitive, affective, and biological factors, (2) behavior, and (3) environmental influences" (Bandura, 1994, p. 30). Most important for the discussion here are environmental factors. An important part of the environment is social, that is, the people who have an influence on an individual's behavior (e.g., family, close friends, co-workers).

The social environment plays an important role in a person's ability to effectively change behavior. For example, assume for the moment that you wanted to quit smoking. If your friends and roommates are supportive of your effort to quit (e.g., urging you not to smoke and being careful not to smoke in your presence), then you have a better chance of actually kicking the habit than someone who has a social network that is not supportive (e.g., smokes in your presence). As another example, a person will have trouble lowering his or her cholesterol level if he or she is consistently served greasy, deep-fried, foods at mealtimes. Thus, the support and cooperative behavior of those around the person trying to change his or her behavior are important determinants of success.

Bandura (2000) argues that many persuasive communication campaigns, however, do not include a social component. For example, the Domel and colleagues (1993) study on fruit and vegetable consumption found that the students' increased consumption of fruits occurred in school at lunch rather than at home. Since parents likely make most of the decisions in terms of what foods (including fruits and vegetables) are purchased and how they are served, the fact that the campaign lacked a strong social (in this case parental) component limited its effectiveness.

SUMMARY

This chapter examined two models of social influence that can be effectively applied in mass media campaigns. Research on Inoculation Theory documents the effectiveness of this technique for promoting resistance to persuasion. Field experiments document the effectiveness of this technique for promoting resistance to attack messages in political and health promotion campaigns. Social Cognitive Theory reflects a general approach to persuasion and human functioning that stems from observational learning. By observing the rewards and punishments that models receive for their behavior, people learn vicariously to enact socially desirable behaviors. For adolescents, Social Cognitive Theory is a particularly effective method of acquiring behavior. The influence of peer and adult models provides one basis for developing programs to promote prosocial behavior in adolescents. Although neither of the models described in this chapter is inherently a mass media model of social influence, each can readily and successfully be applied in mediated campaigns of social influence. Given the multiplicative power of the media, these theories may ultimately prove to be more effectively applied in media campaigns than in interpersonal influence situations.

NOTES

1. A *model*, in this context, is another person observed performing the behavior. It could be a family member, a valued friend, or a TV, movie, or sports star. The more positively valued the model, the more likely that social learning will occur.
2. It bears mentioning that this reinforcement function serves principally as an informative and motivational operation rather than as a mechanical response strengthener. The notion of "response strengthening" is, at best, a metaphor (Bandura, 1977, p. 21).

References

Ajzen, I. (1985). From intentions to actions: A theory of planned behavior. In J. Kuhland & J. Beckman (Eds.), *Action-control: From cognitions to behavior* (pp. 11–39). Heidelberg, Germany: Springer.

Ajzen, I., & Fishbein, M. (1977). Attitude behavior relations: A theoretical analysis and review of empirical research. *Psychological Bulletin, 84,* 888–918.

Ajzen, I., & Fishbein, M. (1980). *Understanding attitudes and predicting social behavior.* Englewood Cliffs, NJ: Prentice-Hall.

Akers, R. L., Krohn, M. D., Lanza-Kaduci, L., & Radosevich, M. (1979). Social learning and deviant behavior: A specific test of a general theory. *American Sociological Review, 44,* 636–655.

Albarracin, D., Johnson, B. T., Fishbein, M., & Muellerleile, P. A. (2001). Theories of reasoned action and planned behavior as models of condom use: A meta-analysis. *Psychological Bulletin, 127,* 142–161.

Alberts, J. K., Hecht, M. L., Miller-Rassulo, M., & Krizek, R. L. (1992). The communicative process of drug resistance among high school students. *Adolescence, 27,* 203–226.

Alberts, J. K., Miller-Rassulo, M. A., & Hecht, M. L. (1991). A typology of drug resistance strategies. *Journal of Applied Communication Research, 19,* 129–151.

Alexander, N. C., & Campbell, E. Q. (1966). Peer influence on alcohol drinking. *Journal of Studies on Alcohol, 28,* 444–453.

Allen, C., & Metoyer, E. (1987). Crimes of the occult. *Police,* pp. 38–45.

Allen, M. (1991). Meta-analysis comparing the persuasiveness of one-sided and two-sided messages. *Western Journal of Speech Communication, 55,* 390–404.

Allen, M. (1993). Determining the persuasiveness of message sidedness: A prudent note about utilizing research summaries. *Western Journal of Communication, 57,* 98–103.

Allen, M., Hale, J., Mongeau, P., Berkowitz-Stafford, S., Stafford, S., Shanahan, W., Agee, P., Dillon, K., Jackson, R., & Ray, C. (1990). Testing a model of message sidedness: Three replications. *Communication Monographs, 57,* 274–291.

Allen, M., Mabry, E. A., Banski, M., Stoneman, M., & Carter, P. (1990). A thoughtful appraisal of measuring cognition using the Role Category Questionnaire. *Communication Reports, 3,* 49–57.

Allen, M., & Stiff, J. B. (1989). Testing three models for the sleeper effect. *Western Journal of Speech Communication, 53,* 411–426.

Allport, G. W. (1935). Attitudes. In C. Murchison (Ed.), *A handbook of social psychology* (pp. 798–844). Worcester, MA: Clark University Press.

Andersen, P. A., & Guerrero, L. K. (Eds.). (1998). *Handbook of communication and emotion: Research, theory, applications, and contexts.* San Diego, CA: Academic Press.

Anderson, N. H. (1959). Test of a model for opinion change. *Journal of Abnormal and Social Psychology, 59,* 371–381.

Anderson, N. H. (1971). Integration theory and attitude change. *Psychological Review, 78,* 171–206.

Anderson, N. H. (1981). *Foundations of information integration theory.* San Diego, CA: Academic Press.

Anderson, N. H., & Hovland, C. (1957). The representation of order effects in communication research. In C. Hovland (Ed.), *The order of presentation in persuasion* (pp. 158–169). New Haven, CT: Yale University Press.

Andreoli, V., & Worchel, S. (1978). Effects of media, communicator, and message position on attitude change. *Public Opinion Quarterly, 42,* 59–70.

Applegate, J. L. (1980). Person- and position-centered teacher communication in a day care center: A case study triangulating interview and naturalistic methods. *Studies in Symbolic Interaction, 3,* 59–96.

Applegate, J. L. (1982). The impact of construct system development on communication and impression formation in persuasive contexts. *Communication Monographs, 49,* 277–289.

Aristotle. (1960). *The rhetoric of Aristotle* (L. Cooper, Trans.). Englewood Cliffs, NJ: Prentice-Hall. (Original translation published 1932)

Aronson, E. (1968). Dissonance theory: Progress and problems. In R. P. Abelson, E. Aronson, W. J. McGuire, T. M. Newcomb, M. J. Rosenberg & P. H. Tannenbaum (Eds.), *Theories of cognitive consistency: A source-book* (pp. 5–27). Chicago: Rand McNally.

Aronson, E. (1999). *The social animal* (8th ed.). New York: Worth.

Aronson, E., Turner, J. A., & Carlsmith, J. M. (1963). Communicator credibility and communication discrepancy determinants of opinion change. *Journal of Abnormal and Social Psychology, 67,* 31–36.

Asch, S. E. (1955). Opinions and social pressures. *Scientific American, 193,* 31–35.

Asch, S. E. (1956). Studies of independence and conformity: A minority of one against a unanimous majority. *Psychological Monographs, 70*(9, Whole No. 416).

Bacon, S. J. (1974). Arousal and the range of cue utilization. *Journal of Experimental Psychology, 102,* 81–87.

Bandura, A. (1969). *Principles of behavior modification.* New York: Holt, Rinehart & Winston.

Bandura, A. (1973). *Aggression: A social learning analysis.* Englewood Cliffs, NJ: Prentice-Hall.

Bandura, A. (1977). *Social learning theory.* Englewood Cliffs, NJ: Prentice-Hall.

Bandura, A. (1982). Self-efficacy mechanism in human agency. *American Psychologist, 37,* 122–147.

Bandura, A. (1986). *Social foundations of thought and action: A social cognitive theory.* Englewood Cliffs, NJ: Prentice-Hall.

Bandura, A. (2000). Health promotion from the perspective of social cognitive theory. In P. Norman, C. Abraham, & M. Conner (Eds.), *Understanding and changing health behavior: From health beliefs to self-regulation* (pp. 299–339). Amsterdam, The Netherlands: Harwood Academic.

Bandura, A. (2001). Social cognitive theory of mass communication. *Media Psychology, 3,* 265–299.

Bandura, A., Adams, N. E., Hardy, A. B., & Howells, G. N. (1980). Tests of the generality of self-efficacy theory. *Cognitive Therapy and Research, 4,* 39–66.

Bargh, J. A., & Pratto, E (1986). Individual construct accessibility and perceptual selection. *Journal of Experimental Social Psychology, 22,* 293–311.

Baron, P. H., Baron, R. S., & Roper, G. (1974). External validity and the risky shift: Empirical limits and theoretical implications. *Journal of Personality and Social Psychology, 30,* 95–103.

Baumeister, R. F., Stillwell, A. M., & Heatherton, T. F. (1994). Guilt: An interpersonal approach. *Psychological Bulletin, 115,* 243–267.

Baumhart, R. (1968). *An honest profit: What businessmen say about ethics in business.* New York: Holt, Rinehart & Winston.

Beaman, A. L., Cole, C. M., Preston, M., Klentz, B., & Steblay, N. M. (1983). Fifteen years of foot-in-the-door research: A meta-analysis. *Personality and Social Psychology Bulletin, 9,* 181–196.

Beatty, M. (1987). Erroneous assumptions underlying Burleson's critique. *Communication Quarterly, 35,* 329–333.

Beatty, M., & Payne, S. (1984). Loquacity and quantity of constructs as predictors of social perspective taking. *Communication Quarterly, 32,* 207–210.

Beatty, M., & Payne, S. (1985). Is construct differentiation loquacity?: A motivational perspective. *Human Communication Research, 11,* 605–612.

Beck, K. H., & Frankel, A. (1981). A conceptualization of threat communications and protective health behavior. *Social Psychology Quarterly, 44,* 204–217.

Becker, M. H. (1974). *The health belief model and personal health behavior.* Thorofare, NJ: Slack.

Becker, S. L. (1963). Research on emotional and logical proofs. *Southern Speech Journal, 28,* 198–207.

Becker, S. L. (1971). Rhetorical studies for the contemporary world. In L. Bitzer & E. Black (Eds.), *The prospect of rhetoric* (pp. 21–43). Englewood Cliffs, NJ: Prentice-Hall.

Bem, D. J. (1967). Self-perception: An alternative interpretation of cognitive dissonance phenomena. *Psychological Review, 74,* 183–200.

Bem, D. J. (1972). Self-perception theory. In L. Berkowitz (Ed.), *Advances in experimental social psychology* (Vol. 6, pp. 1–62). New York: Academic Press.

Beran, M. K. (1998). *The last patrician: Bobby Kennedy and the end of American aristocracy.* New York: St. Martin's Press.

Berger, C. R. (1997). *Planning strategic interaction: Attaining goals through communicative action.* Mahwah, NJ: Erlbaum.

Berger, C. R., Karol, S. H., & Jordan, J. M. (1989). When a lot of knowledge is a dangerous thing: The debilitating effects of plan complexity on verbal fluency. *Human Communication Research, 16,* 91–119.

Berlo, D. K., Lemert, J. B., & Mertz, R. J. (1969). Dimensions for evaluating the acceptability of message sources. *Public Opinion Quarterly, 33,* 563–576.

Berscheid, E. (1966). Opinion change and communicator–communicatee similarity and dissimilarity. *Journal of Personality and Social Psychology, 4,* 670–680.

Berscheid, E., & Walster, E. (1974). Physical attractiveness. In L. Berkowitz (Ed.), *Advances in experimental social psychology* (Vol. 7, pp. 157–215). San Diego, CA: Academic Press.

Besson, A. L., Roloff, M. E., & Paulson, G. D. (1998). Preserving face in refusal situations. *Communication Research, 25,* 183–199.

Bettinghaus, E. P., & Cody, M. J. (1987). *Persuasive communication.* New York: Holt, Rinehart & Winston.

Bettinghaus, E. P., Miller, G. R., & Steinfatt, T. M. (1970). Source evaluation, syllogistic content, and judgments of logical validity by high- and low-dogmatic persons. *Journal of Personality and Social Psychology, 16,* 238–244.

Biglan, A., Glasgow, R., Ary, D., Thompson, R., Severson, H., Lichtenstein, E., Weissman, W., Faller, C., & Gallison, C. (1987). How generalizable are the effects of smoking prevention programs?: Refusal skills, training, and parent messages in a teacher-administered program. *Journal of Behavioral Medicine, 10,* 613–628.

Biglan, A., McConnell, S., Severson, H. H., Bavry, J., & Ary, D. (1984). A situational analysis of adolescent smoking. *Journal of Behavioral Medicine, 7,* 109–114.

Binder, L. (1971). Crises of political development. In *Crises and sequences in political development* (pp. 3–72). Princeton, NJ: Princeton University Press.

Bingham, S. G., & Burleson, B. R. (1989). Multiple effects of messages with multiple goals: Some perceived outcomes of responses to sexual harassment. *Human Communication Research, 16,* 184–216.

Bochner, S., & Insko, C. A. (1966). Communicator discrepancy, source credibility, and opinion change. *Journal of Personality and Social Psychology, 4,* 614–621.

Boster, F. J. (1988). Comments on the utility of compliance gaining message selection tasks. *Human Communication Research, 15,* 169–177.

Boster, F. J. (1990). Group argument, social pressure, and the making of group decisions. In J. A. Anderson (Ed.), *Communication yearbook 13* (pp. 303–312). Newbury Park, CA: Sage.

Boster, F. J. (1995). Commentary on compliance-gaining message behavior research. In C. R. Berger & M. Burgoon (Eds.), *Communication and social influence processes* (pp. 91–113). East Lansing: Michigan State University Press.

Boster, F. J., Cameron, K. A., Campo, S., Liu, W.-Y., Lillie, J. K., Baker, E. M., & Yun, K. A. (2000). The persuasive effects of statistical evidence in the presence of exemplars. *Communication Studies, 51,* 296–306.

Boster, F. J., & Cruz, M. G. (2002). Persuading in the small group context. In J. P. Dillard & M. W. Pfau (Eds.), *The persuasion handbook: Developments in theory and practice* (pp. 474–494). Thousand Oaks, CA: Sage.

Boster, F. J., Fryrear, J. E., Mongeau, P. A., & Hunter, J. E. (1982). An unequal speaking linear discrepancy model: Implications for the polarity shift. In M. Burgoon (Ed.), *Communication yearbook 6* (pp. 395–418). Beverly Hills, CA: Sage.

Boster, F. J., & Hunter, J. E. (1978). *The effect of dimensions of Machiavellianism on compliance-gaining message selection.* Unpublished manuscript, Department of Communication, Arizona State University.

Boster, F. J., & Mayer, M. E. (1984). Choice shifts: Argument qualities or social comparisons? In R. N. Bostrom (Ed.), *Communication yearbook 8* (pp. 393–410). Beverly Hills, CA: Sage.

Boster, F. J., Mayer, M. E., Hunter, J. E., & Hale, J. L. (1980). Expanding the persuasive arguments explanation of the polarity shift: A linear discrepancy model. In D. Nimmo (Ed.), *Communication yearbook 4* (pp. 165–176). New Brunswick, NJ: Transaction Books.

Boster, F. J., & Mongeau, P. A. (1984). Fear-arousing persuasive messages. In R. N. Bostrom (Ed.), *Communication yearbook 8* (pp. 330–375). Beverly Hills, CA: Sage.

Boster, F. J., & Stiff, J. B. (1984). Compliance gaining message selection behavior. *Human Communication Research, 10,* 539–556.

Boster, F. J., Stiff, J. B., & Reynolds, R. A. (1985). Do persons respond differently to inductively-derived and deductively-derived lists of compliance gaining messages?: A reply to Wiseman and Schenck-Hamlin. *Western Journal of Speech Communication, 49,* 177–187.

Bowman, C. H., & Fishbein, M. (1978). Understanding public reactions to energy proposals: An application of the Fishbein model. *Journal of Applied Social Psychology, 8,* 319–340.

Brehm, J. W. (1966). *A theory of psychological reactance.* New York: Academic Press.

Brehm, J. W., & Cohen, A. R. (1962). *Explorations in cognitive dissonance.* New York: Wiley.

Brock, T. (1965). Communicator–recipient similarity and decision change. *Journal of Personality and Social Psychology, 1,* 650–654.

Brock, T. (1967). Communication discrepancy and intent to persuade as determinants of counterargument production. *Journal of Experimental Social Psychology, 3,* 296–309.

Brown, P., & Levinson, S. C. (1987). *Politeness: Some universals in language usage.* Cambridge, UK: Cambridge University Press.

Brown, R., & Gilman, A. (1989). Politeness theory and Shakespeare's four major tragedies. *Language in Society, 18,* 159–212.

Buller, D. B. (1986). Distraction during persuasive communication: A meta-analytic review. *Communication Monographs, 53,* 91–114.

Burger, J. M. (1986). Increasing compliance by improving the deal: The that's not all technique. *Journal of Personality and Social Psychology, 51,* 277–283.

Burger, J. M. (1999). The foot-in-the-door compliance procedure: A multiple-process analysis and review. *Personality and Social Psychology Review, 3,* 303–325.

Burgoon, J. K., Burgoon, M., Miller, G. R., & Sunnafrank, M. (1981). Learning theory approaches to persuasion. *Human Communication Research, 7,* 161–179.

Burgoon, J. K., Stacks, D. W., & Burch, S. A. (1982). The role of rewards and violations of distancing expectations in achieving influence in small groups. *Communication, 11,* 114–128.

Burgoon, M. (1989). Messages and persuasive effects. In J. J. Bradac (Ed.), *Message effects in communication science* (pp. 129–164). Newbury Park, CA: Sage.

Burgoon, M., Cohen, M., Miller, M. D., & Montgomery, C. L. (1978). An empirical test of a model of resistance to persuasion. *Human Communication Research, 5,* 27–39.

Burgoon, M., & Klingle, R. S. (1998). Gender differences in being influential and/or influenced: A challenge to prior explanations. In D. J. Canary & K. Dindia (Eds.), *Sex differences and similarities in communication: Critical essays and empirical investigations of sex and gender in interaction* (pp. 257–285). Mahwah, NJ: Erlbaum.

Burleson B., Applegate, J., & Newwirth, C. (1981). Is cognitive complexity loquacity?: A reply to Powers, Jordan, and Street. *Human Communication Research, 7,* 212–215.

Burleson, B., Waltman, M., & Samter, W. (1987). More evidence that cognitive complexity is not loquacity: A reply to Beatty and Payne. *Communication Quarterly, 35,* 317–328.

Burleson, B. R., & Wilson, S. R. (1988). On the continued undesireability of item desireability: A reply to Boster, Hunter, and Seibold. *Human Communication Research, 15,* 178–191.

Burleson, B. R., Wilson, S. R., Waltman, M. S., Goering, E. M., Ely, T. K., & Whaley, R. B. (1988). Item desireability effects in compliance-gaining research: Seven studies documenting artifacts in the strategy selection procedure. *Human Communication Research, 14,* 429–486.

Byrne, D. (1971). *The attraction paradigm.* New York: Academic Press.

Cacioppo, J. T., & Petty, R. E. (1982). The need for cognition. *Journal of Personality and Social Psychology, 42,* 116–131.

Cacioppo, J. T., & Petty, R. E. (1984). The need for cognition: Relationship to attitudinal processes. In R. P. McGlynn, J. E. Maddux, C. D. Stoltenberg,

& J. H. Harvey (Eds.), *Social perception in clinical and counseling psychology* (pp. 113–119). Lubbock: Texas Tech Press.

Campbell, D. T., & Stanley, J. C. (1966). *Experimental and quasi-experimental designs for research*. Chicago: Rand McNally.

Canary, D. J., Brossmann, B. G., & Seibold, D. R. (1987). Argument structures in decision-making groups. *Southern Speech Communication Journal, 53*, 18–37.

Canary, D. J., & Dindia, K. (Eds.). (1998). *Sex differences and similarities in communication: Critical essays and empirical investigations of sex and gender in interaction*. Mahwah, NJ: Erlbaum.

Canary, D. J., & Hause, K. S. (1993). Is there any reason to research sex differences in communication? *Communication Quarterly, 41*, 129–144.

Chaiken, S. (1979). Communicator physical attractiveness and persuasion. *Journal of Personality and Social Psychology, 37*, 1387–1397.

Chaiken, S. (1980). Heuristic versus systematic information processing and the use of source versus message cues in persuasion. *Journal of Personality and Social Psychology, 39*, 752–766.

Chaiken, S. (1986). Physical appearance and social influence. In C. P. Herman, M. P. Zanna, & E. T. Higgins (Eds.), *Physical appearance, stigma, and social behavior: The Ontario Symposium* (Vol. 3, pp. 143–177). Hillsdale, NJ: Erlbaum.

Chaiken, S. (1987). The heuristic model of persuasion. In M. P. Zanna, J. M. Olson, & C. P. Herman (Eds.), *Social influence: The Ontario Symposium* (Vol. 5, pp. 3–39). Hillsdale, NJ: Erlbaum.

Chaiken, S., Duckworth, K. L., & Darke, P. (1999). When parsimony fails. *Psychological Inquiry, 10*, 118–123.

Chaiken, S., & Eagly, A. H. (1976). Communicator modality as a determinant of message persuasiveness and message comprehensibility. *Journal of Personality and Social Psychology, 34*, 606–614.

Chaiken, S., & Eagly, A. H. (1983). Communication modality as a determinant of persuasion: The role of communicator salience. *Journal of Personality and Social Psychology, 45*, 241–256.

Chaiken, S., Liberman, A., & Eagly, A. H. (1989). Heuristic and systematic information processing within and beyond the persuasion context. In J. S. Uleman & J. A. Bargh (Eds.), *Unintended thought* (pp. 212–252). New York: Guilford Press.

Chen, S., & Chaiken, S. (1999). The heuristic–systematic model in its broader context. In S. Chaiken & Y. Trope (Eds.), *Dual-process theories in social psychology* (pp. 73–96). New York: Guilford Press.

Christie, R., & Geis, F. L. (1970). *Studies in Machiavellianism*. New York: Academic Press.

Cialdini, R. B. (1987). Principles of compliance professionals: Psychologists of necessity. In M. P. Zanna, J. M. Olson, & C. P. Herman (Eds.), *Social influence: The Ontario Symposium* (Vol. 5, pp. 165–184). Hillsdale, NJ: Erlbaum.

Cialdini, R. B. (2001). *Influence: Science and practice* (4th ed.). Boston: Allyn & Bacon.

Cialdini, R. B., Cacioppo, J. T., Bassett, R., & Miller, J. A. (1978). Low-ball procedure for producing compliance: Commitment then cost. *Journal of Personality and Social Psychology, 36*, 463–476.

Cialdini, R. B., Levy, A., Herman, C. P., & Evenbeck, S. (1973). Attitudinal politics: The strategy of moderation. *Journal of Personality and Social Psychology, 25*, 100–108.

Cialdini, R. B., Levy, A., Herman, C. P., Kozlowski, L. T., & Petty, R. E. (1976). Elastic shifts of opinion: Determinants of direction and durability. *Journal of Personality and Social Psychology, 34*, 663–672.

Cialdini, R. B., & Petty, R. E. (1981). Anticipatory opinion effects. In R. E. Petty, T. M. Ostrom, & T. C. Brock (Eds.), *Cognitive responses in persuasion* (pp. 217–235). Hillsdale, NJ: Erlbaum.

Cialdini, R. B., & Schroeder, D. A. (1976). Increasing compliance by legitimizing paltry contributions: When even a penny helps. *Journal of Personality and Social Psychology, 34*, 599–604.

Cialdini, R. B., Vincent, J. E., Lewis, S. K., Catalan, J., Wheeler, D., & Darby, B. L. (1975). Reciprocal concessions procedure for inducing compliance: The door-in-the-face technique. *Journal of Personality and Social Psychology, 31*, 206–215.

Clark, R. A. (1979). The impact of self interest and desire for liking on the selection of communicative strategies. *Communication Monographs, 46*, 257–273.

Cline, R. (1990). Small group communication in health care. In E. B. Ray & L. Donohew (Eds.), *Communication and health: Systems and applications* (pp. 69–91). Hillsdale, NJ: Erlbaum.

Cody, M. J., Canary, D. J., & Smith, S. W. (1994). Compliance-gaining goals: An inductive analysis of actors' and goal types, strategies, and successes. In J. A. Daly & J. M. Wiemann (Eds.), *Strategic interpersonal communication* (pp. 33–90). Hillsdale, NJ: Erlbaum.

Cody, M. J., & McLaughlin, M. L. (1985). The situation as construct in interpersonal communication research. In M. Knapp & G. R. Miller (Eds.), *Handbook of interpersonal communication* (pp. 263–312). Beverly Hills, CA: Sage.

Cohen, A., Stotland, E., & Wolfe, D. (1955). An experimental investigation of need for cognition. *Journal of Abnormal and Social Psychology, 51*, 291–294.

Cohen, J. (1960). A coefficient of agreement for nominal scales. *Educational and Psychological Measurement, 20*, 37–46.

Cohen, M. R. (1949). *Studies in philosophy and science.* New York: Holt.

Cook, D. T., & Campbell, D. T. (1979). *Quasi-experimentation: Design and analysis issues for field settings.* Chicago: Rand McNally.

Cook, T., Gruder, C., Hennigan, K., & Flay, B. (1979). History of the sleeper effect: Some logical pitfalls in accepting the null hypothesis. *Psychological Bulletin, 86*, 662–679.

Cooper, J., & Fazio, R. H. (1984). A new look at dissonance theory. In L. Berkowitz (Ed.), *Advances in experimental social psychology* (Vol. 17, pp. 229–266). New York: Academic Press.

Cooper, J., Zanna, M. P., & Taves, P. A. (1978). Arousal as a necessary condition for attitude change following induced compliance. *Journal of Personality and Social Psychology, 36*, 1101–1106.

Coulter, R. H., & Pinto, M. B. (1995). Guilt appeals in advertising: What are their effects? *Journal of Applied Psychology, 80*, 697–705.

Cronkhite, G., & Liska, J. (1976). A critique of factor analytic approaches to the study of credibility. *Communication Monographs, 43*, 91–107.

Cronkhite, G., & Liska, J (1980). The judgment of communicator acceptability. In M. E. Roloff & G. R. Miller (Eds.), *Persuasion: New directions in theory and research* (pp. 101–139). Beverly Hills, CA: Sage.

Croyle, D. T., & Cooper, J. (1983). Dissonance arousal: Physiological evidence. *Journal of Personality and Social Psychology, 45*, 782–791.

DeBono, K. G. (2000). Attitude functions and consumer psychology: Understanding perceptions of product quality. In G. R. Maio & J. M. Olson (Eds.), *Why we evaluate: Functions of attitudes* (pp. 195–221). Mahwah, NJ: Erlbaum.

DeBusk, R. G., Miller, N. H., Superko, H. R., Dennis, C. A., Thomas, R. J., Lew, H. T., Berger, W. E., III, Heller, R. S., Rompf, J., Gee, D., Kraemer, H. C., Bandura, A., Ghandour, G., Clark, M., Shah, R. V., Fisher, L., & Taylor, C. B. (1994). A case-management system for coronary risk factor modification after acute myocardial infarction. *Annals of Internal Medicine, 120*, 721–729.

DeFleur, M. L., & Ball-Rokeach, S. (1989). *Theories of mass communication.* New York: Longman.

Delia, J. G., & Clark, R. A. (1977). Cognitive complexity, social perception, and the development of listener-adapted communication in six-, eight-, ten-, and twelve-year old boys. *Communication Monographs, 46*, 326–345.

Delia, J. G., & Crockett, W. H. (1973). Social schemas, cognitive complexity, and the learning of social structures. *Journal of Personality, 41*, 413–429.

Delia, J. G., Kline, S. L., & Burleson, B. R. (1979). The development of persuasive communication strategies in kindergartners through twelfth graders. *Communication Monographs, 46*, 274–281.

Delia, J. G., & O'Keefe, B. J. (1979). Constructivism: The development of communication in children. In E. Wartella (Ed.), *Children communicating* (pp. 157–185). Beverly Hills, CA: Sage.

Deutsch, M., & Gerard, H. B. (1955). A study of normative and informational social influence upon individual judgment. *Journal of Abnormal and Social Psychology, 51*, 629–636.

Devlin, L. P. (2001). Contrasts in presidential campaign commercials of 2000. *American Behavioral Scientist, 44*, 2338–2369.

DiBlasio, E. A. (1986). Drinking adolescents on the roads. *Journal of Youth and Adolescence, 15*, 173–188.

DiBlasio, E. A. (1987). Predriving riders and drinking drivers. *Journal of Studies on Alcohol, 49*, 11–15.

DiBlasio, E. A., & Benda, B. B. (1990). Adolescent sexual behavior: Multivariate analysis of a social learning model. *Journal of Adolescent Research, 5*, 449–466.

Dickerson, C. A., Thibodeau, R., Aronson, E., & Miller, D. (1992). Using cognitive dissonance to encourage water conservation. *Journal of Applied Social Psychology, 22,* 841–854.

DiClemente, R. J., & Peterson, J. L. (Eds.). (1994). *Preventing AIDS: Theories and methods of behavioral interventions.* New York: Plenum Press.

Dillard, J. P. (1988). Compliance gaining message selection: What is our dependent variable? *Communication Monographs, 55,* 162–183.

Dillard, J. P. (1989). Types of influence goals in personal relationships. *Journal of Social and Personal Relationships, 6,* 293–308.

Dillard, J. P. (1990a). A goal-driven model of interpersonal influence. In J. P. Dillard (Ed.), *Seeking compliance: The production of interpersonal influence messages* (pp. 41–56). Scottsdale, AZ: Gorsuch-Scarisbrick.

Dillard, J. P. (1990b). Self-inference and the foot-in-the-door technique. *Human Communication Research, 16,* 422–447.

Dillard, J. P. (1991). The current status of research on sequential-request compliance techniques. *Personality and Social Psychology Bulletin, 17,* 283–288.

Dillard, J. P. (1994). Rethinking the study of fear appeals: An emotional perspective. *Communication Theory, 4,* 295–323.

Dillard, J. P. (1998). Foreword: The role of affect in communication, biology, and social relationships. In P. A. Andersen & L. K. Guerrero (Eds.), *Handbook of communication and emotion: Research, theory, applications, and contexts* (pp. xvii–xxxii). San Diego, CA: Academic Press.

Dillard, J. P., Anderson, J. W., & Knobloch, L. K. (2002). Interpersonal influence. In M. Knapp & J. Daly (Eds.), *Handbook of interpersonal communication* (3rd ed., pp. 425–474). Thousand Oaks, CA: Sage.

Dillard, J. P., Hunter, J. E., & Burgoon, M. (1984). Sequential-request persuasive strategies: Meta-analysis of foot-in-the-door and door-in-the-face. *Human Communication Research, 10,* 461–488.

Dillard, J. P., & Meijnders, A. (2002). Persuasion and the structure of affect. In J. P. Dillard & M. W. Pfau (Eds.), *The persuasion handbook: Developments in theory and practice* (pp. 309–327). Thousand Oaks, CA: Sage.

Dillard, J. P., Plotnick, C. A., Godbold, L. C., Freimuth, V. S., & Edgar, T. (1996). The multiple affective outcomes of AIDS PSAs: Fear appeals do more than scare people. *Communication Research, 23,* 44–72.

Dillard, J. P., Segrin, C., & Hardin, J. M. (1989). Primary and secondary goals in the production of interpersonal influence messages. *Communication Monographs, 56,* 19–38.

Dillard, J. P., Wilson, S. R., Tusing, K. J., & Kinney, T. A. (1997). Politeness judgments in personal relationships. *Journal of Language and Social Psychology, 16,* 297–325.

Dion, K., Baron, R., & Miller, N. (1970). Why do groups make riskier decisions than individuals? In L. Berkowitz (Ed.), *Group processes* (pp. 227–299). New York: Academic Press.

Dion, K., Berscheid, E., & Walster, E. (1972). What is beautiful is good. *Journal of Personality and Social Psychology, 24,* 285–290.

Domel, S. B., Baranowski, T., Davis, H., Thompson, W. O., Leonard, S. B.,

Riley, P., Baranowski, J., Dudovitz, B., & Smyth, M. (1993). Development and evaluation of a school intervention to increase fruit and vegetable consumption among 4th and 5th grade students. *Journal of Nutrition Education, 25*, 345–349.

Doob, L. W. (1950). Goebbels' principles of propaganda. *Public Opinion Quarterly, 14*, 419–442.

Dulany, D. E. (1961). Hypotheses and habits in verbal "operant conditioning." *Journal of Abnormal and Social Psychology, 63*, 251–263.

Dulany, D. E. (1968). Awareness, rules, and propositional control: A confrontation with S–R behavior theory. In D. Horton & T. Dixon (Eds.), *Verbal behavior and S–R behavior theory* (pp. 340–387). Englewood Cliffs, NJ: Prentice-Hall.

Eagly, A. H. (1974). Comprehensibility of persuasive arguments as a determinant of opinion change. *Journal of Personality and Social Psychology, 29*, 758–773.

Eagly, A. H. (1978). Sex differences in influenceabililty. *Psychological Bulletin, 85*, 86–116.

Eagly, A. H., & Carli, L. L. (1981). Sex of researchers and sex-typed communications as determinants of sex differences in influenceability: A meta-analysis of social influence studies. *Psychological Bulletin, 90*, 1–20.

Eagly, A. H., & Chaiken, S. (1976). Why would anyone say that? Causal attribution of statements about the Watergate scandal. *Sociometry, 39*, 236–243.

Eagly, A. H., & Chaiken, S. (1993). *The psychology of attitudes.* Fort Worth, TX: Harcourt Brace Jovanovich.

Eagly, A. H., Chaiken, S., & Wood, W. (1981). An attribution analysis of persuasion. In J. H. Harvey, W. J. Ickes, & R. E. Kidd (Eds.), *New directions in attribution research* (Vol. 3, pp. 37–62). Hillsdale, NJ: Erlbaum.

Eagly, A. H., & Warren, R. (1976). Intelligence, comprehension, and opinion change. *Journal of Personality, 44*, 226–242.

Eagly, A. H., Wood, W., & Chaiken, S. (1978). Causal inferences about communicators and their effect on opinion change. *Journal of Personality and Social Psychology, 36*, 424–435.

Edwards, K. (1990). The interplay of affect and cognition in attitude formation and change. *Journal of Personality and Social Psychology, 59*, 202–216.

Edwards, W. (1961). Behavioral decision theory. *Annual Review of Psychology, 12*, 473–498.

Fazio, R. H. (1987). Self-perception theory: A current perspective. In M. P. Zanna, J. M. Olson, & C. P. Herman (Eds.), *Social influence: The Ontario Symposium* (Vol. 5, pp. 129–150). Hillsdale, NJ: Erlbaum.

Fazio, R. H., Chen, J., McDonel, E. C., & Sherman, S. J. (1982). Attitude accessibility, attitude–behavior consistency, and the strength of the object–evaluation association. *Journal of Experimental Social Psychology, 18*, 339–357.

Fazio, R. H., Sanbonmatsu, D. M., Powell, M. C., & Kardes, F. R. (1986). On the automatic activation of attitudes. *Journal of Personality and Social Psychology, 50*, 229–238.

Fazio, R. H., & Williams, C. J. (1986). Attitude accessibility as a moderator of the attitude–perception and attitude–behavior relations: An investigation of the 1984 presidential election. *Journal of Personality and Social Psychology, 51,* 505–514.

Fazio, R. H., & Zanna, M. P. (1981). Direct experience and attitude–behavior consistency. In L. Berkowitz (Ed.), *Advances in experimental social psychology* (Vol. 14, pp. 161–202). New York: Academic Press.

Fazio, R. H., Zanna, M. P., & Cooper, J. (1977). Dissonance and self-perception: An interactive view of each theory's proper domain of application. *Journal of Experimental Social Psychology, 13,* 464–479.

Fehr, B., & Russell, J. A. (1984). Concept of emotion viewed from a prototype perspective. *Journal of Experimental Psychology, 113,* 464–484.

Fern, E. E., Monroe, K. B., & Avila, R. A. (1986). Effectiveness of multiple request strategies: A synthesis of research results. *Journal of Marketing Research, 23,* 144–152.

Festinger, L. (1953). An analysis of compliant behavior. In M. Sherif & M. O. Wilson (Eds.), *Group relations at the crossroads* (pp. 232–256). New York: Harper & Brothers.

Festinger, L. (1954). A theory of social comparison processes. *Human Relations, 7,* 117–140.

Festinger, L. (1957). *A theory of cognitive dissonance.* Stanford, CA: Stanford University Press.

Festinger, L. (1964). Behavioral support for opinion change. *Public Opinion Quarterly, 28,* 404–417.

Festinger, L., & Carlsmith, J. M. (1959). Cognitive consequences of forced compliance. *Journal of Abnormal and Social Psychology, 58,* 203–210.

Festinger, L., & Maccoby, N. (1964). On resistance to persuasive communication. *Journal of Abnormal and Social Psychology, 68,* 359–366.

Fink, E. L., Kaplowitz, S. A., & Bauer, C. L. (1983). Positional discrepancy, psychological discrepancy, and attitude change: Experimental tests of some mathematical models. *Communication Monographs, 50,* 413–430.

Fishbein, M. (Ed.). (1967). *Readings in attitude theory and measurement.* New York: Wiley.

Fishbein, M., & Ajzen, I. (1975). *Belief, attitude, intention, and behavior.* Reading, MA: Addison-Wesley.

Fishbein, M., & Ajzen, I. (1980). Predicting and understanding consumer behavior: Attitude behavior correspondence. In I. Ajzen & M. Fishbein (Eds.), *Understanding attitudes and predicting social behavior* (pp. 148–172). Englewood Cliffs, NJ: Prentice-Hall.

Fishbein, M., & Coombs, E. S. (1974). Basis for decision: An attitudinal analysis of voting behavior. *Journal of Applied Social Psychology, 4,* 95–124.

Fiske, S. T., & Taylor, S. E. (1991). *Social cognition* (2nd ed.). New York: McGraw-Hill.

Fitzpatrick, M. A., & Winke, J. (1979). You always hurt the one you love: Strategies and tactics in interpersonal conflict. *Communication Quarterly, 27,* 1–11.

Flay, B. R. (1986). Mass media linkages with school-based programs for drug abuse prevention. *Journal of School Health, 56,* 402–406.

Flay, B. R. (1987). Mass media and smoking cessation: A critical review. *American Journal of Public Health, 77,* 153–160.

Fogg, B. J., Lee, E., & Marshall, J. (2002). Interactive technology and persuasion. In J. P. Dillard & M. W. Pfau (Eds.), *The persuasion handbook: Developments in theory and practice* (pp. 765–788). Thousand Oaks, CA: Sage.

Folkes, V. S. (1982). Communicating the reasons for social rejection. *Journal of Experimental Social Psychology, 18,* 235–252.

Forsyth, D. R. (1999). *Group dynamics* (3rd ed.). Belmont, CA: Brooks/Cole.

Francik, E. P., & Clark, H. H. (1985). How to make requests that overcome obstacles to compliance. *Journal of Memory and Language, 24,* 560–568.

Freedman, J. L., & Fraser, S. (1966). Compliance without pressure: The foot-in-the-door technique. *Journal of Personality and Social Psychology, 4,* 195–202.

Freedman, J. L., & Sears, D. O. (1965). Selective exposure. In L. Berkowitz (Ed.), *Advances in experimental social psychology* (Vol. 2, pp. 58–98). New York: Academic Press.

French, J. P. R., Jr., & Raven, B. (1960). The bases of social power. In D. Cartwright & A. Zander (Eds.), *Group dynamics* (pp. 607–623). New York: Harper & Row.

Galanter, M. (1999). *Cults: Faith, healing, and coercion* (2nd ed.). New York: Oxford University Press.

Gallup, G. H. (1977). *The Gallup Poll: Public opinion 72–77.* Wilmington, DE: Scholarly Resources.

Gass, R. H., & Seiter, J. S. (1999). *Persuasion, social influence, and compliance gaining.* Boston: Allyn & Bacon.

Geller, E. S. (1989). Using television to promote safety belt use. In R. E. Rice & C. K. Atkin (Eds.), *Public communication campaigns* (pp. 201–203). Newbury Park, CA: Sage.

German, K., Gronbeck, B. E., Ehninger, D., & Monroe, A. H. (2001). *Principles of public speaking* (14th ed.). New York: Longman.

Gillig, P., & Greenwald, A. (1974). Is it time to lay the sleeper effect to rest? *Journal of Personality and Social Psychology, 29,* 132–139.

Glass, G. V., McGaw, B., & Smith, M. L. (1981). *Meta-analysis in social research.* Beverly Hills, CA: Sage.

Goethals, G. R., & Nelson, R. E. (1973). Similarity in the influence process: The belief–value distinction. *Journal of Personality and Social Psychology, 25,* 117–122.

Goldfarb, L., Gerrard, M., Gibbons, E. X., & Plante, T. (1988). Attitudes toward sex, arousal, and the retention of contraceptive information. *Journal of Personality and Social Psychology, 55,* 634–641.

Gorassini, D. R., & Olson, J. M. (1995). Does self-perception change explain the foot-in-the-door effect? *Journal of Personality and Social Psychology, 69,* 91–105.

Gould, S. J. (1983). *Hen's teeth and horse's toes*. New York: Norton.

Gouldner, A. W. (1960). The norm of reciprocity: A preliminary statement. *American Sociological Review, 25*, 161–178.

Gray, J. (1992). *Men are from Mars, women are from Venus: A practical guide for improving communication and getting what you want in your relationships*. New York: HarperCollins.

Greene, J. O. (Ed.). (1997). *Message production: Advances in communication theory*. Mahwah, NJ: Erlbaum.

Greenwald, A. G. (1975). On the inconclusiveness of "crucial" cognitive tests of dissonance vs. self-perception theories. *Journal of Experimental and Social Psychology, 11*, 490–499.

Greenwald, A. G. (1989). Why are attitudes important? In A. R. Pratkanis, S. J. Breckler, & A. G. Greenwald (Eds.), *Attitude structure and function* (pp. 1–10). Hillsdale, NJ: Erlbaum.

Greenwald, A. G., Brock, T. C., & Ostrom, T. M. (1968). *Psychological foundations of attitudes*. New York: Academic Press.

Greenwald, A. G., & Ronis, D. L. (1978). Twenty years of cognitive dissonance: Case study of the evolution of a theory. *Psychological Review, 85*, 53–57.

Gruder, C., Cook, T., Hennigan, K., Flay, B., Alessis, C., & Halamaj, J. (1978). Empirical tests of the absolute sleeper effect predicted from the discounting cue hypothesis. *Journal of Personality and Social Psychology, 36*, 1061–1074.

Guerrero, L. K., Andersen, P. A., & Trost, M. R. (1998). Communication and emotion: Basic concepts and approaches. In P. A. Andersen & L. K. Guerrero (Eds.), *Handbook of communication and emotion: Research, theory, applications, and contexts* (pp. 5–27). San Diego, CA: Academic Press.

Gunter, G. (1994). The question of media violence. In J. Bryant & D. Zillman (Eds.), *Media effects: Advances in theory and research* (pp. 163–211). Hillsdale, NJ: Erlbaum.

Guttman, L. (1955). A generalized simplex for factor analysis. *Psychometrika, 20*, 173–192.

Haaland, G. A., & Venkatesen, M. (1968). Resistance to persuasive communications: An examination of the distraction hypothesis. *Journal of Personality and Social Psychology, 9*, 167–170.

Hale, J. L., Householder, B. J., & Greene, K. L. (2002). The Theory of Reasoned Action. In J. P. Dillard & M. W. Pfau (Eds.), *The persuasion handbook: Developments in theory and practice* (pp. 259–268). Thousand Oaks, CA: Sage.

Hale, J. L., Lemieux, R., & Mongeau, P. A. (1995). Cognitive processing of fear-arousing message content. *Communication Research, 22*, 459–474.

Hale, J., Mongeau, P. A., & Thomas, R. M. (1991). Cognitive processing of one- and two-sided persuasive messages. *Western Journal of Speech Communication, 55*, 380–389.

Hample, D. (1977). Testing a model of value argument and evidence. *Communication Monographs, 44*, 106–120.

Hample, D. (1978). Predicting immediate belief change and adherence to argument claims. *Communication Monographs, 45*, 219–228.

Hample, D. (1979). Predicting belief change using a cognitive theory of argument and evidence. *Communication Monographs, 46,* 142–151.

Hample, D., & Dallinger, J. M. (1987). Cognitive editing of argument strategies. *Human Communication Research, 14,* 123–144.

Hample, D., & Dallinger, J. M. (1998). On the etiology of the rebuff phenomenon: Why are persuasive messages less polite after rebuffs? *Communication Studies, 49,* 305–321.

Harkins, S. G., & Petty, R. E. (1981). The multiple source effect in persuasion: The effects of distraction. *Personality and Social Psychology Bulletin, 7,* 627–635.

Harmon-Jones, E. (2002). A cognitive dissonance theory perspective on persuasion. In J. P. Dillard & M. Pfau (Eds.), *The persuasion handbook: Developments in theory and practice* (pp. 99–116). Thousand Oaks, CA: Sage.

Harmon-Jones, E., & Mills, J. (Eds.). (1999). *Cognitive dissonance: Progress on a pivotal theory in social psychology.* Washington, DC: American Psychological Association.

Harrington, N. G. (1995). The effects of college students' alcohol resistance strategies. *Health Communication, 7,* 371–391.

Hatfield, E., & Sprecher, S. (1986). *Mirror, mirror . . . : The importance of looks in everyday life.* Albany: State University of New York Press.

Hecht, M. L., Corman, S. R., & Miller-Rassulo, M. (1993). An evaluation of the Drug Resistance Project: A comparison of film versus live performance media. *Health Communication, 5,* 75–88.

Hecht, M., Trost, M. R., Bator, R. J., & MacKinnon, D. (1997). Ethnicity and sex similarities and differences in drug resistance. *Journal of Applied Communication Research, 25,* 75–97.

Heider, E. (1946). Attitudes and cognitive organization. *Journal of Psychology, 21,* 107–112.

Herek, G. W. (1984a). Attitudes toward lesbians and gay men: A factor analytic study. *Journal of Homosexuality, 10,* 39–51.

Herek, G. W. (1984b). Beyond "homophobia": A social psychological perspective on attitudes toward lesbians and gay men. *Journal of Homosexuality, 10,* 2–17.

Herek, G. W. (1987). Can functions be measured?: A new perspective on the functional approach to attitudes. *Social Psychology Quarterly, 50,* 285–303.

Herek, G. W. (1988). Heterosexuals' attitudes toward lesbians and gay men: Correlates and gender differences. *Journal of Sex Research, 25,* 451–477.

Herek, G. M. (2000). The social construction of attitudes: Functional consensus and divergence in the U.S. public's reactions to AIDS. In G. R. Maio & J. M. Olson (Eds.), *Why we evaluate: Functions of attitudes* (pp. 325–364). Mahwah, NJ: Erlbaum.

Hewgill, M. A., & Miller, G. R. (1965). Source credibility and response to fear-arousing communications. *Speech Monographs, 32,* 95–101.

Higgins, E. T. (1996). Knowledge activation: Accessibility, applicability, and salience. In E. T. Higgins & A. W. Kruglanski (Eds.), *Social psychology: Handbook of basic principles* (pp. 133–168). New York: Guilford Press.

Higgins, E. T., King, G. A., & Mavin, G. H. (1982). Individual construct accessibility and subjective impressions and recall. *Journal of Personality and Social Psychology, 43,* 35–47.

Hill, K., & Monk, A. F. (2000). Electronic mail versus printed text: The effects on recipients. *Interacting with Computers, 13,* 253–263.

Hovland, C. I., Janis, I. L, & Kelley, H. H. (1953). *Communication and persuasion.* New Haven, CT: Yale University Press.

Hovland, C., Lumsdaine, A., & Sheffield, E. (1949). *Experiments in mass communication.* Princeton, NJ: Princeton University Press.

Hovland, C. I., & Pritzker, H. A. (1957). Extent of opinion change as a function of amount of change advocated. *Journal of Abnormal and Social Psychology, 54,* 257–261.

Hovland, C., & Weiss, W. (1951). The influence of source credibility on communication effectiveness. *Public Opinion Quarterly, 15,* 635–650.

Hullett, C. R., & Boster, F. J. (2001). Matching messages to the values underlying value-expressive and social-adjustive attitudes: Reconciling an old theory with a contemporary measurement approach. *Communication Monographs, 68,* 133–153.

Hunter, J. E. (1988). Failure of the social desireability response set hypothesis. *Human Communication Research, 15,* 162–168.

Hunter, J. E., & Boster, F. J. (1978, November). *An empathy model of compliance-gaining message strategy selection.* Paper presented at the annual meeting of the Speech Communication Association, Minneapolis, MN.

Hunter, J. E., & Boster, F. J. (1979, November). *Situational differences in the selection of compliance gaining messages.* Paper presented at the annual meeting of the Speech Communication Association, San Antonio, TX.

Hunter, J. E., & Boster, F. J. (1987). A model of compliance-gaining message selection. *Communication Monographs, 54,* 63–84.

Hunter, J. E., Danes, J. E., & Cohen, S. H. (1984). *Mathematical models of attitude change: Change in single attitudes and cognitive structure.* New York: Academic Press.

Hunter, J. E., & Schmidt, F. L. (1990). *Methods of meta-analysis: Correcting error and bias in research findings.* Newbury Park, CA: Sage.

Hunter, J. E., Schmidt, F. L., & Jackson, G. B. (1982). *Meta-analysis: Cumulating research findings across studies.* Beverly Hills, CA: Sage.

Ifert, D. E. (2000). Resistance to interpersonal requests: A summary and critique of recent research. In M. Roloff (Ed.), *Communication yearbook 23* (pp. 125–161). Thousand Oaks, CA: Sage.

Ifert, D. E., & Roloff, M. E. (1994). Anticipated obstacles to compliance: Predicting their presence and expression. *Communication Studies, 45,* 120–130.

Insko, C. A. (1967). *Theories of attitude change.* New York: Appleton Century Crofts.

Insko, C. A., Turnbull, W., & Yandell, B. (1974). Facilitative and inhibiting effects of distraction on attitude change. *Sociometry, 37*, 508–528.

Isenberg, D. J. (1986). Group polarization: A critical review and meta-analysis. *Journal of Personality and Social Psychology, 50*, 1141–1151.

Jaccard, J. J., Knox, R., & Brinberg, D. (1979). Prediction of behavior from beliefs: An extension and test of a subjective probability model. *Journal of Personality and Social Psychology, 37*, 1239–1248.

Jackall, R., & Hirota, J. M. (2000). *Image makers: Advertising, public relations, and the ethos of advocacy.* Chicago: University of Chicago Press.

Jackson, S., & Allen, M. (1987, May). *Meta-analysis of the effectiveness of one-sided and two-sided argumentation.* Paper presented at the annual meeting of the International Communication Association, Montreal, Canada.

Jackson, S., & Jacobs, S. (1983). Generalizing about messages: Suggestions for design and analysis of experiments. *Human Communication Research, 9*, 169–191.

Jackson, S., O'Keefe, D. J., & Jacobs, S. (1988). The search for reliable generalizations about messages: A comparison of research strategies. *Human Communication Research, 15*, 127–142.

Janis, I. L. (1967). Effects of fear arousal on attitude change: Recent developments in theory and research. In L. Berkowitz (Ed.), *Advances in experimental social psychology* (Vol. 3, pp. 166–224). New York: Academic Press.

Janis, I. L., & Feshbach, S. (1953). Effects of fear arousing communications. *Journal of Abnormal and Social Psychology, 48*, 78–92.

Janis, I. L., & Frick, E. (1943). The relationship between attitudes toward conclusions and errors in judging logical validity of syllogisms. *Journal of Experimental Psychology, 33*, 73–77.

Janis, I. L., Kaye, D., & Kirschner, P. (1965). Facilitating effects of "eating-while-reading" on responsiveness to persuasive communications. *Journal of Personality and Social Psychology, 1*, 181–186.

Janis, I. L., & King, B. T. (1954). The influence of role-playing on opinion change. *Journal of Abnormal and Social Psychology, 49*, 211–218.

Janz, N. K., & Becker, M. H. (1984). The health belief model: A decade later. *Health Education Quarterly, 11*, 1–47.

Jessor, R., & Jessor, S. L., (1977). *Problem behavior and psychosocial development: A longitudinal study of youth.* New York: Academic Press.

Johnson, B. T., & Eagly, A. H. (1989). Effects of involvement on persuasion: A meta-analysis. *Psychological Bulletin, 106*, 290–314.

Johnson, B. T., & Eagly, A. H. (1990). Involvement and persuasion: Types, traditions, and the evidence. *Psychological Bulletin, 107*, 375–384.

Kahneman, D. (1973). *Attention and effort.* Englewood Cliffs, NJ: Prentice-Hall.

Kahneman, D., & Tversky, A. (1973). On the psychology of prediction. *Psychological Review, 80*, 237–251.

Kaid, L. L., & Bystrom, D. G. (Eds.). (1999). *The electronic election: Perspectives on the 1996 campaign communication.* Mahwah, NJ: Erlbaum.

Kallgren, C. A., & Wood, W. (1986). Access to attitude-relevant information in memory as a determinant of attitude-behavior consistency. *Journal of Experimental Social Psychology, 22,* 328–338.

Kaminski, E. E., McDermott, S. T., & Boster, F. J. (1977, April). *The use of compliance-gaining strategies as a function of Machiavellianism and situation.* Paper presented at the annual meeting of the Central States Speech Association, Southfield, MI.

Katz, D. (1960). The functional approach to the study of attitudes. *Public Opinion Quarterly, 24,* 163–204.

Kellermann, K. (1980). The concept of evidence: A critical review. *Journal of the American Forensics Association, 16,* 159–172.

Kellermann, K., & Cole, T. (1994). Classifying compliance-gaining messages: Taxonomic disorder and strategic confusion. *Communication Theory, 4,* 3–60.

Kelley, H. H. (1952). Two functions of reference groups. In G. E. Swanson, T. M. Newcomb, & E. L. Hartley (Eds.), *Readings in social psychology* (2nd ed., pp. 410–414). New York: Holt.

Kelley, H. H. (1967). Attribution theory in social psychology. In D. Levine (Ed.), *Nebraska Symposium on Motivation* (Vol. 15, pp. 192–238). Lincoln: University of Nebraska Press.

Kelman, H. C. (1958). Compliance, identification, and internalization: Three processes of attitude change. *Journal of Conflict Resolution, 2,* 51–60.

Kelman, H. C. (1961). Processes of opinion change. *Public Opinion Quarterly, 25,* 57–78.

Kelman, H., & Hovland, C. (1953). Reinstatement of the communicator in delayed measurement of opinion change. *Journal of Abnormal and Social Psychology, 48,* 327–335.

Kerlinger, F. N., & Lee, H. B. (2000). *Foundations of behavioral research* (4th ed.). Fort Worth, TX: Harcourt Brace.

Kiesler, C. A. (1971). *The psychology of commitment: Experiments linking behavior to belief.* San Diego, CA: Academic Press.

Kiesler, C. A., Collins, C. A., & Miller, N. (1983). *Attitude change: A critical analysis of theoretical approaches.* Malabar, FL: Krieger. (Original work published 1969)

Kim, M. S., & Hunter, J. E. (1993a). Attitude–behavior relationships: A meta-analysis of attitude relevance and topic. *Journal of Communication, 43,* 101–142.

Kim, M. S., & Hunter, J. E. (1993b). Relationships among attitudes, behavioral intentions, and behaviors: A meta-analysis. *Communication Research, 20,* 331–364.

King, B. T., & Janis, I. L. (1956). Comparison of the effects of improvised versus non-improvised role playing in producing opinion changes. *Human Relations, 9,* 177–186.

King, W. C., Dent, M. M., & Miles, E. W. (1991). The persuasive effect of graphics in computer-mediated communication. *Computers in Human Behavior, 7,* 269–279.

Kogan, N., & Wallach, M. A. (1967). Risky-shift phenomenon in small decision-making groups: A test of the information exchange hypothesis. *Journal of Experimental Social Psychology, 6*, 467–471.

Kokkinaki, F., & Lunt, P. (1997). The relationship between involvement, attitude accessibility, and attitude–behavior consistency. *British Journal of Social Psychology, 36*, 497–509.

Kruglanski, A. W., & Thompson, E. P. (1999). Persuasion by a single route: A view from the unimodel. *Psychological Inquiry, 10*, 83–109.

Lamm, H., & Myers, D. G. (1978). Group-induced polarization of attitudes and behavior. In L. Berkowitz (Ed.), *Advances in experimental social psychology* (Vol. 11, pp. 145–195). New York: Academic Press.

LaPiere, R. T. (1934). Attitudes vs. actions. *Social Forces, 13*, 230–237.

Larson, C. U. (2001). *Persuasion: Reception and responsibility* (9th ed.). Belmont, CA: Wadsworth.

Lasswell, H. D. (1950). Propaganda and mass insecurity. *Psychiatry: Journal for the Study of Interpersonal Processes, 13*, 283–299.

Latane, B., & Darley, J. M. (1968). Group inhibition of bystander intervention in emergencies. *Journal of Personality and Social Psychology, 10*, 215–221.

Latane, B., & Darley, J. M. (1970). *The unresponsive bystander: Why doesn't he help?* New York: Appleton-Century-Crofts.

Latane, B., & Rodin, J. (1969). A lady in distress: Inhibiting effects of friends and strangers on bystander intervention. *Journal of Experimental Social Psychology, 5*, 189–202.

Lavine, H. (1999). Types of evidence and routes to persuasion: The unimodel versus dual-process models. *Psychological Inquiry, 10*, 141–144.

Lavine, H., & Snyder, M. (2000). Cognitive processing and the functional matching effect in persuasion: Studies of personality and political behavior. In G. R. Maio & J. M. Olson (Eds.), *Why we evaluate: Functions of attitudes* (pp. 97–131). Mahwah, NJ: Erlbaum.

Lenihan, K. J. (1965). *Perceived climates as a barrier to housing desegregation.* Unpublished manuscript, Columbia University, Bureau of Applied Social Research, New York.

Leupker, R. V., Johnson, C. A., Murray, D. M., & Pechacek, T. E. (1983). Prevention of cigarette smoking: Three-year follow-up of an education program for youth. *Journal of Behavioral Medicine, 6*, 53–62.

Leventhal, H. (1970). Findings and theory in the study of fear communications. In L. Berkowitz (Ed.), *Advances in experimental social psychology* (Vol. 5, pp. 119–186). New York: Academic Press.

Levin, K. D., Nichols, D. R., & Johnson, B. T. (2000). Involvement and persuasion: Attitude functions for the motivated processor. In G. R. Maio & J. M. Olson (Eds.), *Why we evaluate: Functions of attitudes* (pp. 163–194). Mahwah, NJ: Erlbaum.

Levine, T. R., & Boster, F. J. (2001). The effects of power and message variables on compliance. *Communication Monographs, 68*, 28–48.

Lewin, K. (1935). *A dynamic theory of personality.* New York: McGraw-Hill.

Liebert, R. M., Neale, J. M., & Davidson, E. S. (1973). *The early window: Effects of television on children and youth.* New York: Pergamon Press.

Lumsdaine, A. A., & Janis, I. L. (1953). Resistance to "counter-propaganda" produced by one-sided and two-sided "propaganda" presentations. *Public Opinion Quarterly, 17,* 311–318.

MacHovec, E. J. (1989). *Cults and personality.* Springfield, IL: Thomas.

Madden, T. J., Ellen, P. S., & Ajzen, I. (1992). A comparison of the theory of planned behavior and the theory of reasoned action. *Personality and Social Psychology Bulletin, 18,* 3–9.

Maio, G. R., & Olson, J. M. (2000a). Preface. In G. R. Maio & J. M. Olson (Eds.), *Why we evaluate: Functions of attitudes* (pp. vii–xi). Mahwah, NJ: Erlbaum.

Maio, G. R., & Olson, J. M. (Eds.). (2000b). *Why we evaluate: Functions of attitudes.* Mahwah, NJ: Erlbaum.

Mandler, G. (1984). *Mind and body: Psychology of emotion and stress.* New York: Norton.

Marshall, L. J., & Levy, V. M., Jr. (1998). The development of children's perceptions of obstacles in compliance-gaining interactions. *Communication Studies, 49,* 342–357.

Marwell, G., & Schmitt, D. R. (1967). Dimensions of compliance-gaining behavior: An empirical analysis. *Sociometry, 30,* 350–364.

Matice, K. (1978). *The effect of source, class, dogmatism, and time on attitude change of police academy recruits.* Unpublished doctoral dissertation, University of Missouri, St. Louis.

Mayer, M. E. (1986). Explaining the choice shift: A comparison of competing effects-coded models. In M. L. McLaughlin (Ed.), *Communication yearbook 9* (pp. 297–314). Beverly Hills, CA: Sage.

McCroskey, J. C. (1966). Scales for the measurement of ethos. *Speech Monographs, 33,* 65–72.

McCroskey, J. C. (1967). The effects of evidence in persuasive communication. *Western Speech, 31,* 189–199.

McCroskey, J. C. (1969). A summary of experimental research on the effects of evidence in persuasive communication. *Quarterly Journal of Speech, 55,* 169–176.

McGuire, W. J. (1960). A syllogistic analysis of cognitive relationships. In C. I. Hovland & M. J. Rosenberg (Eds.), *Attitude organization and change: An analysis of consistency among attitude components* (pp. 65–111). New Haven, CT: Yale University Press.

McGuire, W. J. (1961a). The effectiveness of supportive and refutational defenses in immunizing and restoring beliefs against persuasion. *Sociometry, 24,* 184–197.

McGuire, W. J. (1961b). Persistence of resistance to persuasion induced by various types of persuasive defenses. *Journal of Abnormal and Social Psychology, 64,* 241–248.

McGuire, W. J. (1964). Inducing resistance to persuasion: Some contemporary approaches. In L. Berkowitz (Ed.), *Advances in experimental social psychology* (Vol. 1, pp. 191–229). New York: Academic Press.

McGuire, W. J. (1966). Attitudes and opinions. *Annual Review of Psychology*, *17*, 475–514.

McGuire, W. J. (1968). Personality and attitude change: An information processing theory. In A. G. Greenwald, T. C. Brock, & T. M. Ostrom (Eds.), *Psychological foundations of attitudes* (pp. 171–196). New York: Academic Press.

McGuire, W. J. (1969). The nature of attitudes and attitude change. In G. Lindzey & E. Aronson (Eds.), *Handbook of social psychology* (Vol. 3, pp. 136–314). Reading, MA: Addison-Wesley.

McGuire, W. J. (1999). *Constructing social psychology: Creative and critical processes*. Cambridge, UK: Cambridge University Press.

McGuire, W. J., & Papageorgis, D. (1961). The relative efficacy of various types of prior belief-defense in producing immunity against persuasion. *Journal of Abnormal and Social Psychology*, *62*, 327–337.

McLaughlin, M. L., Cody, M. J., & Robey, C. S. (1980). Situational influences on the selection of strategies to resist compliance-gaining attempts. *Human Communication Research*, *7*, 14–36.

Metts, S., Cupach, W. R., & Imahori, T. T. (1992). Perceptions of sexual compliance resisting messages in three types of cross-sex relationships. *Western Journal of Communication*, *56*, 1–17.

Meyers, R. A. (1989). Persuasive arguments theory: A test of assumptions. *Human Communication Research*, *15*, 357–381.

Meyers, R. A., Brashers, D. E., & Hanner, J. (2000). Majority–minority influence: Identifying argumentative patterns and predicting argument-outcome links. *Journal of Communication*, *50*, 3–30.

Meyers, R. A., & Seibold, D. R. (1990). Perspectives on group argument: A critical review of persuasive arguments theory and an alternative structurational view. In J. A. Anderson (Ed.), *Communication yearbook 13* (pp. 268–302). Newbury Park, CA: Sage.

Millar, M. G., & Millar, K. U. (1990). Attitude change as a function of attitude type and argument type. *Journal of Personality and Social Psychology*, *59*, 217–228.

Miller, G. R. (1963). Studies in the use of fear appeals: A summary and analysis. *Central States Speech Journal*, *14*, 117–125.

Miller, G. R. (1967). A crucial problem in attitude research. *Quarterly Journal of Speech*, *53*, 235–240.

Miller, G. R. (1973). Counterattitudinal advocacy: A current appraisal. In C. D. Mortensen & K. K. Sereno (Eds.), *Advances in communication research* (pp. 105–152). New York: Harper & Row.

Miller, G. R. (1980). On being persuaded: Some basic distinctions. In M. E. Roloff & G. R. Miller (Eds.), *Persuasion: New directions in theory and research* (pp. 11–28). Beverly Hills, CA: Sage.

Miller, G. R., Boster, E. J., Roloff, M., & Seibold, D. (1977). Compliance-gaining message strategies: A typology and some findings concerning effects of situational differences. *Communication Monographs, 44,* 37–51.

Miller, G. R., Boster, E. J., Roloff, M., & Seibold, D. (1987). MBRS rekindled: Some thoughts on compliance gaining in interpersonal settings. In M. E. Roloff & G. R. Miller (Eds.), *Interpersonal processes: New directions in communication research* (pp. 89–116). Newbury Park, CA: Sage.

Miller, G. R., & Burgoon, M. (1978). Persuasion research: Review and commentary. In B. D. Ruben (Ed.), *Communication yearbook 12* (pp. 29–47). New Brunswick, NJ: Transaction Books.

Miller, K. I. (2002). *Communication theories: Perspectives, processes, and contexts.* New York: McGraw-Hill.

Miller, M. A., Alberts, J. K., Hecht, M. L., Trost, M. R., & Krizek, R. L. (2000). *Adolescent relationships and drug use.* Mahwah, NJ: Erlbaum.

Miller, N. (1965). Involvement and dogmatism as inhibitors of attitude change. *Journal of Experimental Social Psychology, 1,* 121–132.

Miller, N., & Pederson, W. C. (1999). Assessing process distinctiveness. *Psychological Inquiry, 10,* 150–156.

Mindred, P. W., & Cohen, J. B. (1979). Isolating attitudinal and normative influences in behavioral intentions models. *Journal of Marketing Research, 16,* 102–110.

Mindred, P. W., & Cohen, J. B. (1981). An examination of the Fishbein–Ajzen behavioral-intentions model's concepts and measures. *Journal of Experimental Social Psychology, 17,* 309–339.

Mongeau, P. A., Hale, J. L., & Alles, M. (1994). An experimental investigation of accounts and attributions following sexual infidelity. *Communication Monographs, 61,* 326–344.

Mongeau, P. A., & Stiff, J. B. (1993). Specifying causal relationships in the elaboration likelihood model. *Communication Theory, 3,* 65–72.

Morley, D. D. (1988a). Meta-analytic techniques: When generalizing to message populations is not possible. *Human Communication Research, 15,* 112–126.

Morley, D. D. (1988b). Reply to Jackson, O'Keefe, and Jacobs. *Human Communication Research, 15,* 143–147.

Moscovici, S., Lage, E., & Naffrechoux, M. (1969). Influence of a consistent minority on the responses of a majority in a color perception test. *Sociometry, 32,* 365–380.

Nabi, R. L. (2002). Discrete emotions and persuasion. In J. P. Dillard & M. Pfau (Eds.), *The persuasion handbook: Developments in theory and practice* (pp. 289–308). Thousand Oaks, CA: Sage.

Naisbitt, J. (1982). *Megatrends: Ten new directions transforming our lives.* New York: Warner Books.

National Gay Task Force. (1984). *Anti-gay/lesbian victimization.* Washington, DC: Author. (Available from National Gay and Lesbian Task Force, 1517 U Street NW, Washington, DC 20009)

Newcomb, T. M. (1953). An approach to the study of communicative acts. *Psychological Review, 60,* 393–404.

Newcomb, T. M., Turner, R. H., & Converse, P. E. (1965). *Social psychology.* New York: Holt, Rinehart & Winston.

Norman, P., Abraham, C., & Conner, M. (Eds.). (2000). *Understanding and changing health behavior: From health beliefs to self-regulation.* Amsterdam: Harwood Academic.

Norman, R. (1976). When what is said is important: A comparison of expert and attractive sources. *Journal of Experimental Social Psychology, 12,* 294–300.

O'Keefe, B. J. (1988). The logic of message design: Individual differences in reasoning about communication. *Communication Monographs, 55,* 80–103.

O'Keefe, B. J. (1990). The logic of regulative communication: Understanding the logic of message designs. In J. P. Dillard (Ed.), *Seeking compliance: The production of interpersonal influence messages* (pp. 87–106). Scottsdale, AZ: Gorsuch-Scarisbrick.

O'Keefe, B. J., & Delia, J. G. (1978). Construct comprehensiveness and cognitive complexity. *Perceptual and Motor Skills, 46,* 548–550.

O'Keefe, B. J., & McCornack, S. A. (1987). Message design logic and message goal structure: Effects on perceptions of message quality in regulative communication situations. *Human Communication Research, 14,* 68–92.

O'Keefe, B. J., & Shepherd, G. J. (1987). The pursuit of multiple objectives in face-to-face persuasive interactions: Effects of construct differentiation on message organization. *Communication Monographs, 54,* 396–419.

O'Keefe, D. J. (1987). The persuasive effects of delaying identification of high- and low-credibility communicators: A meta-analytic review. *Central States Communication Journal, 38,* 64–72.

O'Keefe, D. J. (1990). *Persuasion: Theory and research.* Newbury Park, CA: Sage.

O'Keefe, D. J. (1993). The persuasive effects of message sidedness variations: A cautionary note concerning Allen's (1991) meta-analysis. *Western Journal of Communication, 57,* 87–97.

O'Keefe, D. J. (1997). Standpoint explicitness and persuasive effect: A meta-analytic review of the effects of varying conclusion articulation in persuasive messages. *Argumentation and Advocacy, 34,* 1–12.

O'Keefe, D. J. (1998). Justification explicitness and persuasive effect: A meta-analytic review of the effects of varying support articulation in persuasive messages. *Argumentation and Advocacy, 35,* 61–75.

O'Keefe, D. J. (2000). Guilt and social influence. In M. Roloff (Ed.), *Communication yearbook 23* (pp. 67–101). Thousand Oaks, CA: Sage.

O'Keefe, D. J. (2002). Guilt as a mechanism of persuasion. In J. P. Dillard & M. W. Pfau (Eds.), *The persuasion handbook: Developments in theory and practice* (pp. 329–344). Thousand Oaks, CA: Sage.

O'Keefe, D. J., & Delia, J. D. (1981). Construct differentiation and the relationship of attitudes and behavioral intentions. *Communication Monographs, 48,* 146–157.

O'Keefe, D. J. & Figgé, M. (1997). A guilt-based explanation of the door-in-the-face influence strategy. *Human Communication Research, 24,* 64–81.

O'Keefe, D. J., & Hale, S. L. (1998). The door-in-the-face influence strategy: A random effects meta-analytic review. In M. Roloff (Ed.), *Communication yearbook 21* (pp. 1–33). Thousand Oaks, CA: Sage.

O'Keefe, D. J., & Hale, S. L. (2001). An odds-ratio-based meta-analysis on the door-in-the-face influence strategy. *Communication Reports, 14*, 31–38.

O'Keefe, D. J., Jackson, S., & Jacobs, S. (1988). Reply to Morley. *Human Communication Research, 15*, 148–151.

Osterhouse, R. A., & Brock, T. C. (1970). Distraction increases yielding to propaganda by inhibiting counterarguing. *Journal of Personality and Social Psychology, 15*, 344–358.

Papageorgis, D., & McGuire, W. J. (1961). The generality of immunity to persuasion produced by pre-exposure to weakened counterarguments. *Journal of Abnormal and Social Psychology, 62*, 475–481.

Patch, M. A. (1988). Differential perception of source legitimacy in sequential request strategies. *Journal of Social Psychology, 128*, 817–823.

Perloff, R. M. (2001). *Persuading people to have safer sex: Applications of social science to the AIDS crisis*. Mahwah, NJ: Erlbaum.

Perloff, R. M., & Brock, T. C. (1980). " . . . And thinking makes it so": Cognitive responses to persuasion. In M. E. Roloff & G. R. Miller (Eds.), *Persuasion: New directions in theory and research* (pp. 67–99). Beverly Hills, CA: Sage.

Petty, R. E., & Cacioppo, J. T. (1981). *Attitudes and persuasion: Classic and contemporary approaches*. Dubuque, IA: Brown.

Petty, R. E., & Cacioppo, J. T. (1986). *Communication and persuasion: Central and peripheral routes to attitude change*. New York: Springer-Verlag.

Petty, R. E., & Cacioppo, J. T. (1990). Involvement vs. persuasion: Tradition vs. integration. *Psychological Bulletin, 107*, 367–374.

Petty, R. E., Cacioppo, J. T., & Goldman, R. (1981). Personal involvement as a determinant of argument based persuasion. *Journal of Personality and Social Psychology, 41*, 847–855.

Petty, R. E., Kasmer, J. E., Haugtvedt, C. P., & Cacioppo, J. T. (1987). Source and message factors in persuasion: A reply to Stiff's critique of the elaboration likelihood model. *Communication Monographs, 54*, 233–249.

Petty, R. E., Ostrom, T. M., & Brock, T. C. (1981). *Cognitive responses in persuasion*. Hillsdale, NJ: Erlbaum.

Petty, R. E., & Wegener, D. T. (1998). Attitude change: Multiple roles for persuasion variables. In D. Gilbert, S. Fiske, & G. Lindzey (Eds.), *Handbook of social psychology* (4th ed., pp. 323–390). New York: McGraw-Hill.

Petty, R. E., & Wegener, D. T. (1999). The elaboration likelihood model: Current status and controversies. In S. Chaiken & Y. Trope (Eds.), *Dual-process theories in social psychology* (pp. 41–72). New York: Guilford Press.

Petty, R. E., Wegener, D. T., Fabrigar, L. R., Priester, J. R., & Cacioppo, J. T. (1994). Conceptual and methodological issues in the elaboration likelihood model of persuasion: A reply to the Michigan State critics. *Communication Theory, 3*, 336–363.

Petty, R. E., Wells, G. L., & Brock, T. C. (1976). Distraction can enhance or reduce yielding to propaganda: Thought disruption versus effort justification. *Journal of Personality and Social Psychology, 34,* 874–888.

Petty, R. E., Wheeler, S. C., & Bizer, G. Y. (1999). Is there one persuasion process or more?: Lumping versus splitting in attitude change theories. *Psychological Inquiry, 10,* 156–163.

Petty, R. E., Wheeler, S. C., & Bizer, G. Y. (2000). Attitude functions and persuasion: An elaboration likelihood approach to matched versus mismatched messages. In G. R. Maio & J. M. Olson (Eds.), *Why we evaluate: Functions of attitudes* (pp. 133–162). Mahwah, NJ: Erlbaum.

Pfau, M. (1992). The potential of inoculation in promoting resistance to the effectiveness of comparative advertising messages. *Communication Quarterly, 40,* 26–44.

Pfau, M. (1995). Designing messages for behavioral inoculation. In E. Maibach & R. L. Parrott (Eds.), *Designing health messages: Approaches from communication theory and public health practice* (pp. 99–113). Thousand Oaks, CA: Sage.

Pfau, M., & Burgoon, M. (1988). Inoculation in political communication. *Human Communication Research, 15,* 91–111.

Pfau, M., & Kenski, H. C. (1990). *Attack politics: Strategy and defense.* New York: Praeger.

Pfau, M., Kenski, H. C., Nitz, M., & Sorenson, J. (1990). Efficacy of inoculation strategies in promoting resistance to political attack messages: Application to direct mail. *Communication Monographs, 57,* 25–43.

Pfau, M., & Parrott, R. (1993). *Persuasive communication campaigns.* Boston: Allyn & Bacon.

Pfau, M., & Van Bockern, S. (1994). The persistence of inoculation in conferring resistance to smoking initiation among adolescents: The second year. *Human Communication Research, 20,* 413–430.

Pfau, M., Van Bockern, S., & Kang, J. G. (1992). Use of inoculation to promote resistance to smoking initiation among adolescents. *Communication Monographs, 59,* 213–230.

Powell, M. C., & Fazio, R. H. (1984). Attitude accessibility as a function of repeated attitude expression. *Personality and Social Psychology Bulletin, 10,* 139–148.

Powers, W., Jordan, W., & Street, R. (1979). Language indices in the measurement of cognitive complexity: Is complexity loquacity? *Human Communication Research, 6,* 69–73.

Reardon, K. K. (1981). *Persuasion: Theory and context.* Beverly Hills, CA: Sage.

Pratkanis, A. R., Greenwald, A. G., Leippe, M. R., & Baumgardner, M. H. (1988). In search of reliable persuasion effects: III. The sleeper effect is dead. Long live the sleeper effect. *Journal of Personality and Social Psychology, 54,* 203–218.

Regan, D. T., & Fazio, R. H. (1977). On the consistency between attitudes and behavior: Look to the method of attitude formation. *Journal of Experimental Social Psychology, 13,* 28–45.

Reinard, J. C. (1988). The empirical study of the persuasive effects of evidence:

The status after fifty years of research. *Human Communication Research*, *15*, 3–59.

Reinard, J. C. (1998). The persuasive effects of testimonial evidence. In M. Allen & R. W. Preiss (Eds.), *Persuasion: Advances through meta-analysis* (pp. 69–86). Cresskill, NJ: Hampton Press.

Reynolds, R. A., & Burgoon, M. (1983). Belief processing, reasoning, and evidence. In R. Bostrom (Ed.), *Communication yearbook 7* (pp. 83–104) Beverly Hills, CA: Sage.

Reynolds, R. A., & Reynolds, J. L. (2002). Evidence. In J. P. Dillard & M. Pfau (Eds.), *The persuasion handbook: Developments in theory and practice* (pp. 427–444). Thousand Oaks, CA: Sage.

Rhine, R. J., & Severance, L. J. (1970). Ego-involvement, discrepancy, source credibility, and attitude change. *Journal of Personality and Social Psychology*, *16*, 175–190.

Rogers, E. M. (1985). *Diffusion of innovations*. New York: Free Press.

Rogers, R. W. (1975). A protection motivation theory of fear appeals and attitude change. *Journal of Psychology, 91*, 93–114.

Rogers, R. W. (1983). Cognitive and physiological processes in fear appeals and attitude change: A revised theory of protection motivation. In J. Cacioppo & R. Petty (Eds.), *Social psychophysiology* (pp. 153–176). New York: Guilford Press.

Rohrbach, L. A., Graham, J. W., Hansen, W. B., Flay, B. R., & Johnson, C. A. (1987). Evaluation of resistance skills training using multitrait-multimethod role play skill assessment. *Health Education Research, 2*, 401–407.

Rokeach, M. (1968). *Beliefs, attitudes and values: A theory of organization and change*. San Francisco: Jossey-Bass.

Roloff, M., & Barnicott, E. E, Jr. (1978). The situational use of pro- and anti-social compliance-gaining strategies by high and low Machiavellians. In B. D. Ruben (Ed.), *Communication yearbook 2* (pp. 193–205). New Brunswick, NJ: Transaction Books.

Roloff, M., & Barnicott, E. E., Jr. (1979). The influence of dogmatism on the situational use of pro- and anti-social compliance gaining strategies. *Southern Speech Communication Journal, 45*, 37–54.

Ronis, D. L., & Greenwald, A. G. (1979). Dissonance theory revised again: Comment on the paper by Fazio, Zanna, and Cooper. *Journal of Experimental Social Psychology, 15*, 62–69.

Roskos-Ewaldson, D. R., Apran-Ralstin, L., & St. Pierre, J. (2002). Attitude accessibility and persuasion: The quick and the strong. In J. P. Dillard & M. W. Pfau (Eds.), *The persuasion handbook: Developments in theory and practice* (pp. 39–61). Thousand Oaks, CA: Sage.

Rule, B. G., Bisanz, G. L., & Kohn, M. (1985). Anatomy of a persuasion schema: Targets, goals, and strategies. *Journal of Personality and Social Psychology, 48*, 1127–1140.

Ryan, M. J. (1982). Behavioral intention formation: A structural equation analysis of attitudinal and social influence interdependency. *Journal of Consumer Research, 9*, 263–278.

Sadler, O., & Tesser, A. (1973). Some effects of salience and time upon interpersonal hostility and attraction during social isolation. *Sociometry, 36,* 99–112.

Samp, J. A., & Solomon, D. H. (1998). Communicative responses to problematic events: I. The variety and facets of goals. *Communication Research, 25,* 66–95.

San Miguel, C. L., & Millham, J. (1976). The role of cognitive and situational variables in aggression toward homosexuals. *Journal of Homosexuality, 1,* 11–27.

Sarnoff, D. (1960). Reaction formation and cynicism. *Journal of Personality, 28,* 129–143.

Schachter, S., & Singer, J. E. (1962). Cognitive, social, and physiological determinants of emotional state. *Psychological Review, 65,* 121–128.

Schinke, S. P., & Gilchrist, L. D. (1984). Preventing cigarette smoking with youth. *Journal of Primary Prevention, 5,* 48–56.

Schrader, D. C., & Dillard, J. P. (1998). Goal structures and interpersonal influence. *Communication Studies, 49,* 276–293.

Seibold, D. R. (1988). A response to "Item desireability in compliance-gaining research." *Human Communication Research, 15,* 152–161.

Seibold, D. R., Cantrill, J. G., & Meyers, R. A. (1985). Communication and interpersonal influence. In M. L. Knapp & G. R. Miller (Eds.), *Handbook of interpersonal communication* (pp. 551–611). Beverly Hills, CA: Sage.

Shannon, W. V. (1967). *The heir apparent: Robert Kennedy and the struggle for power.* New York: Macmillan.

Shavitt, S., & Nelson, M. R. (2002). The role of attitude functions in persuasion and social judgment. In J. P. Dillard & M. W. Pfau (Eds.), *The persuasion handbook: Developments in theory and practice* (pp. 137–153). Thousand Oaks, CA: Sage.

Sheppard, B. H., Hartwick, J., & Warshaw, P. R. (1988). The theory of reasoned action: A meta-analysis of past research with recommendations for modifications and future research. *Journal of Consumer Research, 15,* 325–343.

Sherif, C. W., Sherif, M., & Nebergall, R. E. (1965). *Attitude and attitude change.* Philadelphia: Saunders.

Sherif, M., & Hovland, C. I. (1961). *Social judgment: Assimilation and contrast effects in communication and attitude change.* New Haven, CT: Yale University Press.

Sherif, M., & Sherif, C. W. (1956). *An outline of social psychology.* New York: Harper & Row.

Sherif, M., & Sherif, C. W. (1967). Attitude as the individual's own categories: The social judgment–involvement approach to attitude and attitude change. In C. W. Sherif & M. Sherif (Eds.), *Attitude, ego-involvement, and change* (pp. 105–139). New York: Wiley.

Sillars, A. L. (1980). The stranger and the spouse as target persons for compliance-gaining strategies: A subjective expected utility model. *Human Communication Research, 6,* 265–279.

Simons, H. W., Berkowitz, N. N., & Moyer, R. J. (1970). Similarity, credibility, and attitude change: A review and a theory. *Psychological Bulletin, 73,* 1–16.

Simons, H. W., Morreale, J., & Gronbeck, B. (2001). *Persuasion in society.* Thousand Oaks, CA: Sage.

Sivacek, J., & Crano, W. D. (1982). Vested interest as a moderator of attitude-behavior consistency. *Journal of Personality and Social Psychology, 43,* 210–221.

Skinner, B. F. (1938). *The behavior of organisms: An experimental analysis.* Englewood Cliffs, NJ: Prentice-Hall.

Slater, M. D. (1997). Persuasion processes across receiver goals and message genres. *Communication Theory, 7,* 125–148.

Slater, M. D. (2002). Involvement as goal-directed strategic processing: Extending the Elaboration Likelihood Model. In J. P. Dillard & M. W. Pfau (Eds.), *The persuasion handbook: Developments in theory and practice* (pp. 175–194). Thousand Oaks, CA: Sage.

Smetana, J. G., & Adler, N. E. (1980). Fishbein's valence X expectancy model: An examination of some assumptions. *Personality and Social Psychology Bulletin, 6,* 89–96.

Smith, M. B., Bruner, J. S., & White, R. W. (1956). *Opinions and personality.* New York: Wiley.

Snyder, M. (1986). *Public appearances/private realities: The psychology of self-monitoring.* New York: Freeman.

Snyder, M., & DeBono, K. (1985). Appeals to image and claims about quality: Understanding the psychology of advertising. *Journal of Personality and Social Psychology, 49,* 586–597.

Staats, C. K., & Staats, A. W. (1957). Meaning established by classical conditioning. *Journal of Experimental Psychology, 54,* 74–80.

Stahelski, A., & Patch, M. E. (1993). The effect of the compliance strategy choice upon perception of power. *Journal of Social Psychology, 133,* 693–698.

Stiff, J. B. (1986). Cognitive processing of persuasive message cues: A meta-analytic review of the effects of supporting information on attitudes. *Communication Monographs, 53,* 75–89.

Stiff, J. B., & Boster, F. J. (1987). Cognitive processing: Additional thoughts and a reply to Petty, Kasmer, Haugtvedt, and Cacioppo. *Communication Monographs, 54,* 250–256.

Stiff, J. B., McCormack, M., Zook, E., Stein, T., & Henry, R. (1990). The effects of attitudes toward gay men and lesbians on learning about AIDS and HIV transmission. *Communication Research, 17,* 743–758.

Stone, J., Aronson, E., Crain, A. L., Winslow, M. P., & Fried, C. B. (1994). Inducing hypocrisy as a means of encouraging young adults to use condoms. *Personality and Social Psychology Bulletin, 20,* 116–128.

Stoner, J. A. E. (1968). Risky and cautious shifts in group decisions: The influence of widely held values. *Journal of Experimental Social Psychology, 4,* 442–459.

Strack, F. (1999). Beyond dual-process models: Toward a flexible regulation system. *Psychological Inquiry, 10,* 166–169.

Strahan, E. J., & Zanna, M. P. (1999). Content versus process: If there is independence, can there still be two levels of information processing? *Psychological Inquiry, 10,* 170–172.

Stroebe, W. (1999). The return of the one-track mind. *Psychological Inquiry, 10,* 173–176.

Sutton, S. R. (1982). Fear-arousing communications: A critical examination of theory and research. In J. R. Eiser (Ed.), *Social psychology and behavioral medicine* (pp. 303–337). London: Wiley.

Sutton, S. R., & Eiser, J. R. (1984). The effect of fear-arousing communications on cigarette smoking: An expectancy-value approach. *Journal of Behavioral Medicine, 7,* 13–33.

Szabo, E. A., & Pfau, M. (2002). Nuances in inoculation: Theory and application. In J. P. Dillard & M. W. Pfau (Eds.), *The persuasion handbook: Developments in theory and practice* (pp. 233–258). Thousand Oaks, CA: Sage.

Tannenbaum, P. H. (1953). *Attitudes toward source and concept as factors in attitude change through communications.* Unpublished doctoral dissertation, Institute for Communications Research, University of Illinois, Urbana.

Tedeschi, J. T., Schlenker, B. R., & Bonoma, T. V. (1971). Cognitive dissonance: Private ratiocination or public spectacle? *American Psychologist, 26,* 685–695.

Tellis, G. J. (1987). *Advertising, exposure, loyalty, and brand purchase: A two-stage model of choice* (Report No. 87-105). Cambridge, MA: Marketing Science Institute.

Tesser, A. (1978). Self-generated attitude change. In L. Berkowitz (Ed.), *Advances in experimental social psychology* (Vol. 11, pp. 289–338). New York: Academic Press.

Tesser, A., & Conlee, M. C. (1975). Some effects of time and thought on attitude polarization. *Journal of Personality and Social Psychology, 31,* 262–270.

Thompson, E. P., Kruglanski, A. W., & Spiegel, S. (2000). Attitude as knowledge structures and persuasion as a specific case of subjective knowledge acquisition. In G. R. Maio & J. M. Olson (Eds.), *Why we evaluate: Functions of attitudes* (pp. 59–94). Mahwah, NJ: Erlbaum.

Thurstone, L. L. (1928). Attitudes can be measured. *American Journal of Sociology, 33,* 529–544.

Thurstone, L. L. (1931). The measurement of social attitudes. *Journal of Abnormal and Social Psychology, 26,* 249–269.

Todorov, A., Chaiken, S., & Henderson, M. D. (2002). The Heuristic-Systematic Model of Social Information Processing. In J. P. Dillard & M. W. Pfau (Eds.), *The persuasion handbook: Developments in theory and practice* (pp. 195–211). Thousand Oaks, CA: Sage.

Toulmin, S. (1964). *The uses of argument.* Cambridge, UK: Cambridge University Press.

Trafimow, D. (2000). A theory of attitudes, subjective norms, and private versus collective self-concepts. In D. J. Terry & M. A. Hogg (Eds.), *Attitudes, behaviors, and social context: The role of norms and group membership* (pp. 47–65). Mahwah, NJ: Erlbaum.

Trafimow, D., & Finlay, K. A. (1996). The importance of subjective norms for a minority of people: Between-subjects and within-subjects analyses. *Personality and Social Psychology Bulletin, 22*, 820–828.

Trafimow, D., & Fishbein, M. (1994). The moderating effect of behavior type on the subjective norm-behavior relationship. *Journal of Social Psychology, 134*, 755–763.

Trent, J. S., & Friedenberg, R. V. (2000). *Political campaign communication: Principles and practices* (4th ed.). Westport, CT: Praeger.

Triandis, H. C. (1971). *Attitudes and attitude change.* New York: Wiley.

Trodahl, V. C., & Powell, E. A. (1965). A short-form dogmatism scale for use in field studies. *Social Forces, 44*, 211–214.

Trost, M. R., Langan, E. J., & Kellar-Guenther, Y. (1999). Not everyone listens when you "just say no": Drug resistance in relational context. *Journal of Applied Communication Research, 27*, 120–138.

Tversky, A., & Kahneman, D. (1974). Judgment under uncertainty: Heuristics and biases. *Science, 185*, 1124–1134.

Tversky, A., & Kahneman, D. (1982). Judgments of and by representativeness. In D. Kahneman, P. Slovic, & A. Tversky (Eds.), *Judgment under uncertainty: Heuristics and biases* (pp. 163–178). Cambridge, UK: Cambridge University Press.

Tybout, A., Sternthal, B., & Calder, B. J. (1983). Information availability as a determinant of multiple request effectiveness. *Journal of Marketing Research, 20*, 280–290.

Vangelisti, A. L., Daly, J. A., & Rudnick, J. R. (1991). Making people feel guilt in conversation: Techniques and correlates. *Human Communication Research, 18*, 3–39.

Vangelisti, A. L., & Sprague, R. J. (1998). Guilt and hurt: Similarities, distinctions, and conversational strategies. In P. A. Andersen & L. K. Guerrero (Eds.), *Handbook of communication and emotion: Research, theory, applications, and contexts* (pp. 124–154). San Diego, CA: Academic Press.

Vinokur, A., & Burnstein, E. (1974). Effects of partially shared persuasive arguments on group-induced shifts: A group problem-solving approach. *Journal of Personality and Social Psychology, 29*, 305–315.

Vohs, J. L., & Garrett, R. L. (1968). Resistance to persuasion: An integrative framework. *Public Opinion Quarterly, 32*, 445–452.

Warshaw, P. R. (1980). A new model for predicting behavioral intentions: An alternative to Fishbein. *Journal of Marketing Research, 17*, 153–172.

Watson, J. D. (1968). *The double helix: A personal account of the discovery of the structure of DNA.* New York: Atheneum.

Wegener, D. T., & Claypool, H. M. (1999). The elaboration continuum by any other name does not smell as sweet. *Psychological Inquiry, 10*, 176–181.

Wheatly, J. J., & Oshikawa, S. (1970). The relationship between anxiety and positive and negative advertising appeals. *Journal of Marketing Research, 7*, 85–89.

Whittaker, J. O. (1967). Resolution of the communication discrepancy issue in attitude change. In C. W. Sherif & M. Sherif (Eds.), *Attitude, ego-involve-ment, and change* (pp. 159–177). New York: Wiley.

Whittaker, J. O., & Meade, R. D. (1967). Sex of the communicator as a variable in source credibility. *Journal of Social Psychology, 72,* 27–34.

Wicker, A. W. (1969). Attitudes versus actions: The relationship of verbal and overt behavioral responses to attitude objects. *Journal of Social Issues, 25,* 41–78.

Wicklund, R. A., & Brehm, J. W. (1976). *Perspectives on cognitive dissonance.* Hillsdale, NJ: Erlbaum.

Williams, D. L., & Boster, F. J. (1981, May). *The effects of beneficial situational characteristics, negativism, and dogmatism on compliance gaining message selection.* Paper presented at the annual meeting of the International Communication Association, Minneapolis, MN.

Williams, K. D., & Williams, K. B. (1989). Impact of source strength on two compliance techniques. *Basic and Applied Social Psychology, 10,* 149–159.

Wilson, J. D. (1992, September 14). Gays under fire. *Newsweek,* pp. 35–40.

Wilson, S. R. (1997). Developing theories of persuasive message production. In J. O. Greene (Ed.), *Message production: Advances in communication theory* (pp. 15–43). Mahwah, NJ: Erlbaum.

Wilson, S. R., Cruz, M. G., Marshall, L. J., & Rao, N. (1993). An attributional analysis of compliance-gaining interactions. *Communication Monographs, 60,* 1–22.

Wiseman, R. L., & Schenck-Hamlin, W. (1981). A multidimensional scaling validation of an inductively-derived set of compliance-gaining strategies. *Communication Monographs, 48,* 251–270.

Witte, K. (1992). Putting the fear back into fear appeals: The extended parallel process model. *Communication Monographs, 59,* 329–349.

Witte, K. (1994). Fear control and danger control: A test of the extended parallel process model (EPPM). *Communication Monographs, 61,* 113–134.

Witte, K., & Allen, M. (2000). A meta-analysis of fear appeals: Implications for effective public health campaigns. *Health Education and Behavior, 27,* 591–615.

Wodarski, J., & Bagarozzi, D. (1979). *Behavioral social work.* New York: Human Sciences Press.

Wood, J. T. (2001). *Gendered lives: Communication, gender, and culture* (4th ed.). Belmont, CA: Wadsworth.

Wood, W., & Eagly, A. H. (1981). Stages in the analysis of persuasive messages: The role of causal attributions and message comprehension. *Journal of Personality and Social Psychology, 40,* 246–259.

Woodall, W. G., & Burgoon, J. K. (1981). The effects of nonverbal synchrony on message comprehension and persuasiveness. *Journal of Nonverbal Behavior, 5,* 207–223.

Worchel, S., Andreoli, V., & Eason, J. (1975). Is the medium the message?: A study of the effects of media, communicator, and message characteristics on attitude change. *Journal of Applied Social Psychology, 5,* 157–172.

Wyer, R. S. (1970). The quantitative prediction of belief and opinion change: A further test of a subjective probability model. *Journal of Personality and Social Psychology, 16,* 559–570.

Wyer, R. S., & Goldberg, L. (1970). A probabilistic analysis of the relationships among beliefs and attitudes. *Psychological Review, 77,* 100–120.

Wyer, R. S., & Srull, T. K. (1981). Category accessibility: Some theoretical and empirical issues concerning the processing of social stimulus information. In E. T. Higgins, C. P. Herman, & M. P. Zanna (Eds.), *Social cognition: The Ontario Symposium* (Vol. 1, pp. 161–197). Hillsdale, NJ: Erlbaum.

Ybarra, O., & Trafimow, D. (1998). How priming the private self or collective self affects the relative weights of attitudes and subjective norms. *Personality and Social Psychology Bulletin, 24,* 362–370.

Zanna, M. P., & Cooper, J. (1974). Dissonance and the pill: An attributional approach to studying the arousal properties of dissonance. *Journal of Personality and Social Psychology, 29,* 703–709.

Zanna, M. P., & Rempel, J. K. (1988). Attitudes: A new look at an old concept. In D. Bar-Tal & A. W. Kruglanski (Eds.), *The social psychology of knowledge* (pp. 315–334). Cambridge, UK: Cambridge University Press.

Zimbardo, P. G. (1960). Involvement and communication discrepancy as determinants of opinion conformity. *Journal of Abnormal and Social Psychology, 60,* 86–94.

Zimbardo, P. G., & Ebbesen, E. B. (1970). Experimental modification of the relationship between effort, attitude, and behavior. *Journal of Personality and Social Psychology, 16,* 207–213.

Index

About the Authors

James B. Stiff, PhD, is President of Trial Analysts, Incorporated, a litigation consulting firm with offices in Dallas and College Station, Texas. He is involved in a wide variety of jury research and consulting activities, including case theme development, witness preparation, focus group and mock trial research, jury selection, and posttrial juror interviews. Dr. Stiff is coauthor (with Gerald R. Miller) of *Deceptive Communication* (Sage, 1993), and has written numerous book chapters and articles in professional journals. He previously taught at Michigan State University, Arizona State University, and the University of Kansas. Dr. Stiff's teaching and research interests include persuasion, credibility assessment, and human information processing.

Paul A. Mongeau, PhD, is a Professor at the Hugh Downs School of Human Communication at Arizona State University. He previously spent 15 years teaching at Miami University in Oxford, Ohio. His teaching and research interests center upon interpersonal communication and social influence. Dr. Mongeau's recent research has focused on several aspects of communication in dating relationships. In the social influence arena, his research has focused on the cognitive processing of persuasive messages in small group and public settings. Dr. Mongeau also served a 3-year term as editor of *Communication Studies*.